COMMUNITY POLICING AND PROBLEM SOLVING

Fourth Edition

COMMUNITY POLICING AND PROBLEM SOLVING

Strategies and Practices

KENNETH J. PEAK

University of Nevada, Reno

RONALD W. GLENSOR

Reno, Nevada, Police Department

PEARSON

Prentice
Hall

Upper Saddle River, New Jersey 07458

Library of Congress Cataloging-in-Publication Data

Peak, Kenneth J., 1947–
    Community policing and problem solving: strategies and practices / Kenneth J. Peak,
    Ronald W. Glensor.—4th ed.
        p. cm.
    Includes bibliographical references and index.
    ISBN 0-13-113268-7
        1. Community policing. 2. Crime prevention—United States—Citizen participation.
    3. Police administration. 4. Police-community relations. 5. Community policing—
    United States. 6. Police administration—United States. I. Glensor, Ronald W. II. Title.

HV7936.C83P43 2004
363.2′3—dc22   2003026113

Executive Editor: *Frank Mortimer*
Editor-in-Chief: *Stephen Helba*
Assistant Editor: *Sarah Holle*
Managing Editor: *Mary Carnis*
Production Liaison: *Brian Hyland*
Manufacturing Buyer: *Cathleen Petersen*
Director of Manufacturing and Production: *Bruce Johnson*
Design Director: *Cheryl Asherman*
Senior Design Coordinator: *Miguel Ortiz*
Cover Designer: *Marianne Frasco*
Cover Illustration/Photo: *Tom Carter/PhotoEdit*
Composition/Full-Service Project Management: *nSight/Laserwords*
Printer/Binder: *Courier Westford/Coral Graphics*

Pearson Prentice Hall™ is a trademark of Pearson Education, Inc.
Pearson® is a registered trademark of Pearson plc
Prentice Hall® is a registered trademark of Pearson Education, Inc.

Pearson Education LTD.   Pearson Education Singapore, Pte. Ltd
Pearson Education, Canada, Ltd   Pearson Education–Japan
Pearson Education Australia PTY, Limited   Pearson Education North Asia Ltd
Pearson Educaçion de Mexico, S.A. de C.V.   Pearson Education Malaysia, Pte. Ltd

10 9 8 7 6 5 4 3 2 1
ISBN 0-13-113268-7

To three who share a common name, an uncommonly kindred spirit, and the ability to give me a life away from my computer: Kathryn Ann, Tiffany Ann, and Lori Ann.

—K. J. P.

To my wife, Kristy, and children, Breanne and Ronnie, for their continuing love, support, and patience.

—R. W. G.

BRIEF CONTENTS

CONTENTS

3 Attending to the "Customer": Community Oriented Government 44

4 Community Oriented Policing and Problem Solving: "COPPS" 63

5   Crime Prevention: For Safe Communities   93

6   Planning and Implementation: Translating Ideas into Action   118

10 New Strategies for Old Problems: COPPS on the Beat   198

11 The "Devil's Advocate": Addressing Concerns with COPPS   222

12   Evaluating COPPS Initiatives   236

13   Selected American Approaches   254

14 In Foreign Venues: COPPS Abroad   274

PREFACE

This book is about policing at its most important and challenging levels—in neighborhoods and in communities across the nation and abroad. It is about a new policing, one that encourages collaboration with the community and other agencies and organizations that are responsible for community safety. It is a style of policing that requires officers to obtain new knowledge and tools such as problem solving, and it is grounded in strategic thinking and planning to enable agencies to keep up with the rapid societal changes such as homeland defense. This policing style also allows agencies to make the necessary organizational and administrative adjustments to maintain a capable and motivated workforce.

The book is grounded on the assumption that the reader is most likely an undergraduate or graduate student studying criminal justice or policing. Or, perhaps the reader is a police practitioner with a fundamental knowledge of police history and operations, or is working in a government agency outside policing and is interested in learning about community policing and problem solving. Citizens who are collaborating with police to resolve neighborhood problems in innovative ways can also be served well by reading this book.

This fourth edition also imparts some of the major underpinnings, prominent names, theories, practices (with myriad examples), and processes that are being implemented under COPPS to control and prevent crime, disorder, and fear. A considerable number of textbooks have already been written about community policing. Most of them, however, emphasize its philosophy and provide little information about its *practical* aspects—putting the philosophy into daily practice. The application of community policing is the primary focus of this book, as indicated in its title.

While some fundamental components of COPPS contribute to its success, no one single model of COPPS exists—there is no cookie-cutter approach that can guarantee success. COPPS is an individualized, long-term process that involves fundamental institutional change, going beyond such simple tactics as foot and bicycle patrols or neighborhood police stations. It redefines the role of the officer on the street, from "crime fighter" to problem solver. It forces a cultural transformation of the entire police agency, involving changes in recruiting, training, awards systems, evaluations, and promotions.

It has been said that problem solving is not new in policing, that police officers have always tried to solve problems in their daily work. As is demonstrated throughout this text, however, problem solving is not the same as solving problems. Problem solving in the context of COPPS is very different and considerably more complex. It requires that officers identify and examine the underlying causes of recurring incidents of crime and disorder. Such policing also seeks to make thinking "street criminologists" of our police officers, teaching them to expand their focus on offenders to include crime settings and victims. Such an approach presents great challenges for those patrol officers who are engaged in analytical work.

Given the extent to which COPPS has evolved since the publication of our third edition, the authors understand the challenges involved with writing this text. Like its three predecessors, this fourth edition might still be viewed as a work in progress; today's "snapshot" of what is occurring nationally with respect to COPPS may need to be drastically revised in the future.

We also emphasize that this book is not a call to ignore or discard policing's past methods, nor do we espouse an altogether new philosophy of policing in its place. Rather, we recommend that the police borrow from the wisdom of the past and adopt a holistic approach to the way police organizations are learning to address public safety more successfully.

We are quite pleased with the work that has been done by many police practitioners and academicians here and abroad who have made substantive contributions to the COPPS approach. But the traditional, reactive, "cops-as-pinballs" philosophy is still very much alive in many agencies. Merely creating a "crime prevention specialist" position, putting an officer on foot or bicycle patrol, or anticipating the receipt of federal dollars does not equate with implementing COPPS. Such activities not only misrepresent the true potential and functions of COPPS but also set unrealistically simplistic goals and expectations for its work.

This book describes how many agencies should, and are, quietly going about the process of revolutionizing their philosophy and operations.

Organization and Content of the Book

Like its three predecessors, this book is distinguished by its *applied* approach. In doing so, it showcases more than 50 exhibits and provides dozens of additional case studies and examples of problem solving in the field.

While providing updated information about crime in the United States, with particular emphasis placed on terrorism, new sections have also been added concerning rave parties, school bullying, street racing, burglar alarms, and 911 calls. Also newly addressed are adult- and problem-based learning. Chapter sections on such major problems as racial profiling and hate crimes have also been updated, and the chapter on the future has received a major revision.

To understand the methods and challenges of COPPS, we first need to look at the big picture. Thus, in the first three chapters we discuss (1) the history of policing and the major transformations over time that led to the present community policing era, (2) some of the many changes occurring in America and what the police must do to confront them, and (3) how governments and the police should turn to and involve their "customers," the public, in making neighborhoods safer places in which to live and work. These initial three chapters help to set the stage for Chapter 4, which is the "heart and soul" of the book, and for the later discussions of COPPS. Following is a chapter-by-chapter breakdown of the book's 15 chapters.

Chapter 1 begins with a brief discussion of Britain's and Sir Robert Peel's influence and the Metropolitan Police Act in England. Next we review the evolution of policing in America, followed by a look at police and change. Then we examine the community problem-solving era, including its principal components, why it emerged, and how it evolved. We will also examine the elevated importance of COPPS in this time of terrorism and homeland defense.

Chapter 2 opens with an examination of the many rapid changes that are occurring in the United States. Next is a consideration of the changing nature of criminality in this country. Then we examine fear of crime and its effects on neighborhoods. These variables—people and crime—are the reason and justification for COPPS.

Chapter 3 explores collaborative partnerships, and how governments and the police should and do conduct business with respect to their customers' needs. This reinvention of government empowers citizens to reclaim their neighborhoods and to improve their overall quality of life. Some local governments refer to this "community oriented government" movement as the next step in community policing.

As indicated above, the foundation of the book is Chapter 4, which includes separate discussions of the concepts of community policing and problem oriented policing. We maintain throughout the book that these are complementary core components. Included are in-depth discussions of collaborative partnerships and problem solving. The problem-solving process is introduced as the officers' primary tool for understanding crime and disorder. Crime analysis and mapping tools used to support problem solving are also discussed. The chapter concludes by delineating what approaches work and what approaches do not appear to be successful for crime prevention.

Crime prevention involves much more than developing programs and distributing brochures. Chapter 5 looks at two important and contemporary components of crime prevention: crime prevention through environmental design (CPTED) and situational crime prevention. These methods help officers understand how opportunities for crime can be blocked and how environments can be designed or changed to lessen a person's or location's vulnerability to crime.

Chapter 6 examines the need for police organizations to engage in strategic thinking in order to be prepared for future challenges. This chapter also discusses the strategic planning process and how to assess local needs and develop a planning document as a roadmap. Then it shifts to the implementation of COPPS per se, considering some vital components: leadership and administration, human resources, field operations, and external relations. Included are several general obstacles to implementation.

In Chapter 7 we recognize that police agencies have a life and culture of their own and address how police agencies must modify their culture from top to bottom in order to fully embrace COPPS. The separate roles and responsibilities of chief executives, middle managers, and rank-and-file officers are included, as are some case studies of agencies that have modified their culture for adopting the COPPS approach. We also stress the importance of developing a *learning organization* for facilitating the change process more smoothly.

Another difficult challenge for those agencies involved in COPPS is the training and education of police officers and others. After looking in Chapter 8 at why police officers comprise a challenging learning audience, we consider means and approaches for training, including a training needs assessment. Then we discuss some methods and review some available technologies for conducting training. Included are some ideas for the curriculum of a COPPS training program. We also discuss how adult and problem-based learning techniques are being infused into these training programs, which focus on problem solving.

Chapter 9 examines the history of relations between the minorities and the police, and how COPPS can enhance those relations. Included are discussions of bias-based policing and racial profiling, cultural differences, customs, and problems; diversity in police organizations; police responses to hate crimes; and some scenarios.

Today's police struggle with an almost overwhelming array of social problems. Chapter 10 describes the application of COPPS to several of those problems, including drug violations, gangs, special populations (the mentally ill, the homeless, and those addicted to alcohol), domestic violence, school violence, rental-property and neighborhood disorder, prostitution, traffic problems, and others. Exhibits and case studies are included throughout this chapter and demonstrate the power of collaborative partnerships and problem solving.

Some writers have raised concerns and criticisms of COPPS. The literature reveals more resistance to community policing than to problem solving. This is largely due to academics and practitioners who have incorrectly associated community policing with community relations. Chapter 11 examines these concerns—what we have termed the "devil's advocate" position toward COPPS. We believe that it is important for these concerns to be aired and given a response. Nine issues or problems that have been raised are addressed.

Although COPPS has been implemented and praised across our nation as well as in foreign venues, what has remained in question is the degree to which the success of these programs has been accurately measured. Chapter 12 confronts the issue of evaluation, beginning with the rationale for evaluating COPPS and social interventions generally, and then reviewing the different methods for evaluation and criteria that can be employed to assess agencies' efforts. Case studies of agencies and research are presented.

Chapter 13 highlights agencies' efforts to implement COPPS in the United States. Featured are case studies in 21 jurisdictions: seven large (categorized as having more than 250,000 population), nine medium-sized (between 50,000 and 250,000 population), and five small (less than 50,000 population). In addition, brief descriptions of such initiatives appear in several exhibits throughout the chapter.

COPPS has indeed gone international, and much can be learned from looking at the activities and approaches undertaken in foreign venues. In Chapter 14 we travel to Canada, Japan, Australia, Great Britain, and other selected locations (Scotland, Israel, Hong Kong, New Zealand, the Isle of Man, and the Netherlands). Other venues are also discussed in chapter exhibits.

Chapter 15 explores the future, with a look at those forces that may influence COPPS in years to come; highlighted are homeland defense, technology, and the role of the rank-and-file police officer.

An Appendix includes several award-winning case studies of excellent problem solving, and examples of a community survey and a strategic plan.

We believe that this book comprehensively lays out how COPPS is being embraced around the world. Perhaps one of the book's major strengths lies with its many case studies and a large number of other examples, which demonstrate how the concept is planned and implemented, operationalized, and evaluated.

We are grateful for the helpful suggestions made by the following reviewers of this book: Alex del Carmen, University of Texas–Arlington; Steven Egger, University of Houston–Clearlake; David Graff, Kent State University–Tuscarawas; William Parks, University of South Carolina–Spartanburg; and Bruce Smith, Ohio University–Chillicothe.

Ken Peak
Ron Glensor

ABOUT THE AUTHORS

Kenneth J. Peak, Ph.D., is professor and former chairman of the criminal justice department at the University of Nevada, Reno (UNR). Beginning his career at UNR in 1983, he has been named "Teacher of the Year" by the UNR Honor Society and served as acting director of public safety. He has authored or coauthored 14 textbooks on general policing, community policing, justice administration, and police supervision and management, and has published more than 50 journal articles and additional book chapters on a wide range of justice-related subjects. He has served as chairman of the Police Section, Academy of Criminal Justice Sciences, and is a past president of the Western and Pacific Association of Criminal Justice Educators. Dr. Peak entered municipal policing in Kansas in 1970 and subsequently held positions as criminal justice planner for southeast Kansas; director of the Four-State Technical Assistance Institute, Law Enforcement Assistance Administration; director of university police, Pittsburg State University; and assistant professor at Wichita State University. He received two gubernatorial appointments to statewide criminal justice committees while in Kansas and holds a doctorate from the University of Kansas.

Ronald W. Glensor, Ph.D., is a deputy chief of the Reno, Nevada, Police Department (RPD). He has more than 28 years of police experience and has commanded the department's patrol, administration, and detective divisions. In addition to being actively involved in the RPD's implementation of community oriented policing and problem solving (COPPS) since 1987, he has provided COPPS training to thousands of officers, elected officials, and community members representing jurisdictions throughout the United States and in Canada, Australia, and the United Kingdom. Dr. Glensor was the 1997 recipient of the prestigious Gary P. Hayes Award, conferred by the Police Executive Research Forum, recognizing his contributions and leadership in the policing field. Internationally, he is a frequent featured speaker on a variety of policing issues. He served a six-month fellowship as problem oriented policing coordinator with the Police Executive Research Forum in Washington, D.C., and received an Atlantic Fellowship in public policy, studying repeat victimization at the Home Office in London. He is coauthor of *Police Supervision and Management in an Era of Community Policing* (with K. Peak and L. K. Gaines) and coeditor of *Policing Communities: Understanding Crime and Solving Problems* (with M. Correia and K. Peak); he has also published in several journals and trade magazines. Dr. Glensor is an adjunct professor at the University of Nevada, Reno (in the CJ department's bachelor of arts degree program in COPPS) and instructs at area police academies and criminal justice programs. He holds a doctorate in political science and a master's of public administration from the University of Nevada, Reno.

FOREWORD

QUINT C. THURMAN
Texas State University

Dr. Quint C. Thurman is a professor of criminal justice and departmental chairperson at Texas State University in San Marcos, Texas. Previously he was employed as program director and director of graduate studies in the School of Community Affairs at Wichita State University, after directing the Criminal Justice Program at Washington State University. His publications include three books and more than 30 refereed articles, and he has received and/or administered approximately $1,500,000 in external grants and has produced numerous technical reports. He recently completed a second edition of Community Policing in a Rural Setting *(with coauthor Edmund McGarrell), and is coauthoring a new book,* Contemporary Policing: Controversies, Challenges, and Solutions. *He teaches graduate classes in evaluation research methods and advanced criminological theory as well as undergraduate classes in criminal justice. He received a doctorate in sociology from the University of Massachusetts, Amherst, in 1987.*

These are challenging times for public safety and police personnel. It was but a few short years ago that American policing and police agencies worldwide seemed set on a course of unprecedented change from a traditional ("just the facts ma'am") law enforcement approach to one distinguished by an awareness of the nexus of public safety within a larger social community. Rather than simply continuing to put up with a public that they were called to protect and serve, as they had been doing for several decades, great expectations were becoming evident about the much larger role of local citizens in shaping the work that the police would do. No longer could the police view the public only as a factory that produced victims in want of a police report or criminal offenders in need of an arrest, but as potential partners who might be helpful in identifying crime problems and suggesting solutions, as well as volunteering their time working with the police to prevent crime and make their streets and homes safer.

Today's world may or may not be a more precarious place after the events of September 11, 2001. For example, security measures have substantially improved (or at least become more stringent) across many facets of American life, from boarding an airplane to immigration, as compared with the relatively nonchalant ways we used to fly or enter this country prior to 9/11. Regardless of whether Americans are safer or not, questions remain about the effectiveness of our response and our feelings about our safety. Now that we have embarked on a path devoted to expending considerable resources for homeland security, a phrase invented after that fateful day, we may ask if we are a country safer or less safe than before, or better yet, do we feel more or less confident in public safety measures that are now in place, and why? We might also ask whether the events of that day stopped the progress of American policing, or simply temporarily interrupted it?

Inasmuch as public perceptions of reality are founded upon our beliefs about the measures that we are taking to ensure that 9/11 will not repeat itself, it is important to look at actual public safety approaches that are in place which might impact citizens' beliefs and expectations about what ought to be done to protect our homes, possessions, and loved ones. The fourth edition of *Community Policing and Problem Solving* provides just such a blueprint.

Terrorism represents a global problem. But it does not—for most of us who live our lives on a more local, social setting—present itself as something that will likely infringe upon our daily lives in a particularly direct sense. The life-threatening or life-altering challenges that most people in this country face each and every day of their lives are those that occur much less infrequently or might occur at some appreciably higher probability level in their lifetimes if left unchecked. These challenges range from those that are medical or accidental in nature to those that the propertied must endure when there are those around them who are propertyless. In the same way that good eating habits and proper exercise can help us manage medical risks, good public safety programs can help to make neighborhoods and communities safer for the residents who inhabit them by reducing known risk factors.

Professor Peak and Deputy Chief Glensor's fourth edition of *Community Policing and Problem Solving* is written in the spirit of helping scholars, practitioners, and students learn what is known in order to help make our communities safer. While we can all follow the news about what is happening around the world and in our nation to lessen the threat of terrorism among the international community, the reality is that most of us live out our entire lives with people and in places that are all too familiar to us. Proactively solving problems that form the basis for crime is largely within the capacity of local police agencies to achieve with the backing and support of the residents who live there. All we need really is the knowledge and the will to do so.

With roots deeply planted in our local communities, we need to come the realization that homeland security should begin at home. Neighbors have an inherent investment in local problem solving. Just as we cannot expect the police to act alone to solve pervasive social problems that are the primary causes of crime, federal agencies cannot be expected to be effective as the singular resource for keeping citizens safe in local jurisdictions. Rather, it is by working together with the local police to coproduce order that crime and disorder will be held in check in a community.

This textbook provides direction after 9/11 for guiding local public safety agencies in the task of keeping our communities safe. In so doing, its authors provide crucial momentum for the continued evolution of community policing as the most logical response to a world that has been forever changed. Rather than sitting numbly in shock and awe of world events, Drs. Peak and Glensor's fourth edition invites readers to work together to gauge the public safety needs of their communities and to interact with the police to make a positive difference in the cities and towns in which they live. It is just such a connection that is needed to ensure the quality of life that Americans expect from a free and democratic society.

INTRODUCTION

It is difficult to accurately establish the beginning of community oriented policing in America. This is possibly due to the fact that the notion of community policing is not altogether new; parts of it are as old as policing itself, emanating (as will be seen later) from concerns about policing that arose in the early nineteenth century.

We also must mention at the outset of this book that community policing and problem solving (COPPS) is not a unitary concept but rather a collection of related ideas. Several prominent individuals, movements, studies, and experiments have brought policing to where it is today. In this chapter we examine the principal activities involving the police for more than a century and a half—activities that led to the development of community policing and problem solving.

This historical examination of policing begins with a brief discussion of Britain's and Sir Robert Peel's influence and the Metropolitan Police Act in England. Then we review the evolution of policing in America, including the emergence of the political era and attempts at reform through the professional crime fighter model. Next we look at police and change, including how "sacred cow" policing methods have (1) been debunked by research, (2) demonstrated the actual nature of police work, and (3) shown the need for a new approach.

Following is an examination of the community problem solving era, including the principles of this new model, why it emerged, and how it evolved. In this connection we discuss how local police departments and sheriff's offices have evolved and rewritten their agency's history by adopting the community oriented policing and problem solving strategy, including how they have greatly expanded their use of the Internet to do so.

—1—

THE EVOLUTION OF POLICING

Past Wisdom and Future Directions

To understand what is, we must know what has been, and what it tends to become.
—OLIVER WENDELL HOLMES

Human history becomes more and more a race between education and catastrophe.
—H. G. WELLS

BRITISH CONTRIBUTIONS

The population of England doubled between 1700 and 1800. Parliament, however, took no measures to help solve the problems that arose from the accompanying social change.[1] London, awash in crime, had whole districts become criminal haunts and thieves become very bold. In the face of this situation, Henry Fielding began to experiment with possible solutions. Fielding, appointed in 1748 as London's chief magistrate of Bow Street, argued against the severity of the English penal code, which provided for the death penalty for a large number of offenses. He felt the country should reform the criminal code in order to deal more with the origins of crime. In 1750 Fielding made the pursuit of criminals more systematic by creating a small group of "thief-takers."[2] When Fielding died in 1754, his half-brother John Fielding succeeded him as Bow Street magistrate. By 1785, his thief-takers had evolved into the Bow Street Runners—some of the most famous policemen in English history.

Later, Robert Peel, a wealthy member of Parliament, felt strongly that London's population and crime merited a full-time, professional police force. But many English people and other politicians objected to the idea, fearing possible restraint of their liberty. They also feared a strong police organization because the criminal law was already quite harsh (by the early nineteenth century there were 223 crimes in England for which a person could be hanged). Indeed, Peel's efforts to gain support for full-time, paid police officers failed for seven years.[3]

Peel finally succeeded in 1829. His bill to Parliament, entitled "An Act for Improving the Police In and Near the Metropolis," and known as the Metropolitan Police Act of 1829, was passed. The *General Instructions* of the new force stressed its preventive nature, saying that: ". . . the principal object to be attained is 'the prevention of crime'. The security of persons and property will thus be better effected, than by the detection and punishment of the offender after he has succeeded in committing the crime."[4] It was decided that constables would don a uniform (blue coat, blue pants, and a black top hat) and be armed with a short baton (known as a truncheon) and a rattle (for raising an alarm). And each constable was to wear his individual number on his collar where it could be easily seen.[5]

Peel proved very farsighted and was keenly aware of the needs of a community oriented police force as well as the needs of the public, which would be asked to maintain it. Indeed, Peel perceived that the poor quality of policing was a contributing factor to the social disorder. Accordingly, he drafted several guidelines for the force, many of which focused on improving the relationship between the police and the public. He wrote that the power of the police to fulfill their duties depended on public approval of their actions; that as public cooperation increased, the need for physical force by the police decreased; that the officers needed to display absolutely impartial service to law; and that force should be employed by the police only when the attempt at persuasion and warning had failed, and then they should use only the minimal degree of force possible. Peel's statement that "The police are the public, and the public are the police" emphasized his belief that the police are first and foremost members of the larger society.[6]

Peel's attempts to appease the public were well-grounded; during the first three years of his reform effort he encountered strong opposition. Peel was denounced as a potential dictator; the *London Times* urged revolt, and *Blackwood's Magazine* referred to the bobbies as "general spies" and "finished tools of corruption." A national secret body was organized to combat the police, who were nicknamed the "Blue Devils" and the "Raw Lobsters." Also during this initial five-year period, Peel endured one of the largest police turnover rates in history. Estimates range widely, but it is probably accurate to accept the figure of 1,341 constables resigning from London's Metropolitan Police from 1829 to 1834.[7]

Peel drafted what have become known as "Peel's Principles" of policing, most if not all of which are still apropos to today's police community. They are presented in Box 1-1.

COMMUNITY POLICING AND PROBLEM SOLVING

BOX 1-1

"Peel's Principles" of Policing

1. The basic mission for which the police exist is to prevent crime and disorder as an alternative to the repression of crime and disorder by military force and severity of legal punishment.

2. The ability of the police to perform their duties is dependent upon public approval of police existence, actions, behavior, and the ability of the police to secure and maintain public respect.

3. The police must secure the willing cooperation of the public in voluntary observance of the law to be able to secure and maintain public respect.

4. The degree of cooperation of the public that can be secured diminishes, proportionately, the necessity for the use of physical force and compulsion in achieving police objectives.

5. The police seek and preserve public favor, not by catering to public opinion, but by constantly demonstrating absolutely impartial service to the law, in complete independence of policy, and without regard to the justice or injustice of the substance of individual laws; by ready offering of individual service and friendship to all members of the society without regard to their race or social standing; by ready exercise of courtesy and friendly good humor; and by ready offering of individual sacrifice in protecting and preserving life.

6. The police should use physical force to the extent necessary to secure observance of the law or to restore order only when the exercise of persuasion, advice, and warning is found to be insufficient to achieve police objectives; and police should use only the minimum degree of physical force which is necessary on any particular occasion for achieving a police objective.

7. The police at all times should maintain a relationship with the public that gives reality to the historic tradition that the police are the public and that the public are the police; the police are the only members of the public who are paid to give full-time attention to duties which are incumbent on every citizen in the interest of the community welfare.

8. The police should always direct their actions toward their functions and never appear to usurp the powers of the judiciary by avenging individuals or the state, or authoritatively judging guilt or punishing the guilty.

9. The test of police efficiency is the absence of crime and disorder, not the visible evidence of police action in dealing with them.

Source: W. L. Melville Lee, *A History of Police in England* (London: Methuen, 1901), Chapter 12.

POLICING COMES TO AMERICA

Americans, meanwhile, were observing Peel's overall successful experiment with the bobbies on the patrol beat. Industrialization and social upheaval had not reached the proportions that they had in England, however, so there was not the urgency for full-time policing that had been experienced in England. Yet by the 1840s, when industrialization began in earnest in America, U.S. officials were watching the police reform movement in England more closely.

To comprehend the blundering, inefficiency, and confusion that surrounded nineteenth-century police, we must remember that this was an age when the best forensic techniques could not clearly distinguish the blood of a pig from that of a human, and the art of criminal detection was little more than divination. Steamboats blew up, trains regularly mutilated and killed pedestrians, children got run over by wagons, injury very often meant death, and doctors resisted the germ theory of disease. In the midst of all this, the police

Early Beginnings

The New York Model

New York police department officers initially refused to wear uniforms because they did not want to appear as "liveried lackeys." A blue frock coat with brass buttons was adopted in 1853. (*Courtesy* NYPD Photo Unit)

would eventually be patrolling—men who at best had been trained by reading pathetic little rule books that provided them little or no guidance in the face of human distress and disorder.[8]

The movement to initiate policing in America began in New York City. (Philadelphia, with a private bequeath of $33,000, actually began a paid, daytime police force in 1833; however, it was disbanded in three years.) In 1844, the New York state legislature passed a law establishing a full-time, preventive police force for New York City. This new body was very different from that adopted from Europe, deliberately placed under the control of the city government and city politicians. The mayor chose the recruits from a list of names submitted by the aldermen and tax assessors of each ward; the mayor then submitted his choices to the city council for approval. Politicians were seldom concerned about selecting the best people for the job; instead, the system allowed and even encouraged political patronage and rewards for friends.[9]

The police link to neighborhoods and politicians was so tight that the police of this era have been considered virtual adjuncts to political machines.[10] The relationship was often reciprocal: political machines recruited and maintained police in office and on the beat, while police helped ward leaders maintain their political offices by encouraging citizens to vote for certain candidates. Soon other cities adopted the New York model. New Orleans and Cincinnati adopted plans for a new police force in 1852; Boston and Philadelphia followed in 1854, Chicago in 1855, and Baltimore and Newark in 1857.[11] By 1880, virtually every major American city had a police force based on Peel's model, pioneered in New York City.

BEAT MAP, circa 1911

MAP SHOWING HOW PATROL "POSTS ARE ARRANGED *under* NEW SYSTEM. STARS ★ SHOW STATIONARY "POSTS." DOTTED LINES ENCLOSE DISTRICTS COVERED *by* PATROLLING POLICE

Operation of the Stationary Post System.

In effect from 11 p.m to 7 a. m.

DIAGRAM SHOWING HOW POSTS ARE COVERED.
Ⓐ SHOWS STATIONARY POLICEMEN *in* MIDDLE *of* STREET Ⓑ SHOWS PATROLLING POLICEMEN COVERING ROUTE INDICATED *by* ARROWS(→)

Foot patrol was the primary strategy for policing neighborhoods during the early 1900s. (*Courtesy* NYPD Photo Unit)

These new police were born of conflict and violence. An unprecedented wave of civil disorders swept the nation from the 1840s until the 1870s. Few cities escaped serious rioting, caused by ethnic and racial conflicts, economic disorder, and public outrage toward such things as brothels and medical school experiments. These occurrences often made for hostile interaction between citizens and the police, who were essentially a reactive force. Riots in many major cities actually led to the creation of the "new police." The use of the baton to quell riots, known as the "baton charge," was not uncommon.[12]

Furthermore, while large cities in the east were struggling to overcome social problems and establish preventive police forces, the western half of America was anything but passive. When people left the wagon trains and their relatively law-abiding ways, they attempted to live together in communities. Many different ethnic groups—Anglo-Americans, Mexicans, Chinese, Native Americans, freed blacks, Australians, Scandinavians, and others—competed for often scarce resources and fought one another violently, often with mob attacks. Economic conflicts were frequent between cattlemen and sheepherders, often leading to major range wars. There was constant labor strife in the mines. The bitterness of the slavery issue remained, and many

From the East to the Wild, Wild West

men with firearms skills learned during the Civil War turned to outlawry after leaving the service. (Jesse James was one such person.)[13]

Despite these difficulties, westerners established peace by relying on a combination of four groups who assumed responsibility for law enforcement: private citizens, United States marshals, businessmen, and town police officers.[14] Private citizens usually helped to enforce the law by joining a posse or through individual efforts, such as vigilante committees.[15] While it is true that they occasionally hanged outlaws, they also performed valuable work by ridding their communities of dangerous criminals.

Federal marshals were created by Congressional legislation in 1789. As they began to appear on the frontier, the vigilantes tended to disappear. United States marshals enforced federal laws, so they only had jurisdiction over federal offenses, such as theft of mail, crimes against railroad property, and murder on federal lands. Their primary responsibility was in civil matters arising from federal court decisions. Finally, when a territory became a state, the primary law enforcement functions usually fell to local sheriffs and marshals. Sheriffs quickly became important officials, but they spent more time collecting taxes, inspecting cattle brands, maintaining jails, and serving civil papers than they did actually dealing with outlaws.[16]

Politics and Corruption

During the late nineteenth century, large cities gradually became more orderly. American cities absorbed millions of newcomers after 1900, without the social strains that attended the Irish immigration of the 1830s to 1850s.[17]

Partly because of their closeness to politicians, police during this era provided a wide array of services to citizens. Many police departments were involved in crime prevention and order maintenance as well as a variety of social services. In some cities they operated soup lines, helped find lost children, and found jobs and temporary lodging for newly arrived immigrants.[18] Police organizations were typically quite decentralized, with cities being divided into precincts and run like small-scale departments—hiring, firing, managing, and assigning personnel as necessary. Officers were often recruited from the same ethnic stock as the dominant groups in the neighborhoods, and they lived in the beats they patrolled, having considerable discretion in handling their individual beats. Decentralization encouraged foot patrol, even after call boxes and automobiles became available. Detectives operated from a caseload of "persons" rather than offenses, relying on their caseload to inform on other criminals.[19]

The strengths of the political era centered on the fact that police were integrated into neighborhoods. This strategy proved useful because it helped contain riots and the police assisted immigrants in establishing themselves in communities and finding jobs. There were weaknesses as well: The intimacy with the community, closeness to politicians, and a decentralized organizational structure (and its inability to provide supervision of officers) led to police corruption. The close identification of police with neighborhoods also resulted in discrimination against strangers, especially minority ethnic and racial groups. Police often ruled their beats with the "end of their nightsticks" and practiced "curbside justice."[20] The lack of organizational control over officers also caused some inefficiencies and disorganization; thus the image of Keystone Cops—bungling police—was widespread.

In summary, the nineteenth-century police officer was essentially a political operative rather than a modern-style professional committed to public service. Because the police were essentially a political institution and perceived as such by the citizenry, they did not enjoy a widespread acceptance by the public. And, as political appointees, officers enjoyed little job security. Salaries were determined by local political factors. Primitive communications technology of the era meant that police chiefs were unable to supervise their captains at the precinct level; thus policy was greatly influenced by the prevailing political and social mores of the neighborhoods. As a consequence, police behavior was very much influenced by the interaction between individual officers and individual citizens. The nature of that interaction, later termed the problem of police-community relations, was perhaps even more complex and ambiguous in the nineteenth century than in the late twentieth century.[21]

The Emergence of Professionalism

The idea of policing as a profession, however, began to emerge slowly in the latter part of the nineteenth century. Reform ideas first appeared as a reaction to the corrupt and politicized state of the police. Reformers agreed that partisan politics was the heart of the problem. Even reformers in the National Prison Association bemoaned the partisan politics that hindered the improvement of the police. Slowly, the idea of policing as a higher calling (higher than the concerns of local politics, that is), as a profession committed to public service, began to gain ground. Two other ideas about the proper role of the police in society also appeared. One emphasized improvement in the role of police with respect to scientific techniques of crime detection, and the other was that police could play more of a social work role; by intervening in the lives of individuals, police officers could reform society by preventing crime and keeping people out of the justice system. These reformers were closely tied to the emerging rehabilitative ideal in correctional circles.[22]

There were several important developments in policing during the late 1800s. Policing realized the beginning of a body of literature. Most authors were closely tied to the police and thus painted an inaccurate picture in some respects (e.g., the corruption that existed in many police departments), but their writings were also very illuminating. They provided glimpses into the informal processes that governed police departments and focused on the individual officer—a focus that would be lost in the later professionalization movement with its emphasis on impersonal, bureaucratic standards. Furthermore, the late 1800s witnessed improvements in the areas of testing and training. The physical and mental qualifications of police officers concerned new police commissioners, and formal schools of instruction were developed (the best being Cincinnati's, which required a total of 72 hours of instruction). There was also the appearance of police conventions during the late 1800s, such as the National Police Chiefs Union [later named the International Association of Chiefs of Police (IACP)] and fraternal and benefit societies.[23]

Movement Toward Reform

New Developments and Calls for Reform

August Vollmer, pioneer of police professionalism from 1905 to 1932, rallied police executives around the idea of reform during the 1920s and 1930s, emerging as the leading national spokesman for police professionalism. What is often overlooked among the abundance of Vollmer's contributions to policing was his articulate advocacy of the idea that the police should function as social workers. The belief that police officers should do more than merely arrest

August Vollmer, a national spokesman for and early pioneer of police professionalism, established one of the first fingerprint bureaus and formal police schools while he was chief of police in Berkeley, California. (*Courtesy* Samuel G. Chapman)

offenders, that they should actively seek to prevent crime by "saving" potential or actual offenders, was an important theme in police reform. It was an essential ingredient in the notion of professionalism. Indeed, in a series of addresses to the IACP Vollmer advanced his ideas in "The Policeman as a Social Worker" (1918) and "Predelinquency" (1921). He began by arguing that the "old methods of dealing with crime must be changed, and newer ones adopted."[24]

Vollmer's views were very prescient for today, especially given the contemporary movement toward community policing. Vollmer felt that traditional institutions and practices were no longer adequate for a modern and complex industrial society. He believed that the police should intervene and be involved with people before they entered lives of crime, and he suggested that police work closely with existing social welfare agencies and become advocates of additional reform proposals. Vollmer also suggested that police inform voters about overcrowded schools and support the expansion of recreational facilities, community social centers, and anti-delinquency agencies. Basically, he was suggesting that the police play an active part in the political life of the community. Yet the major thrust of police professionalization had been to insulate the police from politics. This contradiction illustrated one of the fundamental ambiguities of the whole notion of professionalism.[25]

Other reformers continued to reject political involvement by police, and civil service systems were created to eliminate patronage and ward influences in hiring and firing police officers. In some cities, officers could not live in the same beat they patrolled, to isolate them as completely as possible from political influences. Police departments, needing to be removed from political influence, became one of the most autonomous agencies in urban government.[26] However, policing also became a matter viewed as best left to the discretion of police executives to address. Police organizations became *law enforcement* agencies, with the sole goal of controlling crime. Any non-crime activities they were required to do were "social work." The "professional model" of policing was in full bloom.

The scientific theory of administration was adopted, as advocated by Frederick Taylor during the early twentieth century. Taylor had studied the work process, breaking down jobs to their basic steps and emphasizing time and motion studies, all toward maximizing production. From this emphasis on production and unity of control flowed the notion that police officers were best managed by a hierarchical pyramid of control. Police leaders routinized and standardized police work; officers were to enforce laws and make arrests whenever possible. Discretion was limited to the extent possible. When special problems arose, special units (e.g., vice, juvenile, drugs, tactical) were created, rather than assigning problems to patrol officers.

The early 1900s also became the age of the crime commission, including the Wickersham Commission reports in 1931. President Herbert Hoover, concerned with the lax enforcement of prohibition and other forms of police corruption, created the National Commission on Law Observance and Enforcement, popularly known as the Wickersham Commission, after its chairman, former U.S. Attorney General George W. Wickersham. This commission completed the first national study of crime and criminal justice, issuing 14 reports and recommending that the corrupting influence of politics be removed from policing, police chief executives be selected on merit, patrol officers be tested and meet minimal physical standards, police salaries and working conditions be decent, and police women be used in juvenile and female cases. Many of these recommendations represented what progressive police reformers had been wanting over the previous 40 years; unfortunately, President Hoover and his administration could do little more than report the Wickersham Commission's recommendations before leaving office.

Crime Commissions and Early Police Studies

The most important change in policing during this decade was the advent of the automobile and its accompanying radio. Gradually the patrol car replaced foot patrol, expanding geographic beats and further removing people from neighborhoods. There was also prohibition (which affected the police very little in a long-term way), a bloody wave of racial violence in American cities, and the rise and defeat of police unionism and strikes. The impact of two-way radios was also felt, as supervisors were able to maintain a far closer supervision of patrol officers; and the radio and telephone made it possible for citizens to make heavier demands for police service. The result was not merely a greater burden on the police but also an important qualitative redefinition of the police role.[27]

The 1930s marked an important turning point in the history of police reform. The first genuine empirical studies of police work began to appear, and O. W. Wilson emerged as the leading authority on police administration. The major development of this decade was a redefinition of the police role and the ascendancy of the crime fighter image. Wilson, who took guidance from J. Edgar Hoover's transformation of the Federal Bureau of Investigation (FBI) into an organization of high prestige, became the principal architect of the police reform strategy.[28] Hoover, appointed FBI director in 1924, had raised eligibility and training standards of recruits, giving FBI agents stature as upstanding moral crusaders and developing an incorruptible crime-fighting organization. He also developed impressive public relations programs that presented the Bureau in the most favorable light. Municipal police found Hoover's path a compelling one. Following Wilson's writings on police administration, they began to shape an organizational strategy for urban police that was analogous to that pursued by the FBI.

Also by the 1930s the policewomen's movement, begun in the early 1900s, had begun losing ground. Professionalism came to mean a combination of managerial efficiency, technological sophistication, and an emphasis on crime fighting. The social work aspects of policing—the idea of rehabilitative work, which had been central to the policewomen's movement—fell into almost total eclipse. The result was a severe identity crisis for policewomen as they were caught between a social work orientation and a law enforcement ideology. Later, by the 1960s, women would occupy an extremely marginal place in American policing.[29]

In sum, under the reform era's professional model of policing, officers were to remain in their "rolling fortresses," going from one call to the next with all due haste. As Mark Moore and George Kelling observed, "In professionalizing crime fighting, the 'volunteers,' citizens on whom so much used to depend (were) removed from the fight. If anything has been learned from the history of American policing, it is that, whatever the benefits of professionalization (e.g., reduced corruption, due process, serious police training), the reforms . . . ignored, even attacked, some features that once made the police powerful institutions in maintaining a sense of community security."[30]

The Professional Crime Fighter

Emphasis on Efficiency and Control

The decade of the 1930s ended the first phase in the history of police professionalization. From the 1940s through the early 1960s police reform continued along the lines that were already well established. Police professionalism was defined almost exclusively in terms of managerial efficiency, and administrators sought to further strengthen their hand in controlling rank-and-file officers. Many of the old problems persisted, however, such as racial unrest and an unclear definition of the police role. Nonetheless, by the late 1930s and early 1940s there was a clear sense of mission for the police, a commitment to *public* service where one had not existed before.[31] Also, policing had begun to develop its own sense of professional autonomy. And, ironically perhaps, the most articulate groups and the most creative thinking were to be found in nonpolice groups: the National Prison Association, the social work profession, and the field of public administration. The efforts by reformers to remove political influence over police, though not entirely successful, were beginning to take hold as police boards and totally powerful police chiefs met their demise. Police unions reappeared, however, and the emergence of careerism among police officers significantly altered their attitudes toward the job and the public they served.

The professional model demanded an impartial law enforcer who related to citizens in professionally neutral and distant terms, personified by television's Sgt. Friday on "Dragnet": "Just the facts, ma'am." The emphasis on professionalization also shaped the role of citizens in crime control. Like physicians caring for health problems, teachers for educational problems, and social workers for social adjustment problems, the police would be responsible for crime problems. Citizens became relatively passive in crime control, mere recipients of professional crime control services. Citizens' responsibility in crime control was limited to calling police and serving as witnesses when asked to do so. Police were the "thin blue line." The community "need" for rapid response to calls for service (CFS) was sold as efficacious in crime control. Foot patrol,

NYPD's Emergency Services was formed in 1926 to drive criminals, gangsters, and disorderly characters from the streets. (*Courtesy* NYPD Photo Unit)

when demanded by citizens, was rejected as an outmoded, expensive frill. Professionalism in law enforcement was often identified in terms of firearms expertise, and the popularity of firearms put the police firmly in the anti-gun-control camp.[32]

Citizens were no longer encouraged to go to "their" neighborhood police officers or districts. Officers were to drive marked cars randomly through streets, to develop a feeling of police omnipresence. The "person" approach ended and was replaced by the case approach. Officers were judged by the numbers of arrests they made or the number of miles they drove during a shift. The crime rate became the primary indicator of police effectiveness.

While much of the country was engaged in practicing and "selling" police reform embodied in the professional model of policing, a movement was beginning in Michigan to bring the police and community closer together. Louis Radelet served on the executive staff of the National Conference of Christians and Jews (NCCJ) from 1951 to 1963, when he became a professor in what was then the School of Police Administration and Public Safety at Michigan State University (MSU). In 1955, Radelet, having conducted many NCCJ workshops dedicated to reducing tensions between elements of the community, founded the National Institute on Police and Community Relations (NIPCR) at MSU; he served as institute director from 1955 to 1969, and was also coordinator of the university's National Center on Police and Community Relations, created to conduct a national survey on police-community relations, from 1965 to 1973.[33]

The Institute held five-day conferences each May during its 15-year existence, bringing together teams of police officers and other community leaders to discuss common problems. In peak years, more than 600 participants came from as many as 165 communities and 30 states and several foreign countries. As a result of the institute's work, such programs proliferated rapidly across the nation. We believe the stated purposes of the many

Reestablishing Communication: Police-Community Relations

programs initiated during this period are still applicable today, and should be listed here:

1. To encourage police-citizen partnership in the cause of crime prevention.
2. To foster and improve communications and mutual understanding between the police and the total community.
3. To promote interprofessional approaches to the solution of community problems and to stress the principle that the administration of justice is a total community responsibility.
4. To enhance cooperation among the police, prosecution, the courts, and corrections.
5. To assist police and other community leaders to achieve an understanding of the nature and causes of complex problems in people-to-people relations and especially to improve police-minority relationships.
6. To strengthen implementation of equal protection under the law for all persons.[34]

The NIPCR was discontinued at the end of 1969. Radelet wrote that its demise was "a commentary on the evolution of issues and social forces pertinent to the field. The purposes, assumptions, and institute design of past years may have been relevant in their time. But it became imperative now to think about police-community relations programs in different terms, with more precise purposes that could be better measured."[35]

Problems Overwhelm the Professional Model

Problems with the professional model of policing began to arise during the late 1960s:

During the 1960s, for the first time in history, Americans watched police on television respond to anti-war and civil rights demonstrations and were shocked at the treatment of students and minorities by the police. (A scene from the Walker Report of the 1968 Chicago Democratic National Convention)

Crime began to rise and research suggested that conventional police methods were not effective. The 1960s were a time of explosion and turbulence. Inner city residents rioted in several major cities, protestors denounced military involvement in Vietnam, and assassins ended the lives of President John F. Kennedy, Robert F. Kennedy, and civil rights leader Rev. Martin Luther King. The country was witnessing tremendous upheaval, and incidents such as the so-called "police riot" at the 1968 Democratic National Convention in Chicago raised many questions about the police and their function and role. Largely as a result of this turmoil, five national studies looked into police practices during the 1960s and 1970s, each with a different focus: the President's Commission on Law Enforcement and the Administration of Justice (termed the "President's Crime Commission," 1967); the National Advisory Commission on Civil Disorders (1968); the National Commission on the Causes and Prevention of Violence (1968); the President's Commission on Campus Unrest (1970); and the National Advisory Commission on Criminal Justice Standards and Goals (1973). Of particular note was the aforementioned President's Crime Commission of 1967, charged by President Lyndon Johnson to find solutions to America's internal crime problems. Among the Commission's recommendations for the police were: hiring more minorities as police officers to improve police-community relations, upgrading the quality of police officers through better educated officers, and better applicant screening and intensive preservice training.[36]

The President's Crime Commission brought policing "full circle," restating several of the same principles laid out by Sir Robert Peel in 1829: that the police should be close to the public, that poor quality of policing contributed to social disorder, and that the police should focus on community relations.

Police administrators became more willing to challenge traditional assumptions and beliefs and to open the door to researchers. That willingness to allow researchers to examine traditional methods led to the growth and development of two important policing research organizations, the Police Foundation and the Police Executive Research Forum (PERF).

Fear rose. Citizens abandoned parks, public transportation, neighborhood shopping centers, churches, and entire neighborhoods. What puzzled police and researchers was that levels of fear and crime did not always correspond: Crime levels were low in some areas, but fear high, and vice versa. Researchers found that fear is more closely associated with disorder than with crime. Ironically, order maintenance was one of the functions that police had been downplaying over the years.

Many minority citizens did not perceive their treatment as equitable or adequate. They protested not only police mistreatment but lack of treatment. This, despite attempts by most police departments to provide impartial policing to all citizens.

The antiwar and civil rights movements challenged police. The legitimacy of police was questioned: Students resisted police, minorities rioted against them for what they represented, and the public, for the first time at this level, questioned police tactics. Moreover, minorities and women insisted that they be represented in policing if police were to be legitimate.

Some of the myths on which the reform era was founded—that police officers use little or no discretion and their primary duty is law enforcement—could no longer be sustained. Over and over, research underscored the use of discretion at all levels and that law enforcement comprised but a small portion of police officers' activities.[37] Other research findings shook the foundations of old assumptions about policing; for example, two-person patrol cars are neither more effective nor safe than one-person cars in reducing crime or catching criminals.[38] Other "sacred cows" of policing that were debunked by research are discussed later.

Although managers had tried to professionalize policing, line officers continued to have low status. Police work continued to be routinized; petty rules governed officer behavior. Meanwhile, line officers received little guidance in the use of discretion and had little opportunity for providing input concerning their work. As a result, many departments witnessed the rise of militant unionism.

The police lost a significant portion of their financial support. Many police departments were reduced in size, demonstrating an erosion of public confidence.

Police began to acquire competition: private security and the community crime control movement. Businesses, industries, and private citizens began to seek alternative means of protecting themselves and their property, further suggesting a declining confidence in the capability of police to provide the level of services that citizens desired. Indeed, today there are more than 1.5 million private police personnel employed in the United States—two to three times more personnel than there are in all federal, state, and municipal police agencies combined.[39] The social changes of the 1960s and 1970s obviously changed the face of policing in America. Not to be overlooked is the impact of the courts during this period as well. A number of major landmark Supreme Court decisions curtailed the actions of police and, concurrently, expanded the rights of the accused.

THE CHANGING WISDOM OF POLICING

More Recent Studies of Police Work

As a result of the problems mentioned earlier and civil unrest that occurred during the professional era of policing, research evolved a new "common wisdom" of policing. As will be shown, much of this research shook the foundation of policing and rationalized the changes in methods we offer in later chapters. We discuss what might be termed the two primary "clusters" of police research that illuminated where policing has been and what officers actually do.

The first cluster of research actually began in the 1950s and would ultimately involve seven empirical studies of the police: the early work of sociologist William Westley concerning the culture of policing;[40] the ambitious studies of the American Bar Foundation;[41] the field observations of Jerome Skolnick;[42] the work of Egon Bittner analyzing the police function on Skid Row;[43] Parnas's study of the police response to domestic disturbances;[44] James Q. Wilson's analysis of different policing styles;[45] and the studies of police-citizen contact by Albert Reiss.[46] These studies collectively provided a "new realism" about policing:

- Informal arrangements for handling incidents and behavioral problems were found to be more common than was compliance with formally established procedures.
- Workload, public pressures, interagency pressures, and the interests and personal predilections of functionaries in the criminal justice system were found

in many instances to have more influence on how police and the rest of the criminal justice system operated than the Constitution, state statutes, or city ordinances.

- Arrest, commonly viewed as the first step in the criminal process, had come to be used by the police to achieve a whole range of objectives in addition to that of prosecuting wrongdoers; for example, to investigate, harass, punish, and provide safekeeping.
- A great variety of informal methods outside the criminal justice system had been adopted by the police to fulfill their formal responsibilities and to dispose of the endless array of situations that the public, rightly or wrongly, expected them to handle.
- Individual police officers were found to be routinely exercising a great deal of discretion in deciding how to handle the tremendous variety of circumstances with which they were confronted.[47]

These findings also underscored that the police had, in the past, depended too much on the criminal law in order to get their job done; that they were not autonomous, but rather accountable, through the political process, to the community; and that dealing with fear and enforcing public order are appropriate functions for the police.[48] Other early studies indicated that less than 50 percent of an officer's time was committed to calls for service, and of those calls handled, over 80 percent were noncriminal incidents.[49]

The five national studies of policing practices during the riots and Vietnam War of the 1960s and 1970s (discussed in the previous section) began a quest for new directions. Later, a second cluster of police research occurred that provided further knowledge about police methods. The Kansas City Preventive Patrol Experiment of 1973 questioned the usefulness of random patrol in police vehicles.[50] Other studies showed that officers and detectives are limited in their abilities to successfully investigate crimes[51] and that detectives need not follow up every reported unsolved crime.[52] In short, most serious crimes were unaffected by the standard police actions designed to control them.

Since the 1970s additional studies have dispelled many assumptions commonly held by police about their efficiency and effectiveness. For example, preventive patrol has been shown to be costly, producing only minimal results toward a reduction of crime.[53] Rapid response to calls has been shown less effective at catching criminals than educating the public to call the police sooner after a crime is committed.[54] We now know that police response time is largely unrelated to the probability of making an arrest or locating a witness. The time it takes to report a crime is the major determining factor of whether an on-scene arrest takes place and whether witnesses are located.[55] And, despite their best efforts, police have had little impact on preventing crime.[56]

Box 1-2 shows several studies and experiments in policing that were undertaken from 1972 to the present.

What did the studies mentioned previously mean for the police? Was the professional model of policing (discussed earlier) completely off base? No; in fact, it still has a place in a police agency lacking organization, control, and efficiency. However, these studies do show that the police erred in doggedly investing so much of their resources in a limited number of practices that were based on a rather naive and simplistic concept of the police role.[57] Furthermore, as we noted above, the police got caught up in the "means over ends" syndrome,

Viewing "Sacred Cow" Police Methods with Caution

BOX 1-2

Police Studies and Experiments, 1972–present

Year	Subject	Focus
2000	COPS Program—National Evaluation	Federal Office of Community Oriented Policing Services (COPS) grants
2000	National Evaluation of the Problem Solving Partnerships Project for federal COPS office	Success of 447 police agencies receiving problem solving grants
1999	National Evaluation of Project Weed and Seed (discussed in Chapter 12)	Proactive drug enforcement and prevention
1998	National Evaluation of Youth Firearms Violence	Approaches to reduce firearms related violence
1998	Information Systems Technology Enhancement Project	Technology uses for COPPS
1997	Federal Study of Crime Prevention Programs	Broad range of programs
1995	Repeat Victimization	Prevention of revictimization
1995	Integrated Criminal Apprehension Program	Crime analysis based deployment
1993	"Tipping Point" Studies	Examination of crime epidemics
1992	Crime Prevention through Environmental Design	Designing out crime
1992	Situational Crime Prevention	Reducing crime opportunities
1991	Quality Policing in Madison, Wisconsin	Quality management study
1990	Minneapolis "Hot Spot" Patrolling	Intensive patrol of problem areas
1988	Police Decoy Operations	Criminal targeting tactic
1987	Problem Oriented Policing, Newport News, Virginia	Crime problem solving model
1987	Houston and Newark Fear of Crime Studies	Fear reduction study
1985	Repeat Offender Programs	Target career criminals
1984	Minneapolis Domestic Violence Experiment	Analysis of effective police action
1983	Differential Police Response Field Test	Call priority and alternative reporting
1982	Directed Patrol National Survey	Survey of patrol strategies
1981	Newark Foot Patrol Experiment	Cost benefits of foot patrol
1977	Split Force Patrol Experiment, Wilmington, Delaware	Patrol deployment study
1977	Patrol Staffing in San Diego	One- vs. two-officer cars
1976	Kansas City Response Time Study	Police response to crimes
1975	RAND Study of Investigations	Detective and patrol effectiveness
1975	Field Interview Study, San Diego	Linking field interviews to crime
1974	Kansas City Preventive Patrol Experiment	Effectiveness of random patrol
1973	Team Policing Experiment in Seven U.S. Cities	Team vs. traditional policing
1973	Police-Community Relations	Study of organizational orientation
1972	Policewomen on Patrol	Evaluation of women on patrol

measuring their "success" by the numbers of arrests, quickness of responses, and so on, while often neglecting the outcome of their work: the ends.

As we have seen, the "We've always done it this way" mentality, still pervading policing to a large extent, may be not only an ineffective means of organizing and administering a police agency but also a costly squandering of valuable human and financial resources. For many police agencies today operating under the traditional, incident-driven style of policing, the *beat*, rather than the *neighborhood*, is, to borrow a term from research methodology, the "unit of analysis." Under this time-worn model, officers have been glued to their police radios, flitting like pinballs from one call for service to the next as rapidly as possible. Furthermore, police officers seldom leave their vehicles to address incidents except when answering CFS. They know very little about the underlying causes of problems in the neighborhoods on their beats.

The results of employing conventional police methods have been inglorious. Problems have persisted or been allowed to go unnoticed and grow while neighborhoods deteriorate. Officers become frustrated after they repeatedly handle similar calls, with no sign of progress. Petty offenses contributed to this decline and drove stable community members away once the message went out to offenders and vandals that "no one cares" about the neighborhood. Yet many in the police field are unaware of or refuse to accept that the old ways are open to serious challenge.

Time for a New Approach

We believe it is clear from all we've discussed thus far that police agencies must change their daily activities, their management practices, and even their view of their work in order to confront the changes that are occurring. We maintain that, given the current levels of violence and the public's fear of it, the disorder found in countless American neighborhoods, poor police community relations in many cities, and the rapidly changing landscape of crime and demographics in America, the police need to seriously consider whether a "bureaucratic overhaul" is needed to meet the demands of the future.

Police research also demonstrated the need for agencies to evaluate the effectiveness of their responses. Both quantitative and qualitative data should be used as a basis for evaluation and change. Departments need to know more about what their officers are doing. Agencies are struggling to find enough resources for performing crime trend analyses; most also do not conduct proper workload analyses to know how much uncommitted time is available to their officers.

Research has also provided the realization that policing consists of developing the most effective means for dealing with a multitude of troublesome situations. For example, problem solving is a whole new way of thinking about policing and carries the potential to reshape the way in which police services are delivered.[58]

One of several things the police must do to accomplish their mission is to reacquaint themselves with members of the community by involving citizens in the resolution of neighborhood problems. Simply stated, police must view the public as well as other government and social services organizations as "a part of" as opposed to "apart from" their efforts. This change in conventional thinking advocates efficiency with effectiveness, quality over quantity, and encourages collaborative problem solving and creative resolutions to crime and disorder.

THE COMMUNITY PROBLEM SOLVING ERA

Team Policing, Foot Patrol, and Shattered Myths

In the early 1970s it was suggested that the performance of patrol officers would improve more by using job redesign based on "motivators."[59] This suggestion later evolved into a concept known as "team policing," which sought to restructure police departments, improve police-community relations, enhance police officer morale, and facilitate change within the police organization. Its primary element was a decentralized, neighborhood focus on the delivery of police services. Officers were to be generalists, trained to investigate crimes and basically to attend to all of the problems in their area with a team of officers being assigned to a particular neighborhood and responsible for all police services in that area.

In the end, however, team policing failed, for several reasons. Most of the experiments were poorly planned and hastily implemented, resulting in street officers not understanding what they were supposed to do. Many mid-management personnel felt threatened by team policing and, as a result, some sabotaged the experiment. Furthermore, team policing did not represent a completely different view of policing. As Samuel Walker observed, "It was essentially a different *organizational approach* to traditional policing: responding to calls for service (CFS), deterring crime through patrol, and apprehending criminals" (emphasis in original).[60]

There were other developments for the police during the late 1970s and early 1980s. Foot patrol became more popular and many jurisdictions (such as Newark, New Jersey; Boston; and Flint, Michigan) even demanded it. In Newark, an evaluation found that foot patrol was readily perceived by residents and that it produced a significant increase in the level of satisfaction with police service, led to a significant reduction of perceived crime problems, and resulted in a significant increase in the perceived level of safety of the neighborhood.[61] Flint researchers reported that the crime rate in the target areas declined slightly; CFS in these areas dropped by 43 percent. Furthermore, citizens indicated satisfaction with the program, suggesting that it had improved relations with the police.[62]

These findings and others discussed below shattered several long-held myths about measures of police effectiveness. In addition, research conducted during the 1970s suggested that *information* could help police improve their ability to deal with crime. These studies, along with those of foot patrol and fear reduction, created new opportunities for police to understand the increasing concerns of citizens' groups about disorder (e.g., gangs, prostitutes) and to work with citizens to do something about it. Police discovered that when they asked citizens about their priorities, citizens appreciated their asking and often provided useful information.

The Community Patrol Officer Program (CPOP), instituted by the New York City police department in 1984, was similar in many respects to the Flint foot patrol program. Officers involved in this program were responsible for getting to know the residents, merchants, and service providers in their beat area; identifying the principal crime and order maintenance problems confronting the people within their beat; and devising strategies for dealing with the problems identified.[63]

Principles of the New Model

Simultaneously, Herman Goldstein's problem oriented approach to policing was being tested in Madison, Wisconsin; Baltimore County, Maryland; and Newport News, Virginia. These studies found that police officers enjoy operating with a holistic approach to their work, have the capacity to do problem solving successfully, and can work with citizens and other agencies to solve problems. Also, citizens seemed to appreciate working with police. Moreover, this approach was a rethinking of earlier strategies of handling CFS: Officers were given more autonomy and trained to analyze the underlying causes of problems and find creative solutions. These findings were similar to those of the foot patrol experiments and fear reduction experiments.

The community oriented policing and problem solving (COPPS) model requires not only new police strategies but a new organizational approach as well. There is a renewed emphasis on community collaboration for many police tasks. Crime control remains an important function, but equal emphasis is given to *prevention*. Police officers return to their wide use of discretion under this model, and move away from routinization and standardization of addressing their tasks. This discretion pushes operational and tactical decision making to the lower levels of the organization.

Participative management is greatly increased, and fewer levels of authority are required to administer the organization; middle-management layers are reduced. Concurrently, many cities have developed what are, in effect, "demarketing" programs, actively attempting to rescind programs (such as the idea of rapid response to CFS, and 911 except for dire emergencies) that had been actively sold earlier.

Community problem solving has helped to explain what went wrong with team policing in the 1960s and 1970s. It was a strategy that innovators mistakenly approached as a tactic. Team policing also competed with traditional policing in the same departments, and they were incompatible with one another. A police department might have a small team policing unit or conduct a team policing experiment, but the reform, professional model of policing was still "business as usual."

The classical theory of police organization that continues to dominate many agencies is likewise alien to the community problem solving strategy. The new strategy will not accommodate the classical theory of traditional policing; the latter denies too much of the real nature of police work, continues old methods of supervision and administration, and creates too much cynicism in officers attempting to do creative problem solving.

Risks come with attempting the new strategy. The risks, however, "for the community and the profession of policing, are not as great as attempting to maintain a strategy that faltered on its own terms during the 1960s and 1970s."[64]

Although we will discuss COPPS in greater detail in Chapter 4, following is a summary of the factors that set the stage for the emergence of COPPS:

- The narrowing of the police mission to crime fighting
- Increased cultural diversity in our society, and concern with police violation of minority civil rights
- The detachment of patrol officers in patrol vehicles and administration from officer and community input
- Increased violence in our society
- A downturn in the economy, and, subsequently, a "do more with less" philosophy toward the police
- Increased dependence on high-technology equipment rather than contact with the public

Why the Emergence of Community Oriented Policing and Problem Solving?

- The emphasis on organizational change, including decentralization and greater officer discretion
- A desire for greater personalization of government services
- Burgeoning attempts by the police to adequately reach the community through crime prevention, team policing, and police-community relations

Most of these elements contain a common theme: the isolation of the police from the public and success being measured by the numbers of arrests, quickness of responses, and so on, as noted earlier. For many decades, this isolation often resulted in an "us versus them" mentality on the part of both the police and the citizenry. The notion of community policing, therefore, "rose like a phoenix from the ashes of burned cities, embattled campuses, and crime-riddled neighborhoods."[65]

Community policing "rewrites police history" with a greater willingness to engage the public. (*Courtesy* Fort Lauderdale, Florida, police department)

COPPS is the established paradigm of contemporary policing, both at home and abroad (see Chapter 14); it enjoys a large degree of public acceptance[66] and receives widespread attention by academicians who have published a growing number of journal articles and doctoral dissertations on the topic.[67] Furthermore, it has now moved through three generations, according to Willard Oliver: innovation, diffusion, and institutionalization.[68]

1. The innovation generation of COPPS spans the period of 1979 through 1986, beginning with the seminal work of Herman Goldstein concerning needed improvement of policing,[69] coupled with the "broken windows" theory by Wilson and Kelling.[70] Early concepts of community policing during this generation were often called "experiments," "test sites," and "demonstration projects," and were often restricted to larger metropolitan cities. The style of policing that was employed was predominately narrow in focus, such as foot patrols, problem solving methods, or community substations. These small-scale test sites provided a source of innovative ideas for others to consider.

2. The second generation, diffusion, spans the period from 1987 through 1994. The concepts and philosophy of community policing and problem solving spread rapidly among police agencies through a variety of communication means within the policing subculture. Adoption of the strategy was fast becoming a reality during this generation as evidenced by the fact that, in 1985, slightly more than 300 police agencies had adopted some form of community policing,[71] whereas by 1994 it had spread to more than 8,000 agencies.[72] The practice of community policing during this generation was still generally limited to large and medium-sized cities, and the style of policing during this generation was much broader than the first, being more involved with neighborhood and quality-of-life issues. The strategies normally targeted drug and fear of crime issues while improving police-community relationships. Much more emphasis was placed on evaluating outcomes through the use of appropriate research methodologies.

3. The third generation, *institutionalization*, is from 1995 to the present and has seen widespread implementation of community policing and problem solving across the United States: today nearly 7 in 10 (68 percent) of the nation's 17,000 local police agencies, *employing 90 percent of all officers*, have adopted this strategy.[73] This generation has seen COPPS become deeply entrenched within the political process and has featured federal grant money through the Violent Crime Control and Law Enforcement Act of 1994. This act authorized $8.8 billion over six years to create the Office of Community Oriented Policing Services (COPS) in the United States Department of Justice, added community policing officers across the country, created 31 regional community policing institutes (RCPIs) to develop and deliver community policing training, and allowed agencies of all sizes to apply for community policing grants. (As of January 2003, the COPS office had provided funding assistance to nearly 13,000 jurisdictions through 27 different grant programs, including funding for about 116,500 community policing officers across the country. Table 1-1 shows the history of funded programs and personnel of the COPS office, from 1994 to the present.) The style of policing under this generation has extended to such programs as youth firearms violence, gangs, and domestic violence, while extending into geo-mapping software and crime prevention through environmental design (CPTED, discussed in Chapter 5).

TABLE 1-1.   History of the Federal Office of Community Oriented Policing Services

1994

- The Violent Crime Control & Law Enforcement Act passes both the House and the Senate, authorizing an $8.8 billion expenditure over six years. The Office of Community Oriented Policing Services is created to distribute and monitor these funds.
- COPS launches three new programs: Accelerated Hiring, Education and Deployment (AHEAD), Funding Accelerated for Smaller Towns (FAST), and Making Officer Redeployment Effective (MORE).
- COPS awards $200 million to 392 agencies for 2,700 additional community policing professionals.
- Total program funding for fiscal year 1994: $148.4 million.

1995

- COPS funds 25,000 more officers.
- COPS announces the Universal Hiring Program (UHP), which incorporates FAST and AHEAD.
- COPS awards grants totaling $10 million through the Youth Firearms Violence Initiative.
- Total program funding for fiscal year 1995: $1,225.1 million.

1996

- COPS funds more than 52,000 officers through UHP.
- COPS announces its Anti-Gang Initiative and Community Policing to Combat Domestic Violence Program.
- COPS announces its Problem-Solving Partnership initiative.
- Total program funding for fiscal year 1996: $1,209.2 million.

1997

- COPS publishes and releases a report entitled *Police Integrity: Public Service with Honor*.
- COPS funding establishes a nationwide network of Regional Community Policing Institutes (RCPIs).
- Total program funding for fiscal year 1997: $983.9 million.

1998

- COPS has now funded 75,000 new community policing professionals nationwide.
- COPS introduces three new programs: Distressed Neighborhoods Pilot Project, Police Corps Program, and Small Communities Grant Program.
- COPS launches the Methamphetamine Program, through which it awards $34 million throughout the fiscal year.
- COPS awards a total of $38 million through its Technology Program.
- Total program funding for fiscal year 1998: $1,490.7 million.

1999

- COPS announces its COPS in Schools (CIS) grant program.
- COPS funds its 100,000th community policing professional in May of 1999.
- COPS announces its Tribal Resources Grant Program (TRGP).
- Total program funding for fiscal year 1999: $1,127.7 million.

(continued)

TABLE 1-1.   (continued)

2000

- COPS launches its Police as Problem-Solvers and Peacemakers program, through which it awards $1 million to five law enforcement agencies.
- COPS announces its Justice-Based After School (JBAS) and Value-Based Initiatives (VBI) programs.
- COPS awards $12 million to 41 state law enforcement agencies for the purchase of 2,900 in-car cameras.
- Total program funding for fiscal year 2000: $685.3 million.

2001

- COPS launches two new series of publications: COPS Innovations and Problem-Oriented Policing Guides.
- COPS awards $600,000 through JBAS to seven law enforcement agencies.
- COPS supports the NYPD and Arlington County police department as they respond to the September 11 attacks.
- Total program funding for fiscal year 2001: $558.1 million.

2002

- COPS awards more than $70 million through the Methamphetamine Program.
- COPS awards more than $154 million through the Technology Program.
- COPS announces $128 million in UHP grants that allow 367 agencies to hire 1750 community policing professionals.
- Total program funding for fiscal year 2002: $656.9 million.

Source: Washington, D.C.: U.S. Department of Justice, Office of Community Oriented Policing Services. *http://www.cops.usdoj.gov/Default.asp?Item=44* (Accessed January 20, 2003).

COPPS is obviously the culture of many police organizations, affecting and permeating their hiring processes, recruit academies, in-service training, promotional examinations, and strategic plans. COPPS is also having an impact in the form of community oriented government and in the criminal justice system. There is little doubt that COPPS is the future of policing. The possible shape of things to come, and what the next generation of community policing might be, is discussed in Chapter 15.

Table 1-2 summarizes the three eras of policing that were discussed previously: the political, reform, and community eras.

TODAY'S PREMIER CHALLENGE: HOMELAND SECURITY

Unquestionably, historians of the future will maintain that terroristic acts of the early twenty-first century changed forever the nature of policing efforts in the United States. Words are almost inadequate to describe how the events of September 11, 2001, forever modified and heightened the fears and concerns of all Americans with regard to domestic security and the methods necessary for securing the general public. Within the 50 states, there are thousands of

TABLE 1-2. The Three Eras of Policing

	Political Era 1840s to 1930s	Reform Era 1930s to 1980s	Community Era 1980s to present
Authorization	Politics and law	Law and professionalism	Community support (political), law and professionalism
Function	Broad social services	Crime control	Broad provision of services
Organizational design	Decentralized	Centralized, classical	Decentralized, task forces, matrices
Relationship to community	Intimate	Professional, remote	Intimate
Tactics and technology	Foot patrol	Preventive patrol and rapid response to calls	Foot patrol, problem solving, public relations
Outcome	Citizen, political satisfaction	Crime control	Quality of life and citizen satisfaction

Source: Adapted from George L. Kelling and Mark H. Moore, *The Evolving Strategies of Policing* (Washington, D.C.: U.S. Department of Justice, National Institute of Justice Perspectives on Policing, November 1988).

counties and cities that must be protected. The job of getting law enforcement, emergency services, public health agencies, citizens, and private enterprises coordinated and working together at local, state, and federal levels is a daunting task.

Police have several possible means to address domestic terrorism. First, and perhaps the most fruitful, is military support of domestic law enforcement. The Posse Comitatus Act of 1878 prohibits using the military to execute the laws, generally; the military may be called upon, however, to provide personnel and equipment support for certain special occurrences, such as domestic terrorist events involving weapons of mass destruction. On a larger level, dealing with terrorist organizations requires that the police: gather intelligence on terrorist organizations; determine what measures can be taken to counter, or thwart, terrorist activities; develop rapid response and containment of the damage should such attacks occur; and apprehend and convict terrorists and dismantle their organizations.

Clearly the police are challenged more than ever before, but because COPPS helps to build trust between police and their communities, they can deal more effectively with community concerns. And since COPPS helps the police to develop knowledge of community activity, the problem solving model is well-suited to the prevention of terrorism.

In later chapters we discuss how the analysis portion of problem solving can enhance work in the counterterrorism arena through investigation, prevention, and emergency operations, and we discuss recruiting persons into policing who demonstrate problem-solving skills.

COMMUNITY POLICING BY INTERNET

A look at the Internet's Web pages of many city police departments and county sheriff's offices reveals many such agencies presenting a history of their organization, including their conversion to the COPPS initiative. In a sense these agencies are explaining to the public and their own employees how they have

The terrorist attacks on New York's World Trade Center linked forever the concepts of community policing, problem solving, and homeland security.

evolved at the local level. This approach serves a twofold purpose. First, it serves to educate those persons *outside* the agency concerning the agency's history and identity, and to underscore that COPPS is not to be viewed as a temporary, independent "program" but as a part of the agency's method of service delivery. Second, it conveys to those persons who are employed *inside* the organization a sense of who they are and the agency's philosophy.[74]

A search of police Web sites on a popular search engine revealed nearly 1,000 sites. Often the site was used for public information purposes, such as: letting the community report crimes; listing programs and initiatives, recruitment and employment, special events and activities; and posting contact information and frequently asked questions. Some go further, posting crime statistics (including hate crimes), wanted and missing person reports, sex offender alerts, and annual reports; transmitting intelligence information to detectives in the field; and even allowing people to pay parking tickets and make anonymous tips. The Chicago police department's Web site consists of 1,500 pages of information, which are color-coded and have header bars to help categorize and navigate the site.[75] Some jurisdictions even have chat rooms for citizens, and allow informants to continuously provide information to police.[76]

SUMMARY

This chapter has shown the evolution of policing in America. Problems with some of the old methods, as well as the willingness of police leaders to rethink their basic role and develop new strategies, led us to community oriented policing and problem solving. It is much more than a simple "return to the basics"; it is instead a retooling of the basics, or coming full circle.[77]

The incorporation of past wisdom and the use of new tools, methods, and strategies via COPPS offers the most promise for crime detection and prevention, addressing crime and disorder, and improving relations with the public. These partnerships are essential for addressing the "broken windows" phenomenon[78]—an influential theory asserting that once the process of physical decay begins, its effects multiply until some corrective action is taken. The lesson is that we should redirect our thinking toward improving police handling of "little" problems. In short, the police need to be thinking like what might be termed "street-level criminologists," examining the underlying causes of crime rather than functioning like bureaucrats. This theme will be echoed at various points throughout the book.

NOTES

1. David R. Johnson, *American Law Enforcement History* (St. Louis: Forum Press, 1981), p. 11.

2. Ibid., p. 13.

3. Ibid., p. 14–15.

4. Leon Radzinowicz, *A History of English Criminal Law and Its Administration from 1750*, Vol. IV: *Grappling for Control* (London: Stevens & Son, 1968), p. 163.

5. Johnson, *American Law Enforcement History*, pp. 19–20.

6. A. C. Germann, Frank D. Day, and Robert R. J. Gallati, *Introduction to Law Enforcement and Criminal Justice* (Springfield, IL: Charles C. Thomas, 1962), p. 63.

7. Clive Emsley, *Policing and its Context, 1750–1870* (New York: Schocken Books, 1983), p. 37.

8. Eric H. Monkkonen, *Police in Urban America, 1860–1920* (Cambridge, U.K.: Cambridge University Press, 1981), pp. 1–2.

9. Johnson, *American Law Enforcement History*, pp. 26–27.

10. See K. E. Jordan, *Ideology and the Coming of Professionalism: American Urban Police in the 1920s and 1930s* (Dissertation, Rutgers University, 1972); Robert M. Fogelson, *Big-City Police* (Cambridge, Mass.: Harvard University Press, 1977).

11. Johnson, *American Law Enforcement History*, p. 27.

12. James F. Richardson, *Urban Policing in the United States* (New York: Oxford Press, 1970), p. 51.

13. Johnson, *American Law Enforcement*, p. 92.

14. Ibid., p. 92.

15. Ibid., p. 92.

16. Ibid., pp. 96–98.

17. Ibid.

18. Monkkonen, *Police in Urban America, 1860–1920*, p. 158.

19. John E. Eck, *The Investigation of Burglary and Robbery* (Washington, D.C.: Police Executive Research Forum, 1984).

20. See George L. Kelling, "Juveniles and Police: The End of the Nightstick," in Francis X. Hartmann (ed.), *From Children to Citizens, Vol. II: The Role of the Juvenile Court* (New York: Springer-Verlag, 1987).

21. Samuel Walker, *A Critical History of Police Reform: The Emergence of Professionalism* (Lexington, Mass.: Lexington Books, 1977), pp. 8–9, 11.

22. Ibid., p. 33.

23. Ibid., pp. 33–34, 42, 47.

24. Ibid., p. 81.

25. Ibid., pp. 80–83.

26. Herman Goldstein, *Policing a Free Society* (Cambridge, Mass.: Ballinger, 1977).

27. Albert Reiss, *The Police and the Public* (New Haven, Ct.: Yale University Press, 1971).

28. See Orlando Wilson, *Police Administration* (New York: McGraw-Hill, 1950).

29. Walker, *A Critical History of Police Reform: The Emergence of Professionalism*, pp. 93–94.

30. Mark H. Moore and George L. Kelling, "'To Serve and Protect': Learning from Police History," *The Public Interest* 70 (Winter 1983):49–65.

31. Peter K. Manning, "The Police: Mandate, Strategies, and Appearances," in Jack D. Douglas (ed.), *Crime and Justice in American Society* (Indianapolis, Ind.: Bobbs-Merrill, 1971), pp. 149–163.

32. Walker, *A Critical History of Police Reform: The Emergence of Professionalism*, p. 161.

33. Louis Radelet, *The Police and the Community* (4th ed.)(New York: Macmillan, 1986), p. ix.

34. Ibid., p. 17.

35. Ibid., p. 21.

36. William G. Doerner, *Introduction to Law Enforcement: An Insider's View* (Englewood Cliffs, N.J.: Prentice Hall, 1992), pp. 21–23.

37. Mary Ann Wycoff, *The Role of Municipal Police Research as a Prelude to Changing It* (Washington, D.C.: Police Foundation, 1982).

38. Jerome H. Skolnick and David H. Bayley, *The New Blue Line: Police Innovation in Six American Cities* (New York: The Free Press, 1986), p. 4.

39. William C. Cunningham, John J. Strauchs, and Clifford W. Van Meter, *The Hallcrest Report II: Private Security Trends, 1970–2000* (McLean, Va.: Hallcrest Systems, 1990).

40. William Westley, *Violence and the Police: A Sociological Study of Law, Custom, and Morality* (Cambridge, Mass.: MIT Press, 1970).

41. American Bar Foundation, *The Urban Police Function*. Approved draft. (Chicago: American Bar Association, 1973).

42. Jerome Skolnick, *Justice Without Trial: Law Enforcement in Democratic Society* (New York: John Wiley & Sons, 1966).

43. Egon Bittner, "The Police on Skid Row: A Study of Peace Keeping," *American Sociological Review* 32 (1967):699–715.

44. Raymond I. Parnas, "The Police Response to the Domestic Disturbance," *Wisconsin Law Review*, (1967) 914–955.

45. James Q. Wilson, *Varieties of Police Behavior: The Management of Law and Order in Eight Communities* (Cambridge, Mass.: Harvard University Press, 1968).

46. Albert J. Reiss, Jr., *The Police and the Public* (New Haven, Conn.: Yale University Press, 1971).

47. Goldstein, *Policing a Free Society*, pp. 22–24.

48. Ibid., p. 11.

49. Elaine Cumming, Ian Cumming, and Laura Edell, "Policeman as Philosopher, Guide, and Friend," *Social Problems* 12 (1965):285; T. Bercal, "Calls for Police Assistance," *American Behavioral Scientist* 13 (1970):682; Albert J. Reiss, *The Police and the Public* (New Haven, Conn.: Yale University Press, 1971).

50. George Kelling, Tony Pate, Duane Dieckman, and Charles E. Brown, *The Kansas City Preventive Patrol Experiment: A Summary Report*. (Washington, D.C.: Police Foundation, 1974).

51. Peter W. Greenwood, Joan Petersilia, and Jan Chaiken, *The Criminal Investigation Process*. (Lexington, Mass.: D. C. Heath, 1977); John E. Eck, *Managing Case Assignments: The Burglary Investigation Decision Model Replication* (Washington, D.C.: Police Executive Research Forum, 1979).

52. Bernard Greenbert, S. Yu Oliver, and Karen Lang, *Enhancement of the Investigative Function, Vol. 1, Analysis and Conclusions*, Final Report, Phase 1 (Springfield, Va.: National Technical Information Service, 1973).

53. Kelling, Pate, Dieckman, and Brown, *The Kansas City Preventive Patrol Experiment: A Summary Report*.

54. Ibid.

55. Joan Petersilia, "The Influence of Research on Policing," in Roger C. Dunham and Geoffrey P. Alpert (eds.), *Critical Issues in Policing: Contemporary Readings* (Prospect Heights, Ill.: Waveland Press, 1989), pp. 230–247.

56. James Q. Wilson, *Thinking About Crime* (New York: Vintage Books, 1975).

57. Herman Goldstein, *Problem-Oriented Policing* (New York: McGraw-Hill, 1990), p. 13.

58. Ibid., p. 3.

59. Thomas J. Baker, "Designing the Job to Motivate," *FBI Law Enforcement Bulletin* 45 (1976):3–7.

60. Samuel Walker, *The Police in America: An Introduction* (2d ed.) (New York: McGraw-Hill, 1992), p. 185.

61. Police Foundation, *The Newark Foot Patrol Experiment* (Washington, D.C.: Author, 1981).

62. Robert Trojanowicz, *An Evaluation of the Neighborhood Foot Patrol Program in Flint, Michigan* (East Lansing, Mich.: School of Criminal Justice, Michigan State University, 1982).

63. Michael J. Farrell, "The Development of the Community Patrol Officer Program: Community-Oriented Policing in the New York City Police Department." In Jack R. Greene and Stephen D. Mastrofski (eds.), *Community Policing: Rhetoric or Reality* (New York: Praeger, 1988), pp. 73–88.

64. George L. Kelling and Mark H. Moore, "The Evolving Strategy of Policing" (Washington, D.C.: National Institute of Justice, November 1988), p. 14.

65. Robert Trojanowicz and Bonnie Bucqueroux, *Community Policing: A Contemporary Perspective* (Cincinnati, Ohio: Anderson, 1990), p. 67.

66. George Gallup, *Community Policing Survey* (Wilmington, N.Y.: Scholarly Resources, 1996).

67. Willard M. Oliver, "The Third Generation of Community Policing: Moving Through Innovation, Diffusion, and Institutionalization," *Police Quarterly* 3 (December 2000):367–388.

68. Ibid.

69. Herman Goldstein, "Improving Policing: A Problem-Oriented Approach," *Crime and Delinquency* 25 (1979):236–258.

70. James Q. Wilson and George L. Kelling, "Broken Windows: The Police and Neighborhood Safety," *Atlantic Monthly* (March 1982):29–38.

71. Samuel Walker, *The Police in America: An Introduction* (New York: McGraw-Hill, 1985).

72. T. McEwen, *National Assessment Program: 1994 Survey Results* (Washington, D.C.: National Institute of Justice, 1995).

73. U.S. Department of Justice, Bureau of Justice Statistics, *Law Enforcement Management and Administrative Statistics: Local Police Departments 2000* (Washington, D.C.: Author, January 2003), p. iii.

74. See, for example, Donna Rogers, "Online Police Resources: How Departmental Web Sites and Internet Services Are Making a Difference," *Law Enforcement Technology* (November 2001):70–74.

75. Ibid., p. 71.

76. Chad Nilson and Tod W. Burke, "Policing by Internet: High Tech Community Policing," *Law and Order* (August 2002):36–39.

77. Stephanie Thompson, "Community Policing Comes Full Circle," *American City and County* (February 1991):33–41.

78. Wilson and Kelling, "Broken Windows: The Police and Neighborhood Safety," pp. 29–38.

INTRODUCTION

What kind of country do we live in? What is the nature of its demographics and crime, and where is it headed? Have conventional policing methods of the past been effective and are they sufficient for the future? Or, rather, do the police need to prepare for change and begin putting strategic plans into motion? This chapter examines some of the many changes occurring in the United States and explores what the police must do to confront them.

The chapter begins by examining the changes that are occurring in this nation, beginning with its people—demographics, immigration, the elderly and the young, and the effects of technology. Next is a consideration of the nature of our criminality, including violence, computer and juvenile crimes, and crime accelerators (guns, drugs, and alcohol). Then we examine fear of crime, and the police goal of keeping neighborhoods safe.

—2—

A NATION IN FLUX

Changing People, Crime, and Policing

A state without the means of some change is without the means of its conservation.
—EDMUND BURKE

There is, in public affairs, no state so bad, provided it has age and stability on its side, that it is not preferable to change and disturbance.
—MICHEL DE MONTAIGNE

THE CHANGING FACE OF AMERICA

Demographics: Who Are We?

In 2004, it is projected that nearly 285 million people will be living in America, a little more than half (51 percent) being female. The population of the United States grew nearly 10 percent during the 1990s. Approximately 81 percent of the estimated population of the U.S. are white, 13 percent are black, and 6 percent are Asian, Pacific Islander, Native American, Eskimo, and Aleut; about 13 percent, furthermore, are Hispanic. Nearly two in three of all Americans own their own homes; there are about 2.63 persons per household, and about one-fourth (27.6 percent) of all households are headed by one person.[1]

The mean age of Americans in 2004 is estimated to be 36.5 years (from projections); one-fourth of the population is under 18 years of age, while about 12.5 percent are over 65. About 59 percent of the population are married and live with their spouse; about 19.8 million adults (6.9 percent) are divorced.[2] Also, in connection with the nation's youth, divorce rate, and number of single-parent homes, there is an increasing number of fatherless children—children who are more prone to delinquency and other social pathologies. Between 1960 and 1990, the percentage of children living apart from their biological fathers increased from 17 to 36 percent. By 2000, that number had increased to about half. Of the 26 percent of all children in 2000 under 18 years old who lived with one parent, about 96 percent of them lived with their mother. Many problems in crime control are strongly related to father absence: 90 percent of all homeless and runaway youths are from fatherless homes, as are 71 percent of high school dropouts, 70 percent of youths in state institutions, 75 percent of adolescent patients in substance abuse centers, and 85 percent of rapists who were motivated by displaced anger.[3] The oldest old (persons 85 years old and over) are a small but rapidly growing group and are projected to be the fastest-growing part of the elderly population well into the twenty-first century.[4]

Many changes are expected in the demographics of the United States between now and the year 2035. For example, life expectancy is expected to increase from 76.0 years to 82.6 years, and the median age of the population will increase from 34.0 (in 1994) to 39.1, the increase being driven by the aging baby boomer population born after World War II (1946–1964).[5]

Coming to America: Immigration

With almost one-third of the current population growth being caused by immigration,[6] the influx of immigrants has placed significant demands on the infrastructure of the nation's public service sector, particularly the criminal justice system.[7] Each year between 660,000 and 1 million aliens are lawfully admitted into this country for permanent residence; hundreds of thousands of others are legally residing in this country with temporary immigrant visas, pending a decision on their residency applications.[8] Another estimated 5 million undocumented immigrants reside in the United States as well, and there is an estimated increase of about 275,000 illegal aliens entering and residing in this country each year. Many, about 2.1 million (41 percent), entered legally on a temporary basis and failed to depart.[9]

Between 1990 and 1998, the Hispanic population in the United States grew by an estimated 35 percent (the Asian population, meanwhile, grew 41 percent). Currently, the nation's population is 13 percent Hispanic. The Hispanic and Asian groups—younger and with larger families—are projected to account for more than half of the nation's population growth over the next 50 years.[10]

A police officer works with Asian business owners to improve a shopping center that was rundown and was experiencing increased crime. (*Courtesy* Community Policing Consortium)

COMMUNITY POLICING AND PROBLEM SOLVING

Hispanics account for approximately 54 percent of the illegal immigrant population in the United States. (*Courtesy* Harold Beasley)

The influence of immigration to America and the growth of minority group populations in general cannot be overstated. America now accepts nearly 1 million newcomers each year (with a net immigration of about 880,000 persons, which could increase or decrease in future years), or about 10 million new residents each decade (excluding their offspring) even if immigration rates do not rise.[11]

Exhibit 2-1 discusses the extremely diverse nature of two of the nation's largest cities, Los Angeles and Chicago.

EXHIBIT 2-1   A Tale of Two Cities: Los Angeles* and Chicago**

The City of Los Angeles is one of the most diverse cities in the western hemisphere. This poses a particular problem for the police in trying to gain voluntary compliance with the law as well as build community partnerships. Many people arrived there from their native lands with myriad different customs and cultural practices, some of which may even be deemed illegal in this country. There are over 112 different nationalities of people and more than 100 different languages spoken. With the Russian, Armenian, Korean, Farsi, Spanish, and Thai speaking communities and their cultural barriers, walls are often created and a lack of cooperation fostered between police and the community, with a distrust among the people of either reporting a crime or stepping forward as a witness.

Chicago is the third most popular destination city for new immigrants. Since the 1990 census, the city has become home to tens of thousands of newly documented immigrants from Mexico alone as well as large numbers of undocumented immigrants. Smaller numbers of immigrants also have arrived from the Middle East, the Philippines, and Poland. The city's Chinatown neighborhood is expanding in several directions, and refugees from Southeast Asia are forming new communities of their own. Members of each group arrive with established views of how to relate to the police, and find themselves accommodating these views to a new environment and America's big-city problems.

*Adapted from David Kalish, "West Bureau Community Access Seminars," *http://lapdonline.org/community/op_west__bureau6.htm*, p. 1 (Accessed January 29, 2003).

**Adapted from U.S. Department of Justice, National Institute of Justice, *Community Policing and "The New Immigrants": Latinos in Chicago* (Research Report) (Washington, D.C.: Author, July 2002), p. 3.

In addition to documented and undocumented immigration to the United States, another challenge has been posed for the law enforcement community with the advent of new forms of organized crime activity, particularly Russian groups. While there is no formal organized structure (as with the American "Mafia") among Russian criminal individuals and groups, there is a mix of opportunistic groupings of individuals with a small number of networks that are loosely organized; there is a significant amount of criminal activity that is attributable to those who have come from the states of the former Soviet Union. The structure of Soviet prison camps and the financial and social collapse of Russia created a class of professional criminals who now form a Russian Mafia there as well as in America. This is perceived to be a growing crisis.[12]

Destabilizing Factors

The above described demographic makeup of the nation poses additional challenges for the police. For example, single-occupant households represented 17 percent of the total in 1970, 25 percent in 1997, and are projected to increase to 27 percent in 2010; average household size has been steadily decreasing from 3.14 in 1970 to 2.64 in 1997. Likewise, the percentage of married couples declined from 70 percent in 1970 to 53 percent in 1997, with a continued decline predicted.[13] These figures represent threats to societal stability because the smaller the household, the less the commitment of a population to each other and the less likely deviance will be managed at the household level, thus necessitating governmental intervention. Marriage is our most stable family structure; between 1980 and 1997, however, there was a 20 percent increase in the never-married category—highest among blacks and Hispanics.[14]

Another destabilizing force is the number of people who in a given year change where they live. The average person moves once every six years. But approximately 17 percent of the population moves each year. Thus, long-term neighborhood stability is the exception rather than the rule. Home ownership, another stability factor, is another concern, with 72 percent of blacks and Hispanics and 38 percent of whites unable to afford a modestly priced home.[15]

The Graying of America: Implications and Concerns

We live in a "graying" country as well, in which a growing age group of between 55 and 65 will represent an estimated 12.6 percent of the total population.[16] The golden years for baby boomers represents a graying of the population. The first boomers reached age 50, or midlife, in 1996; soon they will command the aging agenda as they prepare for retirement in 2010 through 2030.

The rapid growth of the elderly, particularly the oldest old, represents a triumph of efforts to extend human life, but these age groups also require a large share of special services and public support. There will be large increases in some very vulnerable groups, such as the oldest old living alone, older women, elderly racial minorities living alone, and elderly unmarried persons with no living children or siblings.[17]

The good news is the elderly are less likely than younger people to become victims of violence, personal theft, and household crimes, and less likely to be injured during a violent crime (but their injuries, with brittle bones, are more severe). Victimization can be permanently disabling. Being on fixed income, they cannot receive the best medical care; most are female. They also have a high fear of crime, but are less likely to take protective measures than younger people and more likely to report a crime. They can also be victimized in nursing homes and hospitals. They are also targeted more for financial fraud than other people, which can lead to severe depression and other serious health problems. Their isolation leads to a high percentage of their victimization occurring in their homes.[18]

Finally, the elderly offer a tremendous workforce resource as volunteers, which will be discussed in more detail in Chapter 3.

A Generational Divide

In addition to the "graying" of America, this nation also has a sizable youthful contingent that will affect the country's social fabric, workforce, and crime in the future. These youthful cohorts are obviously significant in terms of their problems, size, and societal impact. The baby boomers, however—by virtue of their sheer numbers (a total of 76 million were born, constituting roughly a third of the total nation's population in the late 1990s), age, and influence—can fairly be said to presently control America's politics and boardrooms. They are the nation's leaders and include its chief executive officers, sheriffs, and police chiefs; they are conservative, influential policymakers, and leaders in the nation's current get-tough-on-crime movement, carrying the banner for such movements as "three strikes" laws and zero tolerance for crime in general.

The Gen-X (also known as baby busters) cohort, born between 1965 and 1976, are now about 17 percent of the population. They are overall more knowledgeable about technology than earlier generational groups, and are probably more mobile and less concerned at present about a long-term career and retirement.

There is also the baby boomlet generation, born between 1977 and 1995; these are offspring of the baby boomers, who created a generation that is approaching boom status in its size and scope. Boomlet births began to rise in the late 1970s and have been above 4 million a year since 1989. These young people are very high-technology in their orientation and very mobile as well, and tend to be very concerned about real world issues.

Finally, there are the echo boomers, known as Generation Y, constituting a massive demographic group between the ages of 14 and 25 and now felt to be behind a quiet revolution across America. It can be seen in their clothes, hair, and penchant for technology.

How does this generational divide affect policing? First, the police need to understand the perspective of each group's members. Americans aged 18 and younger will soon form a generation as big as the original baby boom. They will likely be quicker to challenge the status quo and higher authority than earlier generations and, for that reason, can make recruiting, hiring, and training of future police officers more difficult. They are also much more multi-cultural and opinionated, accepting of shifting sex roles, and differ widely from their predecessors in race, living arrangements, and socioeconomic class.

High Technology: New Developments, New Problems

Today the world is also rapidly becoming more technological to the extent that there now exists what can be termed a serious "digital divide" (see Exhibit 2-2). The ability to produce and analyze information has become as important to our country as economics in terms of a person's social standing or ability to get a job.

Access to the Internet is no longer a luxury; now more than 42 million people per month use the Internet to upgrade job skills, gather medical data, make major financial or investment decisions, or seek a new job. Three-quarters of this nation's households with incomes greater than $75,000 have a computer, however, compared with only one-third of households with incomes between $25,000 and $35,000. This unbalanced access worries people who are serving on a 26-member President's Information Technology Advisory Committee, who have had a lot of discussion on what is called the "digital divide." The committee wants to ensure that economic or geographic barriers do not prohibit anyone from using advanced communication technologies, especially at this point in time when more women and minorities need to be trained for information technology careers. Fortunately, the federal government is investing in information technology in a national Technology Opportunities Program that established Community Technology Centers (CTCs) so that low income people can access digital technology and the Internet; in fiscal years 2002 and 2003, nearly $50 million in funding was awarded by Congress for this purpose.

More information about CTCs and their funding can be found at: *http://www.ed.gov/offices/ovae/adulted/ctc/* (Accessed April 28, 2003).

"Smokestack America" is largely gone; today there are fewer blue-collar jobs and more white-collar positions. The fastest-growing careers are those requiring more language, mathematics, and reasoning skills. In sum, today's economy is based on knowledge and the ability to process information; whereas employers in the past mostly wanted muscle, today more and more jobs presuppose skills, training, and education.

For dropouts and unskilled workers, finding family wage jobs with benefits will become more difficult in the twenty-first century. The globalization of the economy and technology are producing greater productivity and competition, larger profits, and fewer family wage jobs. Technology will not only eliminate some jobs in industries such as banking and manufacturing, it will also change the educational skills needed for the new jobs. Not everyone has, uses, or knows how to use technology.[19]

Many have-not Americans report possessing a bleak lifestyle. One Gallup study found that about a quarter of Americans consider themselves to be have-nots in other ways as well, saying they worry about household finances "most" or "all" of the time, have not had enough money to pay for basic necessities at some time during the past year, perceive their financial situation as being worse than that of their parents, and labeled their financial situation as "poor" or "lower income."[20] Furthermore, many Americans have seen little benefit from the much-hyped economic boom of the late 1990s. While many stock and dot-com company owners became wealthy during that boom, there were many employee layoffs and relatively lower labor prices.

The growing rift between this country's haves and have-nots is fostered in part by the differences between people in terms of access to, and knowledge of, computer technology. As a result, street crimes and other crimes by the underclass may also increase dramatically as the underclass sees hope decline even further. The poor will become poorer, which could contribute to levels of youth violence.

Crimes committed with computers and by juveniles are discussed next.

We reside in a violent country. One only need look at TV news, read the papers, or, in some cases, merely observe the environment to realize that life and the property of others are almost valueless to a large number of Americans (sce Exhibit 2-3).

A Violent America

The nation's crime rate fell from 1992 to through 2003, however, to its lowest point in a generation. Certainly a robust economy (prior to the recession that began following September 11, 2001 and the overall aging of the country contributed in large fashion to those declines. More and more, however, experts are also pointing to the prominent contribution of community oriented policing and problem solving (COPPS). The nature of crime is also changing rapidly in the United States due in great measure to the introduction of high technology, discussed below. Annually, there are about 23 million violent and property crime victimizations in the country[21] (Table 2-1 depicts four measures of serious violent crime).

Americans now spend about $147 billion per year for federal, state, and local criminal justice activities (including law enforcement, courts, and corrections agencies). Nearly half ($65.3 billion, or 45 percent) of this amount is

---

EXHIBIT 2-3 Signs of the Times: Crime-Related Bulletins from Across the Nation

Following are some "typical" crime news accounts occurring in the nation. They do not involve "household name" serial killers, offenders, or victims, but they do reflect the kinds of crimes that are reported with startling regularity across the country each year. Each case represents a terrible tragedy and involves a tremendous degree of trauma to be borne by the victims or their survivors. Reflected in some of the accounts is the viciousness on the part of some of our nation's youth.

- Santa Ana, California, police arrested two brothers, ages 20 and 15, suspected of killing their mother and trying to escape detection by chopping off her head and hands the way they saw it done on the cable TV series *The Sopranos* (Associated Press, January 2003).
- In a desolate Queens, New York, park, a gang of five homeless men dragged a woman into their squalid encampment, raping and beating her for two hours; the men's huts were so filthy that one officer threw away his shoes after stepping inside (*New York Daily News*, December 22, 2002).
- Nearly every day of the year, a woman is fatally shot by either her husband or boyfriend during the course of an argument, according to a survey by the Violence Policy Center in Washington, D.C. (*LEN*, October 31, 2002, p. 8).
- Serial killer Aileen Wuornow, 46, was executed in October 2002 in Florida, making her the 10th woman executed in the United States since 1976. She murdered six men along Florida highways while working as a prostitute (*LEN*, October 31, 2002, p. 2).
- A chief deputy in Richland, South Carolina, who was about two years away from retirement, was sentenced to more than 18 years in prison for four armed robberies. In one robbery, he pointed a gun at police during a high-speed chase (*LEN*, October 31, 2002, p. 2).
- Two months after serving four years for raping a child, a 17-year-old Akron, Ohio, boy was involved in a fight at school, then ran from the school and knocked on the door of an elderly couple nearby, where he stabbed them (*LEN*, November 15, 2002, p. 3).
- The Clayton, Oklahoma, police chief was charged with having sex with a fellow officer's 15-year-old daughter (*LEN*, October 15, 2002, p. 3).

Source: LEN is a reference to *Law Enforcement News*, a publication of John Jay College of Criminal Justice, City University of New York, 555 W. 57th St., New York, N.Y. Used with permission.

TABLE 2-1. Four Measures of Serious Violent Crime

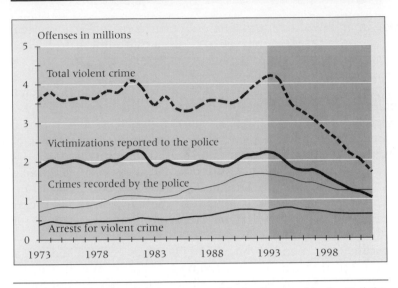

Offenses in millions

Total violent crime

Victimizations reported to the police

Crimes recorded by the police

Arrests for violent crime

1973   1978   1983   1988   1993   1998

Source: Washington, D.C.: U.S. Department of Justice, Bureau of Justice Statistics. *http://www.ojp.usdoj.gov/bjs/glance/cv2.htm* (Accessed January 30, 2003).

for police protection, while $32.1 billion (21.8 percent) is for the courts, and $49 billion (33.3 percent) is for corrections.[22] On any given day there are about 2 million persons incarcerated in this nation's prisons and jails; state and federal prisons hold about 1.3 million inmates, while local jails hold about 630,000 men and women.[23]

A number of factors contribute to these figures: immediate access to firearms, alcohol and substance abuse, drug trafficking, poverty, racial discrimination, and cultural acceptance of violent behavior.[24]

Computer Crimes An estimated 54 million households, or 51 percent, are now plugged into cyberspace, and more enter the online world each day.[25] The Internet has revolutionized the way people communicate, shop, entertain, learn, and conduct business. But as the saying goes, "the fleas come with the dog"; this high-tech revolution in our homes and offices has opened a whole new world for the criminal element as well. Indeed, the problem of cybercrime has become so prevalent that a new Computer Crime and Intellectual Property Section of the Criminal Division of the U.S. Department of Justice has been created; it can be accessed at *www.cybercrime.gov.* Furthermore, CyberAngels, an organization founded by a 21-year-old man that assists victims of Internet crimes, receives 650 online stalking complaints every day. Today the Federal Trade Commission receives more than 18,000 Internet-related complaints each year. The Internet has at least 300 Web sites that offer counterfeit driver's licenses, law enforcement credentials, passports, Social Security cards, and military identification cards.[26]

Pornographers and pedophiles are also on the Web, as well as other criminal types who now dot the landscape: better educated, upscale, older, and increasingly female. Computer crimes include identity theft; cyberterrorism; software piracy; industrial espionage; credit card, consumer, and stock market fraud; rigged baby adoption scams; and embezzlement. These crimes will compel the development of new investigative techniques, specialized and ongoing training for police investigators, and the employment of individuals with a highly technological background. Obviously, the police must become better educated and equipped and more adaptable.[27]

The technology staff of many if not most police agencies are civilians, who are generally kept away from the operational side of the organization. They understand what computers do, but not necessarily how that capability supports the operational needs of the police officer on the street. Thus, the sworn officer or detective is generally unprepared for the above-described host of criminal schemes.[28] This situation must be changed in the future.

Juvenile Crime

Although juvenile crime rates appear to have fallen since the mid-1990s (there is no system in place to monitor the accuracy or completeness of reported juvenile crimes), this decline has not alleviated concerns about crimes by this group; juvenile crime remains one of the nation's serious problems. News accounts of serious crimes committed by children and adolescents have encouraged a general belief that young people are increasingly violent and uncontrollable and that the response of the juvenile justice system has been inadequate. Most states have enacted laws that make the juvenile system more punitive and that allow younger children and adolescents to be transferred to the adult system for a greater variety of offenses and in a greater variety of ways. Indeed, at 645 per 100,000, the U.S. incarceration rate is second only to that of Russia at 685 per 100,000 population.[29]

Community policing, curfews, after-school activities, and conflict resolution classes have also been offered as reasons for the aforementioned juvenile crime rate decline. Curfews probably have had little overall effect, however, because studies show that most juvenile offenses are committed between 3:00 and 7:00 P.M.; furthermore, the value of conflict resolution programs in high school is also probably negligible because they miss the worst violators who are typically no longer in school. But, as one author

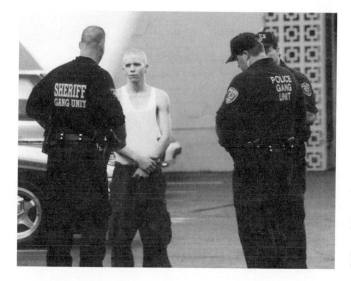

While juvenile crime has been declining, concern about youth crime and violence continues. (*Courtesy* Washoe County, Nevada, Sheriff's Office)

noted, community policing mobilizes community resources to address the problems of our youth, "from clergy to women's clubs, mental health professionals and businesses, all tired of being victimized by a generation in crisis."[30]

Crime Accelerators: Guns, Drugs, and Alcohol

Notwithstanding the recent declining crime wave among juveniles, discussed above, there are still several ingredients for disaster that will afflict this nation unless dramatic changes are effected. Three possible "accelerators"—guns, drugs, and alcohol—might still increase the risk of victimization and a general fear of crime.

There are nearly 200 million guns in private hands in the U.S., with 74 percent of gun owners possessing two or more. Interestingly, gun ownership is highest among middle-aged, college educated people of rural America, primarily for recreation. A little more than half of all privately owned firearms are stored unlocked.[31] Gun violence in the United States is both a criminal justice and a public health problem, with gun-related crime peaking in the late 1980s and early 1990s (in 1997, the national homicide rate declined to a 30-year low of 7 murders per 100,000 residents).

But homicide rates still remain unacceptably high, and firearms are still the weapons most frequently used for murder, being the weapons of choice in nearly two-thirds of all murders. The impact of gun violence is even more pronounced on juveniles and young adults. For persons aged 15 to 24, the homicide rate of 15.2 per 100,000 population is higher than the combined total homicide rate of 11 industrialized nations. Strategies and programs to reduce gun violence include interrupting sources of illegal guns, deterring illegal possession and carrying of guns, and responding to illegal gun use.[32]

Alcohol and drugs are also major factors in crime and violence, with almost 4 in 10 violent crimes involving alcohol. An estimated 65% of adult male arrestees in 2000 had recently used at least one of five drugs (opiates, marijuana, methamphetamine, cocaine and PCP) based on urinalysis testing.[33] With respect to drugs, more than 277,000 offenders are in prison for a drug law violation: 21 percent of state prisoners and over 60 percent of federal prisoners. More than 80 percent of state prisoners and 70 percent of federal prisoners have engaged in some form of illicit drug use. One-third of state prison inmates and 22 percent of federal prisoners report they were under the influence of drugs when they committed the crime for which they are in prison.[34]

FEAR OF CRIME

- The parking lots of fast-food restaurants in the downtown area witness a nightly invasion of youths who gather to drink, fight, and vandalize; restaurant owners complain frequently of litter and damaged property.
- A high-rise apartment complex is plagued with crime, especially against the elderly and on weekends, with rapes and robberies continuing to rise in number.
- Young men sell drugs openly on the street corner in front of a particular residence. Drive-by shootings by gang members have begun occurring. Neighbors have complained numerous times, but to no avail; the citizens, upset with the seemingly meaningless effect of an officer's occasional cruise by the area, threaten to take the law into their own hands.

- During a three-month period, detectives investigate a string of seemingly un-related strong-armed robberies in one area of the city.

- A small band of youths begins to commit a series of nighttime car burglaries and are able to remove a car stereo in less than two minutes.

- A middle-class married couple, apparently happy by day, commence drinking heavily each summer's night; the police are summoned when the couple eventually begin shouting at and assaulting one another. During a two-month period, officers are summoned to their domestic disturbances on 47 occasions.

Crime, fear, and disorder of the nature depicted above frightens Americans. Understandably, one of the greatest fears in the United States is fear of crime. The fear of crime alone is the number one factor keeping businesses out of high-poverty neighborhoods.[35] It costs America over $1 trillion annually. Violent crime alone, including arson and drunk driving, costs an estimated $426 billion per year, including $105 billion in medical costs, lost earnings, and victim assistance.[36]

Drunks, panhandlers, and the homeless add to people's perceptions of safety as much as do actual crimes.

We know that neighborhood disorder affects a person's perception of safety as much as crime does. People express greater fear of strangers loitering near their homes than they do the threat of murder. They fear being bothered by people they view as sinister: panhandlers, drunks, addicts, rowdy teens, mental patients, and the homeless. They also fear *physical* disorder: litter, abandoned buildings, potholes, broken street lights and windows, wrecked cars, and other indicators of neighborhood decline.

Thomas Hobbes wrote in 1651 that the "fundamental purpose of civil government is to establish order, protecting citizens from a fear of criminal attack that can make life nasty, brutish, and short."[37] It would appear, using this Hobbesian scale, that "the current level and distribution of fear indicate an important government failure."[38] For the past 30 years the dominant police strategy has emphasized motorized patrol, rapid response time, and retrospective investigation of crimes. Those strategies were designed not for addressing root community problems but instead for criminal detection and apprehension—the "crime-fighter" cop.

People create organizations to carry out missions. In the United States the police have adopted the notion that their principal mission is to control crime and maintain order. And they believe that they should carry out this mission through legal systems such as traffic courts, the criminal justice system, the juvenile justice system, and other legal processes.[39] Police administrators, in assessing their officers' effectiveness, ask questions such as how fast officers get to victims, how many arrests are made, and what percentage of cases are cleared.

In Chapter 4 we include a discussion of what community oriented policing and problem solving (COPPS) can do to address the fear of crime.

THE OVERARCHING GOAL: KEEPING NEIGHBORHOODS SAFE

Neighborhoods become vulnerable to the changing crime patterns surrounding them, and vary in their capacity to resist crime. A neighborhood is less vulnerable if it is physically insulated from intrusion by outsiders (especially offenders), and if it is able to resist changes in commercial or other activities that attract offenders. Neighborhoods are also vulnerable to demographic changes, especially when a growing population must be accommodated in a housing market and in the trickle-down of housing in that market. Especially important is the influx of single-parent households and of unrelated individuals[40] mentioned earlier. As these transitional processes get under way there is often little effort to repair the physical state of deterioration or to counter their symbolic significance. Albert Reiss stated that

> Inattention and its cumulative effects are rapid—a matter of a few years rather than of decades. Property crime . . . gives way to crimes against persons. The final stage in this transition to a high crime rate is a community that is physically deteriorated, has less residential and commercial property, and fewer residents. These rates eventually stabilize at a level that is high in relation to other neighborhoods in the city.[41]

From the standpoint of community life, the control of property crimes may be more consequential for quality of life and for preventing a transition to a high crime rate. This is true for several reasons. First, the destruction of property often leaves such communities with a deficit of acceptable property and

An abandoned residence vandalized with gang graffiti shows how quickly a neighborhood may decline. (*Courtesy* Sgt. Dominic Licavoli, LAPD)

the symbolic evidence of growing crime. Second, the effects are rapidly cumulative. Moreover, crimes against property are responsible for an exodus from the community and a subsequent decline in property values. Furthermore, crimes against property from arson to malicious destruction of property (vandalism) and a disregard for its value (such as the abandonment of vehicles in the streets) are more the crimes of juveniles than adults.[42]

As we noted briefly in Chapter 1 and will discuss more thoroughly in Chapter 4, we must first realize that the conventional style of reactive, incident-driven policing that has been employed during the professional era has several drawbacks. That type of police department has been hierarchical, impersonal, and rule-based, with most important policy decisions made at the top; line officers can make few decisions on their own.

It has been shown that the police will certainly face powerful challenges in the years ahead. The methods of addressing those challenges must certainly change as well.

SUMMARY

This chapter examined a number of changes that are occurring in America, particularly with respect to its people and the nature of its crimes. While violent crime has been declining of late, the years ahead certainly may not be tranquil. We cannot afford to "hurtle into the future with our eyes fixed firmly on the rearview mirror."[43] Social, political, and economic events of today are causing policing to change forever. A failure to strategically plan for what many police practitioners predict will be a turbulent and complex future could produce untenable consequences. "Business as usual" will not suffice.

In many ways these are difficult times for American police agencies. It will be shown in later chapters that community oriented policing and problem solving offers the best hope for proactive police administrators to strategically plan for the challenges posed to their agencies.

NOTES

1. U.S. Census Bureau, "Projections of Total Residents Population by 5 Year Age Groups, Middle Series 2001–2005." *www.census.gov/population/projections/nation/summary/np/t3-b.txt* (Posted January 13, 2000; Accessed February 24, 2003).
2. U.S. Census Bureau, *Statistics in Brief: Population and Vital Statistics* (Washington, D.C.: Author, 2000), pp. 13–16.
3. Ibid., p. 11.
4. Frank B. Hobbs, "The Elderly Population" (Washington, D.C.: U.S. Census Bureau, 1999), p. 2.
5. Jennifer Cheeseman Day, *National Population Projections* (Washington, D.C.: U.S. Census Bureau, 1999), pp. 1–2.
6. Ibid., p. 2.

7. U.S. Department of Justice, National Institute of Justice, *Community Policing and "The New Immigrants": Latinos in Chicago* (Research Report)(Washington, D.C.: Author, July 2002), p. 1.

8. U.S. Department of Justice, Immigration and Naturalization Service, *Legal Immigration, Fiscal Year 1998* (Washington, D.C.: Author, May 1999), pp. 1–3.

9. U.S. Census Bureau, Illegal Alien Resident Population (Washington, D.C.: Author, 2000), p. 1.

10. U.S. Department of Justice, National Institute of Justice, *Community Policing and "The New Immigrants"*, p. 3.

11. Day, *National Population Projections*, p. 1.

12. Gerald J. Russello, review of James O. Finckenauer and Elin J. Waring, *Russian Mafia in America: Immigration, Culture, and Crime* (Boston: Northeastern University Press, 1998), *http://www.bsos.umd.edu/gvpt/lpbr/subpages/reviews/finckena.html* (Accessed January 29, 2003).

13. Police Futurists International, Visioning 21st century crime and justice. *http://www.policefuturists.org/fall99/21crime.htm* (Accessed October 20, 2000):1–2.

14. Ibid.

15. Ibid.

16. Cicero Wilson, "Economic Shifts that will Impact Crime Control and Community Mobilization." In U.S. Department of Justice, National Institute of Justice, *What Can the Federal Government Do to Decrease Crime and Revitalize Communities?* (Washington, D.C.: Author, 1998), p. 4.

17. Jennifer Cheeseman Day, *Population Projections of the United States by Age, Sex, Race, and Hispanic Origin: 1995 to 2050, Current Population Reports* (Washington, D.C.: U.S. Census Bureau, 1996), p. 10.

18. Andrew Karmen, *Crime Victims: An Introduction to Victimology* (3d ed.) (Belmont, Calif.: Wadsworth, 1996), pp. 263–264.

19. Don Tapscott, *Growing Up Digital: The Rise of the Net Generation* (New York: McGraw-Hill, 1998), p. 255.

20. Gallup News Service, "Have and Have Nots" (Princeton, N.J.: The Gallup Organization, 2000), p. 1.

21. U.S. Department of Justice, Bureau of Justice Statistics, "Criminal Victimizations 2002." *http://www.ojp.usdoj.gov/bjs/cvictgen.htm* (Accessed December 17, 2003).

22. U.S. Department of Justice, Bureau of Justice Statistics, *Justice Expenditure and Employment in the United States, 1999, http://www.ojp.usdoj.gov/bjs/pub/pdf/jeeus99.pdf* (Accessed February 24, 2003).

23. U.S. Department of Justice, Bureau of Justice Statistics, *Key Facts at a Glance, Correctional Statistics. http://www.ojp.usdoj.gov/bjs/glance/tables/corr2tab.htm* (Accessed February 24, 2003).

24. Lee P. Brown, "Violent Crime and Community Involvement," *FBI Law Enforcement Bulletin* (May 1992):2–5.

25. U.S. Census Bureau, "Home Computer and Internet Use in the United States; August 2000." *http://www.census.gov/prod/2001pubs/p23-207.pdf* (Accessed November 4, 2003).

26. Ibid., p. 45.

27. D. Pettinari, "Are we there yet? The future of policing/sheriffing in Pueblo—or in Anywhere, America." *http://www.policefuturists.org/files/yet.html* (Accessed February 13, 2001).

28. G. W. Schoenle, Jr., "Mobile computing police perspectives: The Buffalo experience," *The Police Chief* (September 2001):36–42.

29. Joan McCord, Cathy Spatz Widom, and Nancy A. Crowell (eds.), *Juvenile Crime, Juvenile Justice: Panel on Juvenile Crime, Prevention, Treatment, and Control* (Washington, D.C.: National Academy Press, 2001), pp. 1, 25.

30. Abshire, "Fact and Fiction About Youth Violence," p. 56.

31. U.S. Department of Justice, National Institute of Justice, *Guns in America: National Survey on Private Ownership and Use of Firearms* (Washington, D.C.: Author, 1997), pp. 1–2.

32. David Sheppard, *Strategies to Reduce Gun Violence* (U.S. Department of Justice, Office of Juvenile Justice and Delinquency Prevention Fact Sheet #93, February 1999), p. 1.

33. U.S. Department of Justice, Office of Justice Programs, *Annual Report: Arrestee Drug Abuse Monitoring 2000* (Washington, D.C.: Author, 2003), p. 7.

34. U.S. Department of Justice, Bureau of Justice Statistics Press Release, "More Than Three-Quarters of Prisoners Had Abused Drugs in the Past," January 5, 1999.

35. See James K. Stewart, "The Urban Strangler: How Crime Causes Poverty in the Inner City," *Policy Review* (Summer 1986):6.

36. Moffit and Mulhausen, "Crime: Making America Safer," *Issues 2000: The Candidate's Briefing Book*, p. 5.

37. Thomas Hobbes, *Leviathan* (1651), ed. C.B. Macpherson (Baltimore, Md.: Pelican Books, 1968).

38. Mark H. Moore and Robert C. Trojanowicz, "Policing and the Fear of Crime" (Washington, D.C.: National Institute of Justice, 1988), p. 2.

39. Robert Fogelson, *Big City Police* (Cambridge, Mass.: Harvard University Press, 1977).

40. Albert J. Reiss, "Crime Control and the Quality of Life," *American Behavioral Scientist* 27 (September/October 1983):52–53.

41. Ibid., pp. 53–54.

42. Ibid., p. 55.

43. Neil Postman, quoted in David Osborne and Ted Gaebler, *Reinventing Government: How the Entrepreneurial Spirit is Transforming the Public Sector* (Reading, Mass.: Addison-Wesley, 1992), p. 19.

INTRODUCTION

To better understand community oriented policing and problem solving (COPPS, discussed thoroughly in Chapter 4), this chapter examines one of the basic premises upon which that strategy is founded: how government and the police should and do conduct business with respect to their "customers." This includes the need to "reinvent" government by empowering citizens to assist in reclaiming their neighborhoods from crime and disorder. Specifically, we discuss the independent nature of the American people and their occasionally forgotten ability to control their own affairs.

—3

ATTENDING TO THE "CUSTOMER"

Community Oriented Government

We must all hang together, or assuredly we shall all hang separately.
—BENJAMIN FRANKLIN

The significant problems we face cannot be solved at the same level of thinking we were at when we created them.
—ALBERT EINSTEIN

We begin by discussing citizens as clients and customers and as communitarians and volunteers. Next is a vital aspect of community oriented government: building community through collaboration. We follow that with a discussion of a concept that can assist in a COPPS initiative: total quality management (TQM). Then we try to determine whether or not the police truly have the ability to be a catalyst and be entrepreneurial in reinventing government, as some authors have suggested they can and should.

The chapter concludes with discussions and examples of how police, courts, and corrections organizations are collaborating with communities to address problems and to improve their quality of life while enabling community oriented government.

CITIZENS AS CLIENTS AND CUSTOMERS

Individualism Versus Clienthood

Do the majority of citizens today feel like they are a valued customer when they visit a police station or some other agency of criminal justice? Any agency of government? If we believe that question must be answered in the negative, it is because the public has been shut out of many of these agencies over time. Unfortunately, many public agencies would probably have considerable difficulty merely attempting to define exactly who their customers are. Furthermore, they may have forgotten long ago that quality is determined only by customers.[1] This situation must be corrected, supplanted with one in which the public and their government representatives/employees enjoy a closer linkage.

Indeed, it is important that the public be empowered by government to engage in the identification and resolution of neighborhood concerns. It is well established that people act more responsibly when they control their own environments than when they are controlled by others. Empowerment is an American tradition.[2] Yet, with the public's business, we seem to forget our independent spirit. We get locked into the "it's always been done this way" mindset and bar the community from getting involved to any significant extent.

The community, for its part, allows government workers to dictate policy and procedure. This practice undermines public confidence in the community; it creates *dependency* and *clienthood*. From a COPPS perspective, clienthood is an undesirable trait of community life:

> Clients are people who are dependent upon and controlled by their helpers and leaders. Clients are people who wait for others to act on their behalf. Citizens, on the other hand, are people who understand their own problems in their own terms. Good clients make bad citizens. Good citizens make strong communities.[3]

COMMUNITARIANISM AND VOLUNTEERISM

Citizens Fulfilling Responsibilities

A relatively new concept that has begun to get the attention of academics and politicians alike—one that has application to problem solving and the general notion of community involvement in problem solving—is "communitarianism." This term, promulgated by prominent sociologist Amitai Etzioni and other academics, argues that we have gone too far toward extending rights to our citizens and not far enough in asking them to fulfill responsibilities to the community as a whole. Focusing not so much on politics as on the process of government, "it is a mindset that says the whole community needs to take responsibility for itself. People need to actively participate, not just give their opinions . . . but instead give time, energy, and money."[4]

In this view, communitarianism is an attempt to nurture an underlying structure of "civil society": sound families, caring neighbors, and the whole web of churches, Rotary clubs, block associations, and nonprofit organizations that give individuals their moral compass and communities their strength. Communitarians have tapped into a rich vein of frustration with public behavior that has been eating away at the quality of community life, from drug dealing to aggressive panhandling. Communitarians see our political culture as being in very bad shape, not just because elected officials have done a bad job but also because citizens have not attended to what citizenship is all about.[5]

As a result, communitarians support processes such as problem solving, where neighborhoods have taken matters into their own hands, closing off streets and creating other physical barriers to disrupt the drug trade, working to overcome problems of homelessness and panhandling, and so on. This is where communitarians overlap with the objectives of community problem solving: the recognition that many of the answers to community problems lie not with government but in the community at large.

Volunteers in Action

A related concept is the need for greater support for volunteerism. It is estimated by Independent Sector, a group that studies and represents nonprofit organizations, that there are now 93 million volunteers in America, donating a stunning 20.3 billion hours of their time—an average of 218 hours per person. Only about 8.4 percent of those 93 million volunteers, however, work in "human services," a broad category that includes aiding the homeless, family counseling, and helping the Red Cross; only about 1.2 percent volunteer as mentors or substance-abuse prevention counselors.[6]

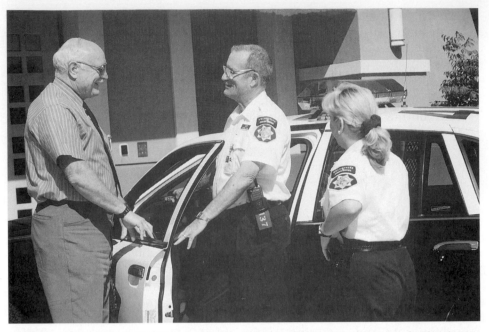

Volunteers provide a vital service to communities. (*Courtesy* Concord, California, police department)

Volunteers are viewed by some as people who do not have anything better to do with their time. Nothing could be further from the truth. Most are simply looking for a meaningful opportunity to contribute and give something back to their communities. Most prefer to have challenging assignments that combine the knowledge and skills they have developed in their professional career with new applications in policing.[7] Volunteering can build a sense of community, break down barriers between people, and raise our quality of life.

Volunteers quickly lose interest if not given meaningful work; therefore, police and other government agencies and nonprofit organizations need to ensure that their volunteers are active. Also, the attitude that "volunteers who work for free can't be valuable" must be cast aside. Such community efforts as COPPS need to be focused and powerful and involve working with other people. This is the form of volunteering that is most likely to get at society's core problems.[8]

Exhibit 3-1 provides examples of how some police agencies have used, and benefited from, the public's interest in volunteerism.

EXHIBIT 3-1   Volunteers in Action: Volunteering in Sun City, Florida

A volunteer effort keeps the 16,000-resident retirement community's crime rate the lowest in its county—reducing overall crime by 60 percent and burglaries by more than 90 percent during its first year of operation. The nonprofit group has five cars and more than 1,450 volunteers who patrol 3,200 acres and 120 miles of road, every day of the year. Each patrol car has a lightbar and an assigned district and carries two people (who have completed a required classroom orientation session), a radio, and an assortment of flares, maps, and spotlights. The volunteers never put themselves at risk; their job is to watch, listen, and report. Minor calls and reports that may be a waste of time for sworn officers are taken by the units as well. Funding is provided by donations and a community foundation.

Source: Eileen Courter, "All Eyes Open: Community Volunteer Patrol," *Law and Order* (April 2002):42–46.

There are "four R's" in volunteer programming: researching, recruiting, retaining, and recognizing.

1. *Researching* includes identifying needs and developing related job descriptions and handbooks (for both volunteers and supervisors).
2. *Recruiting*—at such places as job fairs, colleges, senior centers, and in newspaper and radio ads—entails putting volunteers through a complete background check, drug testing, fingerprinting, and polygraph testing.
3. *Retaining* involves showing the volunteers that they are valued and needed, so that they will continue to give of their time.
4. *Recognizing* occurs in the form of service awards, social events, birthday cards, and so on; volunteers must be rewarded on a regular basis, because recognition is the volunteer's paycheck.[9]

BUILDING A COMMUNITY THROUGH COLLABORATION

Where police/community relationships are concerned, it is important to note that communicating, coordinating, cooperating, and collaborating can all mean different things, and involve different levels of participation. Collaboration is the most involved, difficult, and critical of these police/community relationships. Next we will see what these terms mean and generally how they operate.

When to Collaborate

Police agencies should engage in collaboration with other individuals or organizations when stakeholders have a common, long-term goal, are committed to working together as a team, and cannot achieve the goal more efficiently as independent entities. Not all police relationships must be collaborative. Under some circumstances, it may be appropriate for officers just to establish a good communication plan. Under other circumstances, cooperation between two individuals might be sufficient. Collaboration is, however, critical for many COPPS endeavors.

Prior to looking at an example of police/community collaborative effort, it should first be noted that the following measures can be taken for problem solving.[10]

Collaborative Problem Solving Measures

- **Build a relationship:** Find out where the problem areas are, and then ask, "Who is directly involved? Who has a stake in getting this problem cleaned up?" Once a specific issue and potential allies have been identified, police can then try to partner with citizens to help ensure that the right people will be brought together to solve the problem. Begin with the problem and then decide who is best suited to help. Remember that nonprofit agencies can make valuable partners. Develop timelines as problems are recorded on a large sheet of paper.[11]
- **Define the problem:** Go through the list of problems with the community, one by one, identifying whether the problems may be influenced or controlled. Ask the community to focus on and prioritize the problems identified. The number one priority is the starting point for the group's problem-solving efforts.

SAN DIEGO POLICE DEPARTMENT

Neighborhood Policing

*A Guide for Building a
Police/Community Partnership*

PD-1175 (Rev. 2-93)

This guide to partnerships explains the San Diego police department's Neighborhood Policing Program and emphasizes the importance of collaborative partnerships with the public. (*Courtesy* San Diego police department)

- *Ask questions about the problem:* Look at who is affected by the problem. Does it include children, families, police, prostitutes, drug dealers, social service agencies, probation and parole officers, and/or prosecutors? From this list, have the group decide who should be included in the problem-solving effort. Invite the appropriate people to future meetings. The next question is, "What do we want to know about the problem?" List everything that the group can think of that they want to know. Then ask, "Where do we go to get the information?" Once you identify the source of the information, people can volunteer to get the answers to the questions.

- *Set short-term and long-term goals:* Initially, aim for small wins. What short-term goal can the group reach that will create hope and enthusiasm? Then look at the big picture. What underlying conditions or root causes of the problem need to be addressed? Is it possible to eliminate the problem (such as prostitution, for example)? The community knows what the problem looks like now.

- **Take action:** If the right questions have been asked and the group understands what it can influence, responses to problems become clear. Get the action rolling.
- **Assess effectiveness:** Was the problem solved? If more work needs to be done, do you need to start with Step One or can you reenter the problem-solving process at another step? The most important question at this point is, "Where does the group want to go from here?"

An Illustration

The example that follows outlines how two individuals, representing different organizations but with similar interests, applied the aforementioned problem-solving measures as they progressed from a relationship of communication to cooperation, then to coordination and collaboration:

[Communication] A county sheriff and school principal meet at a community meeting. The principal relates to the sheriff that over the past several weeks some students have complained about problems involving their vehicles in the school parking lot: trash dumped inside them, key marks scratched on them, and backpacks stolen from them.

[Cooperation] The sheriff asks the principal to call the dispatcher if another incident occurs, so a deputy can investigate and look for evidence at the scene.

[Coordination] The two agree that a copy of the offense report will be given to the school for filing; if a deputy cannot come to the school immediately, the principal offers to collect available information, obtain witness and victim statements, and fax the information to the sheriff's office.

[Collaboration] Weeks later, the sheriff calls the principal to suggest that their organizations initiate a problem-solving project (which could use some of the problem-solving measures presented above), and that a sheriff's deputy and a school coach lead the effort. During the next few months, other stakeholders are brought into the partnership to discuss the kinds of tasks [e.g., interviews with student and neighborhood victims; crime prevention through environmental design (CPTED, discussed in Chapter 5) activities; a review of police/school incident reports; mapping locations of incidents; interviews with suspects; a review of parking lot access; and so on] that might be undertaken. They develop a timeline and assign tasks, review resource needs, and continue meeting to exchange information, report progress, and plan their activities. After achieving major results (e.g., reductions in parking lot and neighborhood thefts and vandalism), the collaborators are given awards by the sheriff and principal for their efforts.[12]

IMPROVING CUSTOMER SERVICE: TOTAL QUALITY MANAGEMENT

Definition and Rationalization

Today, citizens want to know what services government provides, how much these services actually cost, how effectively they are delivered and how performance is measured, and whether they can be provided more efficiently.

What can be done to improve the problems now experienced by government agencies, described above? Total quality management (TQM), developed by W. Edwards Deming in 1950, is a philosophical concept for organizations that provides a practical means of meeting this challenge.

The following are the key characteristics of the TQM process:

- *Customer focus:* realizing that the customer or client is the most important ingredient in the feedback loop of all organizational processes.
- *Alignment:* both internal (having each employee and department understand the organization's vision) and external (where the organization is capable of meeting the customer's requirements).
- *Total involvement:* rests on the assumptions that people want to do good work and can identify the problems that keep work from being accomplished, and that leadership must remove the barriers to getting work done effectively and efficiently. *Continuous improvement* means that people in every part of the organization must believe that it is part of their job to continuously improve all they do.
- *Leadership commitment:* also important because TQM requires people who can see the big picture and work for their people.[13]

Entrepreneurial governments that have adopted the TQM concept measure the performance of their agencies by outcomes rather than inputs and are driven by their goals instead of their rules and regulations. They redefine their clients as customers and espouse participatory management. Objectives set the specific targets for each unit of government. For example, in policing, a Sunnyvale, California, objective is to keep the city "within the lowest 25 percent of Part I crimes for cities of comparable size, at a cost of $74.37 per capita."[14]

TQM *can* be adapted to many disparate kinds of government agencies; cities, counties, and states now have official offices of quality, directors of quality services, or offices of excellence. They have started "quality institutes" to do training and have established "quality networks" to share resources and information. They are giving out quality awards.[15] TQM involves the complete rethinking and redesigning of the way a job is performed or a service is rendered.

Table 3-1 shows what TQM is and is not.

Next we discuss TQM's principal elements and its application to COPPS (with which there are several common elements[16]), use by leadership, and some success stories.

TABLE 3-1. What Total Quality Management Is and Is Not

It Is	It Is Not
A structured approach to solving problems	"Fighting fires"
A systematic way to improve products and services	A new program
Long term	Short term
Conveyed by management's actions	Conveyed by slogans
Supported by statistical quality control	Driven by statistical quality control
Practiced by everyone	Delegated to subordinates

Source: U.S. Department of Justice, Federal Bureau of Investigation, Administrative Services Division, *Total Quality Management* (October 1990), no page number.

The principal elements of TQM—the customer, a long-term commitment, teamwork, internal communication, measurement, training, and rewards and recognition—embrace a common-sense approach to management.

TQM has two primary concepts at its foundation: participative management and total involvement.[17] And who decides what "quality" is? The customers, inside and outside of each organization. Every functional unit has a *customer*, and the police are no different.[18]

A key aspect of TQM and COPPS is decentralization. In TQM, managers listen to all voices in the organization including dissenters, and are always open to ideas for improvement from all sources. Managers also push power and decision making in the organization downward by delegating authority and encouraging problem solving at the lowest appropriate levels. In TQM (as with the COPPS strategy), managers demonstrate respect for people by treating everyone in the organization with honor and dignity and by recognizing their potential for growth and development. The manager also allows subordinates the freedom to make mistakes and, sometimes, even fail.

A *long-term commitment* is also essential; substantial gains can be attained in customer satisfaction and organizational efficiency only after management becomes committed, usually for five years or more, to improving quality. Top management, therefore, must be the driving force behind TQM. Full employee involvement is also key. Each employee must be a partner in achieving quality goals. *Teamwork* involves managers, supervisors, and employees in improving service delivery, solving systemic problems, and correcting errors in all parts of work processes. Together, managers emphasize planning rather than "fighting fires."

Internal communication, both vertical and horizontal, is also central to employee involvement. Regular and meaningful communication must occur at all levels, allowing the agency to adjust its ways of operating and reinforcing its commitment to TQM at the same time. In the old style of management (including policing), information was something to be guarded. Information begat knowledge, which begat power, which was not to be shared. Today there is no shame in making mistakes, only in trying to hide them.

Police storefronts and substations provide convenience and improved customer service to neighborhoods. (*Courtesy* Huntington Beach, California, police department)

Measurement is the backbone of involvement, allowing the organization to initiate corrective action, set priorities, and evaluate progress. Standards and measures should reflect customer requirements and changes that need to be introduced in the internal business of providing those requirements. *Training* is also vital to the success of TQM. This normally includes "awareness" training concerning the concept for teams of top-level managers, courses for teams of mid-level managers, and courses for non-managers. TQM is a process and not a program. One can only learn TQM by education and training, followed by practice.

Rewards and recognition are also part of the package. Most private sector companies and federal agencies practicing TQM have given wide latitude to managers in issuing rewards and recognition. A common theme is that individual financial rewards are not as appropriate as awards to groups or team members because most successes are group achievements.

TQM asks police managers to accept ownership of the environment and "culture" of their organizations. They must realize that a shift to TQM will, in many cases, require a substantive shift in management approaches and a cultural change. This notion is consistent with problem solving. Much like TQM, the problem-solving process seeks to identify the role of all parties who may have responsibility for solving a problem. At its simplest level, TQM involves identifying problems, assessing needed corrective action, and taking those actions. It also requires that someone take responsibility for solving a problem, and then solve it.

Experience has shown that mid-level management is the slowest group to accept TQM. They require special help in adjusting to their new role as facilitators of problem recognition and problem solving.

Implementing principles of TQM into an organization does not occur overnight. It presents a difficult and challenging task for police leadership. As Deming stated, "A big ship, traveling at full speed, requires distance and time to turn."[19]

Exhibit 3-2 provides several principles of quality leadership that assisted the Madison, Wisconsin, police department with implementing TQM into the organization.

Challenges remain, however. For example, a recent survey of 97 police commanders and supervisors in 18 police agencies across the nation indicated

---

EXHIBIT 3-2 Principles of Quality Leadership

Following are some of the principles of quality leadership developed by the Madison, Wisconsin, police department (emphases theirs):

- Be committed to the PROBLEM SOLVING process; use it and let DATA, not emotions, drive decisions.
- Seek employees' INPUT before you make key decisions.
- To improve the quality of work or service, ASK and LISTEN to employees who are doing the work.
- Have a CUSTOMER orientation and focus toward employees and citizens.

- Avoid "top down," POWER-ORIENTED decision-making whenever possible.
- Encourage CREATIVITY through RISK-TAKING and be TOLERANT of honest MISTAKES.
- Be a FACILITATOR and COACH. Develop an OPEN atmosphere that encourages providing and accepting FEEDBACK.
- With TEAMWORK, develop with employees agreed-upon GOALS and a PLAN to achieve them.

Source: David C. Couper, "Management for Excellence," International Association of Chiefs of Police, *The Police Yearbook 1988*:76–84.

Citizen surveys provide police departments with vital information about their performance and citizens' concerns. (*Courtesy* Reno, Nevada, police department)

that police leadership is not altogether prepared for community policing and needs to adopt a professional managerial strategy that focuses on such objectives and total quality management. Specifically, these police executives—who averaged 17 years of experience, and 10 years as a supervisor—tended to demonstrate "enforcer skills" instead of "facilitative skills"; in other words, the respondents largely mirrored managerial characteristics typical of a *traditional* police strategy as opposed to a community policing philosophy.[20]

Specifically, this study found that only about one-fourth of these police executives and supervisors felt that organizational change was always or often something an excellent leader should be concerned with; 64 percent felt that excellent leaders should be "tough" very often. Only 4 percent of the participants reported that trust of their subordinates should always be a characteristic of an excellent police leader, and fewer than half (46 percent) felt that delegation of responsibility to others should always be practiced. None of these participants reported that excellent leaders should be visionaries all of the time.

These findings certainly fly in the face of what David Couper stated are important principles of quality leadership under COPPS, as just shown in Exhibit 3-2.

USE OF SURVEYS

A number of communities have found that a beneficial method of allowing community participation is through the survey process. In fact, a key part of both COPPS and TQM is for organizations to constantly ask their customers what they want, then to shape their entire service and production processes to produce it.

As an example, since 1987 the Reno, Nevada, police department has engaged in a semiannual scientific telephone survey of the community, seeking to reach 1 percent of the total city population of 180,000, or about 1,500 completed surveys per year. And in 1987, the Madison, Wisconsin, police department began mailing a survey to every 35th person it encountered, whether a victim of a crime, a witness, a complainant, or even a criminal. Further discussion of community surveys is provided in Chapter 11.

CAN THE POLICE REALLY "REINVENT GOVERNMENT"?: OSBORNE AND GAEBLER REVISITED

Need for a Different "M.O."?

Notwithstanding the good news concerning the recently declining crime rates in the United States, there is still much room for concern. The U.S. still has some of the highest numbers of violent crime incidences in the world. Our courts and prisons are so full that criminals know real punishment is unlikely. And the system is stretching state and county government budgets to the limit, particularly since the economic downturn of 9-11.

Much of the problem, David Osborne and Ted Gaebler argued in their 1992 bestselling book, *Reinventing Government*,[21] stems in part from the outmoded way that government agencies approach problems:

> For the most part, our governments do not play a catalytic role, trying to work with other sectors of society to strengthen families and communities and thus reduce crime. They simply hire more public employees to staff the assembly line. Our governments rarely give communities and citizens any control over public safety; they leave that to the police. They rarely offer their customers any choices. They rarely let the police define a mission and go after it; they tie them up in rules and red tape.[22]

The key, they argue, is the ability of the police to act as a catalyst to coalesce community resources and to provide resources, education, and training to the community. The police must realize that if they empower citizens, they help themselves.

A major part of the Osborne and Gaebler argument is based on the premise that the public sector needs to establish "entrepreneurial government" through the use of private-sector techniques such as reorganization, downsizing, privatization, and total quality management (discussed earlier). The police and the private sector do share many values and concerns. High performance, quality service, customer satisfaction, generation of funding, teamwork, quality supervision, employee development and morale, and ethics are just a few examples. Both are striving for effectiveness (the ability to produce intended or expected results), and efficiency (producing the result with minimum waste expense and unnecessary effort).[23] The private sector has largely succeeded with both of these outcomes. The police have similar goals and can learn from private industry. The biggest hurdle is overcoming the perception that policing has nothing in common with the private sector. The reality, however, is that both the private sector and the police provide services that enhance the quality of life, they need and desire more money, and they want high-performing employees who derive satisfaction from their jobs.[24]

Gennaro Vito and Julie Kunselman[25] examined whether or not contemporary police middle managers agreed with the views of Osborne and Gaebler as set forth in *Reinventing Government* in which the authors single out middle managers as enemies of change. Vito and Kunselman surveyed 35 police middle managers who were attending an advanced management institute to determine which of Osborne and Gaebler's ideas were viewed as "best" and which were "worst" as they applied to policing. The three ideas that were rated as "best" by the respondents were:

1. Community-owned government—Empowering communities to participate in government agencies and ensure accountability of programs to community-based groups (as noted earlier, community policing stresses collaboration with citizens).

2. Customer-driven government—Empowering citizens as customers to participate in government agencies (this is a closely aligned extension of the first).
3. Decentralized government—A shift in agency structure to empower workers to be responsible and accountable in decision making processes (we discuss decentralization more in later chapters).

The following three ideas were rated as "worst":

1. Enterprising government—The police managers felt it promotes profit making; that is it unethical and unfair for police departments to charge additional fees for service (such as unlocking cars for citizens or rolling fingerprints for businesses).
2. Competitive government—The introduction of competition between public and private sectors to promote efficiency is viewed as unhealthy by many; an example is giving largely untrained private security officers arms and authority to "clean up" areas.
3. Results-oriented government—Implementation of evaluation and performance measures that emphasize outcomes rather than inputs. Respondents felt that because crime is fluid, some programs are cut, new leaders are installed, and the level of attention the public wants given to crime changes, it is unfair to try to evaluate and fund based on income.

Vito and Kunselman concluded that the Osborne and Gaebler customer analogy is flawed when it is applied to the police. Customers demand satisfaction, and the police cannot satisfy the demands of complaining victims and/or suspects simultaneously. Overall, they counsel cautious support for the changes expressed in *Reinventing Government*. It should be mentioned in closing, however, that many chief executives in both the public and private sectors have embraced many of the tenets of this book.

PARTNERS IN COMMUNITY JUSTICE

Recently, as the police began rethinking their mission and approach, and COPPS began to develop and be diffused around the country, the courts and corrections components also began to change their strategies and approaches toward a concept of community justice. Community justice is a new way of thinking about the criminal justice system; it is a systematic approach to public safety, emphasizing problem solving and focusing on community concerns. Increasingly, all segments of society as well as the nation's criminal justice system are realizing that the only viable approach to mediating their problems is community-wide participation and cooperation.[26]

Closely related to the concept of community justice is restorative justice, the elements of which include repairing harm (the idea that we should first take care of the victim who suffered the harm prior to trying to help the offender become a better citizen), reducing risk (managing the offender in such a way that he or she will not commit another crime), and building community (taking responsibility for the behavior of its members and becoming involved in the resolution process, not just turning crime over to government to be dealt with). Table 3-2 compares restorative justice, which gives concerns of active involvement of victims and the community, with the traditional standard of retributive justice.

TABLE 3-2. Comparison of Retributive and Restorative Justice

Old Retributive Justice	*New Restorative Justice*
Crime defined as a violation of the state	Crime defined as a violation of one person by another
Focus on establishing blame, on guilt, on the past	Focus on problem solving, liabilities, and future obligations
Adversarial relationships	Dialogue and negotiation
Imposition of pain to punish, the goal being to deter/prevent	Restitution a means of restoring both parties; restoration is the goal
The community as a passive observer represented by the state	The community as facilitator; process is restorative
A "debt" is owed to society	A "debt" to the victim is recognized

Source: adapted from Michael Phillips, "The New Paradigm of Justice," *Government Technology (Special Report: Building Digital Government in the 21st Century* (February 1, 2001), p. 41.

Criminal justice executives must plan a systematic approach to be in a strategic position to focus on community cooperation. The following steps are essential: *identifying the issues* (knowing what specific problems are facing the community and what is being done to address them), *identifying key partners* (persons who are key to the solution of problems), *formulating a message* (communicating what needs to be done to accomplish goals), *establishing relationships* (using friendships, common interests, social service agencies, the corporate sector, other justice agencies, and so on), and *establishing evaluation procedures* (monitoring and measuring community efforts according to previously established criteria).[27]

Community justice services aim to identify and solve the problems that foster crime and injustice. Next, though, we present some of the means by which courts and corrections components of the justice system have worked successfully to revitalize their communities.

Prosecution

Community prosecution focuses on criminal and civil problems in a specific neighborhood and develops a long-term, proactive partnership between the district attorney's office, police agencies, the community, and public and private organizations. The community prosecutor steps out of the traditional role; instead of reacting to a crime after it happens and a suspect is arrested, he or she looks beyond the individual case to the broader public safety problem that negatively affects the quality of life in a given community.[28]

Instead of being handed cases from the police to prepare for trial, the community prosecutor works with police to identify the problems and develop the best responses, whether through administrative means or through the courts. Community prosecutors attend meetings of community groups to become familiar with neighborhood issues and to familiarize residents with the program; become familiar with COPPS efforts in the area, the major problems officers confront, and the results of their activities; meet with community leaders, police, and nonprofit social services and health groups; evaluate data from community surveys; and create a priority list to address the problems.[29]

Educating citizens is an important function for community prosecutors; constitutional issues are explained at community meetings, and mock trials are even conducted to demonstrate the difficulty of establishing proof beyond a reasonable doubt in certain crime situations. Similarly, community prosecutors advise the police on what they can and cannot do, and provide an alternative channel of communication to citizens to access the legal system.[30]

Community policing and community prosecution share many similarities. Both strive to prevent crime before it occurs rather than to react to crime after it happens. Both empower communities to take control of their own destinies. The presence of community police officers and community prosecutors in the neighborhoods, in attendance at community meetings and accessible to community members, shows their human side and makes them seem less intimidating to the average citizen.

Defense

A Neighborhood Defender Service (NDS) experiment in Harlem, New York[31] aimed to develop and test new ways of organizing and deploying public defenders that can solve problems of justice in the community. The NDS was based in the community rather than a courthouse and represented indigent defendants, encouraging citizens to call the office at any time, thus giving lawyers more time to visit with their clients and creating a new attorney-client relationship. Each client is represented by a team, consisting of attorneys, community workers (who helped former clients avoid problems while on probation and parole that might otherwise produce new cases), an administrative assistant, and a senior attorney/team leader.

Defenders know about their clients and the communities from which they come; the staff began to see Harlem as a series of interconnected family networks, and NDS became a family service. Relatives often called the office out of concern for the person's safety as he or she entered the justice system. The program provides a deeper understanding of clients through continuity of representation and better investigation, better presentation of sentencing options through greater connection to community resources, and greater ability to represent residents' support for a less severe sentence. Program savings through shorter sentences alone were about 150,000 bed days or about $10 million.

Courts

Community courts can also assume a problem-solving role in the life of a community, bringing people together and helping craft solutions to problems that communities face. These courts have developed individual programs that differ in important ways, experimenting with a broader range of matters, including juvenile delinquency, mental illness, and housing code violations. They focus on neighborhoods and are designed to respond to particular concerns of their community.[32] They provide new ways of doing business, and bring new resources to the criminal justice system.

Following are two descriptions of actual community courts and their activities; these courts are generally representative of the programs in which community courts engage.[33]

Midtown Community Court, New York City

Launched in 1993, the Midtown Community Court targets quality-of-life offenses such as prostitution, illegal vending, graffiti, shoplifting, fare beating, and vandalism in midtown Manhattan. Residents, businesses, and social service agencies collaborate with the court by supervising projects and providing onsite services, including drug treatment, health care, and job training. Social services located in the court provide the judge with these services as well as a health education class for prostitutes and "johns," counseling for young offenders and mentally ill persons, and employment training. For offenders with lengthier records, the court offers a diversionary program. Many defendants return to court voluntarily to take advantage of these services, including English as a second language and General Educational Development (GED) classes.

Hartford, Connecticut, Community Court

The Hartford program began because citizens wanted something to be done about low-level crimes. The community court works closely with problem-solving committees in the city's 17 neighborhoods, articulating priorities for each neighborhood and sending a representative to the court's advisory board. The court sends community service crews to, and assigns offenders to perform community service in, the neighborhoods. The court regularly employs voluntary mediation in resolving criminal cases, in which an agreement is reached between the parties and trials are avoided. Each defendant in community court is required to meet with a social service team, which includes staff from the city's departments of human services, social services, and mental health and addiction. Defendants are then linked with necessary social services.

Other partnerships that can involve the courts and citizens include child care during trials for victims and witnesses, law-related education, and job training and referral for offenders and victims. A community-focused court practices *restorative justice*, emphasizing the ways in which disputes and crimes adversely affect relationships among community residents, treating the parties to a dispute as real individuals rather than abstract legal entities, and using community resources in the adjudication of disputes.[34]

Corrections

With the recent spate of domestic violence, stalking, and child sexual abuse crimes, today the public demands more information about who the offenders are, where they are living, and what the criminal justice system is going to do about them. As a result, the corrections end of the criminal justice spectrum—probation and parole—is steadily taking on a more visible role within the community policing strategy. Collaborative efforts are being made to make communities safer. Interagency groups monitor offenders who are at risk of committing new offenses and find ways of directing them away from criminal activity, and engaging the community in the process. Community corrections officers and police officers are working as teams, with the community as a partner, to provide a range of prevention, intervention, and support services to the offenders.

A good example of such an initiative is an area of Maricopa County, Arizona, where probation officers saw community blight (graffiti, crack houses, and vandalism) as an opportunity to make a visible, positive impact on the area. The officers mobilized work crews of neighborhood probationers and set about replacing a damaged community center roof. They also landscaped the grounds and made repairs inside the center. "Reformed" gang members performed community service by assisting police and neighborhood youth organizations in speaking to "at-risk" teens on the dangers of gang involvement.

Sentencing low-risk offenders to community work projects is one community-based corrections strategy. (*Courtesy* Washoe County, Nevada, Sheriff's Office)

Select residents and probation and police officers now work side by side in the ongoing effort to close down and clean up crack houses. Vacant lots are kept clean, and graffiti is painted over with murals.[35]

Maricopa County's use of offenders repaying their social debt by completing unpaid community service in their own neighborhood served to break down barriers and prejudice. As community members and police came to know the probationers in a social context and on a somewhat more personal level, they were no longer viewed as merely "criminals" but as neighbors who, under proper supervision, can safely remain in a community setting and offer a meaningful contribution to the community as well.[36]

In other jurisdictions, such as Richmond, Virginia, where 820 probation and parole officers supervise more than 36,000 offenders, officers have frequent interaction with the police and work side by side with community policing officers. One very successful program in Bristol, Virginia, involved a probation and parole services office that was opened in a housing project, where officers work closely with local police and simply walk or bicycle through the community, talking with local residents.[37]

EXAMPLES OF COMMUNITY ORIENTED GOVERNMENT

Next we provide two examples of activities and successes that police agencies are realizing when they collaborate with, engage, and empower their citizens toward addressing problems and improving their quality of life.

Fort Wayne, Indiana

During the 1980s, the Fort Wayne, Indiana, police department experienced a 95 percent increase in calls for service; crime was on the rise. The city's mayor began looking for ways to stem the increase in violence. Part of the answer was in the initiation of community policing. Then, in the early 1990s, a task force was established and charged with implementing the philosophies of community policing throughout city government. Out of the task force grew community oriented government, an approach that takes community policing one step further and gives primary responsibility for problem solving to neighborhood leadership. Community oriented government in Ft. Wayne encourages individual citizens to take issues to one of 197 organized neighborhood associations. Associations prioritize concerns and work with city staff to find solutions. Issues that concern more than one neighborhood are addressed in one of four Area Partnerships, a coalition of neighborhood leaders that meet monthly to discuss and solve problems. This system makes citizens the true "boss." They dictate up the chain of command and tell their "employees"—city staff—which issues require the most attention.[38]

Lawrence, Massachusetts

Serving a diverse community of 70,000 people, the Lawrence police department had begun to feel out of touch with its citizens; its authoritarian management style had led department members to feel disenfranchised. A commitment was made to customers—the first step in meeting and exceeding their needs. The second step was to obtain valuable input using a variety of means that included customer surveys (done annually), citizen advisory committees, customer comment cards, and small focus groups. Other tools used to identify true customer needs included a flow chart, cause-and-effect diagram, affinity diagram, check sheet, and run chart. These in-depth means of identifying needs have been fruitful. For example, using an affinity diagram the department found that while its customers were calling for more foot patrols and more police officers, what they really wanted was to feel safe in neighborhoods free of disorder.

Techniques employed in small groups for obtaining citizen input include the nominal group technique (individuals silently develop ideas and prioritize by voting and ranking), idea writing, brainstorming, Delphi technique (ideas of a panel of experts resulting in a consensus being reached), and interpretive structural modeling. The department believes that using TQM methods has allowed it to become more focused on customers; it has also found citizens to be happier with services provided and that employees are more satisfied because of their input, and that the "job is done not only better but often more cheaply."[39]

CLOSURE

What is needed is nothing short of a shift in the basic model of governance that is used in America—a shift that is already under way. Justice administrators must look beyond tomorrow and anticipate the future. As Peter F. Drucker observed:

> Every government agency, every policy, every program, every activity should be confronted with these questions: "What is your mission? Is it still the right mission? Is it still worth doing? If we were not already doing this, would we now go into it?"[40]

A shift to consideration of the client/customer perspective creates opportunities for police administrators to rethink what their organizations really do and how they do it—to steer rather than row, with a clear map in hand.

TQM and COPPS give police officers enough free rein to experiment and see what works. And the police must continually communicate to people—both those within and outside the department—that community problem solving is in everybody's best interest.

We must also emphasize the important role of persons working with other government (including social service) agencies. The police do not function in a vacuum; representatives from other agencies must be mobilized in the problem-solving endeavor. These agencies include but are not limited to housing, zoning, health, street, fire, and other agencies.

These are important partnerships for problem solving, and representatives from these agencies are key problem-solving actors who must know how they can best assist the police in shutting down crime and disorder and must also be trained in the philosophy and methods that underlie problem solving. We address the issue of training in Chapter 8.

SUMMARY

We propose in this chapter that it is time for government—specifically criminal justice and especially the police—to "get under the hood of its car" to see where problems might be repaired. The theme of this chapter was that government must expand its commitment to customer service, much of which can be achieved through partnerships and borrowed wholly or in part from the total quality management philosophy. It is time for a new, cooperative partnership between the public and its government. This partnership is essential for mending the "broken windows" that plague many of our neighborhoods. This new relationship offers hope for the future and is based on shared accountability for outcomes. It empowers citizens to take charge of their own destiny and reclaim their neighborhoods. In turn, citizens may indeed be safer and realize an improvement in their quality of life.

NOTES

1. David Couper and Sabine Lobitz, *Quality Policing: The Madison Experience* (Washington, D.C.: Police Executive Research Forum, 1991), p. 65.

2. David Osborne and Ted Gaebler, *Reinventing Government: How the Entrepreneurial Spirit is Transforming the Public Sector* (Reading, Mass.: Addison-Wesley, 1992), p. 51.

3. Tom Dewar, quoted in David A. Lanegran, Cynthia Seelhammer, and Amy L. Walgrave (eds.), *The Saint Paul Experiment: Initiatives of the Latimer Administration* (St. Paul, Minn.: City of St. Paul, 1989), p. xxii.

4. Rob Gurwitt, "Communitarianism: You Can Try It at Home," *Governing* 6 (August 1993):33–39.

5. Ibid., p. 39.

6. Michael J. Gerson, "Do do-gooders do much good?" *U.S. News and World Report* (April 28, 1997):27.

7. Karen Siemsen, "For a Full Menu of Policing Services, Partner with Volunteers," *Community Policing Exchange* (September/October 1998):8.

8. Ibid., pp. 33–34.

9. Ronnie L. Paynter, "Helping Hands," *Law Enforcement Technology* (March 1999):30–34.

10. Adapted from Nancy McPherson, "Solution-Driven Partnerships: Just Six Steps Away." In *Partnerships* (Washington, D.C.: Community Policing Consortium, 1995–1998 Edition), pp. 10–11.

11. "Getting the Job Done through Partnerships." In Ibid., p. 4.

12. Adapted from *COPS Collaboration Toolkit: Collaboration Fundamentals* (Washington, D.C.: Office of Community Oriented Policing Services, 2002).

13. Stephen J. Harrison, "Quality Policing and the Challenges for Leadership," *The Police Chief* (January 1996):26, 31–32.

14. City of Sunnyvale, California, *Resource Allocation Plan: 1989–90 to 1998–99 Fiscal Years, 10 Year Operating Budget* (Sunnyvale, Calif.: Author, no date).

15. Jonathan Walters, "TQM: Surviving the Cynics," *Governing*, (September 1994):40.

16. The reader is also encouraged to see Howard S. Gitlow and Shelly J. Gitlow, *The Deming Guide to Quality and Competition* (Englewood Cliffs, N.J.: Prentice Hall, 1987).

17. Ibid., p. iv.

18. Ibid., p. 172.

19. W. Edwards Deming, quoted in U.S. Department of Justice, Federal Bureau of Investigation, *Total Quality Management*, (Washington, D.C.: Author, October 1990), no page number.

20. Dennis J. Stevens, "Improving Community Policing: Using Managerial Style and Total Quality Management," *Law and Order* (October 2000):197–204.

21. Cited in note 2.

22. Ibid., p. 319.

23. Lorne C. Kramer and Mora L. Fiedler, "Beyond the Numbers: How Law Enforcement Agencies Can Create Learning Environments and Measurement Systems," *The Police Chief* (April 2002):164–169.

24. Ibid.

25. Gennaro F. Vito and Julie Kunselman, "Reinventing Government: The Views of Police Middle Managers," *Police Quarterly* 3 (September 2000):315–330.

26. Laurie J. Wilson, "Placing Community-Oriented Policing in the Broader Realms of Community Cooperation," *The Police Chief*, (April 1995):127.

27. Ibid., p. 128.

28. Karen McDonough, "Oceanside's Community Prosecution," *Law and Order* (August 2002):114–116.

29. Ibid.

30. U.S. Department of Justice, National Institute of Justice, *Community Prosecution in Washington, D.C.: The U.S. Attorney's Fifth District Pilot Project* (Washington, D.C.: Author, April 2001), pp. 14, 34.

31. Ibid., pp. 41–45.

32. U.S. Department of Justice, Office of Justice Programs, *Community Courts: An Evolving Model* (Washington, D.C.: Author, October 2000).

33. Ibid.

34. Ibid., pp. 46–51.

35. Leslie D. Ebratt, "Giving Probation a Stake in the Neighborhood," *Community Policing Exchange*, (May/June 1999):5.

36. Ibid.

37. Ray Arp, Sr., "COPPS: Crossing Over Boundary Lines," *Community Policing Exchange* (May/June 1999):5.

38. Paul Helmke, "Community-Oriented Government," *http://www.fwi.com/cofw/community-oriented_government/cog.html*, July 9, 2000.

39. Allen W. Cole, "Better Customer Focus: TQM & Law Enforcement," *The Police Chief* (December 1993):23–26.

40. Peter F. Drucker, "Really Reinventing Government," *The Atlantic Monthly*, (February 1995):49–61.

INTRODUCTION

According to one source, community oriented policing "has become a mantra for police chiefs and mayors in cities big and small across the country."[1] What is this concept that is sweeping the nation? How did it develop, and how does it operate? What are its component parts?

This chapter, the "heart and soul" of the book, addresses those questions. First we discuss the concept of community policing, examining basic principles of the concept and how community oriented and traditional policing differ, and how community policing is distinguished from earlier attempts to engage the community. Next we analyze problem oriented policing, including its origin, how it broadens the role of the street officer, and the four-stage problem-solving process.

Although the two concepts, community policing and problem oriented policing, are commonly treated as separate and distinct, we maintain here and throughout the remainder of the book that they are complementary core components. Therefore, we devote considerable attention in this chapter to an examination of community oriented policing and problem solving—COPPS—which we believe to be the most effective and efficient approach to policing for the future. Then we review some very important considerations and types of tools for police problem solving: establishing and locating a crime analysis unit, the analyst's role in counterterrorism, crime mapping, police reports, calls for service (CFS) analysis, surveys, and software. The chapter concludes with an example of community mobilization, which is the foundation of COPPS.

It should be noted that the following chapter examines a concept that is integral to COPPS—crime prevention—and offers a cost-effective means of making communities safer. Two closely related concepts of COPPS are analyzed in Chapter 5: crime prevention through environmental design, and situational crime prevention.

—4—

COMMUNITY ORIENTED POLICING AND PROBLEM SOLVING

"COPPS"

No problem can be solved by the same consciousness that created it. We must learn to see the world anew.
—Albert Einstein

Before we can communicate, let us define our terms.
—Voltaire

COMMUNITY POLICING

Basic Principles

As we discussed in Chapter 3 (and will necessarily restate in later chapters), there is a growing awareness that the community can and *must* play a vital role in problem solving and crime-fighting. A fundamental aspect of community policing has always been that the public must be engaged in the fight against crime and disorder. And as we noted in Chapter 1, Robert Peel emphasized the police and community working together in the 1820s when setting forth his "principles" of policing: "The police are the only members of the public who are paid to give full-time attention to duties which are incumbent on every citizen in the interest of the community welfare."[2]

Unfortunately, as Herman Goldstein posited, the police have erred in recent decades by pretending that they could take on themselves, and successfully discharge, all of the responsibilities that are now theirs:

> It is simply not possible for a relatively small group of individuals, however powerful and efficient, to meet those expectations. A community must police itself. The police, at best, can only assist in that task. We are long overdue in recognizing this fact.[3]

In the early 1980s, the notion of community policing emerged as the dominant direction for thinking about policing. It was designed to reunite the police with the community. "It is a philosophy and not a specific tactic; a proactive, decentralized approach, designed to reduce crime, disorder, and fear of crime, by involving the same officer in the same community for a long-term basis."[4]

No single program describes community policing. It has been applied in various forms by police agencies in the United States and abroad and differs according to the community needs, politics, and resources available.

Differences in Community Policing and Traditional Policing

The major points where community policing is intended to depart from traditional policing may be seen in Table 4-1. Note that the definition, role, priorities, and assessment of the police differ considerably between the two models.

Many past and present practitioners have become staunch proponents of the concept. For example, former Atlanta, Houston, and New York City police chief Lee P. Brown wrote:

> I believe that community policing—the building of problem solving partnerships between the police and those they serve—is the future of American law enforcement.

Working partnerships with residents to create safer and more secure neighborhoods are vital in community policing. (*Courtesy* Keith Richards, City of Charlotte, North Carolina)

TABLE 4-1. Traditional Versus Community Policing: Questions and Answers

Question	Traditional Policing	Community Policing
Who are the police?	A government agency principally responsible for law enforcement.	Police are the public and the public are the police: The police officers are those who are paid to give full-time attention to the duties of every citizen.
What is the relationship of the police force to other public service departments?	Priorities often conflict.	The police are one department among many responsible for improving the quality of life.
What is the role of the police?	Focusing on solving crimes.	A broad problem-solving approach.
How is police efficiency measured?	By detection and arrest rates.	By the absence of crime and disorder.
What are the highest priorities?	Crimes that are high value (e.g., bank robberies) and those involving violence.	Whatever problems disturb the community most.
With what, specifically, do police deal?	Incidents.	Citizens' problems and concerns.
What determines the effectiveness of police?	Response times.	Public cooperation.
What view do police take of service calls?	Deal with them only if there is no real police work to do.	Vital function and great opportunity.
What is police professionalism?	Swift, effective response to serious crime.	Keeping close to the community.
What kind of intelligence is most important?	Crime intelligence (study of particular crimes or series of crimes).	Criminal intelligence (information about the activities of individuals or groups).
What is the essential nature of police accountability?	Highly centralized; governed by rules, regulations, and policy directives; accountable to the law.	Emphasis on local accountability to community needs.
What is the role of headquarters?	To provide the necessary rules and policy directives.	To preach organizational values.
What is the role of the press liaison department?	To keep the "heat" off operational officers so they can get on with the job.	To coordinate an essential channel of communication with the community.
How do the police regard prosecutions?	As an important goal.	As one tool among many.

Source: Malcolm K. Sparrow, "Implementing Community Policing" (Washington, D.C.: U.S. Department of Justice, National Institute of Justice: U.S. Government Printing Office, November 1988), pp. 8–9.

In essence, we are bringing back a modern version of the 'cop on the beat.' We need to *solve* community problems rather than just *react* to them. It is time to adopt new strategies to address the dramatic increases in crime and the fear of crime. I view community policing as a better, smarter and more cost-effective way of using police resources.[5]

It should be emphasized, however, that community oriented policing is a long-term process that involves fundamental institutional change. One scholar warned police managers that "if you approach community oriented policing as a program, you will likely fail. Beware of the trap that seeks guaranteed, perfect, and immediate results."[6]

Community policing goes beyond simply implementing foot and bicycle patrols or neighborhood stations. It redefines the role of the officer on the street, from crime-fighter to problem solver and neighborhood ombudsman. It forces a cultural transformation of the entire department, including a decentralized organizational structure and changes in recruiting, training, awards systems, evaluation, promotions, and so forth. Furthermore, this philosophy asks officers to break away from the restrictions of incident-driven policing and to seek proactive and creative resolution to crime and disorder.

A Community Policing Officer's Typical Workday

To demonstrate the point about community policing and problem solving being different from traditional policing, see Table 4-1, "Traditional Versus Community Policing: Questions and Answers," as well as Figure 4-1 ("Traditional Policing versus Community Oriented Policing, Problem Oriented Policing, and Neighborhood Police Officers") and Box 4-1 ("A community policing officer's day").

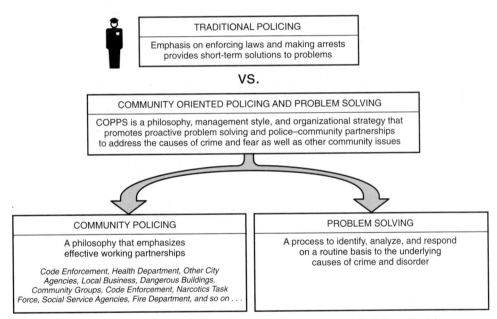

Figure 4-1. Traditional Policing versus Community Oriented Policing, Problem Oriented Policing, and Neighborhood Police Officers.

BOX 4-1

A Community Policing Officer's Day

In addition to traditional law enforcement activities, such as patrol and responding to calls for service, the day might include

- Operating neighborhood substations
- Meeting with community groups
- Analyzing and solving neighborhood problems
- Conducting door-to-door surveys of residents
- Talking with students in schools
- Meeting with local merchants
- Making security checks of businesses
- Dealing with disorderly people

Source: Stephen D. Mastrofski, "What Does Community Policing Mean for Daily Police Work?" *National Institute of Justice Journal* (August 1992): 23–27.

Problem solving is not new; police officers have always tried to solve problems (we define "problem" below). The difference is that in the past, officers received little guidance, support, or technology from police administrators for dealing with problems. But the routine application of problem-solving techniques is new. It is premised on two facts: that problem solving can be applied by officers throughout the agency as part of their daily work and that routine problem-solving efforts can be effective in reducing or resolving problems.

Problem oriented policing (POP) was grounded on principles different from community oriented policing (COP), but they are complementary. POP is a strategy that puts the COP philosophy into practice. It advocates that police examine the underlying causes of recurring incidents of crime and disorder. The problem-solving process, discussed in later chapters, helps officers to identify problems, analyze them completely, develop response strategies, and assess the results.

Herman Goldstein is considered by many to be the principal architect of problem oriented policing. His book *Policing a Free Society* (1977)[7] is among the most frequently cited works in police literature. A later work, *Problem Oriented Policing* (1990),[8] provided a rich and complete exploration into problem oriented policing. Goldstein first coined the term problem oriented policing in 1979 out of frustration with the dominant model for improving police operations: "More attention (was) being focused on how quickly officers responded to a call than on what they did when they got to their destination."[9] He also bemoaned the linkage between the police and the telephone:

> The telephone, more than any public or internal policy, dictates what a police agency does. And that problem has been greatly aggravated with the installation of 911.[10]

As a result, Goldstein argued for a radical change in the direction of efforts to improve policing—a new framework that should help move the police from their past preoccupation with form and process to a much more direct, thoughtful concern with substantive problems. To focus attention on the nature of police business and to improve the quality of police response in the course of their business, Goldstein argued that several steps must be taken:

1. Police must be equipped to define more clearly and to understand more fully the problems they are expected to handle. They must recognize the relationships between and among incidents; for example, incidents involving the same behavior, the same address, or the same people.
2. The police must develop a commitment to analyzing problems. It requires gathering information from police files, from the minds of experienced officers, from other agencies of government, and from private sources as well. It requires conducting house-to-house surveys and talking with victims, complainants, and offenders.
3. Police must be encouraged to conduct an uninhibited search for the most effective response to each problem, looking beyond just the criminal justice system to a wide range of alternatives; they must try to design a customized response that holds the greatest potential for dealing effectively with a specific problem in a specific place under specific conditions.[11]

Basic Principles

In earlier chapters we mentioned the limitations of traditional methods of policing in trying to deal with incidents. The first step in problem oriented policing, therefore, is to move beyond just handling incidents, recognizing that incidents are often merely overt symptoms of problems. It requires that officers take a more in-depth interest in incidents by acquainting themselves with some of the conditions and factors that cause them. Everyone in the department contributes to this mission, not just a few innovative officers or a special unit or function.[12]

Figure 4-2 shows incident-driven policing as it attempts to deal with each incident. Like Band-aid application, this symptomatic relief is valuable but limited. Because police leave unresolved the underlying condition that created the incidents, the incidents are very likely to recur.

A problem oriented police agency would respond as described in Figure 4-3. Officers use the information in their responses to incidents, along with information obtained from other sources, to get a clearer picture of the problem. Then they address the underlying conditions. As James Fyfe asked, "Can anyone imagine the surgeon general urging doctors to attack AIDS without giving any thought to its causes?"[13] If successful, fewer incidents may occur; those that do occur may be less serious. The incidents may even cease.[14]

The problem oriented approach also addresses a major dilemma for the police: the lack of meaningful measures of their effectiveness in the area of

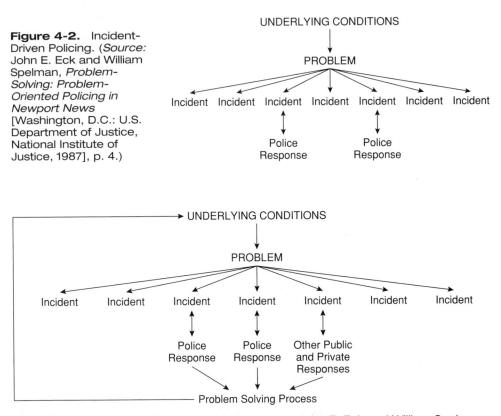

Figure 4-2. Incident-Driven Policing. (*Source:* John E. Eck and William Spelman, *Problem-Solving: Problem-Oriented Policing in Newport News* [Washington, D.C.: U.S. Department of Justice, National Institute of Justice, 1987], p. 4.)

Figure 4-3. Problem Oriented Policing. (*Source:* John E. Eck and William Spelman, *Problem-Solving: Problem-Oriented Policing in Newport News* [Washington, D.C.: U.S. Department of Justice, National Institute of Justice, 1987], p. 4.)

crime and disorder. Crime rate statistics are virtually useless because they collapse all the different kinds of crime into one global category and they are an imperfect measure of the actual incidence of criminal behavior.[15] Goldstein also maintained that the police should "disaggregate" the different problems they face and then attempt to develop strategies to address each one.[16] Domestic disturbances, for instance, should be separated from public intoxication; murder should be separated from sexual assault. In this respect, problem oriented policing is primarily a *planning process.*

A Broader Role for the Street Officer

A major departure of problem oriented policing from the conventional style lies with POP's view of the line officer, who is given much more discretion and decision-making ability, and is trusted with a much broader array of responsibilities. Problem oriented policing values thinking officers, urging that they take the initiative in trying to deal more effectively with problems in the areas they serve. This concept more effectively uses the potential of college-educated officers, "who have been smothered in the atmosphere of traditional policing." [17] It also gives officers a new sense of identity and self-respect; they are more challenged and have opportunities to follow through on individual cases—to analyze and solve problems—which will give them greater job satisfaction. We ought to be recruiting as police officers people who can "serve as mediators, as dispensers of information, and as community organizers."[18]

Under problem oriented policing, officers continue to handle calls, but they also do much more. They use the information gathered in their responses to incidents together with information obtained from other sources to get a clearer picture of the problem. They then address the underlying conditions.

Seeking information from a variety of resources (e.g., business owners) will assist officers in understanding the underlying conditions and factors related to problems. (*Courtesy* Community Policing Consortium)

"S.A.R.A.": The Problem-Solving Process

The Newport News task force designed a four-stage problem-solving process (depicted in Figure 4-4) known as S.A.R.A.: the process involves *scanning, analysis, response*, and *assessment*.[19]

Scanning: Problem Identification

Scanning means problem identification. As a first step, officers should identify problems on their beats, and look for a pattern or persistent, repeat incidents. At this juncture the question might well be asked, "What is a 'problem'?" A problem has been defined as:

A group of two or more incidents that are similar in one or more respects, causing harm and therefore being of concern to the police and the public.

Incidents may be *similar* by various means, including

- *Behaviors* (this is the most frequent type of indicator, including such activities as drug sales, robberies, thefts, graffiti, and so forth);
- *Location* (problems occur in area hot spots, such as downtown cruising, housing complexes plagued by burglaries, parks where gangs commit crimes, and so forth);
- *Persons* (can include repeat offenders or victims; both account for a high proportion of crime);
- *Time* (seasonal, day of week, hour of day; examples include traffic congestion, bar closing, tourist activity); and
- *Events* (crimes may peak during such events as university spring break, rallies, gatherings, etc.).

There does not appear to be any inherent limit on the types of problems patrol officers can work on; there are several types of problems that are appropriate for problem solving. The following list demonstrates the diversity of problems identified and addressed in several jurisdictions:

- A series of burglaries from trailers at a construction site
- Drug activity, drinking, and disorderly conduct at a community park
- Suspected drug activity at a private residence
- Thefts from autos at a shopping mall
- Juvenile loitering at a shopping center and near a bar
- Vagrants panhandling downtown
- Problems with false and faulty alarms at commercial addresses
- Parking and traffic problems
- Street prostitution and related robberies in a downtown neighborhood

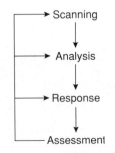

Figure 4-4. A Problem Solving Process. (*Source:* John E. Eck and William Spelman, *Problem-Solving: Problem-Oriented Policing in Newport News* [Washington, D.C.: U.S. Department of Justice, National Institute of Justice, 1987], p. 43.)

- A high rate of burglaries at a rundown apartment complex
- Repeat domestic assault calls to certain addresses[20]

If the incidents police are responding to do not fall within the definition of a problem, the problem-solving model is not applicable and police should handle the incident according to normal procedure.

There are numerous resources available to the police to identify problems, including CFS data, especially repeat calls from the same location or a repeated series of similar incidents. Other ways are through citizen complaints, census data, data from other government agencies, newspaper and media coverage of community issues, officer observations, and community surveys.

The primary purpose of scanning is to conduct a preliminary inquiry to determine if a problem really exists and whether further analysis is needed. During this stage, priorities should be established if multiple problems exist and a specific officer or team of officers should be assigned to handle the problem. Scanning initiates the problem-solving process.

Determining Problem Nature and Extent The second stage, *analysis*, is the heart of the problem-solving process. For this reason, we will dwell on it at greater length. Comprehensively analyzing a problem is critical to the success of a problem-solving effort. Effective, tailor-made responses cannot be developed unless people know what is causing the problem. Thus the purpose of analysis is to learn as much as possible about problems in order to identify their causes; officers must gather information from sources inside and outside their agency about the scope, nature, and causes of problems.

Analysis: The Heart of Problem Solving

Motels converted to daily and weekly rentals often result in an increase in calls for service and crimes in the area.

A complete analysis includes identifying the seriousness of the problem, all the persons/groups involved and affected, all of the causes of the problem, and assessing current responses and their effectiveness.

Many people essentially skip the analysis phase of S.A.R.A., believing that the nature of the problem is obvious, succumbing to pressure to quickly solve the problem, or feeling that the pressure of CFS precludes their having time for detailed inquiries into the nature of the problem. Problem solvers must resist these temptations, or they risk addressing a problem that does not exist and/or implementing solutions that are ineffective in the long run.

For example, computer-assisted dispatch (CAD) data in one southeastern police department indicated that there was a large auto theft problem at a local shopping mall. However, after reviewing incident reports and other records, it became clear that many of the reported "thefts" actually involved shoppers misplacing their cars and then mistakenly reporting them as stolen.[21]

Identifying the Harms   A discussion of harms is important to analyzing problems and responding to them. The problem of gangs serves as an example. We must begin by asking, why are gangs a problem? We can find the answer to this question by focusing on harmful behaviors. Not all gang members are criminals or engage in harmful behaviors. It is therefore important that each community examine the behaviors of its gangs, determine which behaviors are harmful, and design responses appropriate to deal with those behaviors.

Common gang behaviors may include wearing "colors," spreading graffiti, drug use and sales, and a threatening presence. For example, the wearing of colors to school creates fear among students and teachers and may result in fights between rival gang members.

These behaviors present harm to the community and should be the focus of police problem-solving efforts. By identifying harmful behaviors, gangs—a huge, nondescriptive term/problem—is broken down into smaller, more manageable problems. This helps to identify the underlying causes or related conditions that contribute to illegal gang activity and is the basis for officers' responses.

Seeking "Small Wins"   Karl Weick explained that people often look at social problems on a massive scale. The public, media, elected officials, and government agencies often become fixated on problems and define them by using the simplest term (gangs, homelessness, poverty, mental illness, violent crime, and so forth). Viewing problems in this manner leads to defining problems on a scale so massive that they are unable to be addressed, thus becoming overwhelmed. For this reason, Weick introduced the concept. One must understand that some problems are too deeply ingrained or too rooted in other complex social problems to be eliminated. Conversely, however, adopting the "small wins" philosophy helps to understand the nature of our analysis and response to problems.

As indicated above, the more appropriate response to these problems is to break them down into smaller, more controllable problems. Although an individual small win may not seem important, a series of small wins may have a substantial impact on the overall problem. Eliminating the harms (graffiti, drug sales, and so on) is a sensible and realistic strategy for reducing the impact of gang behaviors. Therefore, it makes sense to address a large problem at a level where there can be a reasonable expectation of success.

The idea of small wins is also helpful when prioritizing problems and working together in a group. We have discussed the benefits of a collaborating with the community and other outside agencies to address problems. Small wins can help the group understand the problem better, select realistic objectives, and formulate more effective strategies. It also helps to build confidence and trust among group members.[22]

The Problem Analysis Triangle   Generally, three elements are needed for a problem to occur: an *offender*, a *victim*, and a *location*. The "Problem Analysis Triangle" helps officers visualize the problem and understand the relationship between the three elements. Additionally, it helps officers analyze problems, suggests where more information is needed, and helps with crime control and prevention.

The relationship between these three elements can be explained as follows: If there is a victim, and he or she is in a place where a crime can occur, but there are no offenders, no crime occurs; if there is an offender and he or she is in a place where crimes occur, but there is nothing or no one to be victimized, then no crime will occur; and if an offender and victim are not in the same place, there will be no crime. Part of the analysis phase involves finding out as much as possible about the victims, offenders, and locations where problems exist in order to understand what is prompting the problem and what to do about it.

The three elements must be present before a crime or harmful behaviors—problems—can occur (see Figure 4-5): an *offender* (someone who is motivated to commit harmful behavior), a *victim* (a desirable and vulnerable target must be present), and a *location* (the victim and offender must both be in the same place at the same time; we discuss locations more below). If these three elements show up over and over again in patterns and recurring problems, removing one of these elements can stop the pattern and prevent future harms.[23]

As an example, let us apply the analysis triangle to the problem of graffiti, using Figure 4-6. The "place" is marked buildings and areas immediately around them. The "victims" are the owners and users of the buildings; the "offenders" are the writers of the graffiti (see the inside triangle of Figure 4-6; the outside triangle is discussed below). Removing one or more of these elements will remove the problem. Strategies for removing one of these elements are only limited to an officer's creativity, availability of resources, and ability to formulate collaborative responses.

Some jurisdictions, for example, are setting aside an area for graffiti "artists," even having graffiti contests, or using nonadhesive paint on buildings and property (protecting locations) to discourage taggers ("offenders") or give them an outlet to their illegal tagging activities; other jurisdictions have contemplated outlawing the sale of spray paint, or limiting the sale of broad-tip

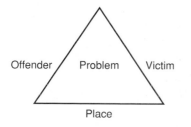

Figure 4-5.   Problem Analysis Triangle. (*Source:* U.S. Department of Justice, Bureau of Justice Assistance, *Comprehensive Gang Initiative: Operations Manual for Implementing Local Gang Prevention and Control Programs* [Draft, October 1993], p. 3.)

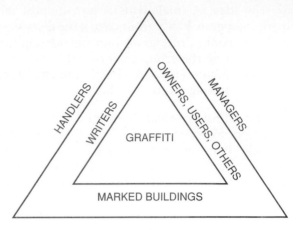

Figure 4-6. Graffiti Problem Triangle: The Role of Third Parties. (*Source:* Adapted from John E. Eck, "Police Problems and Research: A Short, Furious, Concise Tour of a Complex Field." Unpublished draft 1.2, January 20, 2002, p. 4; and U.S. Department of Justice, Bureau of Justice Assistance, *Comprehensive Gang Initiative: Operations Manual for Implementing Local Gang Prevention and Control Programs* [Draft, October 2003], pp. 3–11. Used with permission.)

markers to juveniles, while still others have enacted graffiti ordinances to help business owners ("victims") to keep their "locations" graffiti-free.

The Role of Third Parties Police engaged in problem solving need to also be aware of the three types of "third parties" that can either help or hinder the problem-solving effort by attempting to act on behalf of one or more of the three elements discussed in the problem analysis triangle in Figure 4-5. We will again use examples and Figure 4-6 to explain the role of third parties.

1. *Handlers or Controllers*: people who, acting in the best interests of the potential offenders, try to prevent these people from committing crimes. Handlers of gang members might be parents, adult neighbors, peers, teachers, and employers. However, these youths may live in a poor, one-parent home or not be attending school or working. Handlers can often restrict the tools used by gang members, such as a retailer putting spray cans in locked bins, parents restricting the wearing of "colors," and legislators passing laws obstructing the sale of semi-automatic and automatic weapons.[24]

2. *Guardians*: there are people or things, exercising control over each side of the triangle so that crime is less likely, called guardians. For instance, if the crime problem is drug dealing in a house, and the offender side of the triangle includes dealers and buyers, then a list of guardians would include police, parents of dealers/buyers, probation and parole officers, the landlord, city codes, health and tax departments, and neighbors. Tools used by guardians include crime prevention techniques (discussed more later).[25]

3. *Managers*: people who oversee locations. For example, apartment managers can help prevent or solve problems by installing security equipment in their buildings, screening tenants carefully, and evicting troublemakers or criminals. Conversely, where managers are absent or lax, risks will be higher.[26]

Police should constantly look for ways to improve the effectiveness of third parties because these groups of individuals have the authority to deal with the problem. There will always be the temptation on the part of society to use the police as handlers, guardians, or managers. Although this may be effective for a short time, there are rarely enough officers to control a recurring problem in the long run.

An important adjunct to our discussion of analysis is a look at situational crime prevention (to include crime prevention through environmental design—CPTED) and crime analysis under community policing, both of which are addressed in Chapter 5.

Additional aspects of analysis are examined later in this chapter.

After a problem has been clearly defined and analyzed, the officer confronts the ultimate challenge in problem oriented policing: the search for the most effective way of dealing with it. This stage of the S.A.R.A. process focuses on developing and implementing responses to the problem. Before entering this stage, an agency must overcome the temptation to implement a response prematurely and be certain that it has thoroughly analyzed the problem; attempts to fix problems quickly are rarely effective in the long term.

To develop tailored responses, problem solvers should review their findings about the three sides of the crime triangle—victims, offenders, and location—and develop creative solutions that will address at least two sides of the triangle.[27] It is also important to remember that the key to developing tailored responses is making sure the responses are very focused and *directly linked* to the findings from the analysis phase of the project.

Responses may be wide-ranging and often require arrests (however, apprehension may not be the most effective solution), referral to social service agencies, or changes in ordinances. Potential solutions to problems can be organized into five groups:

1. *Totally eliminating the problem*. Effectiveness is measured by the absence of the types of incidents that this problem creates. It is unlikely that most problems can be totally eliminated, but a few can.
2. *Reducing the number of incidents the problem creates*. A reduction of incidents stemming from a problem is a major measure of effectiveness.
3. *Reducing the seriousness of the harms*. Effectiveness for this type of solution is demonstrated by showing that the incidents are less harmful.
4. *Dealing with a problem better* (treating more participants more humanely, reducing costs, or increasing the effectiveness of handling incidents). Improved victim satisfaction, reduced costs, and other measures can show that this type of solution is effective.
5. *Removing the problem from police consideration*. The effectiveness of this type of solution can be measured by looking at why the police were handling the problem originally and the rationale for shifting the handling to others.[28]

Box 4-2 provides an elaboration on the possible alternative responses to problems.

Problem solving officers will often seek the assistance of the community, other city departments, businesses, private and social service organizations, and anyone else who can help with their efforts. Box 4-3 is a guide to collaboration, to guide officers in developing networks with people and working with other agencies.

Finally, in the *assessment* stage, officers evaluate the effectiveness of their responses. A number of measures have traditionally been used by police agencies and community members to assess effectiveness. These include numbers of arrests, levels of reported crime, response times, clearance rates, citizen

Response: Formulating Tailor-Made Strategies

Assessment: Evaluating Overall Effectiveness

BOX 4-2

Range of Possible Response Options

1. *Concentrate attention on the individuals accounting for a disproportionate share of the problem.* A relatively small number of individuals usually account for a disproportionate share of practically any problem, by causing it (offenders), facilitating it (controllers, managers, guardians), or suffering from it (victims).

2. *Connect with other government and private services.* A thorough analysis of a problem often leads to an appreciation of the need for (a) more effective referrals to existing governmental and private services, (b) improved coordination with agencies that exert control over some of the problems or individuals involved in the incidents, and (c) initiative for pressing for correction of inadequacies in municipal services and for development of new services.

3. *Use mediation and negotiation skills.* Often the use of mediation and negotiation teams can be effective responses to conflicts.

4. *Convey information.* Relating sound and accurate information is one of the least used responses. It has the potential, however, to be one of the most effective for responding to a wide range of problems. Conveying information can help (a) reduce anxiety and fear, (b) enable citizens to solve their own problems, (c) elicit conformity with laws and regulations that are not known or understood, (d) warn potential victims about their vulnerability and advise them of ways to protect themselves, (e) demonstrate to people how they unwittingly contribute to problems, (f) develop support for addressing a problem, and (g) acquaint the community with the limitations on government agencies and define realistically what can be expected of those agencies.

5. *Mobilize the community.* Mobilizing a specific segment of the community helps implement a specific response to a specific problem for as long as it takes to deal with the problem.

6. *Make use of existing forms of social control.* Solve problems by mobilizing specific forms of social control inherent in existing relationships—for example, the influence of a parent, teacher, employer, or church.

7. *Alter the physical environment to reduce opportunities for problems to recur.* Adapt the principles of crime prevention through environmental design and situational crime prevention to the complete range of problems.

8. *Increase regulation, through statutes or ordinances, of conditions that contribute to problems.* An analysis of a specific problem may draw attention to factors contributing to the problem that can be controlled by regulation through statutes or ordinances.

9. *Develop new forms of limited authority to intervene and detain.* Examination of specific problems can lead to the conclusion that a satisfactory solution requires some limited authority (e.g., to order a person to leave) but does not require labeling the conduct criminal so that it can be dealt with through a citation or a physical arrest followed by a criminal prosecution.

10. *Make more discriminate use of the criminal justice system.* Use of the criminal justice system should be much more discreet than in the past, reserved for those problems for which the system seems especially appropriate, and used with much greater precision. This could include (a) straightforward investigation, arrest, and prosecution; (b) selective enforcement with articulated criteria; (c) enforcing criminal laws that, by tradition, are enforced by another agency; (d) defining with greater specificity that behavior which should be subject to criminal justice prosecution or control through local ordinances; (e) intervention without making an arrest; (f) use of arrest without the intention to prosecute; and (g) attaching new conditions to probation or parole.

11. *Use civil law to control public nuisances, offensive behavior, and conditions contributing to crime.* Because most of what the police do in the use of the law involves arrest and prosecution, people tend to forget that the police and local government can initiate a number of other legal proceedings, including those related to (a) licensing, (b) zoning, (c) property confiscation, (d) nuisance abatement, and (e) injunctive relief.

Source: Adapted from Herman Goldstein, *Problem-Oriented Policing* (New York: McGraw-Hill, 1990, pp. 104–141). Used with permission of McGraw-Hill.

BOX 4-3

Problem Solving: Guide to Collaboration

General Background

1. Develop personal networks with members of other agencies who can give you information and help you with problems on which you may be working.
2. Become familiar with the workings of your local government, private businesses, citizen organizations, and other groups and institutions that you may need to call on for help in the future.
3. Develop skills as a negotiator.

Getting Other Agencies to Help

1. Identify agencies that have a role (or could have a role) in addressing the problem early in the problem-solving process.
2. Determine whether these other agencies perceive that there is a problem.

   a. Which agency members perceive the problem and which do not?
   b. Why is it (or isn't it) a problem for them?
   c. How are police perceptions of the problem similar to and different than the perceptions of members of other agencies?

3. Determine whether there is a legal or political mandate for collaboration.

   a. To which agencies does this legal mandate apply?
   b. What are the requirements needed to demonstrate collaboration?
   c. Who is checking to determine whether collaboration is taking place?

4. Look for difficulties that these other agencies face that can be addressed through collaboration on this problem.

   a. Are there internal difficulties that provide an incentive to collaborate?
   b. Are there external crises affecting agencies that collaboration may help address?

5. Determine how much these other agencies use police services.
6. Assess the resource capabilities of these agencies to help.

   a. Do they have the money?
   b. Do they have the staff expertise?
   c. Do they have the enthusiasm?

7. Assess the legal authority of these other agencies.

   a. Do they have special enforcement powers?
   b. Do they control critical resources?

8. Determine the administrative capacity of these agencies to collaborate.

   a. Do they have the legal authority to intervene in the problem?
   b. What are the internal procedures and policies of the stakeholders that help or hinder collaboration?

Working with Other Agencies

1. Include representatives from all affected agencies, if possible, in the problem-solving process.
2. Look for responses to the problem that maximize the gains to all agencies and distribute costs equitably.
3. Reinforce awareness of the interdependence of all agencies.
4. Be prepared to mediate among agencies that have a history of conflict.
5. Develop problem information sharing mechanisms, and promote discussion about the meaning and interpretation of this information.
6. Share problem-solving decisions among stakeholders, and do not surprise others with already-made decisions.
7. Develop a clear explanation as to why collaboration is needed.
8. Foster external support for collaborative efforts, but do not rely on mandates to further collaboration.
9. Be prepared to negotiate with all involved agencies as to their roles, responsibilities, and resource commitments.
10. When collaborating with agencies located far away, plan to spend time developing a working relationship.
11. Try to create support in the larger community for collaborative problem solving.

When Collaboration Does Not Work

1. Always be prepared for collaboration to fail.
2. Have alternative plans.
3. Assess the costs and benefits of unilateral action.
4. Be very patient.

Source: Adapted from John E. Eck, "Implementing a Problem-Oriented Approach: A Management Guide," mimeo, draft copy (Washington, D.C.: Police Executive Research Forum, 1990), pp. 69–70.

complaints, and various workload indicators, such as CFS and the number of field interviews conducted.[29]

Several of these measures may be helpful in assessing the impact of a problem-solving effort; however, a number of nontraditional measures will shed light on whether a problem has been reduced or eliminated:

- Reduced instances of repeat victimization
- Decreases in related crimes or incidents
- Neighborhood indicators, which can include increased profits for businesses in the target area, increased usage of the area, increased property values, less loitering and truancy, and fewer abandoned cars
- Increased citizen satisfaction regarding the handling of the problem, determined through surveys, interviews, focus groups, electronic bulletin boards, and so forth
- Reduced citizen fear related to the problem[30]

Assessment is obviously key in the S.A.R.A. process; knowing that we must assess the effectiveness of our efforts emphasizes the importance of documentation and baseline measurement. Supervisors can help officers assess the effectiveness of their efforts.

If the responses implemented are not effective, the information gathered during analysis should be reviewed. New information may need to be collected before new solutions can be developed and tested.[31] We discuss assessment (evaluation) in depth in Chapter 11.

A COLLABORATIVE APPROACH: COPPS

Basic Principles

As was mentioned in the introduction, our view is that the two above concepts—community policing and problem oriented policing—are separate but complementary notions that can work together "hand-in-glove." We believe the police are severely hampered when attempting to solve neighborhood and community problems without the full cooperation—a partnership and collaboration—with the community and other resources.

Community policing and problem oriented policing share some important characteristics: (1) decentralization (to encourage officer initiative and the effective use of local knowledge); (2) geographically defined rather than functionally defined subordinate units (to encourage the development of local knowledge); and (3) close interactions with local communities (to facilitate responsiveness to and cooperation with the community).[32]

Goldstein did not see problem oriented policing as an alternative to community policing or in competition with it. However, he asserted that much of what is occurring in community policing projects begs for application of all that has been described under the label of problem oriented policing.

A Definition and Illustration

What exactly is COPPS? How does it function? How would we know it if we saw it? Following is a definition we feel accurately captures the essence of this concept:

Community Oriented Policing and Problem Solving (COPPS) is a proactive philosophy that promotes solving problems that are criminal, affect our quality of life, or increase our fear of crime, as well as other community issues.

COPPS involves identifying, analyzing, and addressing community problems at their source.

To assist in our understanding of this definition, following is an example of how a neighborhood problem is treated under the traditional, reactive style of policing versus the community problem solving approach:

> Police have experienced a series of disturbances in a relatively quiet and previously stable residential neighborhood. Although the neighborhood's zoning had for years provided for late-night cabaret-style businesses, none had existed until the "Nite Life," a live-music dance club, opened. Within a few weeks the police dispatcher received an increased number of complaints about loud music and voices, fighting, and screeching tires late into the night. Within a month's time, at least 50 CFS had been dispatched to the club to restore order. Evening shift officers responded to calls and restored order prior to midnight but graveyard shift officers would have to restore order again when being called back to the scene by complaining neighbors after midnight.

Under the COPPS approach, this same matter might be handled thusly:

> The evening-shift area patrol sergeant identified the disturbances as a problem. The initial scanning phase provided the following information: data showing huge CFS increases in the area on both the evening and graveyard shifts; several realtors had contacted council members to complain about declining market interest in the area and to say that they were considering suing both the owner of the new business and the city for the degradation of the neighborhood; a local newspaper was about to run a story on the increase in vehicle burglaries and damage done to parked vehicles in and around the cabaret's parking lot. The team also determined that the consolidated narcotics unit was investigating both employees and some of the late-night clientele of the business as a result of several tips that narcotics were being used and sold in the parking lot and inside the business.

> The officers and their sergeant gathered information from crime reports, a news reporter about to publish the story, neighboring business owners, and the department's crime analysis unit. Information was also gathered concerning possible zoning and health department violations. Officers then met with the business owner to work out an agreement for reestablishing the quality of life in the neighborhood to its previous levels and to decrease the department's CFS.

> First, the business licensing division and the owner were brought together to both reestablish the ground rules and provide for a proper licensing of all the players. This resulted in the instant removal of an unsavory partner and in turn his "following" of drug users and other characters at the business. The landlord agreed to hasten landscaping and lighting of the parking lots and provide a "sound wall" around the business to buffer the area residents. Agreements were reached to limit the hours of operation of the live music of the business. The cabaret's owner and all of his employees were trained by the area patrol teams in pertinent aspects of the city code (such as disturbing the peace, minors in liquor establishments, and trespassing laws). The police experienced a reduction in CFS in the area. Area residents, although not entirely happy with the continuing existence of the business, acknowledged satisfaction from their complaints; no further newspaper stories appeared regarding the noise and disorder in the neighborhood.

In this example, the police not only responded to the concerns of the neighborhood residents, they also developed a better understanding of both the area's businesses and residents, and established a working relationship with all involved. By co-opting the services of the other municipal entities, police also learned of new and valuable resources with whom to share some of the burden of future demands for government service.

One of the strongest advocates of this kind of approach to policing is the California Department of Justice, which has published several monographs on the subject and has taken the position that

> Community Oriented Policing and Problem Solving is a concept whose time has come. This movement holds tremendous promise for creating effective police-community partnerships to reclaim our communities and keep our streets safe. COPPS is not "soft" on crime; in fact, it is tougher on crime because it is smarter and more creative. Community input focuses police activities; and, with better information, officers are able to respond more effectively with arrests or other appropriate actions. COPPS can unite our communities and promote pride in our police forces.[33]

In order for COPPS to succeed, however, the following measures are required:

- Conducting accurate community needs assessments
- Mobilizing all appropriate players to collect data and brainstorm strategies
- Determining appropriate resource allocations and creating new resources where necessary
- Developing and implementing innovative, collaborative, comprehensive programs to address underlying causes and causal factors
- Evaluating programs and modifying approaches as needed[34]

CRIME ANALYSIS

Although crime analysis was discussed earlier in terms of its application under the S.A.R.A. process, analysis is such an important and broad subject that we expand that discussion here.

Indeed, the importance of analysis in policing's COPPS era can be summed up in the following statement: "Community policing can be distinguished from professional policing because it calls for information from domains that had previously been neglected and for more complex analysis of that information."[35]

It is very important for officers who are engaged in problem solving to understand *how, when, where*, and *why* criminal events occur, rather than merely respond to them. In this vein we do not mean to say that patrol officers should develop expertise in understanding the mental processes and theories that are involved in a person's choosing to commit crimes (although criminology or psychology courses at a college or university would certainly benefit the problem-solving officer); rather, we are referring to what might be termed "street-level criminology." This matter is relatively new to policing at the street level, and it requires that we learn more about crime occurrences through analysis and experimentation with the problem-solving process.

Analyzing Crime: Definition, Functions, and Types

Crime analysis has been defined as "a set of systematic, analytical processes providing timely and pertinent information to assist operational and administrative personnel."[36] There are basically three types of crime analysis:

1. *Tactical*: an analytical process that provides information used to assist operations personnel (patrol and investigative officers) in identifying specific and

immediate crime trends, patterns, sprees, and hot spots, providing investigative leads. Criminal activity is associated by the method, time, date, location, suspect, vehicle, and other types of information.

2. *Strategic*: concerned with long-range problems and projections of long-term increases or decreases in crime (crime trends); includes the preparation of crime statistical summaries, resource acquisition, and allocation studies.

3. *Administrative*: focuses on provision of economic, geographic, or social information.

In more closely "dissecting" crime, crime analysis is also indispensable toward identifying the underlying characteristics of criminal behavior. Unfortunately, much of our attempts to control crime treat the symptoms and ignore the disease.

Another reason for engaging in crime analysis is that career criminals are more mobile than the average criminal, often crossing city and even state lines to commit their crimes.[37]

As William Spelman indicated, "So, the offenders we would most like to catch are also the ones we are least likely to catch, at least using present police methods."[38] If we stop concentrating on individual crimes and instead think about series of crimes, all committed by the same offender, we may be able to forecast when and where the offender will commit his or her next crime, and we may be able to link together clues from several crimes to help identify the offender responsible.

Crime analysis has the potential to become increasingly useful to police engaged in problem solving. There are four kinds of analysis functions that may be performed:

- *Crime Series/Pattern Detection*: Crime series detection is identification of offenses that are believed to be committed by the same person or group; crime pattern detection, in contrast, is the number of offenses that have some common characteristics not necessarily unique to a given person or group. The objective of crime series detection is apprehension, and the objective of crime pattern detection is suppression.

Crime analysis information led these repeat offender program officers to the arrest of suspects in a car theft ring. (*Courtesy* Reno, Nevada, police department)

- *Suspect-crime correlations*: These identify perpetrators of known crimes by systematically matching a suspect's physical, vehicle, or MO information from crime reports with similar information from offender-based files.
- *Target/Suspect Profiles*: Target profiles attempt to forecast the nature of the objects that might be attacked or descriptions of the types of structure and victims for a given crime problem. Suspect profiles can be established in the same manner.
- *Crime Potential Forecasts*: These are attempts to determine future crime events based on the historical analysis of cyclical, periodic, or special events and information from crime series/pattern detection.[39]

The value of crime analysis to problem solving also depends on the amount of time crime analysts are allotted to respond to individual officer requests and their ability to become *problem* analysts.

Establishing and Locating a Crime Analysis Unit

One of the first challenges for crime analysis is choosing an analyst and determining whether to use a commissioned officer or to hire a civilian. In either case, the minimum qualifications for an entry-level analyst should be a person with an undergraduate degree in one of the social sciences, familiarity with basic office software, and good verbal and written communication skills.[40] Officers have the advantage of being able to gain the respect of their colleagues, while civilians are often educated specifically for conducting analyses and are much more likely to make crime analysis a career.

Another key decision is where the agency should locate the crime analysis unit. As a rule, these units should be assigned to the division that will benefit most from its expertise; generally, this means the patrol or investigative divisions because that is where the end users are.

With the formation of the International Association of Crime Analysts (IACA), police agencies may obtain assistance in starting such units as well as training and the sharing of ideas, skills, and experiences. According to its Web site (*www.iaca.net*), the IACA is also dedicated to advocating professional standards and creating an international network for the standardization of analytical techniques.[41]

Counterterrorism from the Analyst's Perspective

In the wake of the recent attacks by terrorists on United States soil, the role and functions of crime analysts have become even more crucial. This role with counterterrorism involves two major efforts: investigation and prevention.

Investigation: Terrorists operate according to rules and principles that can be identified, analyzed, and predicted. Although they can be fanatical and fiendish, they behave in a logical fashion, picking their targets with precision. This makes them more vulnerable in the sense that analysts can predict their behavior and disrupt their efforts. Analysts must never work alone, however; they must coordinate with the appropriate federal agency, most often the Federal Bureau of Investigation.

Prevention: This is accomplished by denying the terrorist the opportunity to attack in the first place. The process begins with a threat assessment of the jurisdiction: identifying and evaluating the risk of targets, and constructing countermeasures by using the S.A.R.A. process. Analysts can *scan* for vulnerabilities, *analyze* these methods of attack to determine countermeasures, *respond* by allocating the necessary police resources to try to thwart an attack, and *assess* by performing periodic readiness tests and exercises to determine effectiveness.[42]

Next we discuss the kinds of crime analysis tools that are available to crime problem solvers, including crime mapping, police reports, CFS analysis, and surveys.

Crime mapping has become increasingly popular among law enforcement agencies and is given high visibility at the federal level, in the media, and among the largest police departments in the nation.[43] A federal study found that departments with 100 or more officers used computer crime mapping 35 percent of the time.[44]

The traditional crime map was a jumbo representation of a jurisdiction with pins stuck in it. These maps were useful for showing where crimes occurred, but they had several limitations as well: as they were updated, the prior crime patterns were lost; the maps were static, unable to be manipulated or queried; also, pin maps could be quite difficult to read when several types of crime were mixed together.[45] Consequently, during the 1990s pin maps largely gave way to desktop computer mapping, which have now become commonplace and fast, aided by the availability of cheap color printers.[46]

Computerized crime mapping has been termed "policing's latest hot topic,"[47] providing a way to involve the community in addressing its own problems by observing trends in neighborhood criminal activity. Crime mapping also offers crime analysts graphic representations of crime-related issues, while detectives can use maps to better understand the hunting patterns of serial offenders and to hypothesize where these offenders might live.[48]

The importance of crime mapping is evidenced by the fact that in 1997, the National Institute of Justice established the Crime Mapping Research Center (CMRC) to promote research, evaluation, development, and dissemi-

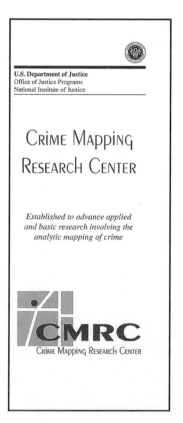

The Crime Mapping Research Center is a national clearing-house for information about crime analysis and mapping.

nation of geographic information systems technology for criminal justice research and practice. The CMRC holds annual conferences on crime mapping to provide researchers and practitioners an opportunity to gain both practical and state-of-the-art information on the use and utility of computerized crime mapping. The CMRC Web site address is *http://www.ojp.usdoj.gov/cmrc.*[49]

Exhibit 4-1 discusses new approaches to crime mapping: interactive crime mapping on the Internet. In a related vein, Figure 4-7 is the initial screen that appears when the user chooses "vehicle and traffic incidents" from the San Diego County Web site, providing information about auto thefts and burglaries as well as traffic accidents. Figure 4-8 shows the Austin, Texas, map viewer.

Computerized crime mapping combines geographic information from global positioning satellites with crime statistics gathered by the department's computer aided dispatching (CAD) system and demographic data provided by private companies or the United States Census Bureau (some agencies acquiring information from the Census Bureau's Internet home page). The result is a picture that combines disparate sets of data for a whole new perspective on crime. For example, maps of crimes can be overlaid with maps or layers of causative data: unemployment rates in the areas of high crime, locations of abandoned houses, population density, reports of drug activity, or geographic features (such as alleys, canals, or open fields) that might be contributing factors.[50] Furthermore, the hardware and software are now available to nearly all police agencies, costing a few thousand dollars.

In 1995 the Chicago police department implemented a system called Information Collection for Automated Mapping, or ICAM—a flexible, user-friendly system that enables all police officers to quickly generate maps of their beats, sectors, or districts, and to search for and analyze crime patterns. ICAM—now officially ICAM2, having already been upgraded with 20 enhancements—is now in use in all of the city's 25 policing districts and can query up to two years and map from a selection of 300 crimes, within specific time ranges; it can also reveal important neighborhood establishments, such as schools, abandoned buildings,

---

EXHIBIT 4-1   Interactive Crime Mapping on the Internet

Following are two examples of interactive crime mapping efforts on the Internet, in San Diego County, California, and Austin, Texas. Such systems not only enable citizens to obtain much more information than was previously available, but it precludes their having to make formal requests for information while freeing crime analysts to devote more time to analyzing crime instead of providing reports to the public.

In 1970, San Diego County's Automated Regional Justice Information System (ARJIS) began allowing all law enforcement agencies in the county to maintain and access crime and arrest information. Recently, however, ARJIS developed the first multi-agency, interactive crime mapping Web site in the nation. Now, anyone in the world can query and view certain crime, arrest, call, and traffic data for the county. Searches can be geographic (by street, neighbor-

hood, police beat, or city, as well as by time of day or day of week. ARJIS serves as a model for making interactive crime maps available to the public on the Internet. People access ARJIS for a variety of purposes, including wanting to learn about crime in their area, for a grant proposal, to support a debate on an issue, for citizen patrol, and even for real estate agent information.

Austin, Texas, unveiled a similarly unique approach to crime mapping on the Web, tripling the amount of information that was previously available and providing aggregated data by patrol areas, ZIP codes, census tracts, and neighborhood associations. Citizens can also see crime totals within 500 feet of any user-inputted address.

Source: Adapted from *Crime Mapping News* (a Police Foundation newsletter) 3 (Summer 2001):1–6.

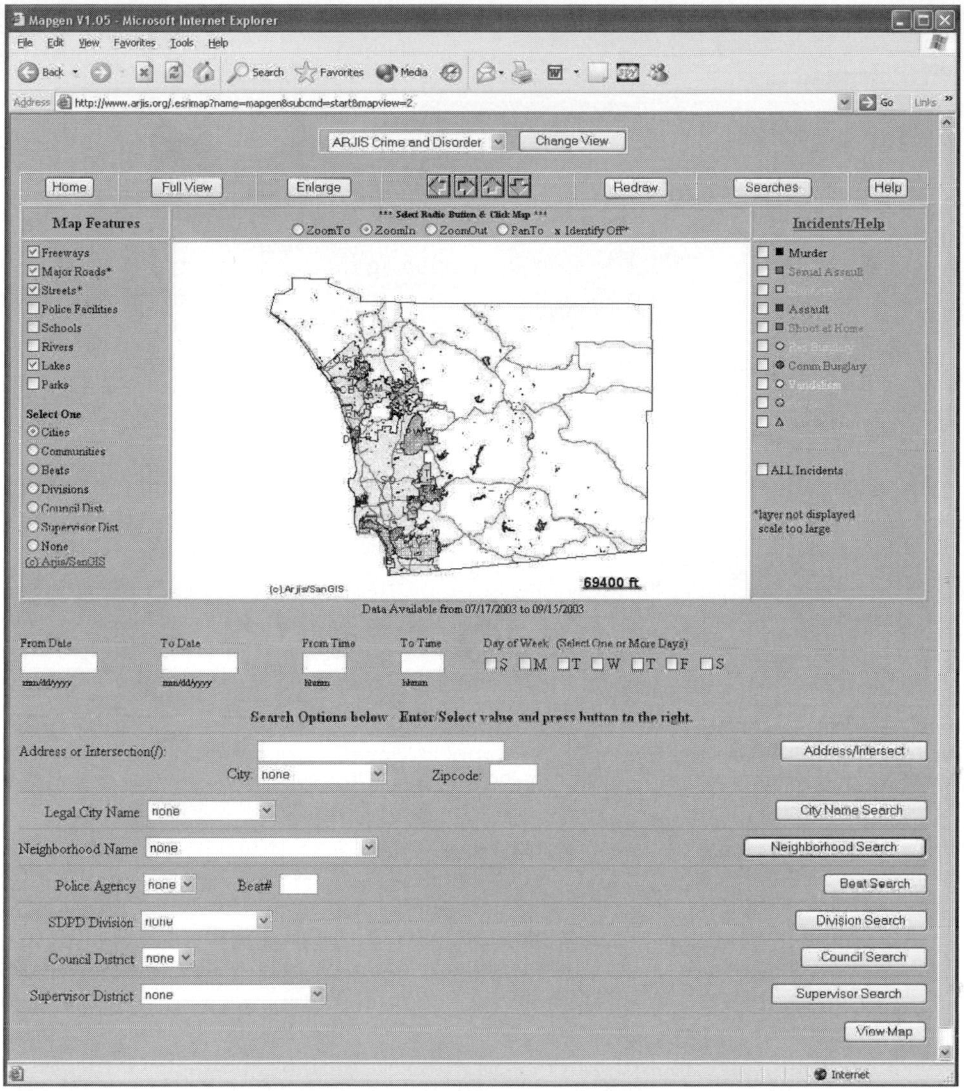

Figure 4-7. San Diego County's Interactive Crime Map.
(*Source: http://www.arjis.org/.esrimap?name=mapgen&subcmd=start&mapview=2*)

and liquor stores. It provides mugshot images within a minute. ICAM can also be an informative tool for the community; many COPPS officers are providing maps detailing crime on a beat during community meetings.[51]

Another example of mapping success is the New York police department's highly touted CompStat program, which provides up-to-the-minute statistics, maps patterns, and establishes causal relationships among crime categories. CompStat also puts supervisors in constant communication with the department's administration, provides updates to headquarters every week, and makes supervisors responsible for responding to crime in their assigned areas.[52]

But crime mapping is a major tool in smaller jurisdictions as well. Following are case studies involving successful outcomes.

- When an armored car was robbed in Toronto, dispatchers helped officers chase the suspects through a sprawling golf course using the mapping feature of the CAD system.

Figure 4-8. The Austin, Texas, Crime Mapping Viewer. (*Source:* Al Johnson, "The Austin Police Department's Crime Mapping Viewer," *Crime Mapping News* [Washington, D.C.: Police Foundation, Summer 2001], p. 5.)

- The Illinois state police map fatality accidents throughout the state and show which districts have specific problems. It can correlate that data with citations written, seatbelt usage, and other types of enforcement data.[53]

A wealth of information and other successful case studies about crime mapping are now provided in publications by the NIJ[54] and the Police Executive Research Forum.[55]

The Tempe, Arizona, police department Crime Analysis Unit's Web site homepage (*http://www.tempe.gov/cau*) allows citizens to learn about crime analysis, view a wide variety of crime statistics and demographics, and learn about ongoing crime studies and available reports and bulletins concerning crime in their community.

Figure 4-9 provides an example of crime mapping of street gang motivated homicide in Chicago.

Police Reports

Police offense reports can be analyzed for suspect characteristics, MOs, victim characteristics, and many other factors. Offense reports are also a potential source of information about high-crime areas and addresses because they capture exact descriptions of locations. However, in a typical department, patrol officers may write official reports on only about 25 to 30 percent of all calls to which they respond. Another limitation is that there may be a considerable lag between when the officer files a report and when the analysis is complete.[56]

Figure 4-9. A Crime Map of Street Gang Motivated Homicide, Chicago.

With the advent of CAD systems, a more reliable source of data on CFS has become available. CAD systems, containing information on all types of calls for service, add to information provided by offense reports, yielding a more extensive available account of what the public reports to the police.[57] The data captured by CAD systems can be sorted to reveal hot spots of crime and disturbances: specific locations from which an unusual number of calls to the police are made.

Many police agencies have the capability to use CAD data for repeat call analysis. The repeat call locations identified in this way can become targets of directed patrol efforts, including problem solving. For example, a precinct may receive printouts of the top 25 calls-for-service areas to review for problem-solving assignments. In Houston, the police and Hispanic citizens were concerned about violence at cantinas (bars). Through repeat call analysis, police learned that only 3 percent of the cantinas in the city were responsible for 40 percent of the violence. The data narrowed the scope of the problem and enabled a special liquor control unit to better target its efforts.[58]

Repeat alarm calls are another example of how CAD data can be used to support patrol officer problem solving. In fact, when the Baltimore County experiment began, some commanders preferred that officers start with alarm

Call For Service Analysis

projects. Data documenting repeat alarm calls by address were readily available, and commanders anticipated that solving alarm problems would be relatively simple, with considerable benefits compared to the investment of time.[59]

Surveys

Not to be overlooked in crime analysis is the use of community surveys to identify or clarify problems. For example, an officer may canvass all the business proprietors in shopping centers on his or her beat. One variation on this theme occurred in Baltimore when an officer telephoned business owners to update the police department's after-hours business contact files. Although the officer did not conduct a formal survey, he used this task to also inquire about problems the owners might want to bring to police attention.

On a larger scale, a team of officers may survey residents of a housing complex or neighborhood known to have particular crime problems. The survey could assist in determining residents' priority concerns, acquiring information about hot spots, and learning more about residents' expectations of police.[60] Residents will also be more likely to keep the police abreast of future problems when officers leave their cards and encourage residents to contact them directly.

Another approach to the survey process involves developing a beat profile. In Tempe, Arizona, COPPS officers began by conducting a detailed profile of a target beat. This involved both door-to-door surveys of residents and businesses and detailed observations of the environment. A survey instrument was developed and pilot tested and all survey team members were trained and given a uniform protocol to follow. The instrument contained questions about socio-demographic characteristics of residents, observed crime and drug problems, fear of crime, perception of city and police services, willingness to participate in and support community policing objectives, and other information. Survey team members also recorded information about the surroundings: condition of buildings, homes, streets, and yards; presence of abandoned vehicles; possible zoning and other code violations; and the existence of graffiti, trash, loiterers, gang members, and other signs of disorder.[61]

SOFTWARE FOR COPPS

Computer software now has analytic power that can work with the S.A.R.A. problem-solving process. Systems such as the "Dynamic Community Policing System" (DCPS) offered by Analysis Central Systems in Tiburon, California, have been specially developed for COPPS and are adaptable to laptop computers. These systems are used by many large and medium-sized police departments in the United States and Canada, including Dallas, Miami, Austin, Long Beach, Sacramento, Virginia Beach, and Vancouver, British Columbia. As advertised, this system is a "proactive computer companion to the officer in finding problems and implementing solutions."[62]

This system can automate beat profiling and demographics, find patterns of problems, help plan daily officer activities, balance beat and officer workloads, and identify current levels of performance. Downloaded information from agency computers is transferred to powerful microcomputers and notebook computers. The system continuously analyzes data using its proprietary decision tools, mathematical analyses, statistical tools, and expert systems. It can scan through hundreds of millions of pieces of data for patterns, trends, or clusters in beats and neighborhoods while ranking and reranking problems. The computer constantly asks itself thousands upon thousands of questions and develops answers.

In the field, the officer simply highlights the neighborhood, beat, or grid to consider, then selects the problem(s) to be worked from a menu the computer has composed. The emphasis for COPPS shifts from "What are the problems in this area?" to "Which of the ranked problems do I want to work and what options do I want to use to solve them?"

AN EXAMPLE OF COMMUNITY MOBILIZATION, THE FOUNDATION OF COPPS

Here we pull together several elements of COPPS that were presented in this chapter, looking at an example of how community mobilization was recently developed and operationalized in the community of San Diego, California.

City Heights is an area of San Diego that has a very diverse population of over 60,000 and contained many drug- and youth-related crime problems. Prior to this mobilization effort, City Heights residents expressed their desire for positive changes, but few actively participated in creating that change. There was a lack of trust between citizens and police, and fear of retaliation reigned, reinforcing silence, submission, and acceptance of crime and decay. Language barriers, cultural clashes, and lack of knowledge concerning community resources and problem-solving techniques served to further exacerbate the situation.

The City Heights Neighborhood Alliance was formed and employed three main mobilization techniques: door-to-door outreach, crisis theory, and community meetings. Door-to-door outreach involved two community organizers mobilizing residents within a 12-block area; they went to every home and apartment to actively engage residents in a partnership with police to solve crime problems. Although labor intensive, this effort established connections and familiarity with former strangers and brought out quality of life problems.

Crisis theory was applied by the organizers as well. They compiled crime statistics and identified crime and problem locations. They also developed flyers to educate residents to the severity and extent of crime in their area, and depicted the state of crisis in the area.

Residents were also invited to attend a community meeting to address their concerns. Organizers distributed flyers regarding the community meeting three days before it was to be held, and placed reminder phone calls to all community residents. A police officer and a community organizer facilitated the meeting, keeping it organized and limiting it to one hour.

To have community residents active in mobilizing, over 200 residents received training in problem-solving and community organization skills. They also met community leaders and governmental officials who could help with their mobilization efforts.

Residents solved several community drug problems. They held community meetings in front of the problem locations, contacted property owners, signed petitions, and brought in outside resources such as code compliance and other officials; they also threatened to picket or file lawsuits when necessary. Three community cleanups were held, and a police assistance team moved in to arrest 320 drug dealers.

This case study demonstrates how COPPS can be taken to a higher level, where police and citizens work together in a true mobilization effort to solve crime and quality of life issues. Such efforts empower community residents with the knowledge, tools, and guidance to forge an effective alliance.[63]

SUMMARY

This chapter, dubbed at the outset the "heart and soul" of this book, has set out the basic principles and strategies of the community policing and problem oriented policing concepts. It also offered a combined approach, which we believe is the best philosophy for the future of policing: community oriented policing and problem solving, or COPPS. We believe that blending these two concepts results in a better, more comprehensive approach to providing quality police service, combining the emphasis on forming a police-community partnership to fight crime with the use of the S.A.R.A. process to solve problems. Other very important elements of this strategy are the expanded role of the street officer and the focus on crime analysis.

NOTES

1. Gordon Witkin and Dan McGraw, "Beyond 'Just the facts, ma'am,'" *U.S. News and World Report* (August 2, 1993):28.

2. W. L. Melville Lee, *A History of Police in England* (London: Methuen, 1901), Chapter 12.

3. Herman Goldstein, "Toward Community-Oriented Policing: Potential, Basic Requirements, and Threshold Questions," *Crime and Delinquency* 33 (1987):17.

4. Robert Trojanowicz and Bonnie Bucqueroux, *Community Policing: A Contemporary Perspective* (Cincinnati: Anderson, 1990), p. 154.

5. Lee P. Brown, "Community Policing: Its Time Has Come," *The Police Chief* 62 (September 1991):10.

6. Jerald R. Vaughn, *Community-Oriented Policing: You Can Make It Happen* (Clearwater, Fla.: National Law Enforcement Leadership Institute, no date), p. 8.

7. Herman Goldstein, *Policing a Free Society* (Cambridge, Mass.: Ballinger, 1977).

8. Herman Goldstein, *Problem-Oriented Policing* (New York: McGraw-Hill, 1990).

9. Herman Goldstein, "Problem-Oriented Policing," paper presented at the Conference on Policing: State of the Art III, National Institute of Justice, Phoenix, Arizona, June 12, 1987.

10. Ibid., p. 4.

11. Ibid., pp. 5–6.

12. John E. Eck and William Spelman, "A Problem-Oriented Approach to Police Service Delivery," in Dennis Jay Kenney (ed.), *Police and Policing: Contemporary Issues* (New York: Praeger, 1989), pp. 95–111.

13. Quoted in Roland Chilton, "Urban Crime Trends and Criminological Theory," in Chris W. Eskridge (ed.) *Criminal Justice: Concepts and Issues* (Los Angeles: Roxbury, 1993), pp. 47–55.

14. Ibid., p. xvii.

15. Samuel Walker, *The Police in America: An Introduction* (2d ed.) (New York: McGraw-Hill, 1992), p. 177.

16. Goldstein, *Problem-Oriented Policing*, pp. 38–40.

17. Goldstein, "Toward Community-Oriented Policing," pp. 6–30.

18. Ibid., p. 21.

19. Ibid., pp. 43–52.

20. Goldstein, *Problem-Oriented Policing*, p. 18.

21. U.S. Department of Justice, Office of Community Oriented Policing Services, *Problem Solving Tips: A Guide to Reducing Crime and Disorder Through Problem-Solving Partnerships* (Washington, D.C.: Author, 2002), p. 10.

22. Karl E. Weick, "Small Wins: Redefining the Scale of Social Problems," *American Psychologist* 39 (1) (January 1984): 40–49.

23. John E. Eck, "A Dissertation Prospectus for the Study of Characteristics of Drug Dealing Places," (College Park, Md.: University of Maryland–College Park, November 1992).

24. Marcus Felson, "Linking Criminal Career Choices, Routine Activities, Informal Control, and Criminal

Outcomes," in Derek Cornish and Ronald Clarke (eds.), *The Reasoning Criminal: Rational Choice Perspectives on Offending* (New York: Springer-Verlag, 1986).

25. Lawrence E. Cohen and Marcus Felson, "Social Change and Crime Rate Trends: A Routine Activity Approach," *American Sociological Review* 44 (August 1979):588–608.

26. Eck, "A Dissertation Prospectus for the Study of Characteristics of Drug Dealing Places."

27. Rana Sampson, "Problem Solving," in *Neighborhood-Oriented Policing in Rural Communities: A Program Planning Guide* (Washington, D.C.: U.S. Department of Justice, Office of Justice Programs, Bureau of Justice Assistance), 1994, p. 4.

28. William Spelman and John E. Eck, "Problem-Solving," *Research in Brief* (Washington, D.C.: National Institute of Justice, January 1987):6.

29. Darrel Stephens, "Community Problem-Oriented Policing: Measuring Impacts," in Larry T. Hoover, *Quantifying Quality in Policing* (Washington, D.C.: Police Executive Research Forum, 1995).

30. U.S. Department of Justice, Office of Community Oriented Policing Services, *Problem Solving Tips: A Guide to Reducing Crime and Disorder Through Problem-Solving Partnerships*, p. 20.

31. Sampson, "Problem Solving," p. 5.

32. Mark H. Moore and Robert C. Trojanowicz, *Corporate Strategies for Policing*. U.S. Department of Justice, National Institute of Justice (Washington, D.C.: U.S. Government Printing Office, 1988), p. 11.

33. California Department of Justice, Attorney General's Office, *Community Oriented Policing and Problem Solving: Definitions and Principles* (Sacramento, Calif.: Author, 1993), p. iii.

34. Ibid.

35. Timothy C. O'Shea and Keith Nicholls, *Crime Analysis in America: Findings and Recommendations* (Washington, D.C.: Office of Community Oriented Policing Services, March 2003), p. 7.

36. Noah Fritz, "Crime Analysis" (Tempe, Arizona: Tempe Police Department, no date), p. 9.

37. Mark A. Peterson and Harriet B. Braiker, "Doing Crime: A Survey of California Prison Inmates" (Santa Monica, Calif.: RAND Corporation, 1980), pp. 131–135.

38. William Spelman, "Crime Analysis: A Review and Assessment" (Washington, D.C.: Police Executive Research Forum, May 1985), p. 3.

39. Bill Blackwood Law Enforcement Management Institute of Texas, TELEMASP Bulletin, "Crime Analysis: Administrative Aspects." Huntsville, Texas, January 1995, p. 1.

40. O'Shea and Nicholls, *Crime Analysis in America*, p. 17.

41. Susan C. Wernicke and Mark A. Stallo, "Steps Toward Integrating Crime Analysis into Local Law Enforcement," *The Police Chief* (July 2000):56–57.

42. Dan Helms, "Closing the Barn Door: Police Counterterrorism After 9-11 From the Analyst's Perspective," *Crime Mapping News* (Police Foundation newsletter) 4 (Winter 2002):1–5.

43. U.S. Department of Justice, National Institute of Justice, *Crime Mapping and Analysis by Community Organizations in Hartford, Connecticut* (Washington, D.C.: Author, March 2001): 1.

44. Donna Rogers, "Getting Crime Analysis on the Map," *Law Enforcement Technology* (November 1999):76–79.

45. U.S. Department of Justice, National Institute of Justice, Crime Mapping Research Center, *Mapping Crime: Principle and Practice* (Washington, D.C.: Author, 1999), p. 1.

46. Ibid., p. 2.

47. Lois Pilant, "Computerized Crime Mapping," *The Police Chief* (December 1997):58.

48. Dan Sadler, "Exploring Crime Mapping" (Washington, D.C.: U.S. Department of Justice, National Institute of Justice, Crime Mapping Research Center, 1999), p. 1.

49. U.S. Department of Justice, National Institute of Justice, *Crime Mapping Research Center* (Washington, D.C.: Author, 2000):1–3.

50. Pilant, "Computerized Crime Mapping," p. 58.

51. Chicago Police Department, *CAPS News* (October 1995):1, 6.

52. Pilant, "Computerized Crime Mapping," pp. 64–65.

53. Ibid., pp. 66–67.

54. See U.S. Department of Justice, National Institute of Justice, Crime Mapping Research Center, *Mapping Crime*, 1999.

55. See Nancy LaVigne and Julie Wartell (eds.), *Crime Mapping Case Studies: Successes in the Field* (Washington, D.C.: Police Executive Research Forum, 1998).

56. Barbara Webster and Edward F. Connors, "Community Policing: Identifying Problems" (Alexandria, Va.: Institute for Law and Justice, March 1991), p. 9.

57. See Lawrence W. Sherman, Patrick R. Gartin, and Michael E. Buerger, "Hot Spots of Predatory Crime: Routine Activities and the Criminology of Place," *Criminology* 27 (1989):27.

58. William Spelman, *Beyond Bean Counting: New Approaches for Managing Crime Data* (Washington, D.C.: Police Executive Research Forum, January 1988).

59. Webster and Connors, "Community Policing," p. 11.

60. For an example of this type of survey process, see William H. Lindsey and Bruce Quint, *The Oasis Technique* (Fort Lauderdale, Fla.: Florida Atlantic University/Florida International University Joint Center for Environmental and Urban Problems, 1986).

61. Webster and Connors, "Community Policing," pp. 14–15.

62. Analysis Central Systems, "Dynamic Community Policing System: Proactive Neighborhood Oriented Systems" (Tiburon, Calif.: Author, no date), p. 3. Also see J. J. Campbell, "Computer Support for Community-Oriented Policing," *FBI Law Enforcement Bulletin* 62 (February 1994):16–18.

63. Recheal Stewart-Brown, "Community Mobilization: The Foundation for Community Policing," *FBI Law Enforcement Bulletin* (June 2001):9–17.

INTRODUCTION

Crime prevention has been defined by the Crime Prevention Coalition of America as

> A pattern of attitudes and behaviors directed both at reducing the threat of crime and enhancing the sense of safety and security to positively influence the quality of life in our society and to help develop environments where crime cannot flourish.[1]

Crime prevention once consisted primarily of exhorting people to "lock it or lose it" and advice from the police on door locks and window bars for their homes and businesses. It typically was (and often still is) an add-on program or appendage to the police agency, which normally included a few officers who were trained to go to citizens' homes and perform security surveys or engage in public speaking on prevention topics.

But times have changed dramatically in this respect. We know that attempting to investigate and solve crimes and prosecute and punish offenders is much more expensive than preventing the offense from occurring in the first place. We are also aware that as the costs of public safety have skyrocketed, governments are extremely hard pressed to continue to afford to build, staff, and operate more jails and prisons. In an era of decreasing resources, crime prevention offers a cost-effective means of making communities safer. Therefore, crime prevention now involves the police and government seeking to influence the civil behavior of individuals, corporations, businesses, and others that are responsible for the creation of criminal opportunities or motivation.[2]

—5—

CRIME PREVENTION

For Safe Communities

The test of police efficiency is the absence of crime and disorder, not the visible evidence of police action in dealing with them.
—Sir Robert Peel's ninth principle of policing, 1829

This chapter examines the multifaceted domain of what contemporary crime prevention has become. We begin with a brief history of how crime prevention evolved and then discuss how today's police are shifting their emphasis to that of crime prevention as an agencywide philosophy. Then the essential role of the community in preventing crime is explored, followed by an overview of how crime prevention relates to community oriented policing and problem solving (COPPS, examined in Chapter 4).

Two very important components of crime prevention and COPPS are then analyzed: crime prevention through environmental design and situational crime prevention. Following that, we review several issues and problems that can accompany crime prevention efforts: the implementation of crime interventions, the displacement of crime when interventions are undertaken, and the evaluation of results. Finally, we view which crime prevention strategies work, which do not work, and which hold promise.

Throughout the chapter the emphasis and common thread—from strategy to strategy, community to community—is the acknowledgment by the police that they alone cannot prevent or address crime and disorder; the community *must* be engaged in a collaborative effort if the physical and social problems that plague communities are to be reduced or eliminated.

Under COPPS, crime prevention is evolving to more comprehensive situational and environmental intervention strategies. This photo depicts a Neighborhood Watch sign vandalized by local gangs.

A BRIEF HISTORY

Crime prevention is not a new idea. Humans have long known that crime is not simply a matter of motivation; it is also a matter of opportunity. Indeed, for as long as people have been victimized, there have been attempts to protect one's self and family. The term *crime prevention*, however, has only recently come to signify a set of ideas for combatting crime.[3]

Our earliest ancestors maximized lighting from the sun and moon and employed defensive placement of homes on the side of cliffs, with only one entrance and exit.[4] Cave dwellers established ownership of a space by surrounding it with large boulders. The Romans developed and enforced complex land laws. Walled cities and castles exist throughout the world. It is a natural human impulse to claim and secure an area to prevent problems.[5]

A more contemporary form of early preventive action was the Chicago Area Project (CAP), based on the research of Shaw and McKay in the 1930s and 1940s, which concerned the altering of the social fabric. Crime and delinquency were concentrated in the central areas of Chicago. Identifying a high level of transiency and an apparent lack of social ties in these areas as the root cause of the problems, Shaw and McKay labeled the problem as "social disorganization," meaning that the constant turnover of residents resulted in the inability of the people to exert any informal social control over the individuals in the area. Consequently, offenders could act with some degree of impunity in these neighborhoods.[6]

Shaw's proposed solution to the problem was to work with the residents to build a sense of pride and community, thereby prompting people to stay and exert control over the actions of the people in the area. CAP was founded in 1931 and generated community support by using volunteers and existing neighborhood institutions.[7]

The 1970s saw the rise of community-based crime prevention programs, such as Neighborhood Watch or Block Watch. These programs used the same premise as physical design approaches—potential offenders will not commit a crime if they perceive citizen activity, awareness, and concern in an area. The focus is on citizen surveillance and action (such as cutting back bushes, installing lighting, removing obstacles to enhance sight lines, organizing security surveys, and distributing crime and crime prevention news). Signs of resident activity and cohesion should work to protect the neighborhood. The police also recognized that they could not stop crime or solve problems on their own; they needed the help of the citizenry.[8]

Crime prevention experienced perhaps its biggest boost, however, with the emergence of physical design as a topic of debate. Led by the work of Oscar Newman in 1972, flaws in the physical environment were identified as causes of, or at least facilitators for, criminal behavior.

In 1969 Newman first coined the term *defensible space*, which, in his mind, did not mean ugly, fortresslike buildings where occupants were prisoners. (Table 5-1 depicts Newman's suggestions for defensible space.) Rather, buildings that are properly designed promote a sense of safety and power to their occupants, making them less afraid and vulnerable.[9]

Newman, an architect, argued that the physical characteristics of an area have the potential to suggest to residents and potential offenders that the area is either well cared for and protected or it is open for criminal activity. Design features conducive to criminal behavior—allowing offenders to commit a crime and escape with minimal risk of detection—would include common entrances for a large number of people, poorly placed windows inhibiting casual surveillance of grounds and common areas, hidden entrances, easy access for illegitimate users, and isolated buildings.[10]

Then, in the 1970s and 1980s, theories of crime were developed that gave added importance to the role of opportunity in crime. Cohen and Felson's

TABLE 5-1. Oscar Newman's Defensible Space Suggestions

1. Reduce the size of a housing estate or block.
2. Reduce the number of dwellings sharing an entrance way.
3. Reduce the number of stories in a building block.
4. Arrange dwellings in groups to encourage social contact.
5. Minimize the degree of shared public space inside and near blocks.
6. Make the boundaries between public and private space very clear.
7. Make public areas clearly visible to nearby housing.
8. Use external rather than internal corridors in blocks of housing so that they are visible.
9. Make entrances flush with the street rather than set back.
10. Do not have entrances facing away from the street because they are not open to surveillance.
11. Avoid landscaping and vegetation that impedes surveillance.
12. Reduce escape routes (elevators, staircases, and multiple exits) for criminals.

Source: U.S. Department of Housing and Urban Development, *Crime Prevention Brief,* "Crime Prevention Through Environmental Design" (no date), p. 2.

The glass stairwell in this parking garage demonstrates how natural surveillance can be designed into a facility. People using the stairwell are easily seen by passers-by, thus reducing the likelihood of victimization.

"routine activity theory" seeks to explain how physical and social environments create crime opportunities by bringing together in one place at a particular time a "likely" offender, a "suitable" target, and the absence of a "capable guardian" against crime (e.g., a police officer or security guard).[11] Routine activity theory was used to explain how large increases in burglary rates occurred in the United States in the 1960s and 1970s, because (1) home electronic goods became lighter, and (2) women increasingly entered the labor force, resulting in more empty homes during the day, which could be entered by burglars.

Another opportunity theory is the "rational choice" perspective, which holds that all crime is purposive behavior designed to benefit the offender.[12] In committing an offense, the offender makes the choice to balance the effort, risks, and rewards with the costs and benefits of alternative legal means of achieving an end.

Wilson and Kelling's 1982 "broken windows" theory extended Oscar Newman's focus on housing projects to entire neighborhoods. "Broken windows" refers to physical signs that an area is unattended: There may be abandoned vehicles and buildings in the area, trash and litter may be present, and there may be broken windows and lights and graffiti.[13] In addition to these physical indicators are social manifestations of the same problems, such as loitering youths, public drunkenness, prostitution, and vagrancy. Both the physical and social indicators are typically referred to as signs of "incivility" that attract offenders to the area.[14]

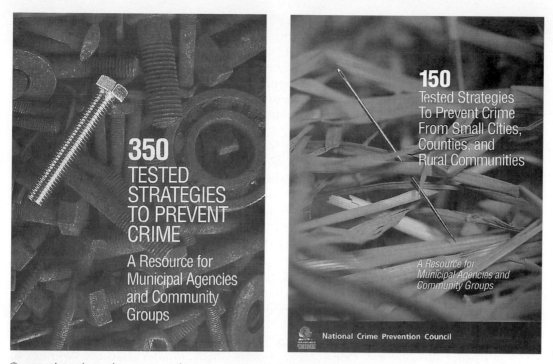

Comprehensive crime prevention resource guides for municipal and rural agencies are available through the National Crime Prevention Council at *http://www.ncpc.org*. (*Courtesy* National Crime Prevention Council)

The most recent movements in crime prevention focus efforts and interventions on attacking specific problems, places, and times. Ronald V. Clarke proposed "situational prevention" as "measures directed at highly specific forms of crime that involve [environmental changes that] reduce the opportunities for crime and increase its risk."[15] Examples of situational prevention include the installation of surveillance equipment in a parking lot experiencing vandalism, erecting security screens in banks to stop robberies, altering traffic patterns in a drug market neighborhood, using electronic tags for library materials, and using caller ID for obscene phone calls.[16] The physical environment as it relates to crime prevention is discussed shortly. Next we discuss the contemporary crime prevention–based philosophy.

TODAY'S SHIFTING EMPHASIS

A simple but profound shift in thinking in contemporary times may help American police organizations to realize new gains in reducing crime, victimization, and fear. Many police agencies now conceive of prevention as the overarching goal of policing rather than as a set of activities. We discuss the following benefits of crime prevention:

- Deterrence of specific kinds of crimes
- Mobilization of residents
- Development of physical and social environments inhospitable to crime[17]

The concept of prevention shifts a police organization's purpose. Police agencies that are operating in a prevention framework must be organized to prevent the next problem from occurring. This reflects Herman Goldstein's call for replacing efficiency with effectiveness as the goal of policing. Once the question becomes "How can we prevent the next crisis?" all kinds of approaches become possible. Police departments and their partners will find themselves embracing approaches that would have been unimaginable under the reactive, traditional policing model.[18]

The Boston police department, for example, partners with probation officers to conduct joint curfew checks on gang members and other high-risk probationers. As the police commissioner noted, "First we tried conventional, police-heavy enforcement tactics. Then we realized we needed a better strategy. We realized the kids needed jobs and opportunities. At that point we gained a new appreciation of our mission."[19]

Understanding prevention as the strategic goal of the policing process rather than as a set of activities for police officers puts into practice Sir Robert Peel's ninth principle of policing, quoted at the beginning of this chapter.[20] Today, prevention means more than simply warning citizens about crime. It means strategically maximizing police resources with those of the community for tangible outcomes.

The core mission of the police is simply to preserve the peace. But they cannot do so alone. Crime prevention is much broader than the confines of the police station house. Still, there is much important work for the police to do in the area of crime prevention. As the International Association of Chiefs of Police Crime Prevention Committee has stated, "Community safety is everyone's responsibility, and crime prevention is everyone's business."[21]

The mission is clear: "Establish the prevention of crime as fundamental to a free and safe society; anchor crime prevention in each department's organizational policy."[22]

NEEDED: COMMUNITY INVOLVEMENT

A number of critical elements must be in place before the community as a whole can be mobilized effectively into positive energy. First, the causes of the problems that contribute to diminished community safety must be identified in order to define appropriate, community-based solutions (see Exhibit 5-1). Second, a community-based, shared vision must be developed with appropriate strategies, including resource allocation, the implementation of specific programs and services, and the identification of measurable results. Third, community-wide mobilization—including the private and corporate sectors, schools, churches, governments, and institutions—must be achieved to solve problems. Finally, dynamic, visionary leaders are needed to provide a voice and example.[23]

These are complex issues. The strategic question, however, is not "Can we do it?" but "Can we afford not to do it?" It is no longer realistic to expect the police to be solely responsible for controlling crime.[24]

Community oriented policing and problem solving (COPPS) argues that the police and the community must stop treating the symptoms of the problem. COPPS requires a "new age" of prevention as well as improvement of prevention efforts.

Altering physical designs of buildings, for example, is not in itself generally sufficient for altering the level of crime; physical design changes cannot stop a truly motivated offender. Furthermore, altering the physical environment does not guarantee that residents will become involved and take action. Direct efforts to enhance active citizen involvement are necessary.[25]

Chapter 3 introduced the concept of communitarianism, a mindset for the whole community to take responsibility for itself, actively participating and giving of time, energy, and money.[26] We noted that communitarians support processes, such as crime prevention and community policing, taking matters into their own hands and closing off streets and creating other physical barriers to disrupt the drug trade, working to overcome problems of homelessness and panhandling, and so forth. Communitarians recognize that many of the answers to community problems lie not with government but in the community at large. Volunteerism can also provide a much needed boost for the police, building a sense of community, breaking down barriers between people, and raising quality of life.

CRIME PREVENTION AND COPPS

Crime prevention and COPPS are close companions, attempting to define a problem, identify contributing causes, seek out the proper people or agencies to assist in identifying potential solutions, and work as a group to implement the solution. The problem drives the solution.[27]

At its heart, COPPS is about preventing crime. COPPS and crime prevention are linked in several areas.

Crime prevention efforts provide information and skills that are essential to community policing. Furthermore, crime prevention and community policing have six major points in common:

- *Each deals with the health of the community.* They acknowledge the many interrelated issues that contribute to crime.

- *Each seeks to address underlying causes and problems.* Although short-term and reactive measures (such as personal security and response to CFS) are necessary, they are insufficient if crime is to be significantly reduced. Looking beyond symptoms to treat the causes of community problems is a strategy that both, at their best, share in full measure.

- *Each deals with the combination of physical and social issues that are at the heart of many community problems.* An abandoned building may attract drug addicts; bored teens may become area burglars. Both approaches examine the broadest possible range of causes and solutions.

- *Each requires active involvement by community residents.* Both have the chief task of enabling people to make themselves and their communities safer by helping them gain appropriate knowledge, develop helpful attitudes, and take useful actions.

- *Each requires partnerships beyond law enforcement to be effective.* Both efforts can and have involved schools, community centers, civic organizations, religious groups, social service agencies, public works agencies, and other elements of the community.

- *Each is an approach or a philosophy, rather than a program.* Neither is a fixed system for delivery of a specific service. Rather, each is a way of doing business and involves the development of an institutional mindset.[28]

The following list of initiatives represents some of the types of crime prevention activities that can help to support community policing. They further the implementation of community policing at the local level; however, cooperation is needed among community organizations, government, and police agencies to create and maintain such activities.

- *Adopt-a-School/Adopt-an-Officer:* The police increase their communication with local schools by having each officer select a school to sponsor. The school has the officer as a primary contact to assist with various service needs.

- *Community Crime Patrol:* Organized citizen patrols in specific neighborhoods provide additional exposure for police services and assistance for police in desired areas.

- *Crime Prevention Month Celebration:* National celebration of crime prevention month in October heightens the awareness and need for crime prevention. Each year a new theme is developed to promote local programming.

- *Cops and Cons:* A coordinated program by the police in which convicts discuss with citizens and businesses why and how they committed their particular crimes; this approach provides awareness of crime prevention and indicates some intervention strategies.

- *Domestic Violence/Sexual Assault Prevention:* Efforts raise the awareness that domestic violence is a crime and should not be tolerated. It also educates victims and others about prevention strategies.

- *Foot Beat/Walk and Talk:* Foot patrol is the oldest method of police patrol; it is an excellent way to get acquainted with citizens and learn about potential neighborhood problems.

- *Hate Crime Prevention:* An initiative designed to address the understanding of bias-motivated crimes and the prevention of criminal acts aimed at particular groups within a neighborhood.

- *Homeless Outreach:* The police and community work together to provide transportation to homeless individuals from city streets to shelter areas.

- *Home Safety and Security Surveys:* Police officers conduct home safety and security surveys to educate community residents on how to better protect their homes.

- *Safe Haven:* An identified area in a public housing community that provides residents a safe place to live and activities for youths as a positive alternative to gang involvement, providing students with a safe place to go after school.

- *Together for a Safer Campus:* An initiative to raise the awareness and importance of crime prevention measures on a college campus to encourage students to take appropriate precautions for their personal safety.
- *Turn Off the Violence:* An initiative to raise the awareness levels among children, teens, and adults so that violence in all of its forms is recognized and dealt with before it escalates beyond control.
- *Weed and Seed:* An initiative of the U.S. Department of Justice, it focuses on the elimination of criminal activity in a particular neighborhood through enforcement and adjudication, while providing a prevention and intervention component to eliminate the illicit activity from recurring in the community.[29]

Crime prevention provides knowledge about ways to involve the entire community in reducing crime, both individually and collectively; community policing practices can spread that knowledge. Community policing officers need to understand and apply techniques to educate and motivate citizens; crime prevention offers these techniques. Because crime prevention addresses both physical and social aspects of neighborhoods, it offers numerous ways for community policing officers to gain entry into community circles. Crime prevention offers resources to help change community attitudes and behaviors.

Exhibit 5-2 provides an example of crime prevention and community policing working hand-in-hand to address a serious set of problems in Bridgeport, Connecticut.

EXHIBIT 5-2   Crime Prevention and Community Policing in Bridgeport, Connecticut

Once a major industrial center on the shore of Long Island Sound, Bridgeport, Connecticut, lost a great deal of its tax base during the 1970s and 1980s. By 1991 the city had filed for bankruptcy. The population of 143,000 included a highly diverse population of 54 separate ethnic groups. The city also faced a major crime crisis, with the highest homicide rate in New England—50 to 60 per year. Many of the victims were juveniles. Drug markets were blatant. There was a long history of police–resident animosity. The police department decided to focus efforts on the toughest area of the city—Eastside, a 1.75-square-mile, high-density area of burned buildings, plagued nightly by automatic weapons gunfire. Gang members walked around openly. Almost half of Eastside's residents were under age 18; most families were too poor to relocate. The police department initiated an outreach to the community, based on community policing and emphasizing that the police wanted to hear residents' concerns. Meanwhile, police stepped up enforcement and surveillance in the area, curbing narcotics traffic by disrupting both sellers and buyers and rescheduling officers to provide for more intensive patrolling in the critical period, 7:00 P.M. to 3:00 A.M. Eventually, community meetings were drawing as many as 200 people. Residents began to more readily report suspicious activities and call 911 or page community officers to report crimes. Community policing was implemented on a neighborhood-by-neighborhood basis, and the emphasis was placed on eradicating blight. Seventy abandoned houses in Eastside were boarded up and vacant lots and graffiti were cleaned up. Crime prevention through environmental design (CPTED, discussed elsewhere in this chapter) tactics were employed, including the installation of concrete diverters and low curbs (to prevent easy access to drug markets by suburban junkies). A sense of community developed, and new programs sprang up from the community policing efforts (such as the group of seniors who conduct a life-skills course for girls ages 13 to 14). Between 1993 and 1997, crime declined 40 percent overall and 75 percent in Eastside; murder rates were down by one-third, as were robberies, burglaries, stolen cars, and fired shots—figures that are even more remarkable because reporting rates in Eastside have increased.

Source: U.S. Department of Justice, Bureau of Justice Assistance, *Crime Prevention and Community Policing: A Vital Partnership* (Washington, D.C.: U.S. Government Printing Office, 1997), pp. 8–9.

CRIME PREVENTION THROUGH ENVIRONMENTAL DESIGN

Crime prevention through environmental design (CPTED) is defined as the "proper design and effective use of the environment that can lead to a reduction in the fear and incidence of crime, and an improvement in the quality of life."[30] At its core are three principles that support problem-solving approaches to crime:

- *Natural access control.* Natural access control uses elements such as doors, shrubs, fences, and gates to deny admission to a crime target and to create a perception among offenders that there is a risk in selecting the target.
- *Natural surveillance.* Natural surveillance includes the proper placement of windows, lighting, and landscaping to increase the ability of those who care to observe intruders as well as regular users, allowing them to challenge inappropriate behavior or report it to the police or the property owner.
- *Territorial reinforcement.* Using such elements as sidewalks, landscaping, and porches helps distinguish between public and private areas and helps users exhibit signs of "ownership" that send "hands off" messages to would-be offenders.[31]

Ironically, in the past the police were not involved in design planning, whereas fire departments have promulgated and enforced national fire codes for about a half-century. Today, in cities such as Tempe, Arizona, if the police are not involved in the preliminary stages of planning a building, they often become very involved afterward, when crimes are committed in or around the structure.[32]

Cities such as Tempe have become leaders in expanding policing's new role in "designing out crime." In the late 1900s Tempe enacted an ordinance requiring that no commercial, park, or residential building permit be issued

This gated storage facility uses an electronic keyed gate for access control.

Advertising obstructions create poor natural surveillance and may contribute to a location's being an attractive target to offenders.

until the police department had approved it, ensuring that the building fully protected its occupants. The department now makes several recommendations, such as keeping landscaping and plants that will be more than two feet high away from parking islands, inside perimeters, or walkways, or within 50 feet of access doors.

Tempe's CPTED officers advocate that walls around the perimeter of a building be at least eight feet high to make them more difficult to scale. River rocks are banned from parking lots because they can be used as weapons. Natural surveillance, which can be obtained from proper lighting and window placement, helps to oversee nearby activities. Transparent fences are better than walls to monitor activities. Light switches in restrooms should be keyed or remotely controlled to prevent tampering that would perhaps facilitate a possible hiding place for an attacker; restrooms should not be located at the ends of hallways where they are isolated. Defensive architecture includes "target hardening" through quality deadbolts and other mechanical means, and includes proper landscaping—thorny bushes, for example, help to keep burglars away.[33] Five types of information are needed for CPTED planning:

1. *Crime analysis information.* This can include crime mapping, police crime data, incident reports, and victim and offender statistics.
2. *Demographics.* This should include resident statistics such as age, race, gender, income, and income sources.
3. *Land use information.* This includes zoning information (such as residential, commercial, industrial, school, and park zones) as well as occupancy data for each zone.
4. *Observations.* These should include details of parking procedures, maintenance, and residents' reactions to crime.
5. *Resident information.* This includes resident crime surveys and interviews with police and security officers.[34]

See Exhibit 5-3 for other successful CPTED case studies.

EXHIBIT 5-3 Successful CPTED Case Studies

Following are brief descriptions of three successful applications of CPTED strategies for solving problems.

Knoxville, Tennessee's "Deal Street," as the name implies, was the locus of drive-through drug dealing for as many as 1,200 cars per day. Based on the neighborhood analysis, the following programs and activities were adopted:

- Cleaning up the area and replacing broken street lights and fixtures
- Closing streets, creating cul-de-sacs, and adding speed bumps in the neighborhoods
- Redesigning parks and rescheduling recreational activities to encourage the use of park facilities
- Training police officers to work with other city staff toward CPTED objectives, and training volunteers in how to conduct security surveys

The result was that only 50 cars per day came into the neighborhood, and children now cross the streets safely to get to and from school.

Richmond, Virginia, had one branch of a bank in a declining area that contained numerous vacant properties and abandoned businesses. The bank installed bullet-resistant enclosures for tellers inside the bank. Another problem arose, however; ATM patrons were being robbed an average of once a month. Robbers would come to the bank after hours and hide around the corner from the ATM, under cover of the darkened drive-up teller area. When a patron conducted the ATM business on foot, the offender would jump from cover and rob the patron. After the bank's officers rejected a number of expensive options for addressing the problem, one of the bank's employees suggested a very simple and cost-effective solution: construction of a fence at the corner of the building to remove any opportunity to jump out and surprise ATM patrons. The bank installed an 8-feet tall, 16-feet long ornamental aluminum picket fence at a cost of $800, totally eliminating robberies at the location.

Gainesville, Florida, was faced with a tremendous increase in the number of convenience store robberies. The police department carried out an evaluation of the problems and possible solutions, finding that nearly every store in the community (96 percent) had been robbed more than once. The city commission enacted an ordinance that required store operators to remove signs from windows to offer clear views to and from cash registers, locate the sales area and cash registers in a place visible from the street, post signs declaring limited cash availability, provide lighted parking areas, install security cameras, and train all employees in robbery prevention. Afterward, the city enjoyed a 64 percent decrease in convenience store robberies.

Source: National Crime Prevention Council, *Designing Safer Communities: A Crime Prevention through Environmental Design Handbook* (Washington, D.C.: Author, 1997), pp. 7–8.

SITUATIONAL CRIME PREVENTION

Situational crime prevention (SCP) departs radically from most criminology in its orientation. It is focused on the settings for crime, rather than on persons committing criminal acts. It seeks to forestall the occurrence of crime, rather than to detect and sanction offenders. It seeks not to eliminate criminal or delinquent tendencies through improvement of society or its institutions but merely to make criminal action less attractive to offenders.[35]

SCP is a targeted means of reducing crime. It provides an analytical framework for strategies to prevent crime in varying settings. It is an "environmental criminology" approach that seeks to reduce crime opportunity by making settings less conducive to unwanted or illegal activities, focusing on the environment rather than the offender.[36] The commission of a crime requires not merely the offender, but, as every detective story reader knows, it also requires the opportunity for crime.[37]

Although the concept of SCP was British in origin, its development was influenced by two independent, but nonetheless related, strands of policy research in the United States: defensible space and crime prevention through environmental design, both of which preceded SCP and were discussed earlier in the chapter. Because of the trans-Atlantic delay in the dissemination of ideas, however, there was no stimulus for the development of SCP.[38]

SCP is a problem oriented approach that examines the roots of a problem and identifies a unique solution to the problem. Experience has shown that

Signage at the entrance to this apartment complex and high school parking lot serves to remove offenders' excuses for loitering and trespassing.

successful SCP measures must be directed against specific crimes and must be designed with a clear understanding of the motives of offenders and the methods they employ. SCP relies on the rational choice theory of crime, which asserts that criminals choose to commit crimes based on the costs and benefits involved with the crime. For example, a potential offender will commit a high-risk crime only if the rewards of the crime outweigh the risks.[39]

Ronald V. Clarke[40] divided crime prevention goals into four primary objectives, each of which is designed to dissuade the criminal from committing the offense by making the crime too hard to commit, too risky, or too small in terms of rewards to be worth the criminal's time. Next we discuss each of these four objectives.

1. *Increasing the effort needed to commit the crime.* Crimes are typically committed because they are easy to commit. A person might see an easy opportunity to commit a crime and do so. Casual criminals are eliminated by increasing the

effort needed to commit a crime. Following are different methods for increasing the effort needed to commit a crime:

Target hardening: installing physical barriers (such as locks, bolts, protective screens, and mechanical containment and antifraud devices to impede an offender's ability to penetrate a potential target).

Access control: installing barriers and designing walkways, paths, and roads so that unwanted users are prevented from entering vulnerable areas.

Deflecting offenders: discouraging crime by giving people alternate, legal venues for their activities (such as decreasing littering by providing litter bins or separating fans of rival teams after athletic events).

Controlling facilitators: Facilitators are accessories who aid in the commission of crimes. Controlling them is achieved by universal measures (such as firearm permit regulations) and specific measures (metal detectors in community centers).

2. *Increasing the risks associated with the crime.* Increasing the risks associated with a crime reduces the incidence of that crime, because criminals like to believe they will not be caught; offenders who believe that they will be caught are less likely to offend. For example, if a video camera monitors all entrances and exits to a convenience store or bank, some potential robbers who know of such surveillance will be less likely to rob such establishments.

Entry and exit screening: using screening methods including guest sign-ins or a required display of identification; ensures that residents and visitors meet entrance requirements.

Formal surveillance: using security personnel and hardware (such as CCTV and burglar alarms) as a deterrent to unwanted activities.

Informal surveillance: the presence of building attendants, concierges, maintenance workers, and attendants to increase site surveillance and crime reporting.

Natural surveillance: the surveillance provided by people as they go about their daily activities, making potential offenders feel exposed and vulnerable.

3. *Reducing the rewards.* Reducing the rewards from crime makes offending not worthwhile to offenders. Methods of reducing rewards include making targets of crime less valuable by the following means:

Target removal: eliminating crime purposes from public areas. Examples include a no-cash policy and keeping valuable property in a secure area overnight.

Identifying property: using indelible marks, establishing ownership, and preventing individuals from reselling the property.

Removing inducements: related to target removal; involves removing temptations that offenders have not targeted in advance but that are likely to become the targets of a spontaneous crime (such as vacant houses or other living units or broken windows and light fixtures).

4. *Removing the excuses.* Many offenders say, "I didn't know any better" or "I had no choice." This strategy involves informing individuals of the law and rules and offers them alternatives to illegal activity by eliminating their excuses for committing crime. For example, a "no trespassing" sign is enforceable if posted. It also involves "rule-setting," such as clearly stating the rules, say, of a housing development, which establishes the procedures of punishment for violators. Such methods prevent offenders from excusing their crimes by claiming ignorance or misunderstanding.

Table 5-2 presents a situational crime prevention matrix for CPTED, specifically the four CPTED objectives discussed. Included are organized (procedural measures), mechanical (providing or removing certain physical objects), and natural (using native aspects of the environment) means of facilitating each.

TABLE 5-2. Situational Crime Prevention Matrix for CPTED

Increasing the Effort (Access Control and Territorial Reinforcement)

	Target Hardening	Access Control	Removing/Deflecting Offenders	Closing Windows to Crime Facilitators
Organized		Kiosks, reception desks	Bus stop placement and stop times, alternate cruising areas	Controlled spray can sales, gun control, alcohol ban, nonbreakable containers, occupying vacant apartments
Mechanical	Locks, bandit screens, tough glass, tamper-proof seals, safes, slug rejectors	Locked gates, fences, entry phones, card keys, ID badges, PINs, vehicle decals, parking lot barriers	Graffiti boards, moving bars and pubs, litter bins, spittoons, public urinals, moving recreational space locations	Credit card photos, Breathalyzer, caller ID, rotary dials on pay phones, removing shopping carts from the premises
Natural	Remove trees that can enable access to upper level units	Shrubbery "fences"	Plants or steep slopes near windows to prevent entry	Greenery or planters in front of graffiti-prone areas

Increasing the Risk (Surveillance)

	Entry and Exit Screening	Formal Surveillance	Surveillance by Employees	Improving Natural Surveillance
Organized	Guest sign-ins, registration	Police patrol, security guards, informant hotline	Bus conductors, place administrative offices in view of development, front desk clerks, maintenance crews	Neighborhood watch, passive surveillance by "eyes on the street"
Mechanical	ID badges, PIN entry, metal sensors	Burglar alarms, hidden cameras, CCTV, radar speed traps	CCTV systems, pay phones in locations visible to employees	Interior and exterior lighting, windows on high-crime areas
Natural	Gates	Remove greenery that obstructs view of crime-ridden areas	Place frequently used service drives in crime-ridden areas	Remove greenery that obstructs view of crime-ridden areas

(continued)

TABLE 5-2. (continued)

	Reducing the Rewards of Crime			
	Removing Crime Targets	*Identifying and Tagging Property*	*Removing Inducements for Crime*	*Boundary and Rule Setting*
Organized	Exact change requirements, limited or no-cash policy, pay by check, safe in administrative offices	Vehicle and bike registration	Rapid graffiti removal, gender-neutral phone lists, off-street parking	Drug-free school zone, public park use sign-up, enforced evictions, applicant screening
Mechanical	Removable car radios in maintenance vehicles, tokens for laundry and vending machines, phone card public phones, remove vending machines, antigraffiti treatments	Property marking, operation ID, Lojack, property serial number databases	Replace metal signs with plastic or wood signs to reduce "drive-by shootings," remove damaged signs, remove abandoned cars	Signs and posted notices of policies and local laws
Natural	Cover graffiti-prone areas with ivy or thorny bushes	Use greenery to define private areas surrounding individual units (gardens, flowers, etc.)	Remove greenery such as trees near windows that can hide or enable criminal activities	Use greenery to define public and private areas

	Removing Excuses and Increasing Shame
Organized	Public posting of trespasser pictures and names, sending postcards to suspected drug purchasers, impounding vehicles of drug purchasers, sign upkeep

Source: U.S. Department of Housing and Urban Development, *Crime Prevention Brief*, "Situational Prevention" (no date), pp. 2–3.

ISSUES AND PROBLEMS

Next we look at three areas that can be problematic for crime prevention: implementation of programs, crime displacement, and evaluation of results.

Implementation

A key issue for any type of intervention is the degree to which it is adequately implemented. Unless implemented properly, interventions have a good chance of failure. For example, a Neighborhood Watch initiative in a crime-ridden, ethnically divided area that gains participation from only 20 percent of the residents from only one of three ethnic groups could not be expected to have much of an impact on the entire neighborhood or community.

Another potential problem is the possibility that key agencies, actors, or community members will only halfheartedly participate. The police and public might develop a "we-versus-them" attitude, there may be a sense that the police have the necessary training and the public does not, or there might be a fear of a return to vigilante justice. Breaking through such attitudes and fears is not easy, but cooperation between the police and public is essential for successful crime prevention programs.[41]

Canada's National Crime Prevention Council asked, "How do we get started?" and developed the following practical answer:

> Crime prevention efforts must begin with an understanding of the underlying causes of crime . . . knowledge that the roots of crime lie, in large part, within the broad social and economic environment of the child. Development of a comprehensive and workable crime prevention strategy will require involvement and improved coordination of all levels of government, criminal justice organizations, social and health services, and community agencies and groups.[42]

Julian Fantino, chief of the London Police Force, Ontario, Canada, argued that one of the critical components concerns children and youth:

> We must move quickly, before the promise of childhood is poisoned by exploitation and neglect. Many chronic young offenders have been victims as children. Clearly, a link exists between child abuse or neglect and later delinquency and antisocial behavior. Society as a whole must embrace the challenge to become more proactive in protecting its most vulnerable citizens—especially children who are preyed upon by adults.[43]

We discuss planning and implementation for COPPS in Chapter 6; many of those same methods, considerations, and approaches can be applied to crime prevention as well.

Displacement of Crime

An issue that emerges in any serious discussion of crime prevention is crime displacement, which refers to the idea that rather than eliminate crime, interventions simply result in the movement of crime to another area, shift offenders to new targets in the same area, alter the methods used to accomplish a crime, or prompt offenders to change the type of crime they commit.[44] Displacement has, therefore, been the Achilles' heel of crime prevention in general. Efforts to control drug dealing and crime in neighborhoods and places are often criticized for having displaced the offending behavior instead of reducing it. If crime or drug dealing has only been moved around without any net reduction in harmful behavior, that would be a valid criticism.

Research indicates, however, that displacement is not inevitable but is contingent on the offender's judgments about alternative crimes. If these alternatives are not viable, the offender may well settle for smaller criminal rewards or for a lower rate of crime. Few offenders other than addicts are so driven by need or desire that they have to maintain a certain level of offending, whatever the cost. For many, the elimination of easy opportunities for crime may actually encourage them to explore noncriminal alternatives.[45] There are six commonly recognized types of displacement:

- *Temporal:* Offenders change the time when they commit crimes (e.g., switching from dealing drugs during the day to dealing at night).
- *Spatial:* Offenders switch from targets in one location to targets in other locations (e.g., a dealer stops selling drugs in one community and begins selling them in another community).

- *Target:* Offenders switch from one type of target to another type (e.g., a burglar switches from apartment units to single-family, detached homes).
- *Method:* Offenders change the way they attack targets (e.g., a street robber stops using a knife and uses a gun).
- *Crime type:* Offenders switch from one form of crime to another (e.g., from burglary to check fraud).
- *Perpetrator:* New offenders replace old offenders who have been removed by police enforcement (e.g., a dealer is arrested and a new dealer begins business with the same customers).[46]

A review of the evidence for displacement shows that when attempts to detect displacement have been made, it is often not found, and, if found, it is far less than 100 percent.[47] John Eck found that of 33 studies that looked for displacement effects, only 3 found evidence of much displacement;[48] Eck concluded that "There is more reason to expect no displacement than a great deal. A reasonable conclusion is that displacement can be a threat, but that it is unlikely to completely negate gains due to an enforcement crackdown or a crime prevention effort."[49]

Research has shown that offenders generally begin offending at places they are familiar with and explore outward into increasingly unfamiliar areas.[50] If opportunities are blocked (by increased enforcement, target hardening, or some other means) close to a familiar location, then displacement to other targets close to familiar areas is most likely. Displacement is most likely to occur in the direction of familiar places, times, targets, and behaviors. Offenders may desist for varying periods of time, or they may even stop offending, depending on how important crime is to their lives.[51]

Though studies have indicated that displacement may not pose a major threat to crime prevention efforts, it is still a phenomenon that police officials must take into account. Ignoring this problem can lead to inequitable solutions to problems; this is particularly true of problem-solving tactics designed to displace offenders from specific locations. Efforts must be made to track those individuals to ensure that they do not create a problem somewhere else.[52]

Evaluation of Results

Crime prevention also suffers from the malady of many other interventions: poor or nonexistent evaluation. The evaluation component of many programs is poorly conceived, marginally funded, and short-lived. A useful form of evaluation is an "outcome" or "impact" evaluation to determine whether the intervention accomplished the expected outcome. Assessments of this type require more planning and effort, and consideration must be given to the selection of comparison groups, time frames, outcome variables, potential confounding factors, and analytic techniques.[53] (Evaluations are discussed more thoroughly in Chapter 12.)

Giving community leaders and residents an indication of the success or failure of crime prevention efforts is critical to maintaining strong ties, ensuring their continued participation, and documenting that headway is being made in efforts to improve the safety and quality of neighborhoods.[54]

What Works and Does Not Work in Crime Prevention

Many crime prevention programs work. Others do not. Most programs have not yet been evaluated with enough scientific evidence to draw conclusions. Enough evidence is available, however, to create tentative lists of what works, what does not work, and what is promising.

Although both adult and juvenile military style boot camps are increasing in number, they have poor results in reducing repeat offending. (*Courtesy* Washoe County, Nevada, Sheriff's Office)

Following are the major conclusions of a 1998 report to Congress, based on a systematic review of more than 500 scientific evaluations of crime prevention practices by the University of Maryland's Department of Criminology and Criminal Justice.[55] This is the first major evaluation of crime prevention programs and has resulted in much attention and debate in the field. There are some surprising findings, particularly in the list of programs that do not hold promise—several of which have become pet projects of police agencies and political leaders.

The following are programs that researchers believed with reasonable certainty would prevent crime or reduce risk factors for crime; these programs are thus likely to be effective in preventing some form of crime:

What Prevents or Reduces Crime

- Providing extra police patrols in high-crime hot spots
- Monitoring repeat offenders to reduce the time on the streets of known high-risk repeat offenders and returning them to prison quickly
- Arresting domestic abusers to reduce repeated abuse by employed suspects
- Offering rehabilitation programs for adult and juvenile offenders that are appropriate to their risk factors to reduce their repeat offending rates
- Offering drug treatment programs in prison to reduce repeat offending after release

Sufficient evidence indicated to the University of Maryland researchers that the following programs failed to reduce crime or reduce risk factors:

What Does Not Appear to Be Successful

- Gun buyback programs failed to reduce gun violence in cities (as evaluated in St. Louis and Seattle).
- Neighborhood Watch programs organized with police failed to reduce burglary or other target crimes, especially in higher-crime areas where voluntary participation often fails.
- Arrests of unemployed suspects for domestic assault caused higher rates of repeat offending over the long term than nonarrest alternatives.
- Increased arrests or raids on drug markets failed to reduce violent crime or disorder for more than a few days, if at all.

- Storefront police offices failed to prevent crime in the surrounding areas.
- Police newsletters with local crime information failed to reduce victimization rates (as evaluated in Newark, New Jersey, and Houston, Texas).
- Correctional boot camps using traditional military training failed to reduce repeat offending after release compared to similar offenders serving time on probation and parole, both for adults and juveniles.
- "Scared Straight" programs that bring minor juvenile offenders to visit maximum security prisons to see the severity of prison conditions failed to reduce the participants' reoffending rates and may increase crime.
- Shock probation, shock parole, and split sentences, in which offenders are incarcerated for a short period of time at the beginning of the sentence and then supervised in the community, did not reduce repeat offending compared to the placement of similar offenders only under community supervision, and increased crime rates for some groups.
- Home detention with electronic monitoring for low-risk offenders failed to reduce offending compared to the placement of similar offenders under standard community supervision without electronic monitoring.
- Intensive supervision on parole or probation did not reduce repeat offending compared to normal levels of community supervision.

What Holds Promise

Researchers determined that the level of certainty for the following programs is too low for there to be positive, generalizable conclusions, but some empirical basis exists for predicting that further research could show positive results.

- Problem-solving analysis is effective when addressed to the specific crime situation.
- Proactive arrests for carrying concealed weapons in gun crime hot spots, using traffic enforcement and field interrogations, can be helpful.
- Community policing with meetings to set priorities reduced community perceptions of the severity of crime problems in Chicago.
- Field interrogations of suspicious persons reduced crime in a San Diego experiment.
- Gang offender monitoring by community workers and probation and police officers can reduce gang violence.
- Community-based mentoring by Big Brothers/Big Sisters of America substantially reduced drug abuse in one experiment, although evaluations of other similar programs showed that it did not.
- Battered women's shelters were found to reduce at least the short-term (six-week) rate of repeat victimization for women who take other steps to seek help.

Many more impact evaluations using stronger scientific methods are needed before even minimally valid conclusions can be reached about the impact of programs on crime. Again, as previously noted, there is much debate in the field about the research findings. The Maryland report to Congress, however, has raised the consciousness of the crime prevention discipline and will, it is hoped, bring about more much needed research and inquiry.

TABLE 5-3. Crime Prevention Matrix

Best Practice Crime Prevention Programs	Boston	Denver	Fort Worth	Hartford	New York City	San Diego
Communities and Crime Prevention						
• Gang violence prevention focused on reducing gang cohesion, but not increasing it	■	■	■	■	■	■
• Volunteer mentoring (Big Brothers/Big Sisters) reduces substance abuse, but not delinquency	■	■	■	■	■	■
• Restorative justice, such as police referral of vandalism cases to repair damage and to community rehabilitation programs	■	■		■		■
• "Coaching" to reduce crime at sporting venues ("Hooliganism")				■		■
Family-Based Crime Prevention						
• Long-term, frequent home visitation combined with preschool prevents later delinquency	■	■				
• Infant weekly home visitation reduces child abuse and injuries	■	■				
• Family therapy by clinical staff for delinquent/predelinquent youth	■	■	■			■
• Reeducation program for men convicted of wife battering	■		■			■
• Battered women's shelters for women who take other steps to change their lives	■	■	■	■		■
• Orders of protection for battered women	■		■	■	■	■
School-Based Crime Prevention						
Crime and Delinquency						
• Programs aimed at building school capacity to initiate and sustain innovation	■	■	■	■		■
• Programs aimed at clarifying and communicating norms about behaviors—by establishing school rules, improving the consistency of their enforcement (particularly when they emphasize positive reinforcement of appropriate behavior), or communicating norms through schoolwide campaigns (e.g., antibullying campaigns) or ceremonies	■	■		■		■
• Comprehensive instructional programs that focus on a range of social competency skills (e.g., developing self-control, stress-management, responsible decision making, social problem solving, and communication) and that are delivered over a long period of time	■	■	■	■	■	■
• Coordinated action between schools and social services		■		■		■
• Antibullying programs using coordinated work between schools, families, and social services				■		■

(continued)

TABLE 5-3. (continued)

Best Practice Crime Prevention Programs	Boston	Denver	Fort Worth	Hartford	New York City	San Diego
• Programs that group youth into smaller "schools-within-schools" to create smaller units, more supportive interactions, or greater flexibility in instruction	■			■		
• Behavior modification and programs that teach "thinking skills" to high-risk youth	■	■		■	■	■
Substance Abuse						
• Programs aimed at clarifying and communicating norms about behaviors	■	■	■	■	■	■
• Comprehensive instructional programs using a range of social competency skills (see above) delivered over a long period of time to continually reinforce skills	■	■	■	■	■	■
• Programs aimed at building school capacity to initiate and sustain innovation	■	■			■	■
• Programs that group youth into smaller "schools-within-schools" to create smaller units, more supportive interactions, or greater flexibility in instruction	■			■		
• Programs that improve classroom management and that use effective instructional techniques	■	■			■	■
Labor Markets and Crime Risk Factors						
• Vocational programs aimed at older male ex-offenders no longer in the justice system	■		■	■		
• Job Corps	■	■		■		■
• Prison-based vocational education programs aimed at adults	■			■	■	■
• Dispersed housing for poverty-level households		■		■		■
Preventing Poverty at Places						
• Nuisance abatement	■		■	■	■	■
• Microneighborhood watch				■		■
• Housing design standards						■
• Supervision by caretakers	■					
• Reduction of access to firearms	■			■	■	
• Burglary reduction programs using the Safer Cities model					■	
• Multiple clerks in commercial stores	■					■
• Store design	■					■
• Server training in bars and taverns	■					
• Metal detectors and guards in airports	■		■	■	■	■
• Street closures in open public spaces	■		■	■	■	■
• Target hardening in public facilities	■		■	■	■	■
• Closed circuit television in public places	■			■	■	
• City guards in public streets				■	■	
Policing for Prevention						
• Increased directed patrols in street-corner hot spots of crime	■	■	■	■	■	■
• Proactive arrests of serious repeat offenders	■		■	■	■	■

(continued)

TABLE 5-3. (continued)

Best Practice Crime Prevention Programs	Boston	Denver	Fort Worth	Hartford	New York City	San Diego
• Proactive drunk driving arrests	■		■	■	■	■
• Arrests of employed suspects for domestic assault	■		■	■		■
• Police traffic enforcement patrols against illegally carried handguns	■		■	■		
• Community policing with community participation in priority setting	■	■	■	■	■	■
• Community policing focused on improving police legitimacy	■		■	■		■
• Zero tolerance of disorder, if legitimacy issues can be addressed	■		■	■	■	
• Problem oriented policing generally	■	■	■	■	■	■
• Adding extra police to cities, regardless of assignments	■		■	■		■
• Warrants for arrest of suspect absent when police respond to domestic violence	■			■	■	■

Criminal Justice and Crime Prevention

Best Practice Crime Prevention Programs	Boston	Denver	Fort Worth	Hartford	New York City	San Diego
• Rehabilitation programs with particular characteristics	■	■		■		■
• Prison-based therapeutic community treatment of drug-involved offenders	■				■	■
• Incapacitating offenders who continue to commit crimes at high rates	■					■
• Effective rehabilitation programs that	■	■				■
• Are structured and focused, use multiple treatment components, focus on developing skills (social, academic, and employment), and use behavioral and cognitive methods (with reinforcements for clearly identified, overt behaviors as opposed to nondirective counseling focusing on insight, self esteem, or disclosure)	■			■		■
• Provide for substantial, meaningful contact with the treatment personnel	■			■		■
• Providing intensive community-based treatment for drug addicts	■	■	■	■		■
• Drug courts combining both rehabilitation and criminal justice control	■		■	■		■
• Day fines	■			■		
• Juvenile aftercare	■	■	■	■		■
• Drug treatment combined with urine testing	■	■	■	■		■

A FEDERAL INITIATIVE

In concluding this chapter on crime prevention, we should mention that the federal government's Bureau of Justice Assistance has initiated a Comprehensive Communities Program (CCP) that stresses crime reduction. It has two primary components—community policing and community mobilization—to help police bring about solutions to local problems, and bring together people most affected by crime problems. As of 2003, 16 highly populated jurisdictions were participating in this initiative.[56]

SUMMARY

It is clear that the field of crime prevention has "matured" from its earlier forms, originally involving strategic placement of rocks by early cave dwellers, or more recently having to do primarily with target hardening one's home with better locks. This chapter has shown its various elements as well as the results of research efforts concerning what good can occur when measures are taken to prevent crimes.

The police are realizing that they alone cannot prevent or address crime and disorder, and that a partnership with the community is essential if the physical and social problems that plague communities are to be reduced or eliminated.

NOTES

1. Crime Prevention Coalition of America, *Crime Prevention in America: Foundations for Action* (Washington, D.C.: National Crime Prevention Council, 1990), p. 64.

2. Ronald V. Clarke, *Situational Crime Prevention: Successful Case Studies* (2nd ed.) (Monsey, N.Y.: Criminal Justice Press, 1997), p. 2.

3. Steven P. Lab, "Crime Prevention: Where Have We Been and Which Way Should We Go?" In Steven P. Lab (ed.), *Community Policing at a Crossroads* (Cincinnati: Anderson, 1997), pp. 1–13.

4. Cynthia Scanlon, "Crime Prevention through Environmental Design," *Law and Order* (May 1996):50.

5. U.S. Department of Housing and Urban Development, "Crime Prevention through Environmental Design," Crime Prevention Brief (Washington, D.C.: Author, no date), p. 2.

6. Lab, "Crime Prevention," p. 5.

7. Ibid.

8. Ibid., p. 7.

9. Scanlon, "Crime Prevention through Environmental Design," p. 50.

10. Lab, "Crime Prevention," p. 6.

11. L. E. Cohen and M. Felson, "Social Change and Crime Rate Trends: A Routine Activity Approach," *American Sociological Review* 44 (1997):588–608.

12. D. B. Cornish and R. V. Clarke, *The Reasoning Criminal: Rational Choice Perspectives on Offending* (New York: Springer-Verlag, 1986).

13. James Q. Wilson and George Kelling, "Broken Windows," *The Atlantic Monthly* 211 (1982):29–38.

14. Lab, "Crime Prevention," p. 6.

15. Ronald V. Clarke, "Situational Crime Prevention: Its Theoretical Basis and Practical Scope." In *Crime and Justice: An Annual Review of Research*, Vol. 4, Michael Tonry and Norval Morris (eds.) (Chicago: University of Chicago Press, 1983), p. 225.

16. Lab, "Crime Prevention," pp. 8–9.

17. U.S. Department of Justice, Bureau of Justice Assistance, *Crime Prevention and Community Policing: A Vital Partnership* (Washington, D.C.: U.S. Government Printing Office, 1997), p. 4.

18. Jim Jordan, "Shifting the Mission: Seeing Prevention as the Strategic Goal, Not a Set of Programs," *Subject to Debate* (Washington, D.C.: Police Executive Research Forum, December 1999), pp. 1–2.

19. Ibid., p. 3.

20. Ibid.

21. Quoted in Julian Fantino, "Taking Crime Prevention Back to the Future!" *The Police Chief* (May 1999):18.

22. Ibid.

23. Ibid., p. 20.

24. Ibid.

25. Lab, "Crime Prevention," p. 6.

26. Rob Gurwitt, "Communitarianism: You Can Try It at Home," *Governing* 6 (August 1993):33–39.

27. Ibid., p. 8.

28. U.S. Department of Justice, Bureau of Justice Assistance, *Crime Prevention and Community Policing: A Vital Partnership*, p. 3.

29. Adapted from The Ohio Crime Prevention Association, *A Citizen Guide to Community Policing* (Dublin, Oh.: Author, 1998), pp. 21–24.

30. C. R. Jeffrey, *Crime Prevention through Environmental Design* (Beverly Hills, Calif.: Sage, 1971), p. 117.

31. National Crime Prevention Council, *Designing Safer Communities: A Crime Prevention through Environmental Design Handbook* (Washington, D.C.: Author, 1997), pp. 7–8.

32. "Building a More Crime-Free Environment: Tempe Cops Have the Last Word on Construction Projects," *Law Enforcement News* (November 15, 1998):7.

33. Scanlon, "Crime Prevention through Environmental Design," pp. 51–52.

34. Ibid., p. 3.

35. Ronald V. Clarke (ed.), *Situational Crime Prevention: Successful Case Studies* (Albany, N.Y.: Harrow and Heston, 1992), p. 3.

36. U.S. Department of Housing and Urban Development, "Situational Prevention," Crime Prevention Brief (Washington, D.C.: Author, no date), p. 1.

37. Clarke, *Situational Crime Prevention*, p. 3.

38. Ibid.

39. Ibid.

40. Clarke, *Situational Crime Prevention*, p. 27.

41. Ibid., pp. 9–10.

42. Ibid., p. 21.

43. Ibid.

44. Lab, "Crime Prevention," p. 12.

45. Ronald V. Clarke, *Situational Crime Prevention: Successful Case Studies* (2nd ed.), p. 2.

46. Robert Barr and Ken Pease, "Crime Placement, Displacement, and Deflection." In *Crime and Justice: A Review of Research*, Vol. 12, Michael Tonry and Norval Morris (eds.) (Chicago: University of Chicago Press, 1990), pp. 146–175.

47. John E. Eck, "The Threat of Crime Displacement," *Criminal Justice Abstracts* 25(3) (September 1993):529.

48. Pat Mayhew, Ronald V. Clarke, A. Sturman, and J. M. Hough, *Crime as Opportunity*, Home Office Research Study No. 34 (London: Her Majesty's Stationery Office, 1976); J. Lowman, "Prostitution in Vancouver: Some Notes on the Genesis of a Social Problem," *Canadian Journal of Criminology* 28(1) (1997):1–16; Barry Poyner and Barry Webb, "Reducing Theft from Shopping Bags in City Center Markets." In Ronald V. Clarke (ed.), *Situational Crime Prevention: Successful Case Studies* (Albany, N.Y.: Harrow and Heston, 1992).

49. Eck, "The Threat of Crime Displacement," pp. 534–536.

50. Ibid., p. 537.

51. Ibid.

52. Ibid., pp. 541–542.

53. Ibid.

54. William Spelman and John E. Eck, "Problem-Solving: Problem Oriented Policing in Newport News." *Research in Brief* (Washington, D.C.: National Institute of Justice, January 1987), p. 83.

55. Lawrence W. Sherman, Denise C. Gottfredson, Doris L. MacKenzie, John Eck, Peter Reuter, and Shawn D. Bushway, "Preventing Crime: What Works, What Doesn't, What's Promising." In National Institute of Justice, *Research in Brief* (Washington, D.C.: Author, 1998), pp. 1–27.

56. "Promising Strategies to Reduce Gun Violence." U.S. Department of Justice, Bureau of Justice Assistance. *http://ojjdp.ncjrs.org/pubs/gun_violence/sect08-a.html* (Accessed April 24, 2003).

INTRODUCTION

Having identified the core components and elements of community oriented policing and problem solving (COPPS) in previous chapters, we now look at how to strategically plan for and implement this concept.

To help conceptualize strategic planning, one might view it as maintaining the tension on the line while fishing—if you reel it in too fast, the line might snap; but if you go too slowly, the fish will not be landed. The strategic plan that the police agency "holds in its hands" outlines bold milestones spread over the next several years.[1]

This chapter begins with a look at the general need for strategic thinking and for police organizations to engage in the strategic planning process. This section also discusses the planning cycle, and how to assess local needs and develop a planning document.

Then we shift to the implementation of COPPS per se, considering some principal components: leadership and administration, human resources, field operations, and external relations. All of this is then brought fully into focus by use of examples, with a view of actual agency strategic planning processes. We conclude the chapter by considering several general obstacles to implementation, and by delineating 10 ways that COPPS can be undermined.

—6—
PLANNING AND IMPLEMENTATION

Translating Ideas into Action

Alice: Cheshire Puss, would you tell me, please, which way I ought to go from here?

Cheshire Cat: That depends a good deal on where you want to get to.

Alice: I don't much care where . . .

Cheshire Cat: Then it doesn't matter which way you go.

—Lewis Carroll, in *Alice's Adventures in Wonderland*, 1865

STRATEGIC THINKING

In order for a chief executive to engage in strategic planning, he or she must first become engaged in strategic *thinking* and then assist the organization in thinking strategically. This means seeing both the big picture and its operational implications. As one author observed,

> The purpose of strategic thinking is to discover novel, imaginative strategies which can rewrite the rules of the competitive game and to envision potential futures, significantly different from the present.[2]

Strategic thinking refers to a creative, divergent thought process. It is a mode of strategy making that is associated with reinventing the future.[3]

Strategic thinking is, therefore, compatible with strategic planning. Both are required in any thoughtful strategy-making process and strategy formulation. The creative, groundbreaking strategies emerging from strategic thinking still have to be operationalized through convergent and analytical thought (strategic planning). Thus, both strategic thinking and strategic planning are necessary, and neither is adequate without the other for effective strategic management (see Figure 6-1).[4] As Loizos Heracleous observed,

It all comes down to the ability to go up and down the ladder of abstraction, and being able to see both the big picture and the operational implications, which are signs of outstanding leaders and strategists.[5]

Strategic planning is a leadership tool and a process (as shown in Figure 6-2); furthermore, as with most tools, it is primarily used for one purpose: to help

Basic Elements

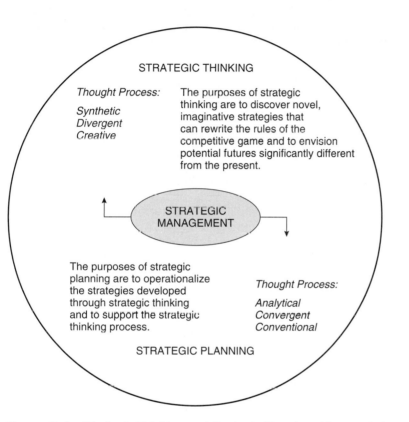

Figure 6-1. Strategic Thinking and Strategic Planning. (*Source:* Loizos Heracleous, "Strategic Thinking or Strategic Planning?" *Long Range Planning* 31 [June 1998]:485. Used with permission.)

Montgomery County, Maryland's multiyear strategic plan was designed for adaptability and continual evaluation. (*Courtesy* Montgomery County, Maryland, police department)

an organization do a better job—to focus its energy, ensure that members of the organization are working toward the same goals, and assess and adjust an organization's direction in response to a changing environment. In short, strategic planning is a disciplined effort to produce fundamental decisions and actions that shape and guide what an organization is, what it does, and why it does it, with a focus on the future.[6]

The history of strategic planning began in the military, in which strategy is "the science of planning and directing large-scale military operations." Although our understanding of strategy as applied to management has been transformed, one element remains: aiming to achieve competitive advantage. Strategic planning also includes the following elements:

- It is oriented toward the future and looks at how the world could be different five to ten years in the future. It is aimed at creating the organization's future.
- It is based on thorough analysis of foreseen or predicted trends and scenarios of possible alternative futures.
- It thoroughly analyzes the organization, its internal and external environment, and its potential.
- It is a qualitative, idea-driven process.
- It is an ongoing, continuous learning process.
- When it is successful, it influences all areas of operations, becoming a part of the organization's philosophy and culture.[7]

Excellent examples of strategic planning abound. For example, see the strategic plan of the U.S. Department of Justice.[8]

For police leaders, strategic planning holds many benefits. It can help an agency anticipate key trends and issues facing the organization, both currently and in the future. The planning process explores options, sets directions, and helps stakeholders make appropriate decisions. It facilitates communication among key stakeholders who are involved in the process and keeps organizations focused on outcomes while battling daily crises. Planning can be used to develop performance standards to measure an agency's efforts. Most important, it helps leaders facilitate and manage change (which is the subject of the following chapter).

The Planning Cycle

A fundamental cycle is used for strategic planning—the initial steps to be taken in the process—with appropriate involvement by all stakeholders. The process is not fixed, however; it must be flexible enough to allow rapid revision of specific strategies as new information develops.

1. *Identify the planning team:* Include the involvement of several key stakeholders, both internal and external to the organization.
   - *Department and city leadership*
   - *Department personnel:* Supervisors, officers, nonsworn staff members, and all members of the department should be included.
   - *The community:* The plan must be developed in partnership with the community it is designed to serve.
   - *Interagency partners:* These include both staff and other government agencies and representatives of key social welfare agencies.
2. *Environmental scanning:* Conduct a needs assessment (discussed later).
3. *Develop a planning document* (discussed later).

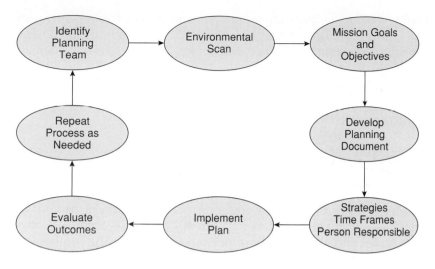

Figure 6-2. Planning Cycle.

Figure 6-2 depicts the various steps that are involved in the planning cycle.

Environmental scanning is a part of the planning cycle that deserves special attention, because it refers to the collection and analysis of information required to determine the nature and extent of crime in a community, community residents' perceptions of crime and how they are affected by it, and information about the environment or conditions of a community. The purpose of the needs assessment is to determine and exchange information about specific types of community crime and disorder problems, their causes and effects, and the resources available to combat them. The needs assessment provides the foundation for a community's entire COPPS effort.

Environmental Scanning: A Needs Assessment

Therefore, in order to develop a comprehensive implementation plan for community policing, a needs assessment should be completed at the earliest possible time, for several reasons:

- to list (in order of priority) and clarify the existing crime and drug problems
- to provide a view of resident perceptions about the crime and drug problems, and to provide an excellent means of involving the community in problem identification
- to provide information to the public about problems
- to provide initial direction for developing a work plan, and to assist in setting program goals, strategies, and objectives
- to provide baseline data for evaluation

Needs assessment is ultimately a process conducted for outlining the current issues of the community and the resources needed to resolve those issues. This document will

- result in a clearer picture of community needs and resources; and
- allow the planning team to develop a strong rationale for decision making.

Information sources for needs assessment include the following:
- city planning reports
- newspaper articles

- police reports [including local crime analysis and dispatch calls for service (CFS) data, as well as police officers' knowledge of the community, the Federal Bureau of Investigation's *Uniform Crime Reports,* and other related sources]
- interviews with community leaders
- community surveys (see "A Strategic Plan Survey in Portland, Oregon" in Appendix C)
- employment, housing, education, and health information

THE PLANNING DOCUMENT: A GUIDE FOR IMPLEMENTATION

Elements and Issues

Strategic planning is both a document and a process. A written document or plan is the product of a planning team's efforts, is helpful for organizing key objectives, and serves as a guide for those persons involved in the implementation process. The detail and structure of a plan may vary greatly. It may be highly detailed and cover goals, objectives, tasks, and timelines, or it may be less formal, identifying general areas targeted for change.

The structure and formality of a plan will depend largely on the needs and capacity of the organization (based on the environmental scanning and needs assessment). Large organizations with funding and staff support may desire a more comprehensive plan to keep track of the many details and numbers of people involved in implementation. Conversely, smaller police organizations may be capable of implementing change with less detailed plans (see Exhibit 6-1).

EXHIBIT 6-1   Shifting to COPPS in Mount Pleasant, South Carolina

Mount Pleasant, South Carolina, is a small oceanside community of about 36,000 citizens. For several years the city's police department—with 71 sworn officers and 28 civilians—had been moving from the traditional policing model to COPPS. The command staff in the police department began a comprehensive training process that included visits to departments in three other states. Staff members met with the agency leaders and observed various COPPS initiatives in action. Each command staff member was given a set of materials to review and critique pertaining specifically to Mount Pleasant. Then the staff developed an implementation process that included

- redefining the department's mission;
- researching COPPS; and
- setting goals, objectives, and tasks for implementation.

After the goals, objectives, and tasks were identified, the department was in a position to establish time frames for completing the tasks associated with program implementation. Time frames allowed agency personnel and community members to schedule pro-

gram activities around their normal responsibilities. The implementation plan also specified the process by which everyone was to be informed about the work to be done and the changes necessary to get it done.

Based on this process, the plan included 133 tasks that the staff was to undertake over a three-year period to ensure a complete transition to COPPS. These tasks included everything from training personnel to seeking alternative sources of revenue to fund agency operations. The plan was presented to the city council and a number of community organizations. COPPS training was completed by January 1993. To obtain citizen input, the department worked closely with a planning committee throughout the process. CFS management, performance evaluations, training, and a rewards system consumed a considerable amount of time during implementation. Today, however, every patrol team in the department practices COPPS, performing research, analyzing data, and developing potential solutions for problems.

Source: Thomas J. Sexton, "Mount Pleasant Plans Strategy for Shift to Community Policing," *Community Policing Exchange* (November/December 1995):5.

Following are some format and content issues for the planning process and the development of a planning document.

1. *Develop statements of vision, mission, and values:*
   - The *vision* is a scenario or description of how the agency and community will change if the plan is successful.
   - The *mission* defines the "business" of COPPS. The statement can be expected to include both traditional aspects of policing (such as public safety, enforcement, "protect and serve") and aspects of COPPS philosophy (community engagement, shared responsibility for public safety).
   - *Values* guide decisions and actions. Prioritize and develop a short list of key principles that people who are involved in COPPS implementation should consider.

2. *Identify primary objectives* that define critical outcomes anticipated from the change to COPPS.

3. *Select strategies* from among various options outlined during the process that clearly outline the primary avenues and approaches that will be used to attain objectives.

4. *Set goals* that are general statements of intent. They are the first step in translating a mission statement into what can realistically be attained. Goals should be obtainable and measurable, often beginning with such phrases as "to increase," "to reduce," or "to expand."

5. *Set objectives*—specific statements of what must be done to achieve a goal or desired outcomes. Usually, several objectives are developed for each goal. A meaningful and well-stated objective should be:

    specific: stating precisely what is to be achieved;
    measurable: answering how much, how many, how well; and
    time-bound: indicating when results will be achieved.

6. *Set activities*, or detailed steps necessary to carry out each strategy; they should be time framed and measurable.

7. *Identify a responsible person* for every task.

8. *Set timelines* for the completion of tasks.

A BRIEF EXAMPLE OF A STRATEGIC PLAN: ASPEN, COLORADO

Aspen, Colorado is a mountain resort community with 27 sworn officers and a population that soars in winter to nearly double its normal size, to about 30,000. Recently the police undertook the task of developing a strategic plan, portions of which are presented. After finalizing their mission, philosophy, vision, and values statements (synthesizing from the work of such luminaries as Tom Peters, W. Edwards Deming, and John Naisbitt), the entire department began developing outcome measures, goals, and service standards. For example, for the goal "To have our services rated as 'good' to 'excellent' by at least 85 percent of our customers," the agency established the following:

Outcome Measurement: This goal will be measured by the department's Customer Satisfaction Survey: to have at least 85 percent of residents agree that they feel safe in the city and in their neighborhoods after dark.

Outcome Measurement: This goal will be measured by analyzing data in the city's annual Citizen Survey: to have at least 80 percent of the residents view the department's staff as knowledgeable, courteous, informative, and service-oriented. There will be no unresolved complaints related to the behavior of department employees.

Other goals were established concerning traffic safety, youth/police relations, staff recruitment and hiring, community relations, and crime analysis.[9]

IMPLEMENTING COPPS

Department-wide Versus Experimental District

Since COPPS came into being, most police executives have implemented the strategy throughout the entire agency; some executives, however, have attempted to implement the concept by introducing it in a small unit or an experimental district[10] and often in a specific geographic area of the jurisdiction.

It is strongly argued that COPPS be implemented on a department-wide basis, because the introduction of a "special unit" seems to exacerbate the conflict between community policing's reform agenda and the more traditional outlook and hierarchical structure of the agency. A perception of elitism is created—a perception that is ironic, because COPPS is meant to close the gap between patrol and special units and to empower and value the rank-and-file patrol officer as the most important functionary of police work.

The key lesson from research on implementation is that there is no "golden" or "bright-line" rule or any universal method to ensure the successful adoption of COPPS. Two general propositions are important, however, for consideration in implementing the concept: the role of the rank-and-file officer and the role of the environment (or "social ecology") in which COPPS is to be implemented.[11] The social ecology of COPPS includes both the internal/organizational and external/societal environments. Both of these factors are discussed later in the chapter.

We also believe that TQM (discussed in Chapter 3) supports putting the responsibility for implementation of COPPS at the door of everyone in the organization. If rank-and-file officers are able to show positive results with COPPS projects, their success can become difficult to criticize among those with whom the philosophy is unpopular.[12]

Principal Components of Successful Implementation

Moving an agency to COPPS is a complex endeavor. Four principal components of implementation profoundly affect the way agencies do business: leadership and administration, human resources, field operations, and external relations.[13]

Management and Administration

Management Approaches. COPPS requires changing the *philosophy of leadership* and management throughout the entire organization. This begins with the development of a *new vision/values/mission statement,* as noted earlier. Leadership should be promoted at all levels, and a shift in management style from *controller to facilitator* is necessary. The organization should invest in *information systems* that will assist officers in identifying patterns of crime and support the problem-solving process. Progressive leaders will need to prepare for the future by *engaging in long-term, strategic management and developing continuous evaluation processes,* but at the same time these leaders should be flexible and comfortable with change. *Finances and resources* will no longer be firmly established within boxes in the organizational chart. Rather, they will be commonly shared across the organization, with other city departments and the public engaged in neighborhood problem solving.

Role of the Chief Executive. It is essential that chief executives communicate the idea that COPPS is department-wide in scope. To get the whole agency involved, the chief executive must adopt four practices as part of the implementation plan:

1. Communicate to all department members the vital role of COPPS in serving the public. Executives must describe why handling problems is more effective than simply handling incidents.

2. Provide incentives to all department members to engage in COPPS. This includes a new and different personnel evaluation and reward system, as well as positive encouragement.

3. Reduce the barriers to COPPS that can occur. Procedures, time allocation, and policies all need to be closely examined.

4. Show officers how to address problems. Training is a key element of COPPS implementation. The executive must also set guidelines for innovation. Officers must know they have the latitude to innovate.[14]

The top management of a police agency must consciously address these four concerns. Failure to do so will result in the COPPS approach being conducted by a relatively small number of officers; as a result, relatively few problems will be addressed.

The general task of the chief executive is to challenge the fundamental assumptions of the organization, its aspirations and objectives, the effectiveness of the department's current technologies, and even the chief's own self-perception. This is an awkward stage in the life of the organization. It seems

Arlington County, Virginia, Police Chief Ed Fynn "walks the talk" of COPPS by appearing at neighborhood clean-up efforts to show his support to residents and officers. (*Courtesy* Arlington County, Virginia, police department)

to be a deliberate attempt by the chief to upset the agency. The remedy lies in the personal commitment of the chief and his or her senior managers and supervisors. Ensuing surveys may well find that morale improves once it becomes clear that the change in direction and style was more than a "fleeting fancy" and that the chief's policies have some longevity.[15]

Middle Managers.   In the early twentieth century, a powerful midlevel management group emerged that extended the reach of chiefs throughout the department and became the locus of the practice and skill base of the occupation. As such, middle managers—captains and lieutenants—became the leading edge in the establishment of decentralized control over police departments' internal environment and organizational operations.[16] Furthermore, in the past one of the basic functions and practices of middle managers was to forestall creativity and innovation.

Times have changed in this regard, however; today these middle managers play a crucial role in planning and implementing COPPS, as well as encouraging their officers to be innovative, to take risks, and to be creative.[17] As George Kelling and William Bratton observed, "Ample evidence exists that when a clear vision of the business of the organization is put forward, when mid-managers are included in planning, when their legitimate self-interests are acknowledged, and when they are properly trained, mid-managers can be the leading edge of innovation and creativity."[18]

First-Line Supervisors.   Research has provided additional information for leaders to consider when implementing a COPPS philosophy. To begin, first-line supervisors and senior patrol officers seem to generate the greatest resistance to community policing, largely because of long-standing working styles cultivated from years of traditional police work and because these officers can feel disenfranchised by a management system that takes the best and brightest out of patrol and (they often believe) leaves them behind. The press of 911 calls also makes it difficult to meet the need for community outreach, problem solving, and networking with other agencies. Officers may also become concerned about the size of the area for which they are responsible; community policing beats are typically smaller than those of radio patrols.

We discuss the role of middle managers and first-line supervisors in greater detail in Chapter 7, on changing the culture of the organization.

Examining the Organization.   An important aspect of COPPS is that its implementation occurs not over a period of days or weeks but more likely over many months or even years. The bigger the organization, the longer it will take to change. Also, throughout the period of change the office of the chief executive is going to be surrounded by turbulence. An executive may be fortunate enough to inherit an organization that is already susceptible to change; however, the executive who inherits a smoothly running bureaucracy, complacent in the status quo, has a tougher job.

With regard to the organization, one of the first steps the executive and managers must take is an *analysis of existing policies and procedures.* Although a need remains for some standing orders and some prepared contingency plans and procedures, in the past such manuals have been used more to allocate blame retrospectively after some error has been discovered. It is not surprising that street officers have adopted a mindset of doing things "by the book." Many executives have deemphasized their policy and procedure manuals in implementing community policing. As an extreme example, the manual of an

English police force had grown to four volumes, each more than three inches thick, totaling more than 2,000 pages of instructions. Under COPPS, the manual was discarded in favor of a one-page "Policy Statement" that gave 11 brief "commandments." These commandments related more to initiative and "reasonableness of action" than to rules and regulations. Each officer was issued a pocket-size laminate copy of the policy statement.[19]

The organization should conduct an *in-depth analysis of the existing departmental rank structure*, which itself can be a principal obstacle to the effective communication of new values and philosophy throughout the organization. A large metropolitan police force may have 10 or more layers of rank. The chief executive must talk with the officers. Therefore, it is necessary to ensure that the message not be filtered, doctored, or suppressed.[20]

Human Resources

Human resources constitutes the basis of organizational culture. Developing COPPS as a part of daily police behaviors and practices presents a major challenge. To accomplish this requires that the mechanisms that motivate, challenge, reward, and correct employees' behaviors comport with the principles of COPPS. They include *recruiting, selection, training, performance evaluations, promotions, honors and awards,* and *discipline,* all of which should be reviewed to ensure that they promote and support the tenets of COPPS.

Modeling Behaviors. Recruiting literature should reflect the principles of COPPS. Agencies should actively recruit students, minorities, and women into their organization. Community groups may be helpful in this respect. Advertisements in newspapers or on television and radio shows that target certain populations are also wise.

COPPS should be integrated into academy training, field training programs, and in-service training. As was discussed in previous chapters, it is also important to provide training and education to the other city agencies and community, business, and social service organizations so that they understand COPPS. Performance evaluations and reward systems should reflect new job descriptions and officers' application of their COPPS training.

Promotion systems should be expanded from their usual focus on tactical decision making to include knowledge of the research on community policing, and they should test an officer's ability to apply problem solving to various crime and neighborhood problems.

Labor Relations. Another challenge for leadership and administration in the implementation of COPPS centers on labor unions. Since the 1960s police unions and associations have evolved quickly, making great strides in improving wages, benefits, and working conditions. Yet there is a concern about police administrators' ability to run their agencies and the impact of unions on police–community partnerships. Unions are often viewed by administrators and the public as a negative force, focusing only on financial gain and control over administrative policy making without regard for the department or community.

Does COPPS conflict with the philosophy of police unions? It is understandable that this approach could be construed as antithetical to union interests. For example, COPPS asks officers to assume a proprietary interest in the neighborhoods where they work and to be flexible and creative in their work hours and solutions to problems. This approach often conflicts with collective bargaining contracts in which unions have negotiated for stability of work hours and compensation when working conditions are altered. The idea of civilianization, reductions of rank, and decentralized investigations can also be viewed as a threat to officers' lateral mobility, promotional opportunities, and career development. Labor organizations are also concerned with any proposed changes in shifts, beats, criteria for selection, promotion, discipline, and so on.

It is wise to include labor representatives in the planning and implementation process from the beginning. When the unions are excluded from the planning process, officers perceive the implementation of COPPS as a public relations gimmick in management's interests. It is also important that union leaders understand management's concerns and collaborate in planning an agency's future.

Remember, COPPS is important from both the labor and management perspectives. Both sides are interested in creating a quality work environment for employees. This translates to a healthy and productive work force. COPPS provides officers the opportunity to use their talents. It removes layers of management and quota-driven evaluations that are often opposed by officers.

Field Operations

Decentralized Services. The need for available time to engage in problem solving presents a supervisory challenge that begins with managing CFS. This requires comprehensive workload analysis, call prioritization, alternative call handling, and differential response methods (discussed in Chapter 4). This information helps an agency when its managers are considering a decentralized approach to field operations that involves assigning officers to a beat and shift for a minimum of one year to learn more about a neighborhood's problems. It is also helpful in reconstructing beat boundaries to correspond more closely with neighborhoods.

Decentralized service is an important part of the general scheme of COPPS. Under the traditional, incident-driven style of policing, officers have little permanent territorial responsibility. They know that they may be dispatched to another area at any time and that they are not responsible for anything that occurs on their beat when they are off duty. This responsibility for their area only during a specific period of time reinforces the officer's focus on incidents rather than on long-term area problems. When the chief executive says to the officer, "This area is yours, and nobody else's," however, the territory becomes personalized. The officer's concern for the beat does not end with a tour of duty. Concerned officers will want to know what occurred on their beat while they were off duty and will often make unsolicited follow-up visits, struggling to find causes of incidents that would otherwise be regarded as inconsequential.[21]

Detectives. A matter that relates to field operations and COPPS involves detectives. The detective division may easily view the introduction of COPPS as a matter strictly for the patrol officers; the detectives might believe that "Our job is still to solve crime."[22] Detectives might maintain that attitude until they are removed from the group that reinforces that perception. They have to be incorporated into the COPPS context (see Exhibit 6-2). Valuable intelligence information gained by detectives through investigations can be fed to the patrol division. Also, detectives must believe that crime prevention is their principal obligation and not the exclusive responsibility of the patrol force.

Detectives have opportunities to establish and enhance positive working relationships with victim-advocacy groups, civic organizations, police district advisory councils, and other stakeholders in the system. Detectives, like patrol officers, should attend regular community meetings and impart valuable knowledge relating to criminal activities, trends, and patterns. In addition, quicker, easier investigative responses can be realized.

EXHIBIT 6-2   Investigations in the COPPS Context

One problematic issue for police departments that are implementing COPPS is the appropriate organization of investigative functions. How can agencies structure investigations to best support these approaches? Who in the organization should conduct which types of investigations? Should agencies decentralize investigative functions? Should there be a separate command structure for detectives?

A group of chiefs leading organizations through the change process first identified this whole issue. The National Institute of Justice will fund a research project surveying 900 law enforcement agencies, all those serving populations of at least 50,000 and having at least 100 sworn personnel. The Police Executive Research Forum will ask these agencies about their status with respect to COPPS, as well as detailed questions about the structure of their investigative functions. Researchers will then develop several models of the investigative function in the COPPS context.

Source: Workshop presentation, Mary Ann Wycoff, Police Executive Research Forum, "The 8th Annual International Problem Oriented Policing Conference: Problem Oriented Policing 1997," November 16, 1997, San Diego, California.

An excellent recent example of bringing detectives into COPPS is that of El Paso, Texas, which witnessed a problem of repetitive, violent acts of domestic violence. After analyzing the problem—and examining the environment of the offenses, including victims' family situation, economics, and social pressures involved in lack of prosecutions—detectives worked with the patrol division to encourage victims to follow through with prosecutions, engage in follow-up investigations, and even devise a rudimentary witness protection unit, with impressive outcomes.[23]

The Top Priority: Patrol Personnel.   There is one very important positive aspect of considering whether to implement a COPPS philosophy, one that all chief executives should remember: It encourages many of the activities that patrol officers would like to do, that is, to engage in more inquiry of crime and

Allowing officers to identify and resolve neighborhood problems can improve morale by making the job more rewarding. (*Courtesy* Community Policing Consortium)

disorder and get more closure from their work. When asked why they originally wanted to enter policing, officers consistently say that they joined in order to help people.[24] By emphasizing work that addresses people's concerns and by giving officers the discretion to develop a solution, COPPS helps make police work more rewarding.

Among the most frequent complaints voiced by patrol officers, however, are that patrol is given little support, they are accorded low esteem by their organization, and they are simply a pool of employees from which to draw for other special assignments. For COPPS to be successful, the agency must ensure that patrol staffing is maintained and that its officers believe that their work is most important to the organization's success.

External Relations

In Chapter 4 we discussed the various stakeholders and partners that police will find in the community for assistance in the COPPS initiative. Enlisting the assistance of the community is often a more complex undertaking than one might assume.

Collaborative responses to neighborhood crime and disorder are essential to the success of COPPS. This requires new relationships and the sharing of information and resources among the police and community, local government agencies, service providers, and businesses. Also, police agencies must educate and inform their external partners about police resources and neighborhood problems using surveys, newsletters, community meetings, and public service announcements. The media also provide an excellent opportunity for police to educate the community. Press releases about collaborative problem-solving efforts should be sent to the media, and news conferences should be held to discuss major crime reduction efforts.

Another essential consideration of implementing COPPS is the solicitation and establishment of political support for the concept. The political environment varies considerably with, say, the strong mayor and council-manager forms of government. These and other rapidly changing political environments make the implementation of COPPS more difficult—especially when we add to the cauldron the at-will employment of most police executives.

Exhibit 6-3 shows how Sacramento, California, approached external relations by providing neighborhood services.

EXHIBIT 6-3 External Relations: Neighborhood Services in Sacramento

Recently Sacramento, California, decided to reorganize its city services into four geographically based system areas. This configuration mirrored the Sacramento police department's (SPD) patrol deployment boundaries. A new city department called Neighborhood Services was developed that included such elements as recreation, housing and building inspections, nuisance abatement, community centers, planning, parks, human services, and code enforcement. The four area managers of this new department and the four SPD patrol captains cooperated to implement new levels of problem solving. The increased contact between the departments and community members occurred simultaneously at several levels. Problem solving is a collaboration among the SPD, Neighborhood Services, and the community, facilitating the dissemination of information and enabling them to identify issues quickly. Community mobilization has spread from community associations to business associations, recreation programs, political action committees, and redevelopment project boards. With this increase of community input, a variety of responses enhances and continues the problem-solving cycle.

Source: Workshop presentation, Mike Busch, Sacramento Police Department, "The 8th Annual International Problem Oriented Policing Conference: Problem Oriented Policing 1997," November 16, 1997, San Diego, California.

Elected officials must provide direction and support through policy development and resource allocation. This may be accomplished in several ways. For instance, in Tempe, Arizona, the city council passed a resolution that established guidelines for the creation of a Neighborhood Assistance Office. The program's goal was "fostering a partnership among the city council, city staff and residents, and the creation of an environment in which citizens are afforded an opportunity to participate in city affairs in an advisory or advocacy role."[25] In essence, the Neighborhood Assistance Office was to be a conduit for communication between the city government and citizens:

> Implementation of the Neighborhood Associations included several important steps on the part of the City: maintaining a register and mailing list of existing organizations and their officers and bylaws; mailing newsletters for Neighborhood Associations; providing insurance coverage for use of school facilities for neighborhood meetings; coordinating annual citywide informational meetings; arranging for city staff and officials to speak at association meetings; and responding to concerns and questions raised by individual associations.[26]

TYING IT ALL TOGETHER

Figure 6-3 ties together these four key areas—management and administration, human resources, field operations, and external relations—illustrating the principal components of implementation.

An Example: Montgomery County, Maryland

Exhibits 6-4 through 6-8 show the Montgomery County, Maryland, Department of Police Strategic Implementation Plan for moving to COPPS. Provided are the plan's vision statement (Exhibit 6-4), mission statement (Exhibit 6-5), statement of organizational values (Exhibit 6-6), and goals and objectives for the problem-solving strategy (Exhibit 6-7); additional goals and objectives are provided in the agency's planning document for accountability, partnership, and organizational development.

Exhibit 6-8 provides Montgomery County's strategies for implementing problem solving. The strategies are quite diverse and number about 30. In ad-

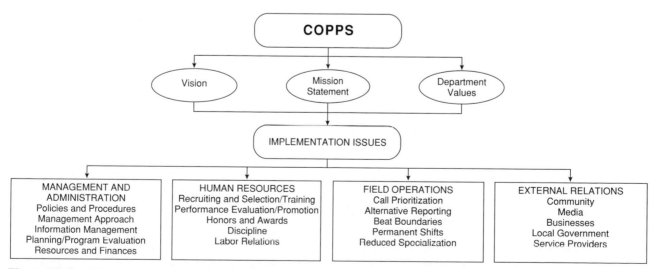

Figure 6-3. Principal Components of Implementation.

EXHIBIT 6-4   Vision Statement

The Montgomery County Police will provide the highest quality of police services by working in partnership with the community to improve the quality of life within Montgomery County, while at the same time maintaining respect for individual rights and human dignity. The Department recognizes the value and importance of its employees and will ensure that all employees are treated equitably and fairly. The Department is committed to providing its members with the quality of leadership, training, and equipment necessary to perform its mission.

EXHIBIT 6-5   Mission Statement

We, the Montgomery County Department of Police, are committed to providing the highest quality of police services by empowering our members and the community to work in partnership with the goal of improving the quality of life within Montgomery County, while at the same time maintaining respect for individual rights and human dignity.

EXHIBIT 6-6   Organizational Values

Partnership
We are committed to working in partnership with the community and each other to identify and resolve issues which impact public safety.

Respect
We are committed to respecting individual rights, human dignity, and the value of all members of the community and the department.

Integrity
We are committed to nurturing the public trust by holding ourselves accountable to the highest standards of professionalism and ethics.

Dedication
We are committed to providing the highest quality of professional law enforcement service to the community with the goal of enhancing the quality of life within Montgomery County.

Empowerment
We are committed to empowering our members and the community to resolve problems by creating an environment that encourages solutions that address the needs of the community.
. . . pride in our community, pride in our department, pride in ourselves.

EXHIBIT 6-7   Goal 2.0: Problem Solving

Community policing emphasizes the need for a problem solving approach to reduce the incidence and the fear of crime. In many instances, it will be more effective and efficient to spend several hours (or even days) to thoroughly address and eliminate a problem than it will be to repeatedly dispatch cars to the same call day after day, week after week, month after month, and in some cases, year after year.

Problem solving requires that officers be allowed to not only try the safe and proven traditional solutions, but also new, imaginative, and even unorthodox solutions. Not all solutions will be successful, as with any solution there is the risk of failure.

Risk taking is a necessity in community policing. Problem solving requires that the Department not only accept risk taking but encourage it. Employees should be commended for their successes and not chastised for their failures. A common axiom in community policing is "zero risk equals zero success."

2.0 Problem Solving
The analysis of a recurring problem to determine its cause and to devise solutions to permanently eliminate it. Problem solving also includes implementing the chosen solution. Problem solving involves risk taking.

Goal Objectives
2.1 Reduce fear of crime and conditions that contribute to crime and disorder through community policing strategies.
2.2 Reallocate individual and unit workloads to facilitate innovation and problem solving opportunities.
2.3 Establish a permanent planning unit to support and facilitate current and future departmental planning strategies.
2.4 Identify changes needed to existing laws and ordinances and propose new legislation to facilitate community policing strategies.

dition to the strategies shown in the exhibit, including training personnel, creating relevant manuals, expanding Neighborhood Watch programs, and developing a Community Services Section within each policing district, others include such tasks as using foot and bicycle patrols, initiating a new Arrest Processing and Transport Unit, adjusting patrol boundaries and beats following workload studies, beefing up the planning unit, and coordinating with other governmental agencies.

To further demonstrate the implementation process, Box 6-1 shows the specific sequential steps taken by the Baltimore, Maryland, police department toward implementation of its COPPS philosophy, following the development of appropriate vision, mission, and values statements for the department.

EXHIBIT 6-8 Goal 2.0: Problem Solving

Strategies	Time Frame (Years)	Fiscal Impact	Assignment of Responsibility
2.1.1 Institute a training program to train all members of the department in the concepts and philosophies of community policing. CALEA 33.6.2	Ongoing	Yes	Office of Comm. Policing Training
2.1.2 Develop a training manual for problem solving techniques. CALEA 33.6.2	Completed	No	Field Svcs. Bureau Office of Comm. Policing Training
2.1.3 Assign beat officers the responsibility of identifying problems within their beat and developing plans to remedy the problem. CALEA 41.2.1, 41.2.5, 54.2.4, 54.2.5	Immediate	No	Field Svcs. Bureau District Commanders
2.1.4 Increase district crime analysts' interaction with beat officers by jointly identifying crime patterns or problem areas through analysis. CALEA 15.1.6	Ongoing	No	Field Svcs. Bureau Central Crime Analyst District Crime Analysts District Commanders
2.1.5 Expand and publicize the Neighborhood Watch Programs. CALEA 45.2.2	1–2	Yes	Field Svcs. Bureau District Commanders Community Svcs. Section District Comm. Svcs. Officer
2.1.6 Reinstitute and publicize "Operation ID." CALEA 45.2.2	1–2	Yes	Field Svcs. Bureau District Commanders Crime Prevention Section District Comm. Svcs. Officer
2.1.7 Train patrol officers in specific skill areas of investigations and innovative investigative techniques. CALEA 33.6.2	1–2	Yes	Training Investigative Svcs. Bureau
2.1.8 Develop and maintain a Community Services Section within each district. This section will coordinate community meetings and serve as a liaison. CALEA 45.2.1	Completed	No	Field Svcs. Bureau District Commanders
2.1.9 Implement a training program to educate resident managers and rental property owners. CALEA 33.7.1	2–3	No	District Comm. Svcs. Officer

BOX 6-1

Implementation in Baltimore, Maryland

Several implementation issues had to be addressed. The values statement was widely disseminated across the community and the department. The public was challenged to come forth when they believed a value standard had been violated. The policing strategy became neighborhood-based and officers were shown that they were respected for the enormous contributions they could and did make to the community. Restructuring of the department, especially the Operations Bureau, was necessary. Each commander was given total responsibility for policing the neighborhoods in that district. There were a number of other important steps in the implementation sequence:

- *Fiscal support*: A commitment by the city was necessary to provide the department with the capital needed for maximum effectiveness, as well as a commitment by the department that resources would be carefully and effectively utilized.
- *Organizational structure and management systems*: The organizational hierarchy was flattened so that there was a minimum of supervisory and management levels between the police commissioner and the officers assigned to field service delivery in the city's neighborhoods. Investigative functions were decentralized as well, and civilianization was increased.
- *Community policing district deployment model*: Decisions had to be made concerning such matters as duties and job descriptions of COPPS officers, functions to be performed, staffing levels, and neighborhood boundaries.
- *Internal and external marketing:* The philosophy had to be marketed in order to succeed. All members of the department had to be oriented to the philosophy and massive changes had to be undertaken with regard to the department's handling of 911 CFS. The city council, other government agencies, and citizens were made fully aware of the changes proposed and positive results to be expected.
- *Deployment:* A new set of district and post boundaries were created that matched the major neighborhood areas of the city, ensuring that key "activity" centers (those areas generating the greatest number of CFS) were in the middle of districts and posts, thus providing for strong accountability for policing those areas. Patrol staffing was given the highest priority in the department.
- *Training:* COPPS training was developed for patrol officers and detectives, based on nationally recognized, state-of-the-art police problem-solving methodology. To support the curricula, new materials were developed reflecting the department's new orientation. Lieutenants, sergeants, and patrol officers were trained in facilitation and COPPS skills.
- *Interagency support:* A problem-solving methodology was developed to link all levels of the department with other agencies of government.
- *Quality control:* A new system was developed for evaluating police success at all levels—as a department, within a district, and on individual posts. A new set of performance standards was developed.
- *Recruitment and personnel management:* A new recruitment strategy was initiated that attracted young men and women to join the department, desiring to serve the community and become neighborhood COPPS officers. This ensured that the department remained on a "fast track" toward guaranteeing that the diversity of the community was reflected in all ranks.
- *Profiling neighborhoods:* Officers in each neighborhood of the city profiled their post, developing a "picture" of the neighborhood's priorities, resources, institutions, and problems of crime, fear, and violence. They also developed an action plan to address the neighborhood's concerns, in collaboration with local residents and businesspeople.

Source: Baltimore Police Department, *Implementation Task Force Report: Assessment of the Department* (Baltimore, Md.: Author, no date), pp. 10–12.

GENERAL OBSTACLES

Several possible obstacles that can militate against the implementation of COPPS have been identified:

1. *Police leadership*. Many police executives pride themselves on being hardline disciplinarians, unbending in the governance of their organizations. They may rule through coercion, fear, and intimidation. Their officers may be legalistic in

style and reactive in nature. There may be a distinct separation between labor and management, as well as an "us-versus-them" schism between the police and the public.

2. *Police organization.* Traditional crime-fighting organizational values provide a strong barrier to COPPS because, in order for implementation of COPPS to occur, the very core of the organization's culture must change (discussed in Chapter 7). There also exists in some organizations what has been termed a "small cadre of nonproductive, abusive malcontents." Not until police officers at all levels begin to clean house will the community accept them as trusting, civil, sensitive, and responsive representatives, which is a vital step toward implementing COPPS.

3. *Political leadership.* Politics are involved in every aspect of policing in America. Every jurisdiction is beholden to some extent to elected politicians, who in turn serve at the pleasure of their constituents. Politicians set the tone for the policing of a community.

4. *Community diversity.* Until officers can fully embrace our diverse communities, it is not likely that the concept can be implemented in those neighborhoods.[27]

Notwithstanding these conceivable obstacles, the potential for their coming into play and creating problems for COPPS implementation will be minimized if the guidelines provided earlier in this chapter are followed.

TEN WAYS TO UNDERMINE COPPS

In closing this chapter on implementation, Exhibit 6-9 offers for the tradition-bound chief John Eck's "ten things you can do to undermine" COPPS[28]—a prescription for preventing COPPS from gaining a foothold for many years to come. Many of these tactics are being practiced today, sometimes out of ignorance and sometimes intentionally. With apologies to the U.S. Surgeon General, we issue a prefatory warning: "Practicing these techniques in a police department may be hazardous to the health of community policing and problem solving."

EXHIBIT 6-9   Ten Ways to Undermine COPPS

1. *Oversell it:* COPPS should be sold as the panacea for every ill that plagues the city, the nation, and civilization. Some of the evils you may want to claim COPPS will eliminate are crime, fear of crime, racism, police misuse of force, homelessness, drug abuse, gangs, and other social problems. COPPS can address some of these concerns in specific situations, but by building up the hopes and expectations of the public, the press, and politicians, you can set the stage for later attacks on COPPS when it does not deliver.

2. *Don't be specific:* This suggestion is a corollary of the first principle. Never define what you mean by the following terms: community, service, effectiveness, empowerment, neighborhood, communication, problem solving. Use these and other terms indiscriminately, interchangeably, and whenever possible. At first, people will think the department is going to do something meaningful and won't ask for details. Once people catch on, you can blame the amorphous nature of COPPS and go back to what you were doing before.

3. *Create a special unit or group:* Less than 10 percent of the department should be engaged in this effort, lest COPPS really catch on. Since the "grand design" is possibly the return to conventional policing anyway (once everyone has attacked COPPS), there is no sense in involving more than a few officers. Also, special units are popular with the press and politicians.

4. *Create a soft image:* The best image for COPPS will be a uniformed female officer hugging a small child. This caring and maternal image will warm the hearts of community members suspicious of

(*continued*)

police, play to traditional stereotypes of sexism within policing, and turn off most cops.

5. *Leave the impression that COPPS is only for minority neighborhoods:* This is a corollary of items 3 and 4. Since a small group of officers will be involved, only a few neighborhoods can receive their services. Place the token COPPS officers in areas like public housing. With any luck, racial antagonism will undercut the approach. It will appear that minority, poor neighborhoods are not getting the "tough on crime" approach they need.

6. *Divorce COPPS officers from "regular" police work:* This is an expansion of the soft image concept. If the COPPS officers do not handle calls or make arrests, but instead throw block parties, speak to community groups, walk around talking to kids, visit schools, and so on, they will not be perceived as "real" police officers to their colleagues. This will further undermine their credibility and ability to accomplish anything of significance.

7. *Obfuscate means and ends:* Whenever describing COPPS, never make the methods for accomplishing the objective subordinate to the objective. Instead, make the means more important than the ends, or at least put them on equal footing. For example, to reduce drug dealing in a neighborhood, make certain that the tactics necessary (arrests, community meetings, etc.) are as important as, or more important than, the objective. These tactics can occupy everyone's time but still leave the drug problem unresolved. Always remember: The means are ends, in and of themselves.

8. *Present community members with problems and plans:* Whenever meeting with community members, officers should listen carefully and politely and then elaborate on how the department will enforce the law. If the community members like the plan, go ahead. If they do not, continue to be polite and ask them to go on a ride-along or witness a drug raid. This avoids having to change the department's operations while demonstrating how difficult police work is, and why nothing can be accomplished. In the end, they will not get their problems solved, but will see how nice the police are.

9. *Never try to understand why problems occur:* Do not let officers gain knowledge about the underlying causes of the problems; COPPS should not include any analysis of the problem and as little information as possible should be sought from the community. Keep officers away from computer terminals; mandate that officers get permission to talk to members of any other agency; do not allow COPPS officers to go off their assigned areas to collect information; prevent access to research conducted on similar problems; suppress listening skills.

10. *Never publicize a success:* Some rogue officers will not get the message and will go out anyway and gather enough information to solve problems. Try to ignore these examples of effective policing and make sure that no one else hears about them. When you cannot ignore them, describe them in the least meaningful way (item 2). Talk about the wonders of empowerment and community meetings. Describe the hours of foot patrol, the new mountain bikes, or shoulder patches. In every problem solved, there is usually some tactic or piece of equipment that can be highlighted at the expense of the accomplishment itself. When all else fails, reprimand the COPPS officer for not wearing a hat.

Source: John E. Eck, "Helpful Hints for the Tradition-Bound Chief," *Fresh Perspectives* (Washington, D.C.: Police Executive Research Forum, June 1992):1–7.

SUMMARY

This chapter has shown how to plan and implement the COPPS concept after assessing community needs and developing a planning document. Four keys to successful implementation—management and administration, human resources, field operations, and external relations—were examined, and we considered several obstacles that can undermine COPPS.

It should be evident that there is no substitute for having a well-thought-out, well laid-out plan of implementation for the COPPS philosophy. As with any new venture, there must be a "road map" to show the executive and the agency how to travel the highway in order to reach the ultimate destination.

NOTES

1. Robert Trojanowicz, quoted in Harry Sloan, Grand Rapids, Michigan, Police Department Web page, *http://www.grpolice.grand-rapids.mi.us/default .htm,* October 20, 2000, p. 1.

2. Eton Lawrence, "Strategic Thinking: A Discussion Paper," Research Directorate, Policy, Research, and Communications Branch, Public Service Commission of Canada, Ottawa, Ontario, Canada, April 27, 1999, p. 6.

3. Ibid., pp. 6–7.

4. Ibid.

5. Loizos Heracleous, "Strategic Thinking or Strategic Planning?" *Long Range Planning* 31 (June 1998):481–487.

6. Internet Nonprofit Center, "What Is Strategic Planning?" (San Francisco, Calif.: Author, Support Center, 2000), p. 1.

7. "Brief History of Strategic Planning," *http://www.des .calstate.edu/glossary.html,* September 24, 2000, p. 2.

8. *http://www.usdoj.gov/jmd/mps/strategic2000_2005/ index.htm.*

9. Aspen, Colorado, Police Department, "Organizational Change and Community Policing," *http:// www.jus.state.nc.us.ncja/module-4* (Accessed February 24, 2003).

10. Herman Goldstein, *Problem-Oriented Policing* (New York: McGraw-Hill, 1990), p. 172.

11. Gregory Saville and D. Kim Rossmo, "Striking a Balance: Lessons from Community-Oriented Policing in British Columbia, Canada" (unpublished manuscript, June 1993), pp. 29–30.

12. Charles S. Bullock and Charles M. Lamb (eds.), *Implementation of Civil Rights Policy* (Monterey, Calif.: Brooks/Cole, 1984).

13. Ronald W. Glensor and Kenneth J. Peak, "Implementing Change: Community-Oriented Policing and Problem Solving," *FBI Law Enforcement Bulletin* 7 (July 1996):14–20.

14. John E. Eck and William Spelman, *Problem-Solving: Problem-Oriented Policing in Newport News* (Washington, D.C.: Police Executive Research Forum, 1987), pp. 100–101.

15. Malcolm K. Sparrow, *Implementing Community Policing* (Washington, D.C.: National Institute of Justice, "Perspectives on Policing," no. 9, November 1988), pp. 2–3.

16. George L. Kelling and William J. Bratton, *Implementing Community Policing: The Administrative Problem* (Washington, D.C.: U.S. Department of Justice, National Institute of Justice, "Perspectives on Policing," no. 17, July 1993), p. 4.

17. Ibid., p. 9.

18. Ibid., p. 11.

19. Sparrow, *Implementing Community Policing*, pp. 4–5.

20. Ibid., p. 5.

21. Ibid., p. 6.

22. Ibid., p. 7.

23. Sylvia Aguilar, "Detectives and Community Oriented Policing," *Law and Order* (September 2002): 222–225.

24. Jesse Rubin, "Police Identity and the Police Role." In *Issues in Police Patrol: A Book of Readings,* Thomas J. Sweeney and William Ellingsworth (eds.) (Kansas City, Mo.: Kansas City Police Department, 1973); John Van Maanen, "Police Socialization: A Longitudinal Examination of Job Attitudes in an Urban Police Department," *Administrative Science Quarterly* 20 (1975):207–228.

25. Don Cassano and Carol Smith, *Establishing and Sustaining Political Support for Problem Oriented/Community Policing* (Tempe, Ariz.: Tempe City Council Representatives, 1992), p. 74.

26. Ibid., pp. 74–75.

27. Adapted from George E. Rush, "Community Policing: Overcoming the Obstacles," *The Police Chief* (October 1992):50, 52, 54–55.

28. John E. Eck, "Helpful Hints for the Tradition-Bound Chief," *Fresh Perspectives* (Washington, D.C.: Police Executive Research Forum, June 1992):1–7.

INTRODUCTION

Police agencies have a life and culture of their own. Powerful forces have a much stronger influence over how a department conducts its business than do managers of the department, the courts, legislatures, politicians, and members of the community. As Herman Goldstein observed, "Against this background, many of the exhortations for change do, indeed, look naive, and the elaborate schemes for 'improving the police' unlikely to succeed."[1] Nonetheless, willingness to change is a fundamental requirement of community oriented policing and problem solving (COPPS); police agencies must modify their culture from top to bottom. This chapter addresses that agency imperative. Change is never easy, however, because there is so much uncertainty accompanying it.

We begin this chapter with a discussion of change within organizations generally, including some obstacles to innovation and the requirements of effecting smooth, planned change. Then we turn specifically to change in police organizations, beginning with a look at some lessons learned and how change must occur to accommodate COPPS. The roles of three key leaders in this process—chief executives (and their precarious political position as innovators), middle managers, and rank-and-file officers—are then covered, including how sufficient time may be allocated for the latter to engage in problem-solving activities. In this vein we also examine some methods and challenges involved with recruiting problem solvers under the COPPS philosophy. We conclude the chapter with some case studies of agencies that have modified their culture for adopting the COPPS approach.

—7—

FROM RECRUIT TO CHIEF

Changing the Agency Culture

Where there is no vision, a people perish.
—Ralph Waldo Emerson

THE KEY TO THE CHANGE PROCESS: "LEARNING ORGANIZATIONS"

To help to effect change in their organizations, police administrators are increasingly turning to the writings of Peter Senge, who studied how firms and organizations develop adaptive capabilities and who developed the vision of a "learning organization," which evolved into a book that popularized the concept, *The Fifth Discipline*.[2]

Senge said that learning organizations are those

> where people continually expand their capacity to create the results they truly desire, where new and expansive patterns of thinking are nurtured, where collective aspiration is set free, and where people are continually learning to see the whole together.[3]

The basic rationale for such organizations is that in situations of rapid change only those that are flexible, adaptive, and productive will excel. For this to happen, organizations need to "discover how to tap people's commitment and capacity to learn at all levels."[4]

For Senge, real learning is necessary because it gets to the heart of what it is to be human and to re-create ourselves. Succinctly put, certain basic disciplines must be mastered, however:

- Systemic thinking—we need to focus on the whole rather than the parts of the organization, and remember that we learn from our experiences
- Personal mastery—organizations learn only through individuals who learn, continually clarifying and deepening our personal vision, focusing our energies, and seeing reality objectively
- Mental models—deeply ingrained assumptions and generalizations influence how we understand the world; we need to hold them rigorously to scrutiny so that people can learn new skills and develop new orientations
- Building a shared vision—people must have the capacity to hold a shared picture of the future in order to excel and learn (the development of a police organizational vision for COPPS was discussed in Chapter 6)
- Team learning—the process of developing the capacities of the team creates results that its members truly desire.[5]

In sum, the learning organization requires a new view of leadership; they are responsible for building organizations where people continually expand their capabilities to understand complexity, clarify vision, and improve shared mental models. Leaders do not teach, but foster learning.

This is the crux of influential writings of Chris Argyris,[6] who believed that people need more activity, relative independence, and greater awareness of themselves to control their own destiny. Argyris viewed an effective organization as one requiring employees to be self-responsible, self-directed, and self-motivated, and noted that the organization has a responsibility to structure the work environment so that employees can grow to become mature. Argyris believed that organizational factors have more impact on work satisfaction than individual characteristics; his theory also suggests that police agencies would be more productive if they moved away from the military model–which one contemporary author said Argyris would likely feel is "futile, empty, and unproductive."[7] In order to create learning organizations in law enforcement, it is important to have an integrative and futuristic approach to planning, and to overcome or at least minimize organizational barriers to change: professional jealousy, problems with staff recruitment and training, and change resistance. Well-planned, gradual change is the least disruptive and most productive way of achieving organizational change.[8]

Organizational change and change process are discussed more below, and the concept of learning organizations is discussed more in Chapter 8, which deals with training.

CHANGE IN ORGANIZATIONS: A FORMULA

Organizational change occurs when an organization adopts new ideas or behaviors.[9] Any change in the organization involves an attempt to persuade employees to change their behavior and their relationships with one another. Therefore, it is not surprising that most people find change uncomfortable. Studies on change in organizations have shown that only about 10 percent of the people in most organizations will actively embrace change. Approximately 80 percent will wait to be convinced or wait until the change is unavoidable.

The remaining 10 percent will actively resist change. For these people, change is very upsetting; they may even seek to subvert or sabotage the process.[10]

This resistance to change is reflected in the "change equation":[11] Discomfort (the case for change) + Vision + Steps must be greater than Resistance to change).

$$D + V + S > R$$

D includes those compelling reasons for and against change in an agency or community, such as existing supports for and barriers against change. *V* requires the leadership to consider changes that will have to occur with respect to related public institutions, management practices, individual behaviors, organizational culture, and the community at large. *S* includes those steps that must be developed in order to leverage supports and overcome barriers to change.[12]

Usually when change is proposed, an innovative idea is introduced and behavioral changes are supposed to follow. Consequently, the ultimate success of any organizational change depends on how well the organization can alter the behavioral patterns of its employees. Employee behavior is influenced by factors such as leadership styles, motivational techniques, informal relationships, and organization and job design. To bring about timely change, managers need to consider why people resist change and how resistance can be overcome.[13]

As indicated earlier, probably the most common characteristic of change is people's resistance to it. Generally, people do not like to change their behavior, and adaptation to a new environment or methods often results in feelings of stress or other forms of psychological discomfort. Resistance to change is likely when employees do not clearly understand the purpose, mechanics, or consequences of a planned change because of inadequate or misperceived communication. If employees are not told how they will be affected by change, rumors and speculation will follow, and resistance and even sabotage can ensue.[14]

Those who resist change are sometimes coerced into accepting it. Although coercion may be immediately effective and lead to compliance, the long-range results will certainly be harmful. Change in police agencies, particularly major

Decentralized decision-making is a key to the success of COPPS.

changes, are frequently characterized by the use of centralized decision making and coercive tactics. Management and employees often have an adversarial relationship. Management might assume that because many employees do not understand the need for the change and will resist it anyway, there is no need to involve them in the process, and they must be forced to go along. Some managers might even hope that those persons resisting the change will retire or resign. These are inappropriate assumptions; coercion should be used as a last resort.[15]

By using task forces, ad hoc committees, group seminars, and other participatory techniques, employees can become directly involved in planning for change. By thoroughly discussing and debating the issues, an accurate understanding and unbiased analysis of the situation is likely to result.[16]

REQUIREMENTS FOR PLANNED CHANGE

Psychologist Kurt Lewin is often considered the father of modern organizational change theory. He coined the term *group dynamics* and was one of the first people to observe that leader behavior could shape culture during organizational change. Working with anthropologist Margaret Mead during World War II, Lewin established the concept of participative management: People are more likely to modify their own behavior and carry out decisions when they participate in problem analysis and solution.

Lewin believed change was a three-phase process: unfreezing, changing, and refreezing (see Table 7-1). He believed that people are naturally resistant to change, but meanwhile the environment is changing. To create change, "unfreezing" the organization is necessary; this includes overcoming the negative forces that cause people to resist change through new or disconcerting information. "Changing" is the change in attitudes, values, feelings, and behaviors of the people, and it occurs when people discuss and plan new actions. "Refreezing" occurs when the organization reaches a new status quo, with the support mechanisms in place to maintain the desired behaviors.

Any police executive contemplating change should do so in a manner that offers the greatest possibility of success. As Charles Swanson, Leonard Territo, and Robert Taylor noted:

> Conventional wisdom about change states that the way to change an organization is to bring in a new top executive, give the individual his or her head (and maybe a hatchet), and let the individual make the changes that he or she deems necessary. What the conventional wisdom overlooks are the long-term consequences of unilateral, top-down change.[17]

The problem, then, with radical and unilateral change is the possibility of a severe backlash in the organization; a complementary problem for changes that are made very gradually is that after many months or a few years of meetings,

TABLE 7-1. Lewin's Process Model of Change

Unfreezing	Changing	Refreezing
The process by which people become aware of the need for change	The movement from the old way of doing things to a new way	Making new behaviors relatively permanent and resistant to change

discussion, and planning sessions, nothing much has actually happened in the organization. Finding an appropriate pace for change to occur—neither too quickly and radically nor too slowly and gradually—is one of the most critical problems of planned organizational change. The readiness of the organization for change is a problem for which no easy resolutions are available.[18]

Sometimes a great deal can be learned by studying the success and failure patterns of organizations that have undertaken planned change. A survey of 18 studies of organizational change found the following "successful" change patterns:

- being spread throughout the organization
- producing positive changes in line and staff attitudes
- prompting people to behave more effectively in solving problems
- resulting in improved organizational performance[19]

CHANGE IN POLICE ORGANIZATIONS

Lessons Learned   Change is difficult for any organization, and is particularly so for police departments, which are paramilitary, bureaucratic, and somewhat socially isolated from the community. How did change come about in those many agencies that have adopted COPPS? A general transition process appears to have emerged.

First, the agencies recognized that traditional approaches did not succeed. Second was a change in attitude about the functions of administrators, line personnel, and citizens. Third, community assessments were performed to identify new police responsibilities. Fourth, new organizational and operational approaches were conceived to meet the newly defined police responsibilities. And fifth, the community was enlisted to work cooperatively with the police to achieve the desired results.[20]

Lessons were also learned about the *political environment* in which police administrators managed change, including the following:

1. There must be a stimulus for change. A leader must have a vision, be willing to take the first step in challenging the status quo and involve people at all levels, and maintain that commitment (reallocating resources, amending policies and procedures, experimenting with new ideas).
2. Change must be grounded in logical and defensible criteria as opposed to effecting change just to "shake things up" in the organization.
3. There must be sufficient time for experimentation, evaluation, and fine-tuning of new ideas.
4. Remember that major change might require a generation; people tend to be impatient, but resocialization of employees and citizens is a long-term endeavor requiring patience and stamina.
5. Recognize that not everyone will "buy into" new ideas.
6. Be flexible in your view of change. Many ideas are "losers," so we must maintain the freedom to fail, even though in our culture success is often mandated.
7. Remember that change carries risks, and that change agents might be placed on the "hot seat" to explain new endeavors; in short, one's political neck may be on the line.
8. Organizational personnel evaluation systems must measure and reward effective involvement in change. Benefits do not have to be monetary, but can

include such things as positive reinforcement, creative freedom, and awards or commendations.

Avoiding the "Bombshell" Technique

Police organizations develop considerable inertia and can develop a resistance to change. Having a strong personal commitment to the values with which they have "grown up" in the organization, patrol officers may find any hint of proposed change in the department extremely threatening. Therefore, the chief executive who simply announces that COPPS is now the order of the day—dropping the "bombshell"—without a carefully designed plan for implementing that change is in danger of "losing traction" and of throwing the entire force into confusion. Additionally, the chief executive confronts a host of difficult issues: What structural changes are needed, if any? How do we get the people on the beat to behave differently? What should we tell the public and when? How fast can we bring about this change? Do we have enough external support?[21]

Changing Organizational Values

A related subject is that of values in police organizations, discussed briefly in Chapter 6. All organizations have values—the beliefs that guide an organization and the behavior of its employees.[22] Police departments are powerfully influenced by their values, and policing styles reflect a department's values.

COPPS reflects a set of values rather than a technical orientation toward the police function. There is a service orientation, which means that citizens are to be treated with respect at all times. And when riding in patrol vehicles, supervisors and managers must listen for the "talk of the department" to determine whether values expressed by officers reflect those of the department.

Also, values are no longer hidden but serve as the basis for citizen understanding of the police function, judgments of police success, and employee understanding of what the police agency seeks to achieve.[23] Values are a guidepost by which the agency will provide service to the community and a means by which the community can evaluate the agency.

The Honolulu police department displays its values—"Integrity/Respect/Fairness"—on its vehicles.

CHANGING TO COPPS

**Potential
for Resistance
and Conflict**

As Fresno, California, police chief Jerry Dyer has observed, managing change in police agencies is not working as it should, for a variety of reasons: officers and labor unions block change by claiming memorandum of agreement violations, filing grievances, utilizing their political influence with council members, or making calls to local news media outlets. Such obstacles my prevent many police leaders from seeking change in their organizations.[24] (Fresno's reorganization effort, and that of the Boston police department, are discussed in the Case Studies section of the chapter, below.)

In the many jurisdictions where COPPS has been implemented and is flourishing and succeeding, however, the traditional orthodoxy of policing, rooted in military command and scientific management theory, had to be changed. In short, the traditional orthodoxy became "taboo."[25] This included management style, performance measures (as one author put it, "Bean-counting performance measures have little meaning in such a system"),[26] and disciplinary measures.[27] A new, required leadership style meant (1) a shift from telling and controlling employees to helping them develop their skills and abilities; (2) listening to the customers in new and more open ways; (3) solving problems, not just reacting to incidents; (4) trying new things and experimenting, realizing that risk taking and honest mistakes must be tolerated to encourage creativity and achieve innovation; and (5) avoiding, whenever possible, the use of coercive power to effect change.[28]

A Washington State University graduate student determined that the three most significant reactions by Spokane officers to the shift to community policing were

> *Meaning:* Some officers saw community policing as a way of validating who they were, allowing them to do the kind of policing they believed they should have been doing all along.

> *Resistance:* Community policing, being a philosophy rather than a program, made it more difficult for management to describe, so some officers who were said to be resistant were merely trying to determine what community policing meant in relation to how they were currently doing their jobs.

> *Sabotage:* Some employees went beyond resistance, engaging in sabotage and being obstructionist; some supervisors would wait until a ranking officer was out of earshot and then proceed to tell their staff "how it's really going to be."[29]

**"We're Too Busy
to Change"**

It is not uncommon for consultants to go into police agencies to assist in implementing or training COPPS and be told, "We're too busy for community policing and problem solving." As William Geller and Guy Swanger noted, it may be true in some organizations that people are too busy to change; this, they said, may be the case

> if the senior leadership insists that middle managers continue doing all the old things they shouldn't be doing plus all the new things they should. The classic problem here is being too busy bailing out the boat to fix the hole in the hull.[30]

Indeed, preoccupation with the task at hand prevents people from pausing to reflect critically on whether what they are doing has any value. As Price Pritchett and Ron Pound observed, "Ditch those duties that don't count much, even if you can do them magnificently well."[31] Beliefs that police are too busy to change can be compounded by fears that COPPS will only intensify the workload. But when the community is an organized, active partner in problem

The following text is taken from the "Community Policing Tutorial" home page of the Santa Clara, California, police department. It presents the reasons the department believes it is time to change to COPPS:

- Public safety is a citywide concern. Crime and disorder in our neighborhoods, parks, and business districts cause citizen frustration, uneasiness, and fear.
- Traditionally, police respond to calls, investigate crimes, and make arrests. This process alone does not reduce crime.

- Crime and public safety issues are community problems. They require the commitment of the community and the police to solve them together.
- The police department is committed to developing a strong relationship with the citizens of Santa Clara through community policing.

Source: Santa Clara, California, Police Department, "What Is Community Policing?" *http://www.scpd.org/community_policing_pg5.htm* (Accessed January 7, 2004).

---

solving, the problem-solving process is not as labor intensive for the police as some have asserted.[32] (Exhibit 7-1 shows how one police department got the community involved in its change to COPPS.)

ROLES OF KEY LEADERS

In Chapter 6 and earlier in this chapter we discussed briefly the roles of chief executives, middle managers, and first-line supervisors in the implementation of COPPS. Here we briefly examine their respective roles in the change process.

The Chief Executive as Change Agent

Risk Takers and Boat Rockers

Of course, the police chief executive is ultimately responsible for all of the facets of COPPS, from implementation to training to evaluation. Therefore, what is needed are chief executives who are willing to do things that have not been done before, or, as one writer put it, "risk takers and boat rockers within a culture where daily exposure to life-or-death situations makes officers natural conservators of the status quo."[33]

These are chief executives who become committed to getting the police and neighborhoods to work together to attack the roots of crime. For them, "Standing still is not only insufficient . . . it is going backwards."[34]

Therefore, police executives must be *viable change agents*. In any hierarchy the person at the top is responsible for setting both the policy and tone of the organization. Within a police agency the chief or sheriff has the ultimate power to make change, particularly one as substantive as COPPS. The chief executive must be both visible and credible and must create a climate conducive to change. Under COPPS, chief executives must focus on the vision, values, mission (all three were discussed in Chapter 6), and long-term goals of policing in order to create an organizational environment that enables officers, government officials, and community members to work together. By building consensus, they can establish programs, develop timelines, and set priorities. They should honor the good work done in the past but exhibit a sense of urgency about implementing change while involving people from the community and the department in all stages of the transition. The chief executive's roles and responsibilities during the change to COPPS include the following:

- articulating a clear vision to the organization
- understanding and accepting the depth of change and time required to implement COPPS
- assembling a management team that is committed to translating the new vision into action
- being committed to removing bureaucratic obstacles whenever possible

Many police organizations boast talented and creative chief executives who, when participating in the change process, will assist in effecting change that is beneficial and lasting. As James Q. Wilson put it,

> The police profession today is the intellectual leadership of the criminal justice profession in the United States. The police are in the lead. They're showing the world how things might better be done.[35]

Middle Managers

Middle managers—lieutenants and captains—also play a crucial role in the operation of a COPPS philosophy. COPPS's emphasis on problem solving necessitates that middle managers draw on their familiarity with the bureaucracy to secure, maintain, and use authority to empower subordinates, helping officers to actively and creatively confront and resolve issues, sometimes using unconventional approaches on a trial-and-error basis.

There are many really significant contributions middle managers can make to the changing culture of the agency to embrace and sustain COPPS. First, they must *build on the strengths* of their subordinates, capitalizing on their training and competence.[36] They do so by treating people as individuals and creating talented teams.[37] They must "cheerlead," encouraging supervisors and patrol officers to actually solve the problems they are confronting.[38] It is also imperative that middle managers *not* believe they are serving the chief executive's best interests by preserving the status quo. The lieutenants are the gatekeepers and must develop the system, resources, and support mechanisms to ensure that the officers, detectives, and supervisors can perform to achieve the best results. The officers and supervisors cannot perform without the necessary equipment, resources, and reinforcement.[39]

Middle managers, like their subordinates, must be allowed the freedom to make mistakes. And good middle managers protect their subordinates from organizational and political recrimination and scapegoating when things go wrong. Put another way, middle managers cannot stand idly by while their people are led to the guillotine, and they must protect their officers from the political effects of legitimate failure.[40] They must not allow their problem-solving officers to revert to traditional methods. They must be diplomats and facilitators, using a lot more persuading and negotiating (toward win-win solutions) than they did under the traditional "my way or the highway" management style.

The roles and responsibilities of middle managers during the change to COPPS include the following:

- assuming responsibility for strategic planning
- eliminating red tape and bottlenecks that impede the work of officers and supervisors
- conducting regular meetings with subordinates to discuss plans, activities, and results
- assessing COPPS efforts in a continuous manner

The general role and outlook for middle managers in a COPPS environment were well described by Kelling and Bratton, who stated that

> The idea that mid-managers are spoilers, that they thwart project or strategic innovation, has some basis in fact. Mid-managers improperly directed can significantly impede innovation. Yet, ample evidence exists that when a clear vision of the business

of the organization is put forward, when mid-managers are included in planning, when their legitimate self-interests are acknowledged, and when they are properly trained, mid-managers can be the leading edge of innovation and creativity.[41]

It is widely held that the most challenging aspect of changing the culture of a police agency lies in changing the attitudes and beliefs of first-line supervisors. The influence of first-line supervisors is so strong that their role warrants special attention.

First-Line Supervisors

The Ultimate Challenge

The primary contact of street officers with their organization is through their sergeant. Indeed, the quality of an officer's daily life is often dependent on his or her immediate supervisor. Most officers do not believe their sergeants are sources of guidance and direction but rather are authority figures to be satisfied (by numbers of arrests and citations, manner in which reports are completed, officer's ability to avoid citizen complaints, and so on). There is just cause for the reluctance of first-line supervisors to avoid change. Herman Goldstein stated that

> Changing the operating philosophy of rank-and-file officers is easier than altering a first-line supervisor's perspective of his or her job, because the work of a sergeant is greatly simplified by the traditional form of policing. The more routinized the work, the easier it is for the sergeant to check. The more emphasis placed on rank and the symbols of position, the easier it is for the sergeant to rely on authority—rather than intellect and personal skills—to carry out [his or her] duties. . . . [S]ergeants are usually appalled by descriptions of the freedom and independence suggested in problem oriented policing for rank-and-file officers. The concept can be very threatening to them. This . . . can create an enormous block to implementation.[42]

Supervisors must be convinced that COPPS makes good sense in today's environment. And they should possess the "Characteristics of a Good Problem Oriented Supervisor," as shown in Exhibit 7-2.

COPPS is not soft on crime—and first-line supervisors are key to its success. (*Courtesy* Washoe County, Nevada, Sheriff's Office)

EXHIBIT 7-2 Characteristics of a Good Problem Oriented Supervisor

1. Allowing subordinates freedom to experiment with new approaches.
2. Insisting on good, accurate analyses of problems.
3. Granting flexibility in work schedules when requests are appropriate.
4. Allowing subordinates to make most contacts directly and paving the way when they are having trouble getting cooperation.
5. Protecting subordinates from pressures within the department to revert to traditional methods.
6. Running interference for subordinates to secure resources, protect them from criticism, and so forth.
7. Knowing what problems subordinates are working on and whether the problems are real.
8. Knowing subordinates' beats and important citizens in it, and expecting subordinates to know it even better.
9. Coaching subordinates through the process, giving advice, helping them manage their time.
10. Monitoring subordinates' progress and, as necessary, prodding them along or slowing them down.
11. Supporting subordinates even if their strategies fail, so long as something useful is learned in the process and the process was well thought through.
12. Managing problem-solving efforts over a long period of time; not allowing efforts to die simply because they get sidetracked by competing demands for time and attention.
13. Giving credit to subordinates and letting others know about their good work.
14. Allowing subordinates to talk with visitors or at conferences about their work.
15. Identifying new resources and contacts for subordinates and making them check them out.
16. Stressing cooperation, coordination, and communication within the unit and outside it.
17. Coordinating efforts across shifts, beats, and outside units and agencies.
18. Realizing that this style of policing cannot simply be ordered; officers and detectives must come to believe in it.

Source: Police Executive Research Forum, "Supervising Problem-Solving" (Washington, D.C.: Author, training outline, 1990).

The roles and responsibilities of first-line supervisors during a change to COPPS include the following:

- understanding and practicing problem solving
- managing time, staff, and resources
- encouraging teamwork
- helping officers to mobilize stakeholders
- tracking and managing officers' problem solving
- providing officers with ongoing feedback and support

Another matter implicating police supervisory personnel concerns the amount of time required for patrol officers to engage in problem-solving activities. We examine that issue next.

"Recapturing Officers' Time" for Problem Solving

One of the ongoing controversies with respect to COPPS—as noted in the "We're Too Busy to Change" section earlier—concerns whether police officers can garner the time required to engage in problem-solving activities. On the one hand, officers complain that they are going from call to call and have little time for anything else. On the other hand, administrators say there is plenty of time for problem solving because calls account for only 50 to 60 percent of an officer's time.

Who is right? According to Tom McEwen,[43] both sides are correct. Table 7-2 describes a hypothetical workload during a unit's shift. In the example shown in the table, the unit starts the shift at 4:00 P.M. and receives an accident call

TABLE 7-2. Example of a Unit's Workload During a Shift

Activity	Time Dispatched	Time Cleared	Time on Call	Time to Next Call
Start of shift	4:00 P.M.			14 minutes
Accident	4:14	4:44 P.M.	30 minutes	18
Robbery	5:02	5:18	16	17
Suspicious activity	5:35	6:38	63	32
Family problem	7:10	7:40	30	28
Theft	8:08	8:26	18	10
Alarm	8:36	8:46	10	47
Emotionally disturbed person	9:33	11:21	108	17
Unwanted person	11:38	11:49	11	11
End of Shift	12:00 A.M.			
Total			286 minutes	194 minues

at 4:14 P.M., which takes until 4:44 P.M. (30 minutes). The next call (robbery) comes in at 5:02 P.M., which means 18 minutes elapsed between calls. The pattern continues throughout the shift, alternating between handling calls for service and having time for other activities. In total, the unit devotes 4 hours 46 minutes (286 minutes) to calls, with the remaining 3 hours 14 minutes (194 minutes) available for other activities.

The time between calls is the key element of the argument as to whether officers have time for problem solving. In this example, more than three hours are available for other activities. An administrator would be correct in pointing out that there is plenty of time available. However, the available time is spread throughout the shift, varying from 10 minutes between calls to 47 minutes. If we assume a problem-solving project takes 45 minutes, then the officer in this unit has only one block of uninterrupted time for an assignment. (Note: Clearly not all problem-solving projects take 45 minutes each day. Some days, all that is needed is 10 minutes to complete a phone call to, perhaps, a building inspector. On other days, such as Friday or Saturday nights, no work will be done on problem oriented policing (POP). POP projects have no due dates; therefore, problem-solving efforts might be best thought of as being accomplished in bits and pieces, not over the course of a day but over the course of a longer period of time. Departments, however, should be striving to find uninterrupted time for officers so that officers can increase their proactive responsibilities.)

The average time between calls is 21 minutes. Officers believe they are going from call to call with no time for anything else because of the relatively short periods of time between calls.

Of course, not all units or shifts will have the same experience as in this example. Time between calls varies considerably depending on the number of calls for a particular shift, the types of calls, and how much time they require. One or two fewer calls can make a big difference in whether there will be stretches of uninterrupted time.

Obviously, citizen calls are important and cannot be ignored. But the aim should be to handle citizen calls in an expeditious manner. The following four methods can be used to overcome the problem of finding time for problem solving while still handling calls effectively.

1. *Allow units to perform problem-solving assignments as self-initiated activities.* Under this approach, a unit would contact the dispatcher and go out of service for a problem solving assignment. The unit would be interrupted only for an emergency call in its area of responsibility. Otherwise, the dispatcher would hold nonemergency calls until the unit becomes available or send a unit from an adjacent area after holding the call for a predetermined amount of time.

2. *Schedule one or two units to devote a predetermined part of their shift to problem solving.* As an example, a supervisor could designate one or two units each day to devote the first half of their shift or even only one hour to problem solving. Their calls would be handled by other units so that they have an uninterrupted block of time for problems. Of course, this approach means that the other units will be busier. The tradeoff is that problem solving gets done and the supervisor can rotate the units designated for these activities.

3. *Take more reports over the telephone.* Many departments take certain nonemergency complaints by telephone rather than dispatch a patrol unit. The information about the incident is recorded on a department report form and entered in the department's information system as an incident or crime. The average telephone report taker can process four times as many report calls per hour compared to a field unit. The department might increase the types of calls handled by telephone, or the staffing for a telephone report unit can be increased to cover more hours of the day.

4. *Review the department policy on "assist" units.* In some departments, several units show up at the scene of a call even though they are not needed. Some units assist out of boredom or curiosity. The units may initiate themselves out of service to assist or the dispatcher may send several units to the scene. This problem is particularly acute with alarm calls. Many departments have a policy of dispatching two or more units to alarms, even when the source has a long history of false alarms. A department should undergo a detailed study on the types of calls for which assist units are actually appearing, with the aim of reducing the number of assists and discouraging officers from assisting other units unless it is necessary.

As a more general approach, a department should review its patrol plan to determine whether units are fielded in proportion to workload. Time between calls is a function not only of the number of incoming calls but also of the number of units in the field. More units result in more time between calls.

Indeed, we can calculate the number of units needed to ensure that the time between calls averages, for example, 35 minutes. A department may also want to consider changes in officer schedules to facilitate overlapping during busy times of the day; however, adjustments within a shift may be the more effective approach.

Delaying response time to calls for service can also provide more time for officers. For example, by refining the manner in which 911 calls are dispatched in non-life-threatening cases, responses may be significantly reduced annually.[44]

Response time research implied that rapid responses were not needed for most calls. Furthermore, dispatchers can advise citizens of an officer's arrival time. Slower police responses to nonemergency calls has been found satisfactory to citizens if dispatchers tell citizens an officer might not arrive right away.

Managers have also garnered more time for officers by having nonsworn employees handle noncrime incidents.[45]

Time between calls is an important, but frequently overlooked, element of any problem-solving strategy. The overall aim should be to provide officers with uninterrupted amounts of time for problem-solving assignments. There are many ways to accomplish this aim, but they require a concerted planning effort by the department.

Box 7-1 shows the 15-step exercise developed for police managers to recapture officers' time while working in a problem-solving framework. If during the "recapturing time" exercise a police manager finds potential ways to effectively solve problems and recapture time lost to repetitive incidents, then problem oriented policing may be a smart approach.

BOX 7-1

A 15-Step Exercise for Recapturing Officers' Time

1. Assemble a group of patrol officers and emergency communications center personnel representing each shift.

2. Have each of them write down three to five locations where the police respond regularly to deal with the same general problem and people repeatedly.

3. Determine the average number of responses to those locations per month and approximately how long the problem has existed.

4. Determine the average number of officers who respond each time to those incidents.

5. Determine the average length of time involved in handling the incidents.

6. Using the information from 3, 4, and 5, determine the total number of staff hours devoted to each of these problem locations. Do this for the week, month, and year.

7. Identify all the key players that either participate in or are affected by the problem—all direct and indirect participants and groups such as the complaining parties, victims, witnesses, property owners and managers, and bystanders.

8. Through a roundtable discussion, decide what it is about the particular location that allows or encourages the problem to exist and continue.

9. Develop a list of things that have been done in the past to try to deal with the problem, and a candid assessment of why each has not worked.

10. In a free-flowing brainstorming session, develop as many traditional and nontraditional solutions to the problem as possible. Try to include alternative sources like other government and private agencies that could be involved in the solution. Encourage creative thinking and risk taking.

11. After you have completed the brainstorming session, consider which of those solutions are: (a) illegal, (b) immoral, (c) impractical, (d) unrealistic, or (e) not affordable.

12. Eliminate all those that fall in categories a and b.

13. For those that fall in categories c, d, and e, figure out if those reasons are because you are thinking in conventional terms like "We've never done it this way," "It won't work," "It can't be done." If you are satisfied that those solutions truly are impractical, unrealistic, or not affordable, then eliminate them, too. If there is a glimmer of hope that some may have merit with just a little different thinking or approach, then leave them.

14. For each remaining possible solution, list what would have to be done and who would have to be involved to make it happen. Which of those solutions and actions could be implemented relatively soon and with a minimum of difficulty?

15. If the solution were successful, consider the productive things officers could do with the time that would be recaptured from not having to deal with the problem anymore.

Source: Jerald R. Vaughn, *Community Oriented Policing: You Can Make It Happen* (Clearwater, Fla.: National Law Enforcement Leadership Institute, no date), pp. 6–7. Used with permission.

ROLE OF THE RANK-AND-FILE OFFICERS

All experts on the subject of police innovation and change emphasize the importance of empowering and using the input from the street officers. Next we discuss these key personnel, including the unique nature of their recruitment, the need to give them a sense of ownership in their work, and means by which they can progress.

Change Begins with Recruitment

Selecting Problem Solvers

Times have changed greatly in hiring police personnel. The specter of liability and the shift to COPPS have forced police agencies to revise the recruiting and training processes (COPPS training is examined in Chapter 8). The shift to community policing has important implications for how we select police recruits, requiring a reevaluation of past practices and the development of more positively oriented selection criteria and procedures.[46]

The patrol officer is now a *problem solver*. Selection favors those who are interested in creating solutions rather than applying learned rules. Furthermore, there is an emphasis on practical intelligence—the ability to quickly analyze key elements of a situation and identify possible courses of action to reach logical conclusions. It is difficult to neatly delineate separate problem-solving elements. A patrol officer might witness, for example, neighborhood youth painting graffiti on a wall. The officer has to analyze the situation and define the problem. Another scenario might be a patrol officer assigned to a beat in which automobiles are smashed and vandalized each night. In order to formulate a response, the officer must define the problem and address the motivations of the offenders.[47]

A recruitment poster illustrates the department's diversity, values, and belief that one person can make a difference. (*Courtesy* Broken Arrow, Oklahoma, police department)

Under COPPS, the patrol officer is expected to recognize when old methods are inadequate and new and different solutions are needed. The officer is expected to display many of the skills demanded in higher-level personnel such as detectives—being creative, flexible, and innovative; working independently; and maintaining self-discipline. Communication skills are also vital. The officer must possess the ability to work cooperatively with others to solve problems, and to listen.[48]

Today there are private corporations that specialize in assisting police organizations in identifying candidates who will become effective officers for community policing. An examination can be administered that assesses more of the whole person, in addition to traditional measures such as accuracy of observation, short-term memory, reading comprehension, and written communication. Such tests of one's community policing abilities additionally measure one's service orientation, accountability, ethics, and problem-solving orientation.[49]

Many police agencies inform their applicants on their Web page and other recruitment materials that they have implemented COPPS and are thus interested in hiring people who can perform under that philosophy.[50]

CASE STUDIES

Following are examples of how three police organizations approached some aspects of needed change with the COPPS philosophy.

Fresno, California: Departmental Reorganization

The Fresno, California, police department undertook a reorganization effort to completely transform its structure, systems, and processes; the purposes of reorganizing included increasing the agency's effectiveness and efficiency, establishing higher levels of trust by the community, allowing for stronger management and accountability, enhancing communication flow, and decentralizing control of authority. The process began with an informational gathering phase to assess the department's status in these areas.

An initial step was to unify the staff and to build a strong management team. A management psychologist interviewed each staff member and conducted a series of team building exercises, including an analysis of behavioral styles and personality profiles and a three-day retreat.

To gain greater community trust, a chief's advisory board was established to share community concerns and enhance communications; a professional standards unit was established to audit police operations and monitor citizen/officer interactions; demographic data was collected to address concerns of racial profiling; new recruiting strategies were employed to focus on a broader candidate pool; and the agency began going through an accreditation process to ensure its compliance with national standards.

Other changes during this year of reorganization included a new vision and mission, a flattened organizational structure, and decentralization of resources into policing districts. The department's labor unions were involved in each step of the process and provided input, and the media were apprised of changes.

The department learned during this process, however, that there are several potential, major costs involved in undertaking significant change that must be minimized if possible:

- Loss of seasoned professionals: Some employees may not feel included in the change plan, take early retirement, lose confidence in leadership, or not accept new assignments.

- Productivity losses: There can be miscommunication between divisions, inadequate policies and procedures as guidelines, disorganization from change itself, and delay in employees assuming new roles.
- Lack of clarity in purpose/mission: Some employees might hate change or refuse to change without substantial preparation or opportunity for input; they might also need a real connection to community feedback to make change stay.[51]

Boston: Revitalization of the Force

In the early 1990s, when a mayoral commission called for major managerial reforms for the Boston, Massachusetts, police department, then-chief William Bratton asked an organizational psychologist to assist with this challenge. Now, more than a decade later, Boston has evolved into one of the country's premier community policing agencies. The psychologist introduced a focus on systemic change, integrating adult-learning models into management training and paying greater attention to the nuances of organizational structure. Each initiative involves systemic changes related to basic policing practices, business processes, technology, and management and leadership development.

A strategic planning initiative used a long-term planning process to address crime, quality of life, and management issues, with 350 people (police, elected officials, clergy, and other officials) working in 17 teams over a six-month period to carve out action plans for each of the city's 11 police districts. It was determined in these meetings, for example, that the traditional system of officer rotations, transfers, and shift changes ran counter to community policing's philosophy of building relationships with the community; structural changes were then made so that officers worked in neighborhood-focused beat teams.

The department has learned that complex problem solving and systemic change are less difficult when traditional views—such as those involving officers' response to calls for service—are minimized or eliminated.[52]

Hayward, California: Hiring, Training, and Evaluating Personnel

After making the decision to change its policing philosophy, a systems change was required that would greatly affect personnel. Therefore, the initial focus was on personnel systems such as recruiting, hiring, training, performance appraisals, and promotability guidelines. To transform the recruiting and hiring processes, the city's personnel department and the police department began exploring the following questions:

1. Overall, what type of candidate, possessing what types of skills, should be recruited?
2. What specific knowledge, skills, and abilities reflect the COPPS philosophy—particularly problem-solving abilities and sensitivity to the needs of the community?
3. How can these attributes best be identified through the initial screening process?

The department also analyzed the city's demographics, finding that it had a diverse ethnic composition. To promote cultural diversity and sensitivity to the needs of the community, a psychologist was employed to develop a profile of an effective COPPS officer in Hayward. These considerations became an integral part of the department's hiring process.

Next the training and performance evaluation systems were reappraised. All personnel, both sworn and civilian, had to receive COPPS training to provide a clear and thorough understanding of the history, philosophy, and transition to COPPS. The department's initial training was directed at management and supervisory personnel and was designed to assist these employees in accomplishing the department's goals of reinforcing COPPS values, modifying the existing police culture, strategically transitioning the organization from traditional policing to the new philosophy, and focusing on customer relations. Rank-and-file officers were given 40-hour blocks of instruction.

Performance and reward practices for personnel were modified to reflect the new criteria. Emphasizing quality over quantity (e.g., arrest statistics, number of calls for service, response times), new criteria included an assessment of how well a call for service was handled and what type of problem-solving approach was used to reach a solution for the problem. Other mechanisms were developed to broadcast and communicate successes, including supervisors' logs, a COPPS newsletter, and citywide recognition of extraordinary customer service efforts.

The department's promotional process was also retooled; a new phase was added to the department's promotional test—the "promotability" phase—to evaluate the candidate's decision-making abilities, analytical skills, communication skills, interpersonal skills, and professional contributions.[53]

SUMMARY

This chapter has been about change: how it can be quite difficult in organizations—especially those police agencies with the traditional, entrenched culture and management styles—as well as the roles of key police leaders and rank-and-file officers in effecting change.

This chapter underscores the importance and means of changing the culture of the police agency, from recruit to chief, to accommodate the new philosophy and the operation of COPPS. Also called for is a requisite, radical change in the way the police organization views itself, hones its values, and conducts its affairs. The chief executive must be a risk taker and all employees, sworn and civilian, must believe that change is needed within the organization if COPPS is to succeed. This modified approach to policing is also required in the view and latitude given the middle managers as well as first-line supervisors and especially the very important problem-solving street officer. We also emphasized the need to examine—and probably shift—the organization's means for recruiting people as police problem solvers.

NOTES

1. Herman Goldstein, *Problem Oriented Policing* (New York: McGraw-Hill, 1990), p. 29.

2. Peter M. Senge, *The Fifth Discipline: The Art and Practice of the Learning Organization* (London: Random House, 1990).

3. Ibid., p. 3.

4. Ibid., p. 4.

5. Mark K. Smith, "Peter Senge and the Learning Organization," *http://www.infed.org/thinkers/senge.htm* (July 14, 2002).

6. Chris Argyris, *Personality and Organization* (New York: Harper & Bros., 1957).

7. Leanne Fiftal Alarid, "Law Enforcement Departments as Learning Organizations: Argyris's Theory as a Framework for Implementing Community-Oriented Policing," *Police Quarterly*, 2(3) (September 1999):321–337.

8. Ibid., p. 333.

9. J. L. Pierce and A. L. Delbecq, "Organization Structure, Individual Attitudes and Innovation," *Academy of Management Review* 2 (1977):27–37.

10. Community Policing Consortium, *Curricula. Module Four: Managing Organizational Change* (Washington, D.C.: Author, August 2000), pp. 4–5.

11. Ibid., p. 6.

12. Ibid., pp. 6–7.

13. Roy R. Roberg and Jack Kuykendall, *Police Management* (2d ed.) (Los Angeles: Roxbury, 1997), p. 370.

14. Ibid., pp. 370–371.

15. Ibid., pp. 375–376.

16. Ibid., p. 376.

17. Charles R. Swanson, Leonard Territo, and Robert W. Taylor, *Police Administration: Structures, Processes, and Behavior* (3rd ed.) (New York: Macmillan, 1993), p. 668.

18. Ibid., pp. 668–669.

19. L. E. Greiner, "Patterns of Organization Change," *Harvard Business Review* 45 (1967):124–125.

20. David L. Carter, "Community Police and Political Posturing: Playing the Game" (Policy Paper for the Regional Community Policing Training Institute, Wichita State University, Wichita, Kansas, 2000).

21. Malcolm K. Sparrow, "Implementing Community Policing" (Washington, D.C.: U.S. Department of Justice: National Institute of Justice, "Perspectives on Policing," no. 9, November 1988), pp. 1–2.

22. Thomas J. Peters and Robert H. Waterman Jr., *In Search of Excellence* (New York: Harper & Row, 1983), p. 15.

23. Robert Wasserman and Mark H. Moore, "Values in Policing" (Washington, D.C.: U.S. Department of Justice, National Institute of Justice, November 1988), pp. 6–7.

24. Jerry Dyer and Keith Foster, "Managing Change: Reorganizing and Building Community Trust," symposium paper entitled "Risk Management Issues in Law Enforcement," Public Entity Risk Institute, Fairfax, Va., *www.riskinstitute.org* (Accessed May 28, 2003).

25. Mark H. Moore and Darrel W. Stephens, *Beyond Command and Control: The Strategic Management of Police Departments* (Washington, D.C.: Police Executive Research Forum, 1991), pp. 1, 3–4.

26. Gordon Witkin and Dan McGraw, "Beyond 'Just the Facts, Ma'am'," *U.S.News and World Report* (August 2, 1993):29.

27. Malcolm K. Sparrow, Mark H. Moore, and David M. Kennedy, *Beyond 911: A New Era for Policing* (New York: Basic Books, 1990), p. 149.

28. California Department of Justice, Attorney General's Office, Crime Prevention Center, *COPPS: Community Oriented Policing and Problem Solving* (Sacramento, Calif.: Author, November 1992), pp. 67–68.

29. Lunell Haught, "Meaning, Resistance, and Sabotage—Elements of a Police Culture," *Community Policing Exchange* (May/June 1998):7.

30. William A. Geller and Guy Swanger, *Managing Innovation in Policing: The Untapped Potential of the Middle Manager* (Washington, D.C.: Police Executive Research Forum, 1995), p. 41.

31. Price Pritchett and Ron Pound, *A Survival Guide to the Stress of Organizational Change* (Dallas: Pritchett and Associates, 1995), p. 12.

32. Warren Friedman, "The Community Role in Community Policing." In *The Challenge of Community Policing: Testing the Promises*, Dennis P. Rosenbaum (ed.) (Thousand Oaks, Calif.: Sage, 1994), p. 268.

33. Mike Tharp and Dorian Friedman, "New Cops on the Block," *U.S. News and World Report* (August 2, 1993):23.

34. John Eck, quoted in ibid., p. 24.

35. James Q. Wilson, "Six Things Police Leaders Can Do About Juvenile Crime." In *Subject to Debate* (newsletter of the Police Executive Research Forum, September/October 1997), p. 1.

36. Geller and Swanger, *Managing Innovation in Policing*, p. 105.

37. Ibid., p. 131.

38. Ibid., p. 109.

39. Ibid., p. 112.

40. Ibid., pp. 137–138.

41. George L. Kelling and William J. Bratton, *Implementing Community Policing: The Administrative Problem* (Washington, D.C.: National Institute of Justice, "Perspectives on Policing" no. 17, 1993), p. 11.

42. Goldstein, *Problem Oriented Policing*, p. 29.

43. Tom McEwen, "Finding Time for Problem Solving," *Problem Solving Quarterly* 5 (Spring 1992):1, 4.

44. Lee P. Brown, "Community Policing: Bring the Community into the Battle against Crime" (speech before the 19th Annual Lehman Lecture Series, Long Island University, New York, March 11, 1992).

45. John Eck and William Spelman, "A Problem-Oriented Approach to Police Service Delivery." In *Police and Policing: Contemporary Issues*, Dennis Jay Kenney (ed.) (New York: Praeger, 1989), pp. 95–111.

46. Eric Metchik and Ann Winton, "Community Policing and Its Implications for Alternative Models of Police Officer Selection." In *Issues in Community Policing*, Peter C. Kratcoski and Duane Dukes (eds.) (Cincinnati: Anderson, 1995), pp. 107–123.

47. Ibid., p. 116.

48. Ibid., p. 119–120.

49. "Community Police Officer Pre-Employment Exam," *Law and Order* (December 2000):125.

50. See the Redding Police Department's Web site: *http://ci.redding.ca.us/personnel/porec.htm.*

51. Dyer and Foster, pp. 1–3.

52. Joan Sweeney, "Revitalizing Boston's Police Force," *http://www.apa.org/monitor/jun02/revitalizing.html* (Accessed February 21, 2003).

53. Joseph E. Brann and Suzanne Whalley, "COPPS: The Transformation of Police Organizations." In California Department of Justice, Attorney General's Office, Crime Prevention Center, *COPPS: Community Oriented Policing and Problem Solving*, p. 72.

INTRODUCTION

This observation by Mark Twain is made more eloquent, powerful, and lucid when reviewing some definitions of *training*, which include: (1) developing or forming the habits, thoughts, or behavior of [another person] by discipline and instruction; (2) making proficient by instruction and practice, as in some art, profession, or work;[1] and (3) imparting specific and immediately usable skills.[2]

As we have noted in previous chapters, the movement toward community oriented policing and problem solving (COPPS) involves a change in the philosophy and the organizational structure of the police agency. A philosophical shift is critical to the development of new skills, knowledge, and abilities, as well as to a reorientation of perceptions and a refining of current skills. This is a difficult challenge for those involved in the training and education of police officers.

This training is of utmost importance, and the challenge greatly enhanced, because the successful implementation of COPPS requires the training of *every* employee inside the agency, as well as an orientation for a number of people and organizations outside the police department. Indeed, police administrators, federal and state criminal justice planning officials, and criminal justice policy advisory groups have rated training as the primary need in order for COPPS to reach its fullest potential. Furthermore, it is important that the police educate the public and other public and private agencies and organizations in the concept because they will be required, at times, to help carry out the COPPS effort. This chapter analyzes COPPS training from these disparate yet related perspectives.

We begin this chapter with a look at challenges and characteristics of training adults, including the need to create a

—8—

TRAINING FOR COPPS

Approaches and Challenges

A man can seldom—very, very seldom—fight a winning fight against his training: the odds are too heavy.
—MARK TWAIN

"learning organization" and employ problem-based learning. Next we consider why having police officers in the classroom constitutes another sort of challenge, and the various means by which training is provided to these individuals (including the recruit academy and via field training, in-service, roll call, and specialized means); included in this section is a brief description of training technologies.

Then we focus on a combined program for accomplishing COPPS training; this comprehensive section includes the extent to which such training is occurring nationally, methods for determining officers' training needs, the components of a COPPS curriculum, and the various audiences that should be exposed to COPPS training.

The chapter concludes with a sample training program. Exhibits containing examples of police training initiatives are provided throughout the chapter.

KEYS TO TRAINING ADULTS

Before examining the training of police officers in the COPPS strategy, it is important to look briefly at the training process in general. In Chapter 7, Peter

The Learning Organization

157

Senge's increasingly influential concept of learning organizations was introduced, particularly as it applies to organizational change. This concept is obviously important for training adult learners. Senge felt the organization must allow its employees to continually expand their capacity to create the results they truly desire, nurture new and expansive patterns of thinking, allow their collective aspiration to be set free, and continually learn to see the whole picture.[3] In the same vein, Malcolm Knowles provided helpful insights concerning the characteristics of, and unique challenges posed by, adult learners:[4] Adults are *autonomous and self-directed*. They need to be free to direct themselves, and teachers must actively involve class participants in the learning process and serve as facilitators for them, through such means as allowing presentations and group leadership. Show participants how to reach their goals.

- Adults have *life experiences and knowledge* that may include work-related activities, family responsibilities, and previous education. They need to connect learning to this base, so try to draw out their experience and knowledge that is relevant to the topic.
- Adults are *goal-oriented* and appreciate an educational program that is organized and has clearly defined elements. Instructors should explain how their course assists participants in obtaining their goals.
- Adults are *relevancy-oriented* and must see a reason for learning something; learning must be applicable to their work or other purposes to be of value to them. Therefore, when possible allow participants to choose projects that reflect their own interests.
- Adults, finally, need to be shown *respect*, and teachers should treat them as equals in experience and knowledge and allow them to voice their opinions freely in class.

Problem-Based Learning

A method of training that facilitates the learning organization, one that is best suited for adult learners, is problem-based learning (PBL). This training approach was developed and widely employed in medical school education. PBL is both a curriculum and a process; the *curriculum* consists of carefully selected problems that demand from the learner acquisition of critical knowledge, problem-solving proficiency, and team participation skills. The *process* involves resolving problems or challenges that are encountered in life and career. With PBL, students assume increased responsibility for their learning, giving them more motivation and feelings of accomplishment.[5]

PBL is now applied to all aspects of police training across the United States and in Canada, in recruit academies, in FTO training, and in instructor development courses that teach officers how to train other officers.

TRAINING POLICE OFFICERS

Anyone who undertakes to train police officers must be mindful of the challenge at hand. Michael E. Buerger provided food for thought concerning police training:

> Training is usually discussed in terms of a benefit provided to the rank-and-file. From the perspective of those receiving it, however, training is easily divided into two main categories: the kind officers like, and the kind they despise. What they like fits into their world view; what they despise is "training" that attempts to change that view.[6]

There are challenges in training officers in the COPPS strategy. First, because policing often attracts action-oriented individuals, officers tend to be more receptive to hands-on skills training, such as arrest methods, weaponless defense, pursuit driving, firearms proficiency, baton usage, and so on. Certainly, these measures are needed from time to time, and for that reason (and because of the specter of liability) police personnel must receive training in those areas. As many studies have demonstrated, however, only a small fraction of the typical officers' work routine involves the use of weapons, defensive tactics, high-speed chases, and so forth. If training is to help officers do their jobs better, it must focus on what they need to know in order to do their job well. It should also be driven by the mission of the agency.

It must also be remembered that police training is best conducted—and is better received by the officers—when it reflects skills with immediately recognizable application to the job and when that message is constantly reinforced throughout training. Thus, it is not surprising that officers prefer to be instructed by persons who both possess expertise in the activity and have "walked the walk" of police patrol, that is, other police officers.[7] It is also worthwhile to remember that an *environment* that is conducive to learning, with a clearly stated *outcome*, inspiring learners' *physical and mental engagement*, and activities that precipitate *critical thinking and problem solving* are important training processes as well.

A simplistic example of a PBL approach that might be applied to a COPPS training course would be the following:

> Officers assigned to your district have been responding to a number of noise complaints, reckless driving, and fight calls in the area of 7500 Commercial Row, which contains a number of restaurants, bars, and several strip malls that attract juveniles and young adults. Within the past week, there have also been three gang-related drive-by shootings and seven gas drive-offs. A majority of the youths are attracted to a dance club located in one of the strip mall centers and two all-night fast food restaurants. All three locations attract large crowds that loiter and drink alcohol in their parking lots. The owners of the shopping centers and restaurants have also complained about thousands of dollars in vandalism by the loitering youths.

> Divide the class into groups. Use the S.A.R.A. model to determine how to address the problem. Each group should select a scribe and a spokesperson to present the group's analysis and responses to the entire class. The instructor will facilitate a discussion of each group's presentation with the entire class. [Note: The problem analysis triangle from Chapter 4 may be used to address this problem; students might need to determine whether two sides of the triangle can be utilized for solutions in the response stage. "Guardians" may also be used to help the area.]

IMPARTING NEW KNOWLEDGE AND RETAINING LEARNED SKILLS

Training can be categorized into five primary areas: academy, field training officer, in-service, roll call, and specialized. Each is extremely important for imparting values and information concerning the COPPS philosophy.

The Recruit Academy

Academy training (the recruit or cadet phase) sets the tone for newly hired officers. It is at the academy that the recruits begin to develop a strong mind-set about their role as police officers.

Ideally, academy training will provide comprehensive instruction in the two primary elements of COPPS—community engagement and problem solving—if the proper philosophical mindset for recruits is to be accomplished. In many cases, this will require that traditional courses, such as those in history, patrol procedures, police–community relations, and crime prevention, be revamped to include the topics and information recommended in this chapter; this information will teach officers to be more analytical and creative in their efforts to address community crime and disorder. A primary emphasis on the nature of crime and disorder and problem-solving methods should be the foundation for this training.

In 1996, Maryland became the first state in the nation to initiate a "community policing academy," with the goal of providing training in COPPS to officers in every local police agency. The academy serves as a central resource for providing agencies with continuing education as well as training in resource development and community involvement.

Field Training Officers

The next phase of training for newly hired officers is the *field training officer* (FTO) program, which is provided immediately on leaving the academy. The field training program was begun in the San Jose, California, police department in 1972,[8] and assists recruits in their transition from the academy to the streets while still under the protective arm of a veteran officer. Most FTO programs consist of an *introductory phase* (where the recruit learns agency policies and local laws); *training and evaluation phases* (the recruit is introduced to more complicated tasks confronted by patrol officers); and a *final phase* (the FTO may act strictly as an observer and evaluator while the recruit performs all the functions of a patrol officer). This phase of the recruit's training can obviously have a profound effect on his or her later career, and whether or not the neophyte officer is allowed to learn and put this strategy into practice.

Many police agencies are retooling their FTO programs to emphasize community policing. Going even further, the Reno, Nevada, police department, with the assistance and funding of the Police Executive Research Forum and the federal Office of Community Oriented Policing Services, has developed a model Police Training Officer (PTO) program that recognizes the importance of problem-solving skills and critical thinking. Known as the Reno Model, PTO uses a number of tools that embrace adult- and problem-based learning and includes a learning matrix that shows "core competencies," which are specific knowledge, skills, and abilities that are essential for community policing and problem solving.

Exhibit 8-1 shows the learning matrix that is used with the Reno Model. Each cell (A1 through D15) has a corresponding list of skills required to achieve competency in the areas listed.

In-Service

In-service training provides an opportunity to impart information and to reinforce new skills learned in the academy and FTO program. In-service classes are useful for sharing officers' experiences in applying COPPS to a variety of problems, as well as for their collaboration with other city agencies, social service organizations, or the community. In-service training is also one of the primary means of changing the culture and attitudes of personnel.[9]

Obviously, a tremendous challenge for large police departments is providing COPPS training for all of the many hundreds or even thousands of officers and civilians. Some large agencies have used videotaped or computer-assisted training. Many departments, using drug-forfeiture funds, have also purchased high-technology equipment for use with training. In addition to

EXHIBIT 8-1 The Learning Matrix for the Reno Model PTO

	Phase A Non-Emergency Incident Response	Phase B Emergency Incident Response	Phase C Patrol Activities	Phase D Criminal Investigation
CORE COMPETENCIES				
Police Vehicle Operations	A1	B1	C1	D1
Conflict Resolution	A2	B2	C2	D2
Use of Force	A3	B3	C3	D3
Local Procedures, Policies, Laws, Philosophies	A4	B4	C4	D4
Report Writing	A5	B5	C5	D5
Leadership	A6	B6	C6	D6
Problem-Solving Skills	A7	B7	C7	D7
Community-Specific Problems	A8	B8	C8	D8
Cultural Diversity & Special Needs Groups	A9	B9	C9	D9
Legal Authority	A10	B10	C10	D10
Individual Rights	A11	B11	C11	D11
Officer Safety	A12	B12	C12	D12
Communication Skills	A13	B13	C13	D13
Ethics	A14	B14	C14	D14
Lifestyle Stressors/ Self-Awareness/ Self-Regulation	A15	B15	C15	D15
Learning Activities	Introduction of Neighborhood Portfolio Exercise Problem-Based Learning Exercise	Continuation of Neighborhood Portfolio Exercise Problem-Based Learning Exercise	Continuation of Neighborhood Portfolio Exercise Problem-Based Learning Exercise	Final Neighborhood Portfolio Presentation Problem-Based Learning Exercise
Evaluation Activities	Weekly Coaching and Training Reports	Weekly Coaching and Training Reports	Weekly Coaching and Training Reports	Weekly Coaching and Training Reports

Source: Reno, Nevada, police department.
http://www.cityofreno.com/pub_safety/police/ptoprogram.html (Accessed April 30, 2003).

COPPS courses and orientations, departmental newsletters can disseminate information to personnel on a regular basis.

Roll Call

Roll call training is that period of time—from 15 to 30 minutes prior to the beginning of a tour of duty—in which supervisors prepare officers for patrol. Roll call sessions usually begin with a supervisor assigning the officers to their respective beats. Information about wanted and dangerous persons and major incidents on previous shifts is usually disseminated. Other matters may also be addressed, such as issuing officers court subpoenas, explaining new departmental policies and procedures, and discussing shift and beat-related matters.

The 14th Annual International Problem-Oriented Policing Conference in San Diego, California, drew more than 1,500 participants worldwide. (*Courtesy* Police Executive Research Forum)

Roll call meetings afford an excellent opportunity for supervisors to update officers' knowledge and to present new ideas and techniques. This is particularly advantageous for small police agencies that have limited training staff and resources. For example, videotapes or problem-solving case studies can be used at briefing sessions to provide relevant information.

Specialized Training

Specialized training involves issues presented at conferences dedicated solely to COPPS. Such conferences have been conducted in San Diego, California (since 1989 San Diego has hosted an annual International Problem-Oriented Policing Conference, attracting more than 1,500 participants from around the world; at this conference the prestigious Herman Goldstein Award for Excellence in Problem-Oriented Policing awards are presented) and elsewhere throughout the United States. Specialized training is also provided by the federal COPS office, PERF, the International Association of Chiefs of Police, the Community Policing Consortium, and many other such entities. Exhibit 8-2 shows what the federal COPS office has done to disseminate training across the country, with its 31 Regional Community Policing Institutes.

It should also be emphasized that with the spread of COPPS across the United States, many public and private universities and colleges (including community colleges) are now offering courses specifically on community oriented policing and problem solving, and even have degree concentrations in this area. These postsecondary courses will become increasingly available and significant as the concept continues to expand.

EXHIBIT 8-2 Regional Community Policing Institutes

The federal Office of Community Oriented Policing Services (COPS) promotes and supports COPPS endeavors through problem-solving tactics and community–police partnerships, recognizing that this strategy brings about challenges and changes in the way the police are trained. Since 1994 the COPS Office has awarded approximately $8 billion to law enforcement agencies and its 31 Regional Community Policing Institutes (RCPI) across the United States. The RCPIs have trained almost 210,000 officers and citizens across the nation, including more than 80,000 hours of training delivered in 174 curricula. Integral to this training is a national cadre of trainers, electronic dissemination of training sessions and content, and the use of multimedia approaches. The Fiscal Year 2003 budget for the COPS office is provided below, as well as a map of its 31 RCPI sites.

Source: U. S. Department of Justice, Office of Community Oriented Policing Services, "COPS Fact Sheet: Regional Community Policing Institutes. *http://www.cops.usdoj.gov* (Accessed April 20, 2003.)

Fiscal Year 2003 Funding for COPS

On February 20, 2003, President Bush signed the bill providing $584,099,514 in 2003 appropriations for COPS. Highlights from this appropriation include:

COPS Hiring Programs	$198,700,000
COPS Technology Grants	$188,719,000
Methamphetamine enforcement and suppression	$56,761,000
Indian Country Grants	$34,743,000
Community Policing Development	$20,528,000
Interoperable Communications Technology Program	$74,620,000
Police Integrity	$16,853,000
Safe School Initiative	$15,111,000

The bill includes language for COPS to use 30 percent of hiring funds ($60 million) to offer an overtime program. The overtime program and the Interoperable Communications Technology Program are new programs for COPS in 2003.

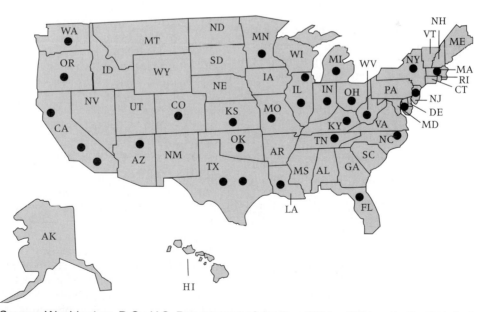

Source: Washington, D.C.: U.S. Department of Justice, Office of Community Oriented Policing Services. *http://www.cops.usdoj.gov/Default.asp?Item=160* (Accessed May 1, 2003).

TRAINING TECHNOLOGIES

As technology progresses, new and better methods of instruction and delivery of material continue to evolve. Such technologies include distance learning, interactive computer disks, satellite television, and even correspondence courses. On-demand learning allows students to receive their training without placing too great a burden on their personal or professional lives.[10] Online training can be self-paced, around-the-clock, and interactive and can contain one-on-one coaching and mentoring. Individuals as well as corporations, colleges, and universities[11] now offer COPPS courses on-line.

Instructor-based training will always exist in some form, but it appears that the instructor may soon augment interactive training rather than vice versa. For example, to be effective CD-ROM training may require a live instructor via telephone, video, or in person to assist the student.[12] Nearly every state is changing its training curricula to reflect some form of interactive learning. Training in the future may be a combination of classroom, interactive, and hands-on practical learning.[13]

Exhibit 8-3 provides informational and training resources that are available on the Internet. Do not overlook training that may be available via e-mail, audio- and videocassettes, teleconferencing, and television programming.

EXHIBIT 8-3 Using the Internet for COPPS

The Internet provides police officers and trainers with a lost-cost means of communicating with their colleagues across the nation or abroad about policies and programs. Following are some Internet addresses where trainers can conduct research and gain information concerning virtually anything about law enforcement.

- *www.usdoj.gov:* U.S. Department of Justice link to all DOJ agencies; includes information about a wide range of research, training, and grants
- *www.officer.com:* Directory related to law enforcement issues
- *www.census.gov/:* U.S. Census Bureau; provides demographic information by jurisdiction
- *www.ssc.msu.edu/~people.cp/:* National Center for Community Policing; center at Michigan State University providing research, training, and information concerning community policing nationwide
- *www.communitypolicing.org/:* Community Policing Consortium; community policing topics are updated monthly and include an array of information such as training sessions and curricula
- *www.usdoj.gov/cops/:* COPS Office; promotes policing strategies and offers a variety of grants, training, and education to state agencies and local communities nationwide
- *www.ncjrs.org:* National Criminal Justice Reference Service; clearinghouse of publications and on-line reference service about a broad range of criminal justice issues
- *www.nlectc.org:* National Law Enforcement and Corrections Technology Center; provides information about new equipment and technologies
- *www.ojp.usdoj.gov/bjs:* Bureau of Justice Statistics; includes a variety of information about criminal justice statistics and provides links to other research Web sites
- *www.ih2000.net/ira/ira.htm:* lists all federal, state, and local agencies on the Web
- *www.policing.com/course1/:* Representative of the kinds of on-line private training courses that are now provided
- *police.sas.ab.ca/:* COPNET; information about police training, job opportunities, links to other agencies, and chat rooms about various subjects

Also, the Police Executive Research Forum (PERF) (1120 Connecticut Avenue, Suite 930, Washington, D.C. 20036) manages an on-line resource known as POPNet that provides a library of successful problem-solving examples. PERF also has literally dozens of COPPS publications that can assist trainers. The Community Policing Consortium (1726 M St. N.W., Suite 801, Washington, D.C. 20036; e-mail: look@aspen-sys.com), furthermore, publishes the *Information Access Guide*, a compilation of community policing practitioners, community organizers, and volunteers, updated and released the first week of every month.

Training is at the heart of COPPS and is expanding as rapidly as the strategy itself. Chapter 1 noted that today nearly 7 in 10 of the nation's local police agencies, *employing 90 percent of all officers*, have adopted the COPPS strategy. Furthermore, two-thirds of these agencies, employing 86 percent of all officers, have full-time community policing officers.[14]

Work remains to be done in terms of providing formal training in COPPS to the agencies' sworn and non-sworn personnel, however. Only about a third (38 percent) of these agencies train *all* new recruits in community policing, and about half provide at least some of their new recruits with such training.[15] Less than one-fourth (21 percent) of the departments provide such training to their in-service officers, while 15 percent train civilian employees in COPPS.

Figure 8-1 shows community policing training in local departments by size of population served.

Population served	Percent of agencies that trained personnel for 8 or more hours in community policing		
	Total	All	Some
New officer recruits			
All sizes	51%	38%	13%
1,000,000 or more	87%	80%	7%
500,000-999,999	90	90	0
250,000-499,999	95	85	10
100,000-249,999	86	77	9
50,000-99,999	87	75	12
25,000-49,999	81	67	14
10,000-24,999	70	53	17
2,500-9,999	54	40	14
Under 2,500	32	21	11
In-service sworn personnel			
All sizes	59%	21%	38%
1,000,000 or more	87%	27%	60%
500,000-999,999	71	34	37
250,000-499,999	83	28	55
100,000-249,999	84	28	56
50,000-99,999	87	33	54
25,000-49,999	83	27	56
10,000-24,999	78	17	61
2,500-9,999	62	20	42
Under 2,500	42	21	21
Civillian personnel			
All sizes	15%	4%	11%
1,000,000 or more	34%	7%	27%
500,000-999,999	31	9	22
250,000-499,999	38	3	35
100,000-249,999	50	10	40
50,000-99,999	45	11	34
25,000-49,999	36	9	27
10,000-24,999	24	6	18
2,500-9,999	15	5	10
Under 2,500	7	2	5

FIGURE 8-1. Community Policing Training in Local Police Departments, by Size of Population Served, 2000. (*Source:* U.S. Department of Justice, Bureau of Justice Statistics, *Local police departments 2000* [Washington, D.C.: Author, January 2003], p. 14.)

EXHIBIT 8-4   Needs Assessment Survey

1. Does our department *currently* have a community policing strategy or plan?

2. Which of the following best describes our department's community policing practice?

   a. All *uniformed* officers are/will be actively involved in community policing.

   b. All *sworn* officers are/will be actively involved in community policing.

   c. Only specifically assigned officers are/will be involved in community policing.

   d. The department does not use community policing.

3. What are our *primary training needs* related to community policing? (Responses might be wide ranging, from community engagement issues to knowledge about crime prevention, the S.A.R.A. process generally, managing patrol time, resources and referrals, organizational change, responsibilities of administrators and supervisors, and so on.)

4. Have any of our officers received community policing training?

   a. Who presented/provided the training?

   b. What percentage of our officers received the training?

5. Does our department have at least one computer with a modem? Access to the Internet?

6. Does our department currently have a Web page?

7. Does our agency currently have e-mail external to the department?

8. Have our officers had any Internet training?

9. Which programs does our department currently have? [Responses might include DARE (Drug Abuse Resistance Education), Neighborhood or Business Watch, ride-along, GREAT (Gang Resistance Education and Training), and so forth.]

Source: Adapted from Andra J. Katz, *The Community Policing Needs Assessment in Kansas and Nebraska: Final Report* (Wichita, Kans.: Regional Community Policing Training Institute, December 1997).

Determining Training Needs

Of primary importance is a needs assessment to provide the trainer with vital information about the new or veteran officers, how they view their daily work, and what obstacles exist that may prevent them from using COPPS training. It can also provide important information for changing officer performance evaluation systems, extending beyond such traditional assessments as traffic citations or numbers of arrests. The assessment is a tool to establish department-wide training needs and can be used for various purposes—academy training, in-service training, supervisory and nonsupervisory training, and so forth—to survey trainees prior to their receiving instruction.

Exhibit 8-4 provides a preliminary COPPS training needs assessment questionnaire. The exhibit shows the kinds of questions that could be used by a police agency to do a preliminary survey of its training needs. Obviously, question 3 of the survey is critical and will require considerable deliberation.

It is also important for COPPS curriculum development that (1) the trainees be determined, (2) a task analysis be conducted, (3) performance measures be constructed by which trainees can be evaluated (to determine successful or unsuccessful course completion), (4) existing courses be identified that might address needs, and (5) the appropriate environment for the training be selected.[16]

Components of a COPPS Curriculum

The overall goal of COPPS training is to provide officers with a level of understanding that allows them to effectively apply community engagement and problem-solving techniques to their daily work. The objectives of such a training curriculum include the following:

- providing participants with an overview of the history of policing and research that serves as the foundation for the COPPS approach

- providing participants with basic problem-solving skills and knowledge of the elements of community engagement
- sharing with participants examples of case studies in jurisdictions where COPPS has been successful
- providing participants with the opportunity to demonstrate the application of the problem-solving model to local problems
- sharing with participants the benefits of collaborating with other government agencies, businesses, social service organizations, and the community in a COPPS approach
- discussing the changes in leadership, management, and supervision styles required to develop an environment conducive to the implementation of COPPS
- helping participants identify the internal and external organizational barriers to COPPS and implement problem oriented policing in their respective agencies
- identifying other external individuals and groups that lend support to COPPS, such as business leaders, other government agencies, social service organizations, and the media

These objectives are discussed in detail in the next sections, following which we examine some sample training curricula that are in use around the country.

Generally, problem solving requires that officers possess research skills, analytical abilities, and communications skills (including knowledge of group processes, such as running public meetings and working with teams).[17] It also requires a more in-depth understanding of CPTED (discussed in Chapter 4).[18]

The University of Delaware offers a "Certificate in Community Policing." Courses include the basic elements of COPPS: problem solving, strategic planning, ethics, and diversity. (*Courtesy* University of Delaware)

The Evolution of Policing

As indicated in Chapter 1, the evolution of policing toward COPPS has followed a logical progression. Policing, like other government organizations and private businesses, has developed new models for providing service based on past experiences and wisdom. It is important, therefore, that trainers begin their instruction on COPPS with an overview of the history and evolution of policing.

Chapter 1 of this book provides an outline for this instruction. It is important to include in this history a discussion of how our society is changing and what the police must do to confront these challenges (Chapter 2) as well as the history of the local agency where the training is being conducted, to personalize the training and to facilitate better understanding of the material. This section of training should end by providing participants with clear definitions of the separate but complementary notions of community oriented and problem oriented policing.

Community Engagement

In this phase of the training program, participants should be introduced to the concept of community policing and its primary components. This segment also provides an opportunity for the participants to interact with one another in examining why their agency is moving into such a method of policing and what changes are likely to occur by doing so. The desired outcomes for this part of the training are for the participants to be able to

- define what is meant by "community" and the concept of "community policing" and its components
- identify why police have a difficult time dealing with crime alone and how a collaborative approach to problem solving can lead to more effective crime control
- know how to develop a community profile that analyzes its problems and identifies its leaders and available resources
- know how to communicate and collaborate with the community (including other city or county departments, local businesses, social services agencies, and so forth) using approaches such as public meetings, newsletters, and contact with leaders, groups, and organizations representing the community
- understand a community's cultural, ethnic, and racial diversity
- discuss community oriented government, including the concepts of a "total quality" or "customer service" orientation in policing
- identify the changes that may arise, both for their agency and for themselves

Diversity Training

COPPS training should include, and provides an excellent opportunity for, a training strategy for policing in a multicultural society. As Chapter 2 described, we live in an increasingly diverse society with many new cultural mores and languages that pose new challenges for police. Policing these new communities requires understanding and new skills. (Chapter 9 addresses diversity, the history of police-minority problems, bias-based and racial policing, and what COPPS can do to build bridges in these areas.) Especially given the current state of world affairs, it is important that police personnel be exposed to different cultures in order to generally make them better and more effective officers, assist in their problem-solving efforts, and hopefully prevent racial profiling.

In attempting to determine the role of training in promoting policing in a manner that is culturally sensitive and responsive, and an approach to training that will yield the greatest success, police agencies must remember the following six principles.

The California Attorney General's Office offers a clearing-house of COPPS resources for agencies, including videos, curricula, Internet sources and links, and trainers and technical assistance.

1. Respect for and sensitivity to the diverse communities served is essential for effective policing.
2. Respect for and sensitivity to ethnocultural communities can best be achieved through a broad-based multicultural strategy.
3. Training must be an essential element of such a strategy.
4. Training must be ongoing and built into the experience of policing; that is, it must be more than a course or two on multiculturalism.
5. A multicultural strategy and the training that supports it will be most effective if they are perceived as integrated aspects of the philosophy and operations of policing.
6. A multicultural strategy and training program must be created in consultation with the ethnocultural communities served by the police.[19]

The problem-based learning (PBL) concept was introduced earlier in this chapter. Here we discuss this approach more specifically as it relates to COPPS.

Problem Solving: Basics and Exercises

    The problem-solving session of training entails teaching officers the basics of conflict resolution, which is the focus of COPPS; it puts philosophy into practice, or "walks the talk" of COPPS. The analysis of problems is the most important component of problem solving. In-depth analysis provides the information necessary for officers to develop effective responses. The S.A.R.A. problem-solving model (scanning, analysis, response, and assessment, which was discussed in detail in Chapter 4) is presented through an interactive lecture and use of case studies. The desired outcomes for this segment include the following:

* identifying each component and principal element of the S.A.R.A. process
* learning the importance of in-depth analysis in the complete identification of a problem

- learning to identify and apply a variety of responses to a problem
- discussing the application of situational crime prevention and CPTED concepts on the environmental influences on crime and disorder
- discussing the importance of both quantitative and qualitative evaluation measures of problem-solving efforts
- discussing how accountability, empowerment, service orientation, and partnership fit into problem solving

Regarding the use of problem-solving exercises, participants should identify current problems in their assigned areas. Facilitators should divide the classes into small work groups and ask them to examine each problem, developing strategies for analyzing, responding to, and assessing the effectiveness of their problem-solving efforts. Figures and tables throughout Chapter 4 can be used to lead officers through the process. Brainstorming should be discussed and used as an appropriate tool to foster innovative and creative thinking in the work groups.[20] The desired outcomes for this segment include the participants' ability to

- identify problems on the officer's beat
- demonstrate an understanding of the problem analysis triangle
- identify the diversity of resources available, the variety of strategies to address the problem, and crime prevention techniques
- evaluate the results using methods similar to those used in the analysis of the problem
- discuss the advantages and disadvantages of the methods used

Once completed, each group will have the opportunity to present its problem to the entire class and explain each step of the S.A.R.A. model. Through these presentations, the participants will be exposed to the problem-solving efforts of the other groups. This method of instruction not only provides officers with a practical exercise but also gives them the opportunity to work through an actual problem on their beat. Their efforts in the classroom can easily be repeated in the field, providing them with their first COPPS projects.

Case Studies

The case studies session provides the trainer with an opportunity to use the S.A.R.A. model of problem solving in addressing an actual situation. Case studies are an excellent training mechanism because they allow the instructor to put the theory (or, as in this case, a problem-solving model) into practice. They also allow the trainer to demonstrate the flexibility of the model as well as emphasize important steps, such as analysis. The desired outcomes of this training segment include the participants' ability to

- demonstrate the steps of S.A.R.A.
- illustrate the importance of thoroughly analyzing a problem using a variety of informational resources and using the problem analysis triangle
- discuss the methods and resources involved in problem solving
- discuss the benefit of the problem-solving model over traditional incident-driven responses

As mentioned above, it is best to localize the case studies, to provide a real-world flavor and to gain a better understanding of the material.

A new and extremely helpful addition to the body of COPPS training literature is the growing array of booklets in the "Problem Oriented Guides for Police Series," published by the COPS office. These guides summarize knowledge about how police can address a variety of problems, including such crime and local problems as street prostitution, graffiti, panhandling, burglary and theft, rave parties, drug dealing, school bullying, false burglar alarms, loud car stereos, robberies at ATMs, and speeding.

There are also several resources from which to obtain and use case studies of successful problem-solving initiatives, including the anthology *Problem Oriented Policing: Crime-Specific Problems, Critical Issues, and Making POP Work* by the Police Executive Research Forum[21] and newspapers such as the free *Community Policing Exchange*, published by the Community Policing Consortium.

Appendix A provides several case studies of problem-solving efforts by police agencies across the United States. These examples show how the S.A.R.A. process was applied to a variety of problems to formulate effective responses.

Leadership and Middle Managers

Executive leadership and middle managers' support are critical to implementing the organizational changes required by the transition to COPPS. Chapters 6 and 7 discussed the role of leadership and management as they relate to the implementation and cultural change of an organization adopting COPPS.

In many instances, the ultimate challenge to a police organization is to change its hierarchical, paramilitary structure. Supervisors, managers, and executives working within a flattened, COPPS oriented organization would require new skills to ensure the successful adaptation and functioning of the police organization.[22] An example of one attempt to support leadership in its transition to COPPS is Seattle, Washington's police department (SPD), which has offered a three-day conference entitled "Leadership Sessions to Support Problem Oriented Policing" for police supervisors, managers, and researchers. Topics included ethical challenges for leaders, politics inside and outside the organization, examining the organization from top to bottom to see how every system and structure supported problem oriented policing, and leadership. The course also includes adult learning theory, gender inclusiveness, and facilitation skills.[23]

The Sergeant as Coach and Manager

As we pointed out in previous chapters, COPPS requires the support of the first-line supervisor. One of the most difficult hurdles for supervisors to overcome is the idea that giving officers the opportunity to be creative and take risks does not diminish the role or authority of the supervisor. Risk taking and innovation require mutual trust between supervisors and line officers.

Supervising in a COPPS environment means a change from being a "controller," primarily concerned with rules, to being a "facilitator" and "coach" for officers involved in problem solving. Supervisors must learn to encourage innovation and risk taking among their officers and be skilled in problem solving. Conducting workload analyses and finding the time for officers to problem solve and engage with the community (discussed in Chapter 4) is an important aspect of supervision. A supervisor must also be prepared to intercede and remove any obstacles to officers' problem-solving efforts. Supervisors must be able to respond to the following questions when officers are confused or resistant to the implementation of COPPS:

- What are the advantages and disadvantages of the traditional form of police supervision?
- What are officers' complaints about management?
- What are officers' complaints about their work?
- What kinds of objections does the supervisor anticipate from officers and detectives when they are told about COPPS?
- How will you respond to such statements as "This is social work and we're not social workers," "We don't have the skills or training to do all this," or "Other cops won't see us as real cops"?[24]

COPPS supervisors should also understand that not all patrol officers or detectives will like this kind of work or be good at it. However, some officers will work on their own unpaid time to solve problems. Furthermore, subordinates will occasionally want to work on problems that really should not be police business and do not deserve a high priority. Supervisors also need to be informed that they must avoid isolating the problem-solving function from the rest of the department. This could create the illusion that problem solving is composed of "privileged prima donnas" who get benefits that other officers do not. Also, supervisors should not allow the COPPS initiative to become a mere public relations campaign; the emphasis is always on results.[25]

The St. Petersburg, Florida, police department identified the characteristics of the "ideal" sergeant under the COPPS philosophy:

Availability	Leader
Flexibility	Champion
Innovative	Trustworthy
Widely experienced	Good speaker
Facilitator	Respected
Open minded	Risk taker
Humorous	Coach
Supportive	Dependable[26]
Buffer	

Finding the time for officers to engage in problem solving and tracking their efforts are also challenges for first-line supervisors. Chapter 4 includes a section on recapturing officers' time.

Barriers and Benefits

A large group discussion may also be facilitated in which participants are asked to identify the internal and external organizational barriers to the success of COPPS. Following the identification of all barriers, strategies are discussed for removing or dealing with the barriers. This discussion helps prepare the trainers for the questions and concerns of the officers in attendance. It also gives the trainers the opportunity to recognize the many benefits of a COPPS approach to policing.

One method of accomplishing this is to divide the class into small groups of 5 to 10 participants. Each group is then asked to identify 10 internal barriers to implementing COPPS (e.g., mindset of officers, supervisory or management practices, time availability, lack of crime analysis, prohibition against officers

It is important to educate the public about community policing. (*Courtesy* Kris Solow, City of Charlotte, North Carolina)

contacting outside agencies, and so forth), 10 external barriers (e.g., lack of support from city council, limited coordination with other city agencies, unrealistic expectations from citizens), and 10 benefits (e.g., reduction in calls for service, improved officer morale, improved police–community relations, increased officer performance). The groups should be given 30 to 45 minutes for this portion of the exercise and instructed not to debate the issues. Each member should participate and the group should prioritize the 10 most important items in each category.

The desired outcomes for this session include providing the trainer with a gauge as to how receptive the participants were to the training; allowing participants to voice their concerns and fears about the agency's transition to new methods of policing; providing command staff with a list of concerns that are most pressing and will need their attention; helping the trainer determine what additional training may be needed; and, finally, allowing the trainer to end the training on a high note by discussing the benefits.

Other Training Considerations

The curriculum discussed provides a basic foundation for COPPS. What has not been discussed are the special considerations for those individuals and groups occupying positions both within and outside the police agency that lend support to COPPS. These groups and individuals include

- support personnel (police)
- the community
- business leaders
- other government agencies
- social service organizations
- elected officials
- the media

Support Personnel

Support personnel provide officers with information that is vital to the success of COPPS. For example, it would be difficult for officers to engage in problem solving if the dispatcher, unaware of the COPPS philosophy, was concerned only with eliminating pending calls and continued to dispatch officers to low-priority calls.

The Community and Business Leaders

As we discussed at length in Chapter 4, the community plays a vital role in COPPS. There are a number of ways in which the department and officers can educate citizens about COPPS, including newsletters, public service announcements, neighborhood meetings, and citizens' academies such as the one discussed in Chapter 9.

It is important that community and business leaders are oriented in the operation of COPPS. Experience has shown that involving the business community can contribute to the success of the COPPS approach. Police executives must never underestimate the level of influence and concern possessed by the business community. Business and industrial leaders can be valuable allies, maybe even providing financial support in causes they believe will help the community. Involving them can foster a cooperative relationship and can have any number of possible beneficial outcomes. Businesspeople might donate time and equipment or provide valuable information for problem-solving efforts. Apartment owners should be informed of the wide array of services officers can provide under a COPPS philosophy, from screening potential tenants to keeping the area free of abandoned vehicles and trash. And business owners who apply CPTED principles may realize significant reductions in crime.

Other Government Agencies

Previous chapters have discussed how problem solving necessarily includes the involvement of agencies other than the police or sheriff's departments. A large percentage of calls for service handled by the police involve noncriminal matters that can be better handled by other city or county agencies. Furthermore, there is considerable overlap between agencies; a deteriorating neighborhood might involve the health, fire, zoning, prosecutor's, street, social services, or other departments as well as the police department. Thus, it is imperative that key persons in those organizations—active partners in problem solving—be trained in the philosophy and workings of COPPS and crime prevention through environmental design (CPTED). This is community oriented government, which is discussed thoroughly in Chapter 3.

Social Service Organizations

With respect to social service agencies, it is not uncommon for these organizations and police agencies to "fire cannon shots across the bow" at one another. When problems arise involving deteriorating neighborhoods and concomitant problems (such as child abuse), which involve both social service and police practitioners, it is particularly important that communication be given top priority. Social service workers must also understand the philosophy and operation of COPPS, because they can serve as a valuable resource and can also provide referrals to the police for solving problems. People who are homeless, mentally ill, survivors of domestic violence, and survivors of schoolyard violence are examples of the people whose calls for service account for a high volume of police responses. Working together, the police and other social service agencies can apply principles of problem solving.

Politicians must be involved and educated early in the planning of COPPS. **Elected Officials**
They often have the final word on whether new ideas or programs will be implemented. The education of politicians regarding COPPS is important for understanding that this philosophy is unique. A police chief may be horrified to hear the mayor announce, in response to a recent tragedy, that henceforth the police would make every effort to arrive no later than 15 minutes after any call for service was received. Politicians must be taught that rapid response to calls is less effective at catching criminals than educating the public to call the police sooner after a crime is committed,[27] and they should be informed that police response time is largely unrelated to the probability of making an arrest or locating a witness.[28] They must also understand that personnel evaluations are to be conducted differently under this strategy and that reported crimes may well increase as the partnership between the police and the public grows.

The local media provide an excellent forum for the police department to pub- **The Media**
licly announce its implementation of COPPS and its goals and objectives. To assist in this endeavor many departments have designated a public information officer (PIO) as the principal spokesperson for the organization. In smaller departments, where a PIO would be unaffordable, the chief or sheriff must master the skills of public relations without the advantage of a PIO buffer.[29]

The most significant facets of effective media relations are truthfulness and reasonable accessibility. Another good tip for the chief executive is to "never alienate anyone who buys ink by the barrel." Of course, this caveat applies to the electronic media as well as the print media.

The chief executive who is attempting to implement COPPS will want and need to market the concept. After the strategy is implemented, COPPS successes should be reported to the community. The media can be of tremendous assistance in this regard.[30]

A SAMPLE TRAINING PROGRAM

Next we look at a sample training program for preparing police personnel for their COPPS duties in Savannah, Georgia. The Savannah police department uses eight training modules, 38 hours in duration, for community oriented policing (COP).

Module I, "Participatory Decisionmaking and Leadership Techniques for Management, Supervision, and Street Officers," is six hours long and is for upper-level supervisors. A professional facilitator presents this orientation, which is based largely on the concept of total quality management (discussed in Chapter 3).

Module II, "Community-Oriented Policing," is an overview that lasts four hours. It begins with the distribution of an in-depth study of crime in Savannah and exacerbating conditions that are found in the same high-crime areas.

Module III explores "Problem-Oriented Policing" (POP) (four hours). POP is viewed by the department as a major component of COP. Themes and advantages are discussed, as are the means by which certain problems can be identified and solved through a structured process (the S.A.R.A. process, discussed in Chapter 4). The resources of the entire community are considered in relation to solving recurring problems. Also discussed are the report forms involved in POP for the officers to use in their duties.

Formal problem-solving training sessions on terrorism awareness have been developed.

Module IV, "Referral System, Materials, City Ordinances" (eight hours), examines the use of referrals and the specific agencies available to help in problem solving. Relevant city codes are reviewed with officers. This block of instruction includes discussions of the several benefits of a good referral system, the key elements of a "good" referral, sources for obtaining materials that explain referral services, and a crime victim brochure.

Module V, "Developing Sources of Human Information," focuses on communicating with citizens in a way that maximizes trust. Four hours in length, it focuses on problematic areas of field interviews and investigative detentions. Included are six barriers to effective communication, seven ways to enhance active listening, and a "citizen's internal checklist after a police–citizen contact." Reasons for conducting a field interview and the means for managing informant information are also included.

Module VI, "Neighborhood Meetings, Survey of Citizen Needs, Tactical Crime Analysis" (four hours), discusses how to organize and conduct neighborhood meetings and community surveys. Topics include identifying groups, formulating questions, pretesting, and gathering and analyzing data.

Module VII is "Crime Prevention Home and Business Surveys" (four hours). Crime prevention is examined in the context of community policing, and officers are trained to conduct security surveys of homes and businesses.

Finally, *Module VIII* (four hours) explores tactical crime analysis; it entails organizing and interpreting crime data, identifying crime trends, and disseminating data in a timely manner.

SUMMARY

This chapter has presented some of the obstacles to learning, an overview of those persons and groups needing to receive COPPS training, and types and component parts of a COPPS training program.

COPPS must become a philosophy before it can become a practice. This change in thinking is the major challenge facing those involved in the training and education of police officers and the public.

This challenge is enhanced because large numbers of police officers and citizens require orientation and training in COPPS.

Police executives who have implemented the COPPS strategy must give due consideration to the training issue—a major aspect of COPPS that is a *sine qua non* of this strategy. Without training, there is nothing.

NOTES

1. P. B. Gove (ed.), *Webster's Encyclopedic Unabridged Dictionary of the English Language* (Springfield, Mass.: Merriam-Webster, 1993), pp. 1502–1503.

2. Larry K. Gaines, Victor E. Kappeler, and Jerald B. Vaughn, *Policing in America* (Cincinnati, Ohio: Anderson, 1994), pp. 88–89.

3. Peter M. Senge, *The Fifth Discipline: The Art and Practice of the Learning Organization* (London: Random House, 1990), p. 3.

4. See Stephen Lieb, "Principles of Adult Learning: Adults as Learners," *http://www.hcc.hawaii.edu/intranet/committees/facdevcom/guidebk/teachtip/adults-2.htm* (Accessed April 30, 2003).

5. "Problem-Based Learning," *http://www.mcli.dist.maricopa.edu/pbl/info.html* (Accessed April 30, 2003).

6. Michael E. Buerger, "Police Training as a Pentecost: Using Tools Singularly Ill-Suited to the Purpose of Reform," *Police Quarterly* 1 (1998):32.

7. Ibid., p. 39.

8. Roger G. Dunham and Geoffrey P. Alpert, *Critical Issues in Policing* (Prospect Heights, Ill.: Waveland Press, 1989), p. 112.

9. Quoted in ibid.

10. Thomas Dempsey, "Cyberschool: Online Law Enforcement Classes," *FBI Law Enforcement Bulletin* (February 1998):10.

11. See, for example, the John Jay College of Criminal Justice School Safety and Security Professional Development course, "Community Policing in Schools," at *www.jjay.cuny.edu/conference/teleconf/*.

12. Richard D. Morrison, "Interactive Training," *Law Enforcement Technology* (January 2000):97.

13. Gregory May, quoted in ibid.

14. U.S. Department of Justice, Bureau of Justice Statistics, *Law Enforcement Management and Administrative Statistics: Local Police Departments 2000* (Washington, D.C.: Author, January 2003), p. iii.

15. Ibid., p. 14.

16. Laurie Austen-Kern, "Training Needs Assessments," *The Law Enforcement Trainer* (November/December 1999):22.

17. Province of British Columbia, Ministry of Attorney General, Police Services Branch, *Community Policing Advisory Committee Report* (Victoria, British Columbia, Canada: Author, 1993), pp. 54–55.

18. Ibid., p. 55.

19. Frum Himelfarb, "A Training Strategy for Policing in a Multicultural Society," *The Police Chief* (November 1991):53–55.

20. Nancy McPherson, "Problem Oriented Policing" (San Diego, Calif.: San Diego Police Department Training Outline, 1992), p. 2.

21. Tara O'Connor Shelley and Anne C. Grant (eds.), *Problem Oriented Policing: Crime-Specific Problems, Critical Issues, and Making POP Work* (Washington, D.C.: Police Executive Research Forum, 1999).

22. Province of British Columbia, Ministry of Attorney General, Police Services Branch, *Community Policing Advisory Committee Report* (Victoria, British Columbia, Canada: Author, 1993), p. 56.

23. Norm Stamper, "A Training Menu to Support Problem Oriented Policing" (Seattle, Wash.: Seattle Police Department, 1997).

24. Police Executive Research Forum, "Supervising Problem-Solving" (Washington, D.C.: Author, training outline, 1990).

25. Ibid., pp. 5–9.

26. Donald S. Quire, "Officers Select 'Ideal' Supervisors" (Washington, D.C.: Community Policing Consortium, *Community Policing Exchange* March/April 1996), p. 8.

27. George L. Kelling, Anthony Pate, Duane Dieck-man, and Charles E. Brown, *The Kansas City Preventive Patrol Experiment: A Summary Report* (Washington, D.C.: The Police Foundation, 1974).

28. Joan Petersilia, "The Influence of Research on Policing." In *Critical Issues in Policing: Contemporary Readings*, Roger C. Dunham and Geoffrey P. Alpert (eds.) (Prospect Heights, Ill.: Waveland Press, 1989), pp. 230–247.

29. Arthur F. Nehrbass, "Promoting Effective Media Relations," *The Police Chief* (January 1989):40, 42–44.

30. See Ken Peak, Robert V. Bradshaw, and Ronald W. Glensor, "Improving Citizen Perceptions of the Police: 'Back to the Basics' with a Community Policing Strategy," *Journal of Criminal Justice* 20 (1992):25–40.

INTRODUCTION

A minority group is a group or category of people who can be distinguished by special physical or cultural traits that can be used to single them out for differential and unequal treatment. We observed in Chapter 2 that U.S. society is rapidly becoming more diverse; it is a cornucopia of multicultural, multiracial, and ethnically rich people with different and competing norms, mores, values, languages, experiences, and expectations. This increase in cultural diversity and languages poses new challenges for the police—who must learn about the diverse cultures if they are to be successful in their objective of providing aid and assistance to all people.

This is not strictly a black and white issue; Latino/Hispanic Americans, Asian/Pacific Americans, and other ethnic minorities have also had difficult relations with the police. Tensions have arisen because many racial and ethnic minorities, homosexuals, and women believed they had been prevented from entering the police field. The most serious problems in police–minority relations, however, have involved African Americans. We, therefore, devote a preponderance of this chapter's discussion to examining race relations between African Americans and police.

We begin this chapter with a brief history of police–minority conflict. Then we examine whether criminal justice in the United States systematically discriminates against minorities, and include discussions of bias-based policing, racial profiling, and hate crimes. Then we consider some means by which police–minority relations can be enhanced, focusing on what community oriented policing and problem solving (COPPS) can do to facilitate that endeavor, including an understanding of cultural customs, differences, and problems.

—9—

POLICE IN A DIVERSE SOCIETY

No man will treat with indifference the principle of race. It is the key of history.
—Disraeli

Following that, we examine "what works": innovative programs in several cities that have built bridges to their minority communities. Next is a discussion of some methods that can be used by police agencies to achieve greater diversity in their ranks. We conclude the chapter with some challenging scenarios involving ethnic customs that police officers might confront.

POLICE AND MINORITIES: A HISTORY OF CONFLICT

In 1900 the African American scholar and activist W. E. B. DuBois said the problem of the twentieth century is the problem of the color line. More than 100 years later we are still proving him right. In the past four decades many changes in society have influenced the nature of police–minority relations:

- The 1954 *Brown v. Topeka Board of Education*[1] decision of the U.S. Supreme Court declared that separate educational facilities were inherently unequal.
- The use of civil disobedience and nonviolent resistance increased in the 1950s and 1960s, and the Civil Rights Act was passed in 1964. Almost all of the riots in the 1960s were sparked by incidents involving the police.[2]

A scene from the Walker Report of the 1968 Democratic National Convention in Chicago.

- The Equal Employment Opportunity Commission was established, and the 1972 Amendment to the Civil Rights Act became law.[3]

Collectively, these actions prohibited discrimination in education, hiring and promotion, voting, and use of public accommodations, among other things.

Of particular importance in the history of U.S. race relations are the events that occurred between 1960 and 1970, when police–minority encounters frequently precipitated racial outbursts. Specifically, Harlem, Watts, Newark, and Detroit all were scenes of major race riots during the 1960s. There were 75 civil disorders involving African Americans and the police in 1967 alone, with at least 83 people killed, mostly African Americans. In addition, many police officers and firefighters were killed or injured. Property damage in these riots totaled hundreds of millions of dollars.[4] The 1970s busing programs that were introduced to integrate schools resulted in white "backlash" and more interracial conflict.

A scene from the Walker Report of the 1968 Democratic National Convention in Chicago.

In the late 1980s police–community relations appeared to worsen, with a major riot in Miami, Florida in 1989. Also in the 1980s, affirmative action programs led to charges of reverse discrimination and more dominant-group backlash.[5] More recently, of course, there has been burning and looting in Miami, Los Angeles, Atlanta, Las Vegas, Washington, D.C., St. Petersburg, Florida, and other cities. These incidents have demonstrated that the same tensions that found temporary release on the streets of African American communities in the past still remain with us.

The police were involved in all of the social changes described. At times police have been used to prevent minority group members from demonstrating on behalf of civil rights, and on occasion police have had to use force against protesting groups. At other times the police have been required to protect those same protesting minorities from the wrath of the dominant group and others who opposed peaceful demonstrations. Over time, alienation has developed from these contacts. Thus, members of both groups today have an uneasy coexistence with a good deal of "baggage" based on what they have seen, heard, or been told of their interactions throughout history. The phrase *police–community relations*, as Samuel Walker wrote, is really a euphemism for *police–race relations*:

> The police have not had the same kinds of conflicts with the white majority community as they do with racial minorities. The most serious aspect of the . . . problem involves *black Americans*. Similar problems exist with respect to other racial-minority groups. In areas with large numbers of *Hispanic Americans* . . . there are also serious conflicts with the police. *Native Americans* . . . have also had conflict with the police. Similar problems exist in cities with large *Asian-American* communities (emphases in original).[6]

Police–community problems are part of a larger problem of racism in our society. The highly respected National Academy of Sciences concluded more than a decade ago that "black crime and the position of blacks within the nation's system of criminal justice administration are related to past and present social opportunities and disadvantages and can be best understood through consideration of blacks' overall social status."[7] Recent mass gatherings in Washington, D.C., engendered by such groups as the Southern Christian Leadership Conference and the Rainbow Coalition, have involved protests against racial profiling (discussed later), police brutality, and other perceived prejudices toward people of color; such assemblies would indicate that the Academy's statement is still valid today. Minority group members remain frustrated because the pace of gains in our society has not kept pace with their expectations.

To many minorities the police are an "occupying force," more concerned with restricting their freedom than providing service to their community. From the police's point of view, minority neighborhoods have not always been supportive of their efforts to combat crime. Which perspective is more accurate? Perhaps that question cannot be answered. However, a key element in police–community relations—and one that is often overlooked—is how the police perceive the public.

MINORITIES AND THE CRIMINAL JUSTICE SYSTEM

A highly influential study addressing whether the justice system discriminates against minorities by the RAND Corporation in 1983 found no consistent, statistically significant, racial differences in the probability of arrest or in case

Systematic Discrimination against Minorities

Minority community members often believe they are unnecessarily detained and interviewed by police. (*Courtesy* Washoe County, Nevada, Sheriff's Office)

processing, even though minority suspects were more likely than whites to be given longer sentences and to be put in prison instead of jail. RAND determined that the criminal justice system did not discriminate against minorities, who were not overrepresented in the arrest population *relative to the number of crimes they actually commit* (emphasis in original), nor were they more likely than whites to be arrested for those crimes.[8]

Recent studies in the late 1990s and the early 2000s, however, paint a different picture and challenge the RAND findings. Research on California's justice system in 1996 raised questions about that state's racial fairness, finding that 39 percent of its African American men in their 20s were in prison, jails, or on probation; the authors concluded that the system was discriminatory. African Americans were charged under California's "three strikes" law at 17 times the rate of whites, and at almost every stage of the justice process, whites fared better than African Americans or Latinos. A member of the NAACP's Legal Defense Fund stated the report showed why the black community does not trust the justice system.[9] Even the San Francisco district attorney was compelled to observe that "The criminal justice system is putting an unfair burden on minorities."[10]

Then, in 2003 the Leadership Conference on Civil Rights (LCCR) issued a report entitled "Justice on Trial," observing that "in one critical area—criminal justice—racial inequality is growing, not receding."[11] The LCCR report bemoaned "unequal treatment of minorities [that] characterizes every stage of the process," and noted that the majority of crimes are not committed by minorities, most minorities are not criminals, and disproportionate numbers of minority arrests perpetuate the belief that minorities commit more crimes, which in turn leads to racial profiling (discussed below).[12] In conclusion, and in complete opposition to the RAND report's findings two decades earlier, the LCCR determined that "our criminal justice system discriminates against minorities."[13]

The above studies would indicate that the American criminal justice system is indeed biased in its treatment of minorities. This has been and continues to be one of the most sensitive charges against the criminal justice system throughout its history, and differential treatment is our next topic of discussion.

Certainly in today's climate there is considerable pressure on the police to be watchful of certain minorities living in our nation who would do us harm. Indeed, since September 11, 2001, law enforcement's targeting of Arabs and Muslims, in their search for suspected terrorists, is viewed by two-thirds of Americans as "understandable."[14] Still, racial profiling has become a despised police practice in the new millennium. (Actually, a more inclusive term is "bias-based profiling," which includes unequal treatment of any persons on the basis of race, ethnicity, religion, gender, sexual orientation, or socioeconomic status.) Bias-based profiling on the basis of race—also known as "driving while black or brown" (DWBB)—where a police officer, acting on a personal bias,[15] stops a vehicle simply because the driver is of a certain race, is given no public support. Such incidents can take various forms, as demonstrated by the following accounts by people who were stopped by police on questionable grounds and subjected to disrespectful behavior or intrusive questioning:

- A young black woman trades her new sports car for an older model because police have repeatedly stopped her on suspicion of possession of a stolen vehicle.
- An elderly African American couple returning from a social event in formal dress are stopped and questioned at length, allegedly because their car resembles one identified in a robbery.
- A prominent black lawyer driving a luxury car is frequently stopped on various pretexts.
- A Hispanic deputy police chief is stopped various times in neighboring jurisdictions on "suspicion."
- A black judge far from her hometown is stopped, handcuffed, and laid face down on the pavement while police search her car (they issue no citations).[16]

This issue has driven a deep wedge between the police and minorities, many of whom claim to be victims of this practice. Indeed, the New Jersey state police superintendent was fired by that state's governor in March 1999 for statements that were perceived as racially insensitive concerning racial profiling.

The best defense for the police may be summarized in two words: *collect data*. Collecting traffic stop data helps chiefs and commanders determine whether officers are stopping or searching a disproportionate number of minorities, and enables them to act on this information in a timely fashion. Technology—including mobile data computers and wireless handheld devices—is available to the police for this purpose.

Exhibit 9-1 shows what the Sacramento, California, police department has done to study and address racial profiling, although no such complaints had been reported in the city.

Recently the International Association of Chiefs of Police issued a comprehensive policy statement on biased policing and data collection. The association "believes that any form of police action that is based solely on the race, gender, ethnicity, age, or socioeconomic level of an individual is both unethical and illegal," but that data collection programs "must ensure that data is being collected and analyzed in an impartial and methodologically sound fashion."[17] Next another minority-related problem is discussed, hate crimes.

EXHIBIT 9-1 Sacramento Searches for Biased Policing

In the late 1990s the Sacramento, California, police department (SPD) began a study on racially biased policing, to determine the degree of intrusiveness of traffic stops, and whether or not such stops were indicative of racially biased policing. Even though there were no reported complaints of such policing, the SPD recognized the importance of responding to national concern toward the problem. The study, by the University of Southern California, and financed by $275,000 in grants from the federal Office of Community Oriented Policing Services and the state's highway patrol, began by collecting reports, editorials, and anecdotal information for insight into approaches taken by other agencies. Meetings were held with the community, civil rights organizations, the police union, and agency staff (officers were invited to provide input on how to conduct the study). Officers filled out data collection forms for each traffic stop, which included data on traffic patterns, type of crimes throughout the city, and officers' badge numbers, age, race, and unit assignments. To broaden

the study, the SPD invited a number of stakeholders—including the American Civil Liberties Union, the Mexican American Legal Defense and Education Fund, and neighborhood associations, all of whom got a better understanding of police work—and who came to the vital realization that rarely could an officer identify the race of the driver or occupants of cars before they were actually stopped. The study did find that traffic stops involving African Americans occurred at a disproportionately higher rate than their overall population, so the study was extended for two years in order to examine whether systems existed that encouraged bias-based policing. Now, as part of its community policing "Police as Problem Solvers/Peacemakers Initiative," the SPD is providing technical assistance to other local police agencies interested in data collection on biased policing.

Source: Tammy Jones, "Sacramento Searches for Bias Policing." In *Community Links* (Washington, D.C.: Community Policing Consortium, February 2003), pp. 1–2.

RESPONDING TO HATE CRIMES

Hate crimes and hate incidents—those that are motivated by an offender's bias against an individual's or group's race, religion, ethnic/national origin, gender, age, disability, or sexual orientation[18]—are also major issues for the police because of their unique impact on victims and the community. Such crimes can have a special emotional and psychological impact. Hate violence can exacerbate racial, religious, or ethnic tensions in a community and lead to a cycle of escalating reprisals. Police executives must demonstrate a commitment to be both tough on hate-crime perpetrators and sensitive to the impact of hate violence on the community.[19]

At present, 41 states and the District of Columbia have crime statutes that enhance the penalties for hate crimes and address hate violence. The 1990 Hate Crime Statistics Act requires the Department of Justice to collect and publish data on bias-motivated crimes across the United States. Furthermore, at the federal level hate crimes are investigated by the FBI's Bias Crimes Unit and the Bureau of Alcohol, Tobacco, Firearms, and Explosives church arson and explosives experts.[20]

In 2002, 7,462 hate crimes were reported in the U.S., 3,642 (48.8 percent) of which were motivated by racial bias, 1,425 (19.1 percent) by religious bias, 1,246 (16.7 percent) by sexual orientation bias, and 1,104 (14.8 percent) by ethnic/national origin bias. Of the 1,425 incidents that were motivated by religious bias, 939 (65.9 percent) were directed against Jews and Jewish institutions.[21]

There is much a law enforcement organization can do with respect to hate crimes to take a leadership role in the community: provide victims with a point of contact in the department to whom they can report hate crimes and express concerns, inform victims on case progress, participate in hate crime training as well as educate the public about these crimes, establish a "zero tolerance" of prejudice within the department, track the criminal activities of hate groups, and sponsor and participate in community events that promote tolerance and diversity.[22] A good example of a police agency's effort to fight hate crimes is that of Madison, Connecticut. At a departmental roll call, every officer receives a laminated hate crimes response card which provides officers important information for responding to hate crimes, working with victims, and pursuing perpetrators. The card includes the definition of a hate crime, questions responding officers should ask, and tips for recognizing signs of organized hate groups. In October 2002, the Anti-Defamation League took the effort further, distributing these cards to more than 7,500 police officers throughout the State of Connecticut.[23]

The Justice Department has developed a new hate-crime training curriculum for police officers, and the Anti-Defamation League has also produced a number of hate-crime resources and prevention initiatives. See Exhibit 9-2 for more information.

IMPROVING POLICE–MINORITY RELATIONS

Given its history and all of the previously mentioned exacerbating factors, we are left to wonder whether police–minority relations can ever be improved.

Complicating Factors, Possible Solutions

Without question, some members of society believe the police have no redeeming qualities. To these people, police officers are, and will always be, symbolic agents of an entire system of injustice, never to be trusted under any circumstances. So long as the police have the duty to enforce the laws and the power to arrest and control the behavior of their fellows, there will be

---

EXHIBIT 9-2 Definition of a Hate Crime

A hate crime is a criminal offense committed against persons, property or society that is motivated, in whole or in part, by an offender's bias against an individual's or a group's perceived race, religion, ethnic/national origin, gender, age, disability or sexual orientation. Legal definitions of hate crimes vary. Check your state statutes for the definition of hate crime in your jurisdiction.

Hate incidents are those actions by an individual or group that, while motivated by bias, do not rise to the level of a criminal offense.

Community Trauma
Hate crimes victimize the entire community and may involve

- Victimization projected to all community members
- Sense of group vulnerability
- Community fear/tension
- Possibility of reactive crimes or copycat incidents
- Community polarization
- Redirection of law enforcement resources
- Loss of trust in criminal justice institutions
- Public damage (i.e., buildings such as churches)

Victim Trauma
Because the basis for the attack is the victim's identity, victim(s) may suffer

- Deep personal crisis
- Increased vulnerability to repeat attack
- Sense of community/system betrayal
- Acute shock and disbelief
- Extreme fear of certain groups
- Hopelessness
- Anger/desire for revenge
- Shame and humiliation

Action to Be Taken at the Scene:

- Explain to the victim(s) and witnesses the likely progression of the investigation
- Report the suspected hate crime to the supervisor on duty
- Refer media representatives to the public information officer or supervisor on duty
- Document the incident thoroughly on the department report forms, noting any particular hate crime indicators and quoting exact wording of statements made by perpetrators

Source: L. E. Technology, "Healing the Hate," p. 58; adapted as "Tear-Out Pocket Guide" by IACP, 515 N. Washington Street, Alexandria, Virginia 22314 (800 THE-IACP; *www.theiacp.org*).

---

inherent problems in obtaining complete public support. "The most difficult of all police problems [is] how to make more palatable the basic regulatory nature of police work."[24] James Baldwin's classic and powerful description of how the police are viewed in the ghetto illustrates the point:

> The only way to police a ghetto is to be oppressive. None of the Police Commissioner's men, even with the best will in the world, have any way of understanding the lives led by the people they swagger about in twos and threes controlling. Their very presence is an insult, and it would be, even if they spent their entire day feeding gumdrops to children. They represent the force of the white world, and that world's criminal profit and ease, to keep the black man corralled up here, in his place. The badge, the gun in the holster, and the swinging club make vivid what will happen should his rebellion become overt. He moves through Harlem, therefore, like an occupying soldier in a bitterly hostile country, which is precisely what and where he is, and is the reason he walks in twos and threes.[25]

WHAT COPPS CAN DO: AGENCY INITIATIVES

Following are some examples of various activities some jurisdictions have undertaken to help address problems and bring about unity among their diverse populations.

Los Angeles: Listening to the Forums

Ethnic diversity defines the City of Los Angeles. To take advantage of that wealth of varied knowledge, the LAPD turned to the community for ideas, establishing six Community Forums to promote community policing with reliance on trust, respect, cooperation, and partnership. Each forum has about 25 members as well as direct access to the police chief. Following are brief descriptions of each.

- Black Forum: As a response to the forum's recent concerns about racial profiling, the LAPD published a pamphlet to improve relations between mo-

Lasting improvements between the police and minorities require that both groups make necessary changes. (*Courtesy* Kris Solow, City of Charlotte, North Carolina)

torists and officers, explain procedures of traffic stops, and a means to commend officers and to lodge complaints.

- Hispanic Forum: This forum's main concerns include immigration rights and the LAPD's policy concerning undocumented aliens, and it attempts to ensure that police comply with a policy against initiating action for the sole purpose of determining a person's immigration status.
- Asian/Pacific Islander Forum: This forum has developed a video on ethnic diversity.
- Gay/Lesbian Forum: Concerns regarding arrests based on lewd conduct and the perceived use of police "baiting" to arrest gays are addressed, and the forum helps police to reduce hate crimes and to hire recruits who respect varied life styles.
- Religious Forum: This forum promotes collaboration among the many religious groups in Los Angeles.
- Youth Forum: This forum exposes young people to the scope of law enforcement so they may better appreciate the importance of laws and justice in their lives.[26]

Santa Ana: A Hands-On Citizen Academy

The Santa Ana, California, police department has launched a unique 12-week citizen police academy that enhances its efforts in community policing by emphasizing problem solving and hands-on activities that expose students to what it is like to be a police officer.

Students are given a simulated burglary case and interview the victim and witnesses, investigate the case, and solve it. They dust for fingerprints, process evidence, and write reports of their activities. Graduates become "ambassadors" for the department; Cesar Dias and Alicia Ramos said the program is a vital source of information about COPPS, and they "go out and spread the word about law enforcement."[27]

In Indiana: Kids Roaming the Internet

Police in Michigan City, Indiana, were determined to befriend and help educate youths in the city's West Side, one of the city's poorer sections. Using a grant from a local group, the department created a new substation and stocked it with four computers, scanners, and printers, as well as a reading library. Each computer has access to the Internet. School liaison and D.A.R.E. officers were transferred to staff the center during weekdays, freeing community policing officers to continue their neighborhood work. Following a U.S. congressman's visit to the center, for which the police bought pizza, the center was packed with young people. In addition to expanding the youths' minds, the center also provides children with a safe place to study and improves community relations.[28]

Lincoln Services Its Non-English Speaking Populations

The Lincoln, Nebraska, police department (LPD) provides a host of services for residents who do not speak English as their primary language. The most common foreign languages spoken in Lincoln are Spanish and Vietnamese, so the LPD makes interpreters available to officers on the street when needed in those and virtually all languages. The LPD Web site contains information in Spanish and Vietnamese and has produced several bilingual videos on various topics for broadcast on cable television. Officers conduct training sessions for new immigrants on a number of topics as well, and LPD provides TDD service to the deaf and hearing impaired; closed captioning is available for the city's public television programs.[29]

Citizens' academies expose people to what it is like to be a police officer, and they help officers understand public concerns.

Office of Community Oriented Policing Services

Finally, it should be mentioned that the U.S. Department of Justice's Office of Community Oriented Policing Services (COPS) recognizes the need for cultural diversity training, which is provided through its 31 Regional Community Policing Institutes across the nation. Specialized training is even being provided for communities that are experiencing rapid demographic changes.[30]

Confronting the Issues

One of the problems with addressing police–minority relations issues is that police and people in general do not like to discuss the topic because "you step on somebody's toes or it's embarrassing."[31]

The COPPS philosophy helps address this complex issue. In addition to getting the two groups talking with each other and, therefore, thwarting conflict, it enables police to pinpoint racial tension in their city. COPPS, by its very nature, encourages officers to find out exactly what is occurring in neighborhoods, including who is involved and what their motives are.

As we've discussed in earlier chapters, supervisors must support officers in this endeavor. Officers must be allowed to interact with different people rather than functioning as mere report-takers. Through this interaction, officers begin to learn the cultural diversity of various racial, ethnic, and religious groups.

What can COPPS do to improve relations between the police and minorities? To begin with, at its most fundamental level COPPS tries to emphasize the interrelationship between the police and the community. COPPS dictates that officers understand their unique, problem-solving relationship with the community as they execute the law. There is no denying that this is at times a huge task, given the history of problems between the two groups.

Indeed, many people are convinced that the U.S. criminal justice system *is* racist. Although COPPS cannot change the outcomes of the above studies by the LCCR and in California, it can humanize the justice system, showing a side of the police that is in stark contrast to these figures.

The acceptance and management of diversity, like the implementation of COPPS, cannot be simply a "program" or strategy. For either to succeed, there must be major personal, personnel, and policy changes from the top to the bottom of the organization.

The key to managing diversity and accommodating cultural differences is training and education. But training in both COPPS and diversity, if not conducted correctly and supported by changes in the organization, is better left undone. As Gayle Fisher-Stewart has noted, too often both COPPS and the management of diversity are introduced

> with a "shot in the arm." A curriculum is developed, and the entire staff of the department is marched through for their inoculation. After the first dose, there are no boosters. The curriculum is not modified on the basis of rank . . . officers are often viewed as the only ones who need training, because they are viewed as the ones causing problems in the community.[32]

In a related vein, Exhibit 9-3 contains 15 appropriate, pointed questions compiled by Minneapolis, Minnesota, chief of police Robert K. Olson, to be considered by police agencies that are attempting to engage in "balancing crime strategies and democratic principles."

Agencies seek to employ a force that is as diverse as the population they serve. (*Courtesy* Fort Lauderdale, Florida, police department)

1. Is your department really doing community-oriented policing: a continual discussion of implementation of crime control strategies involving the direct input of the citizens affected by police action?

2. Does your department routinely give detailed cultural awareness/diversity training to recruits, with follow-up in-services yearly to the rest of the police department?

3. Does your police department have a reputation in the minority community for taking swift internal discipline when serious police misconduct occurs?

4. Have you developed true school liaison and additional police interaction—other than enforcement—with young people?

5. Are there incentives or requirements for the chief and upper staff and/or other members of the department to reside in the city in which they are responsible for policing?

6. Has your department established strong community ties, particularly with the leadership of all relevant organizations representing people of color, so that when crisis happens—and it will—the department will have immediate access and assistance in dealing with it?

7. Has the department and its political leadership made clear to all its employees that racial intolerance will not be permitted, crushed at the slightest hint of its appearance, and that the public, particularly people of color, feel confident that their city will address those issues?

8. Who polices the police or chief in your community? Is there an alternative to internal affairs? Is the police chief held accountable by the appropriate elected body for [e]nsuring a corruption-free police department?

9. Is the chief executive clearly supported by mayor and council in their community policing and other activities designed to include, rather than exclude, all their constituents?

10. Does your department have a hiring process that will not only [e]nsure diversity within the ranks, but is fair and does not exclude people, and is designed to bring in candidates who wish to join for the spirit of service and not the spirit of adventure? Has your department created an internal atmosphere where people of color would want to become a member and have a rewarding, 20-year career?

11. Does each department offer internal promotional and assignment opportunities equally to all? Do the promoted ranks clearly reflect the diversity of the whole organization and the community that it serves?

12. Is the community routinely involved in the discussion of all issues that affect policing within their neighborhoods?

13. Is your police organization structured to ensure there is accountability at every level for the performance and actions of each and every officer who encounters citizens in their daily work?

14. Does your department have consistent institutionalized citizen communication instruments that allow the department to not only keep the citizens informed of police activity, but to receive citizen input on a regular basis on a wide variety of issues?

15. Does your police department have a reasonable standard of behavior and protocol for the stopping of citizens, particularly in high crime areas? Are persons being stopped and clearly being advised of the reason for the stop? Are they being told exactly what the police are doing? Most particularly, does your police training include disengagement techniques—how to get out of a situation where, in fact, the officer may well have been wrong in their assumption, and must appropriately explain and apologize to the citizen for their inconvenience?

Source: List compiled by Chief Robert K. Olson of Minneapolis, Minnesota. Police Executive Research Forum, *Subject to Debate*, 13(6) (June 1999):5. Used with permission.

Understanding Cultural Customs, Differences, Problems

This section discusses the negative consequences of police not understanding the cultural differences of the people they confront. Indeed, actions that are common in mainstream American culture can result in miscommunication and have dire consequences if the police do not recognize cultural nuances. As a fundamental example, it is not uncommon for an officer to get someone's attention by beckoning with a crooked index finger, repeatedly moving it back and forth; although this is an innocuous gesture to Americans, it is an insult to an Ethiopian man, who uses it to call a person a dog.[33]

A more serious example would be the custom of certain Asian cultures to exchange gifts at initial meetings. On meeting with members of such a culture, the COPPS officer can be placed in an uncomfortable position at having to offend those persons whom he or she is there to serve either by not offering a gift or by refusing to accept a gift.[34] These are true ethical if not legal dilemmas that today's police officer—and his or her administrators and supervisors—must address. It has been stated that "law enforcement professionals need to develop cultural empathy."[35]

There are other cultural customs and problems about which the police should be cognizant. For example, during an argument it would not be uncommon for a Mexican American to shout to his friend, "I'm going to kill you if you do that again." In the Anglo culture, this statement would clearly signal one's intent to do harm. However, in the context of the Latino/Hispanic culture, this simply conveys anger. Therefore, the Spanish word *matar* (to kill) is often used to show feelings, not intent. Another example is that Anglo Americans tend to assume that there is a short distance between an emotional, verbal expression of disagreement and a full-blown conflict. For African Americans, though, stating a position with feeling shows sincerity. For most African Americans, threatening movements, not angry words, indicate the start of a fight. In fact, some would argue that fights do not begin when people are talking or arguing, but rather when they stop talking.

Many possible breakdowns in verbal communication can cause difficulties for police officers and those of different cultures.[36] For example, for many Tongans, being handcuffed when arrested for minor crimes is a cultural taboo; that treatment is reserved for only the very worst offenders in their culture. To many Southeast Asians, being asked by an officer to assume a kneeling position with fingers interlocked behind the head is cause for rebellion; to them, this posture is a prelude to being assassinated. For the Chinese, causing someone to lose face through disrespect—such as not being able to use both hands to convey an object—is one of the worst things one person can do to another.[37]

For Latino/Hispanics, the concept of masculine superiority is important, as are the dominance of the father in the family, division of labor according to sex, and the belief that the family is more important than the individual. Arguing politics on street corners is an old tradition that, in its frenzy, might appear to be assaultive behavior. It is culturally taboo for a stranger to touch a small Hispanic girl. The use of surnames and last names may be confusing to some police officers. Latin custom dictates the use of the father's and the mother's last name (e.g., Jose Jesus Leon Flores). The legal name is the surname (Leon); the maternal name is the last name in the series (Flores).[38]

Native Americans, unfortunately, suffer severe social problems. Alcohol has been found to be a factor in 80 percent of all Native American suicides and in 90 percent of all homicides. Alcohol has also been found to play a part in the social, physical, psychological, economic, and cultural disruption experienced by Native Americans.[39]

In addition to these traits, other cultural differences that might be observed by the police include the following.

Criminal justice agencies in the St. Paul, Minnesota, area developed a program to enhance citizens' understanding of the Hmong culture and to train Hmong people in the justice process.

Hmong
Circles of
Peace

A program of the
Upper Midwest
Community Policing
Institute

Integrity, Compassion, Respect,
Honesty, Consensus and Fairness.

Office: (651) 917.2811
Fax: (651) 917.2253

- *Body position:* A police sergeant relaxing at a desk with feet up, baring the soles of the feet, would likely offend a Saudi Arabian or Thai, because the foot is considered the dirtiest part of the body.
- *Facial expressions and expressiveness:* A smile is a source of confusion for police officers when encountering Asian cultures. A smile or giggle can cover up pain, humiliation, or embarrassment; on hearing something sad, they may smile appearing to be a "smart aleck." And, whereas Latin Americans, Mediterranean, Arab, Israeli, and African Americans tend to show emotions facially, other groups tend to be less facially expressive; officers may assume that these persons are not being cooperative.

Pre-service and in-service police training should cover these cultural differences. At the very least, police officers should know what terms are the least offensive when referring to ethnic or racial groups. For example, most Asians prefer not to be called Orientals; they prefer their nationality of origin, such as Korean American.

Many American Indians resent the term "Native American" because that term was invented by the U. S. government. They prefer to be called American Indian or to be known by their tribal ancestry (e.g., Crow, Winnebago). The terms *black American* and *African American* can usually be used interchangeably; however, the latter is more commonly used among younger people. Mexican Americans usually refer to themselves as *Chicanos*, whereas the term *Latino* is preferred by those from Central America.[40]

RECRUITING AND EMPLOYING A DIVERSE POLICE DEPARTMENT

Women and minorities are underrepresented in policing. The organizational culture of policing has been noticeably slow to change in this regard. Female officers may help improve the tarnished image of policing, improve community relations, and foster a more flexible, less violent approach to keeping the peace. Former Houston, Texas, police chief Elizabeth Watson stated that, "Women tend to rely more on intellectual than physical prowess. From that standpoint, policing is a natural match for them."[41]

The recruitment of minority officers remains a difficult task. Probably the single most difficult barrier has to do with the image that police officers have among these groups. Unfortunately, for many African Americans and Latino/Hispanics, police officers are symbols of oppression and have been charged with using excessive brutality; they are often seen as an army of occupation. Meanwhile, many women are reluctant to try to enter what they perceive as a male-dominated, sexist occupation. They may also be aware of high turnover rates of female police officers and the glass ceiling that militates against promotion of women.

Some very successful methods are being used by some law enforcement agencies toward recruiting women and minorities and to generally diversify their workforce. For example, the Philadelphia police department (PPD) has a very informative and easily navigable Web site and visits all the minority communities and such organizations as the Latino Organization; minorities are offered a tour of the police academy to view the training. The Omaha, Nebraska, police department's (OPD) Web site is extensive and takes the reader through the selection process, the command structure, salary and benefits, and the Law Enforcement Code of Ethics. The OPD also works closely with local television, radio, and newspapers to develop videos and publicity spots that highlight various aspects of police work and the department's recruiting efforts. Recruiting information and application forms are disseminated nationally to colleges, universities, community agencies, churches, health clubs, libraries, female/minority owned businesses, special interest groups, and community leaders. Internet job announcements are posted on local, state, and national employment-related job sites, and recruiters attend numerous career fairs to not only disseminate information but also conduct mock interviews for interested candidates.

Similarly, the Chicago police department's (CPD) Web site carries a strong promotional message, offering minorities the opportunity to utilize the latest law enforcement methodologies and technological tools and describing some of the different career and promotional opportunities, benefits, minimum qualifications, and the hiring process. Applications can be downloaded. CPD's diverse recruiting division also visit community and college job fairs, military installations, community meetings, religious organizations, and neighborhood organizations, both in and out of state. CPD's recruiting effort, called the Ambassador Program, is advertised in military transition offices, on local television, and in public service announcements, newspapers, movie theaters, baseball fields, and the mass transit system. A recent innovation is Recruitment Day, in which special invitations are sent to about 7,000 individuals who request them as well as unsolicited invitations to the general public.

Obviously, until more minority and female officers are promoted to administrative levels and can affect policy and serve as role models, there is a higher risk of their being treated unequally and having difficulty being promoted—a classic catch-22 situation. Nonetheless, as the United States generally becomes more diverse, police organizations must take measures to reflect the larger society.

ON THE STREET: SOME PERPLEXING SCENARIOS

Following are five scenarios that are based on actual events and demonstrate some of the situations that might be confronted by COPPS officers. For each scenario we have provided some of the cultural beliefs and practices that might come into play. Try to consider how police officers might best handle each situation and the possible repercussions if they fail to recognize the nonverbal communication and beliefs and practices that are at work in each. Also consider the need for cultural diversity to be incorporated into basic police academy training curricula.

Scenario 1: You witness a traffic violation and when you stop the driver of the vehicle, you notice two things. First, he speaks with a heavy Spanish accent; second, he appears very nervous. You ask for his license and registration. When he gives them to you, you find that he has also enclosed a $100 bill. The traffic offense carries a fine of $25, but now you also have the offense of bribery. How would you handle this situation?[42]

Here, the officer might consider the fact that in some Latin American countries, the way to do business with any public official—especially the police—is to offer money. It is expected, and there are severe penalties for noncompliance. The offense of bribery has been committed and the officer would be well within the law to arrest the driver. After further questioning the driver regarding his country of origin, the officer could explain that the exchange of money is a punishable offense in the United States and charge him only for the traffic offense.

Scenario 2: You are summoned to a local school by the principal, who has been informed of a case of child abuse by a sixth-grade teacher. On arriving at the principal's office, you are shown a Vietnamese girl who had been absent from school for several days with a high fever. The girl has heavy bruising on the left side of her neck. You go to the child's home and question her father, who admits in broken English that he caused the bruising on the girl's neck. What is your reaction?

In parts of Asia, a medical practice called "coining" involves rubbing the skin with a heated coin, leaving highly visible marks on the neck or back. This practice, intended to heal the child, may easily be misinterpreted as child abuse by police, school, or social service agencies. This is a good example of why police officers must avoid being ethnocentric or interpreting what they see through their own cultural "filters."

Scenario 3: You are summoned to a murder scene involving a family picnic in a neighborhood park. On arriving you learn that a Mexican woman had been involved in an extramarital affair and had been bragging about her activities in front of many extended family members in the park. The woman also made comments about her new lover's sexual prowess and her husband's inability to satisfy her. Her husband then left the park. Returning shortly thereafter with a shotgun, he shot and killed his wife. He gives himself up to you. For what criminal charge should the defendant be convicted?

In probably all states, a case such as this would result in a minimum charge of second-degree murder against the defendant. However, in this actual case (in California), because the jury took into consideration the cultural background of this couple, the husband was convicted of a lesser charge of manslaughter. It was argued that the wife's boasting about her lover and the emasculation of her husband created a passion and emotion that completely undermined his "machismo," pride, and honor—what it means to be humiliated in the context of the Latin culture in front of one's family.[43]

Scenario 4: While on foot patrol, a COPPS officer responds to neighbors' complaints. The scene is a brawl at a barbecue party in the backyard of a home where Samoans reside. How should the officer proceed?

The officer could immediately summon backup assistance, and together the officers could make a show of force, breaking up the fighting but also acquiring the undying disrespect of the Samoan community and widening the gap between the two groups. Alternatively, the police could locate the "chief" of this group and let that person deal with the problem in a manner in which he would handle it in Samoa. The chief has a prominent role to play and can serve as a bridge between the police and the community (and keep the matter out of court).[44]

Scenario 5: A police officer stops a Nigerian cabdriver, who moves close to the officer and ignores the officer's command to "step back." He also averts his eyes from the officer, and begins defiantly "babbling to the ground" in a high-pitched tone of voice while making gestures. The officer believes that the cabdriver is out of control, unstable, and possibly dangerous. How should the officer perceive this individual?

In Nigeria, the social distance for conversation is much closer than in the United States; it may be less than 15 inches. Furthermore, Nigerian people often show respect and humility by averting their eyes. What is perceived by the officer as "babbling" is actually the cabdriver's way of sending a message of respect and humility. Most likely, the cabdriver is not even aware that he is perceived as out of control, unstable, and dangerous.

These case studies are not presented to question the rightness or wrongness of any group's values, beliefs, or practices; nor should they be interpreted to mean that serious crimes should be excused on cultural grounds. Rather, the point is to illustrate to the COPPS officer the importance of understanding cultural differences and individual backgrounds.

Obviously the police must take differences in nonverbal communication into account when dealing with people of different cultures. These case studies also reveal that discretion at the police level is much more important than that practiced at the court's level.

It would be unrealistic to expect all police officers to be aware of every possibility for miscommunication or cultural insult. Policing in a multicultural society, however, requires a humanistic approach through which differences are understood and accommodated rather than viewed as cause for conflict. Opponents of COPPS may believe that adding a multicultural focus will soften an allegedly already soft approach to crime prevention; however, not understanding cultural differences can and does result in officer or citizen injury and death and disorder.[45]

SUMMARY

This chapter focused on the often-fractured relations that have historically come between the police and the minority communities they serve.

Ours is not a perfect world. The Constitution notwithstanding, people are *not* created equal, at least with respect to legal, social, political, and economic opportunities. This disparity creates confrontations, mistrust, and enmity between many citizens and the police.

As more studies point to systematic racism within our criminal justice system, the police must work even harder to heal the wounds of the past and to eliminate any vestiges of bias-based policing and vigorously pursue those who would commit hate crimes.

Policing also needs more minorities who are willing to assist as citizens or as police officers to join the cause, as well as more culturally informed police training.

For these reasons, COPPS offers hope for improvement, for this strategy fosters a partnership that is based on trust, communication, and understanding.

NOTES

1. 347 U.S. 483 (1954).

2. Anthony M. Platt (ed.), *The Politics of Riot Commissions* (New York: Collier Books, 1971).

3. Ibid., Chapter 8.

4. See, for example, Allen D. Grimshaw, *Racial Violence in the United States* (Chicago: Aldine, 1969), pp. 269–298; *Report of the National Advisory Commission on Civil Disorders Report* (New York: Bantam Books, 1968).

5. Steven M. Cox and Jack D. Fitzgerald, *Police in Community Relations: Critical Issues,* (2nd ed.) (Dubuque, Iowa: William C. Brown, 1992), p. 129.

6. Samuel Walker, *The Police in America: An Introduction,* (2nd ed.) (New York: McGraw-Hill, 1993), p. 224.

7. National Research Council, *A Common Destiny: Blacks and American Society* (Washington, D.C.: National Academy Press, 1989), p. 453.

8. Joan Petersilia, "Racial Disparities in the Criminal Justice System: Executive Summary of RAND Institute Study, 1983." In *The Criminal Justice System and Blacks,* Daniel Georges-Abeyle (ed.) (New York: Clark Boardman, 1984), pp. 225–258.

9. Greg Krikorian, "Study Questions Justice System's Racial Fairness," *Los Angeles Times,* February 13, 1996, *http://www.pdxnorml.org/LAT.racial.fairness* (Accessed April 28, 2003).

10. *San Francisco Chronicle,* "Racial Gap in Sentences Growing—New Figures Show Blacks Jailed More," February 13, 1996. *http://www.pdxnorml.org/LAT.racial.fairness* (Accessed April 28, 2003).

11. Leadership Conference on Civil Rights, "Justice on Trial: Racial Disparities in the American Criminal Justice System," *http://www.civilright.org/publications/reports/cj/* (Accessed April 28, 2003).

12. Ibid.

13. Ibid.

14. "Since Sept. 11: Racial Profiling of Arabs and Muslims," *http://www.publicagenda.org/specials/terrorism/terror_pubopinion6.htm* (Accessed April 28, 2003).

15. Lorie Fridell, Robert Lunney, Drew Diamond, and Bruce Kubu, *Racially Based Policing: A Principled Response* (Washington, D.C.: Police Executive Research Forum, 2001), pp. 4–5.

16. Ibid., pp. 6–9.

17. G. Voegtlin, "Bias-based Policing and Data Collection," *The Police Chief* (October 2001):8.

18. International Association of Chiefs of Police, *Responding to Hate Crimes: A Police Officer's Guide to Investigation and Prevention* (Arlington, Va.: Author, 2000), p. 27.

19. Michael Lieberman, "Responding to Hate Crimes," *Community Policing Exchange* (Washington,

D.C.: Community Policing Consortium, January/February 2000), p. 3.

20. U.S. Department of Justice, National Criminal Justice Reference Service, "In the Spotlight: Hate Crime Summary." *http://www.ncjrs.org/hate.crimes/summary.html* (Accessed April 28, 2003).

21. *http://www.fbi.gov/ucr/hatecrime2002.pdf* (Accessed November 13, 2003).

22. International Association of Chiefs of Police, "Responding to Hate Crimes: A Police Officer's Guide to Investigation and Prevention," *http://www.theiacp.org/documents* (Accessed April 28, 2003).

23. Madison, Wisconsin, Police Department, "Special Programs: ADL and Police Launch Statewide Effort to Fight Hate Crimes," *http://www.madisonct.org/pdspcprog.htm* (Accessed April 28, 2003).

24. A. C. Germann, Frank D. Day, and Robert R. J. Gallati, *Introduction to Law Enforcement and Criminal Justice* (Springfield, Ill.: Charles C. Thomas, 1976), p. 241.

25. James Baldwin, *Nobody Knows My Name* (New York: Dial Press, 1961), p. 65.

26. Sharon K. Papa, "L.A. Brass Listens to the Forums," *Community Links* (Washington, D.C.: Community Policing Consortium, March 2002), p. 14.

27. Alan Caddell, "Citizen Academy: Hands On Classes Stress Challenges, Responsibilities of Real Thing," *Community Links* (Washington, D.C.: Community Policing Consortium, August 2002), pp. 1–2.

28. Matthew Zolvinski, "Police Help Kids to Roam," *Community Links* (Washington, D.C.: Community Policing Consortium, March 2002), pp. 6–7.

29. "Lincoln Police Department Community Policing Projects," *http://www.ci.lincoln.ne.us/city/police/pdf/cbpprog.html* (Accessed April 28, 2003).

30. U.S. Department of Justice, Office of Community Oriented Policing Services, "COPS Fact Sheet: Regional Community Policing Institutes," *http://www.cops.usdoj.gov* (Accessed April 28, 2003).

31. Willie Williams, quoted in Patricia A. Parker, "Tackling Unfinished Business," *Police* (December 1991):19, 84.

32. Gayle Fisher-Stewart, "Multicultural Training for Police," *MIS Report* 26(9) (September 1994):7.

33. Ibid., p. 4.

34. Ibid., p. 5.

35. Gary Weaver, "Law Enforcement in a Culturally Diverse Society," *FBI Law Enforcement Bulletin* 61 (September 1992):1–7.

36. Ibid.

37. Pamela D. Mayhall, *Police–Community Relations and the Administration of Justice,* (3rd ed.) (Englewood Cliffs, N.J.: Prentice Hall, 1985), pp. 308–309.

38. Ibid., pp. 312–313.

39. Ken Peak and Jack Spencer, "Crime in Indian Country: Another 'Trail of Tears'," *Journal of Criminal Justice* 15 (1987):485–494.

40. Mayhall, *Police–Community Relations*, p. 6.

41. Jeanne McDowell, "Are Women Better Cops?" *Time* (February 17, 1992):70.

42. Fisher-Stewart, "Multicultural Training for Police," p. 8.

43. Adapted from Robert M. Shusta, Deena R. Levine, Philip R. Harris, and Herbert Z. Wong, *Multicultural Law Enforcement: Strategies for Peacekeeping in a Diverse Society* (Englewood Cliffs, N.J.: Prentice Hall, 1995), pp. 21–22.

44. Ibid., p. 22.

45. Fisher-Stewart, "Multicultural Training for Police," p. 4.

INTRODUCTION

As Chekhov indicated, there comes a time when preliminary preparations must cease, and action must be substituted in its place—in the present context, applying community oriented policing and problem solving (COPPS) on the street. Indeed, the litmus test for COPPS is the degree to which it succeeds in addressing crime and disorder in communities and neighborhoods.

This chapter demonstrates that COPPS can be highly effective. Perhaps its focal point is the several examples of COPPS's accomplishments that are provided in the chapter's exhibits, revealing how COPPS has prevailed over crime and disorder. The success of this strategy, however, remains predicated on the police having laid the groundwork well and knowing what is going on in their neighborhoods and beats by using the S.A.R.A. process (discussed in Chapter 4). As Zachary Tumin put it,

—10—

NEW STRATEGIES FOR OLD PROBLEMS

COPPS on the Beat

The time's come: there's a terrific thunder-cloud advancing upon us . . . it's going to blow away all this idleness . . . I'm going to work.
—ANTON CHEKHOV

The role of the professional police officer as a professional is . . . to know the status of his local institutions; to understand how, when, and why they work; to understand their strengths and their vulnerabilities; to know their members or users, that is, to know the people whose relationships comprise the institutions, and why they participate or don't.[1]

This chapter examines several types of problems the police can confront with the problem-solving process. Specifically, it includes the application of COPPS to drug violations (including rave parties), gangs, special populations and problems (the mentally ill, the homeless, and alcohol-related crimes), domestic violence, school violence, rental property and neighborhood disorder, prostitution, and other selected problems (cruising and street racing, false burglar alarms, and misuse and abuse of 911).

The essence of the chapter lies in the case studies, which deal with each type of problem; 11 exhibits as well as numerous examples demonstrate police agencies and other stakeholders collaborating to implement the COPPS strategy.

DRUG VIOLATIONS

That the United States is in the throes of a grave drug problem is no secret. More than 1.5 million U.S. citizens are arrested for drug abuse violations per year; about one-fifth of those arrests are for the sale or manufacturing of drugs.[2] And this is only the tip of the iceberg in comparison with the actual level of manufacturing, use, and trafficking.

The U.S. drug problem—including ubiquitous methamphetamine labs, where a $100 investment can yield $2,000 worth of meth[3]—poses an organizational challenge that now requires new skills, long-range strategies, and coordinated responses of police. Although the potency, cost, and types of drugs that are in high demand might fluctuate, the threat caused by drug abuse—and the seeming inability to get the problem under control—does not. Whereas billions

Operation Seaload, a joint effort of the NYPD, FBI, and U.S. Customs, ended with the seizure of 9.5 tons of marijuana and numerous arrests. (*Courtesy* NYPD Photo Unit)

of dollars have been spent in enforcement, treatment, and education at all levels of government, drug problems show little sign of abatement. Drug buying and selling have eroded the environment, created undesirable role models for many youth, given rise to a wide variety of related criminal acts, and resulted in innumerable gun-wielding gang members across the United States who are fighting to expand their turf.

COPPS has wide applications to the problem of drugs. As will be seen in the following examples, this strategy presents a unique opportunity for police agencies to address the street-level drug dealing that has made urban life a nightmare for many residents in major cities.

A traditional police approach to a citizen's call concerning drug activity involved the officer's arrival and a quick response, often resulting in a misdemeanor arrest. Little analysis or measurement of results occurred. Conversely, although a COPPS officer's arrival might also involve a short-term response (an arrest), there would most likely be an analytical assessment of the situation to determine why the area was the scene of almost constant drug activity: What is the calls for service (CFS) pattern for the location? Are the arrestees youths who are truant from school? When is the activity occurring? Is lighting inadequate? Are grounds littered and vandalized? Are vacant apartments available to foster drug activity? Do abandoned vehicles provide convenient places for drug stashes? The S.A.R.A. process would likely be applied, with follow-up monitoring of the situation. This section examines some COPPS initiatives in cities that were not content with the traditional approach.

COPPS officers are being challenged to use their creative abilities and to do anything legally possible to identify drug users and to attack and harass drug trafficking. West Palm Beach, Florida, police are offering parents a free drug screening kit to use with their children, while others across the nation are parking their patrol vehicles and eating their lunch in front of known drug houses, repeatedly knocking on dealers' doors, or simply standing outside

Delray Beach, Florida, experienced a drug problem that involved a variety of police tactics for resolution. A convenience store (Mario's Market) had been a problem for 20 years, generating hundreds of calls for service for robberies and drug dealing because 30 to 40 drug dealers, users, and robbers hung around the neighborhood. A nearby drug house contributed to the problem, and a T-shaped alley behind the store provided easy ingress and egress for buyers, both on foot and in vehicles. The lighting was poor, and pay phones in the store's front area were constantly used by traffickers. Officers began walking a beat in the area, made videos of the dealing, and made drug buys in the market. They contacted the owner of the drug house near Mario's, but the owner cared little about the problem. Officers initiated a nuisance-abatement suit against the house. They asked the utility company to install bulletproof security lights around and behind the market, and

they erected barriers to prevent vehicles from entering and exiting the alleys. Mario agreed to install a chain-link fence behind the property. The drug dealing decreased because several dealers were sent to prison and others moved out. When dealers began scaling the chain-link fence, officers smeared axle grease on it ("Even drug dealers don't want to get their clothes dirty," an officer commented), slowing drug activity even further. Next, officers offered to paint the market, using paint purchased by Mario and the assistance of probationers. To ward off any remaining dealers, the officers installed a fake video camera at the market's entryway. Annual calls for service declined from more than 100 to 10, thus drastically improving this 20-year-old problem.

Source: Rana Sampson and Michael S. Scott, *Tackling Crime and Other Public Safety Problems: Case Studies in Problem Solving* (Washington, D.C.: U.S. Department of Justice, Office of Community Policing Services, 2000), pp. 23–26.

their homes. Officers and citizens brazenly photograph open drug deals and write down license plate numbers of dealers and sellers. These officers, emphasizing a new partnership with the community, gather tremendous amounts of information from citizens and use their cell phones and the Internet to enhance public contact (the future of "on-line communities" is discussed in Chapter 15). Public chats with citizens are so commonplace that individuals seen talking with officers are not targeted for attack as snitches. Officers meet regularly with Neighborhood Watch and other groups to exchange intelligence information. Preliminary results of applying the COPPS approach are promising.

Exhibit 10-1 provides an example of COPPS strategies against drug dealing in Delray, Florida.

A RELATED PROBLEM: RAVE PARTIES

A serious problem that can involve serious drug abuse is rave parties—dance parties that feature fast-paced, repetitive electronic music and light shows. Drug use is intended to enhance ravers' sensations and boost their energy so they can dance for long periods, usually starting late at night and going into the morning hours. The drug that is most closely associated with rave parties is ecstasy (also known as MDMA, or "Eve"); there is evidence that chronic use of ecstasy can cause permanent brain damage.[4]

Several related problems can flow from rave parties, and in order to understand the extent of the local problem, police should conduct an analysis that answers a number of questions concerning rave incidents, location, and management, and should minimally include the following questions:

- How many medical emergencies are attributable to raves?
- What drugs appear to cause or contribute to these conditions, and to what extent is drug use and trafficking present?

- Does noise from rave venues disturb people?
- How many traffic accidents are involved, and how much traffic congestion?
- To what extent do such problems as thefts from cars, vandalism, and graffiti occur?
- Have any assaults (sexual or nonsexual) occurred that are connected to raves?

Recently, the Portland, Oregon, police bureau assigned its drugs and vice divisions to work "full force" on combating the problem after some youths died as a result of ecstasy use at rave parties.[5]

GANGS

Extent of the Problem

Today, gangs remain a substantial problem in the United States—even in many middle-size and smaller cities and suburban communities—and their members are becoming younger. The typical age range of gang members has been approximately 14 to 24; youngsters generally begin hanging out with gangs at 12 or 13 years of age, join the gang at 13 or 14, and are first arrested at 14.[6] The challenge of responding to today's gang problem is indeed great. According to estimates by the National Criminal Justice Reference Service, there are more than 24,500 gangs and more than 772,000 gang members in the United States, in more than 3,300 jurisdictions.[7] Nearly half of all gang members (48 percent) are African American youth, whereas Hispanic youngsters account for 43 percent and Asians total 5 percent. "Gang-banging" can be quite lucrative. An ethnographic study of street gangs found that one large, now defunct gang that consisted of several hundred gang members realized more than 70 percent of its total annual revenue of approximately $280,000 from the sale of crack cocaine. The gang operated in a neighborhood of roughly four city blocks.[8]

Addressing Gang Violence

Boston, Massachusetts, recently suffered from a youth homicide problem, with 155 young people being either shot or stabbed in three neighborhoods in a four-year period; 60 percent of the homicides were gang related. An interagency group was created, consisting of local, state, and federal law enforcement officers; researchers; probation officers; and gang-intervention street workers. Their responses to the problem focused on both the supply of and demand for guns among the gangs.[9] The guns used in the youth homicides were typically manufactured less than two years before the crimes. This suggested a strategy to the group: identifying and arresting gun traffickers who were supplying guns to the gangs. On the demand side of the problem (why young people carried guns and shot one another), the group identified 61 Boston gangs, with about 1,300 members, representing only about 3 percent of the youth in the affected neighborhoods. Youth homicides, it was determined, were committed by a few gang members who committed many crimes. Enhanced penalties—ranging from strict curfew checks by probation officers to federal prosecutions for street crimes—were enforced against gang members for violent behavior; extraordinary crimes brought extraordinary punishment. The threat of these penalties was communicated to members firsthand. Homicides of young people dropped 67 percent from the mean of the previous seven years.[10]

When gang violence spread in San Mateo, California, primarily because of seven-year warfare between two opposing gangs—involving shootings, stabbings, car bombings, and murder—a street detective requested and received a transfer to the police department's community policing unit. After receiving training in problem solving, he enlisted the support of a local volunteer mediation agency as well as that of the probation department, because of its court-ordered guardianship over many of the seasoned gang members. He also requested a juvenile court judge to waive the nonassociation clause that was a term of most of the gang members' probation, so that they could meet without fear of court-ordered sanctions.[11]

The mediation service arranged for separate meetings with the two rival gangs to be held in a neutral place. Three mediators, two probation officers, and one police officer (the detective) also attended. The groups talked about respect, community racism, the police, and the need to try something new. The idea of a truce was raised, but the two gangs' leaders laughed at the idea. The mediators met individually with each gang four more times; both sides remained curious about the other's commitment, and both seemed tired of the ongoing violence. The gangs finally agreed to meet together. Each gang selected five members as spokespeople who brought a list of items to be addressed; respect was at the top of both lists.[12] An agreement for peace was eventually reached and handshakes were exchanged; all agreed to a follow-up meeting, where 41 gang members agreed to a truce and no more violence. They agreed to respect each other, and if a confrontation arose, they would try to talk through it rather than use weapons.[13] In the four years since this problem-solving effort began, there have been no reports of violence between the two gangs.

Finally, another promising strategy, "designing out" gang homicides and street assaults, has been successful in Los Angeles. When a systematic pattern of opportunity was found—that the majority of drive-by shootings and violent gang encounters occurred in clusters on the periphery of neighborhoods

Youths remove graffiti from a public wall. (*Courtesy* Washoe County, Nevada, Sheriff's Office)

linked to major thoroughfares—police closed all major roads leading to and from the identified hot spots by placing cement freeway dividers at the end of streets that led directly to these roads. An evaluation determined that blocking opportunities reduced homicides and street assaults significantly, and that crime was not displaced to other areas.[14]

GRAFFITI

A problem arising from teen gangs involves graffiti, which is another "harm" that is associated with gangs (harms were discussed in Chapter 4). Reducing the harm can help to reduce the larger problem. The style and quality of graffiti can create and enhance the gang's image; graffiti is even used to advertise those rival gang members they are going to kill. Graffiti also serves to mark the gang's turf; police and neighborhoods have become frustrated with the "tagging" of walls and objects with paint. Graffiti depreciates property values, adds to the deterioration of neighborhoods, and contributes to economic and urban blight.

To combat the problem, some cities have enacted ordinances that require property owners to remove graffiti within a specified period of time. For example, in St. Petersburg, Florida, business owners are required to remove graffiti within 48 hours; in other areas the city will paint over the graffiti for a set fee, usually $50 to $75. (Box 10-1 shows an example of a graffiti ordinance.)

Nonetheless, the problem persists, and the police are working to eradicate the problem in order to diminish the gangs' sense of territory, improve the appearance of the neighborhoods, and make a community statement that gang-type activities will not be tolerated. Following are some means by which

BOX 10-1

Example of a Municipal Antigraffiti Ordinance

WHEREAS, property defaced by gang members is an act of vandalism and is against the law; and

WHEREAS, gang members frequently deface property by painting, drawing, writing, etching, or carving gang graffiti; and

WHEREAS, gang graffiti is the first indication of gang activity; and

WHEREAS, gang graffiti constitutes a public nuisance which causes depreciation of the value of the defaced property, the surrounding property, and contributes to the deterioration of the neighborhood and the City in general; and

WHEREAS, depreciation of property values and deterioration of neighborhoods leads to economic blight, an increase in criminal activity, and is injurious to the public health, safety, morals, and general welfare of the residents of the City,

NOW, THEREFORE, BE IT ORDAINED BY THE CITY COUNCIL OF THE CITY OF LAKEWOOD, COLORADO, THAT:

9.85.060 NOTIFICATION OF NUISANCE. (a) The owner of any property defaced by gang graffiti shall be given written notice to abate the public nuisance on his property by removal within five (5) days after service of the notice. Such notice shall be by personal service to the owner, or by posting the notice on the defaced property together with written notice mailed to the owner by first-class mail. The notice to the property owner shall contain:

1. The location of and a description of the violation;

2. A demand that the owner remove or eradicate the gang graffiti from the property within five (5) days after service of the notice;

3. A statement that the owner's failure or refusal to remove or eradicate the gang graffiti may result in abatement by the City;

4. A statement that if the costs of abatement plus the $75 fee for inspection and incidental costs is not paid to the City within 30 days after notice, an additional $75 will be assessed for administrative and other incidental costs.

Source: Adapted from the Antigraffiti Ordinance of Lakewood, Colorado, O-91-29, Title 9, Article 85, Chapter 9.85.

the police and the public can attempt to reduce the rewards for, and increase the detection of, those who spread graffiti.

- Detect graffiti rapidly and routinely (by monitoring graffiti-prone locations and increasing reporting).
- Remove graffiti rapidly.
- Increase natural observation of graffiti-prone locations, through use of police, security personnel, and citizens.
- Conduct publicity campaigns, combined with beautification efforts and cleanup days.
- Control access to, and vandal-proof, prone locations (using dark or textured surfaces and special products that are resistant to graffiti and are easy to clean).
- Focus on chronic offenders[15]

Special Populations and Problems

Next we examine how COPPS can assist the police in dealing with persons who are mentally ill or homeless, and offenders who are heavily involved with alcohol. Discussed in Chapter 4 (and illustrated in Figure 4-8) was the fact that police need to concentrate efforts on helping or addressing those individuals who account for a disproportionate share of community problems. The mentally ill, homeless, and alcohol-abuser populations would fall into that category.

The Mentally Ill

One of the saddest aspects of police work involves trying to help people who are mentally ill or unstable, many of whom suffer from paranoid schizophrenia, hallucinate, are solitary, engage in illegal activities, and/or are addicted to alcohol or drugs. Many such people are also homeless.

It is estimated that 200,000 people with mental illness are jailed or imprisoned in the United States every day.[16] Ironically, while the population of state psychiatric hospitals declined from 560,000 in 1955 to less than 60,000 today, there has been a significant increase in the number of individuals with mental illness who are incarcerated.[17] A related problem has arisen recently in which individuals who are mentally unstable and who want to die employ a technique that has been termed "suicide by cop"— engaging in a shoot-out with and being killed by the police.

Funding cutbacks and changing laws and policies (such as the deinstitutionalization policies of the 1980s) have concurrently made it more difficult for the police and relatives of the mentally ill to have them committed to institutions; these factors have left many disturbed people—including families—in the streets and alleys and on the riverbanks to fend for themselves. Limited bed space and selective admission practices at detoxification and other alcoholism facilities have also curtailed the ability of the police to transport public inebriates to health care facilities.

What problem-solving strategies can work with these special populations? Several innovative approaches have been undertaken:

- After a Seminole County, Florida, deputy sheriff was killed by a man suffering from paranoid schizophrenia, the deputy's widow and offender's sister created a task force to study treatment for mentally ill people who break the law.
- Several states have enacted legislation to provide early and humane intervention.

- Memphis, Tennessee, police created a Crisis Intervention Team to set a standard of excellence for treatment of mentally ill individuals and to establish individual responsibility and overall accountability for each event. Since CIT started, the number of trained officers has risen from 32 to almost 200; the plan has been modeled in several other cities as well.

- In Florence, Alabama, a police lieutenant not only received training in mental illness but also in geriatrics and substance abuse, and is dispatched to every call when a subject is thought to be mentally ill; assesses the danger posed by the individual; takes the subject to the hospital for evaluation; tries to get people released from jail for treatment; and is establishing a mental health court.[18] The Regional Community Policing Institutes of the federal Office of Community Oriented Policing Services provide training in responding to mental health problems, helping officers to understand and deal with the problem, review medications used in treatment, and know how to apply the S.A.R.A. problem-solving process.[19] Exhibit 10-2 provides another look at how the police are dealing with the mentally ill under COPPS, with a special training program in St. Petersburg, Florida. Similar programs are under way in Albuquerque, New Mexico; Portland, Oregon; and Tampa, Florida.[20]

The Homeless

The homeless—estimates of whom range from 300,000 to three million—often panhandle, use intimidation, and generally are a problem for businesses and citizens using parks and public sidewalks. Most studies indicate that although the homeless have higher overall arrest rates than the general population, the vast majority of their offenses do not involve violence. Rather, the police most often arrest the homeless for public intoxication, theft or shoplifting, and burglary.[21] One study also found that an average of 29 percent of people who are homeless suffer from severe mental disorders. A surprising number of the homeless are military veterans; runaways comprise another sizable category. Many, however, have experienced economic hard times or cannot afford their own housing.[22]

As with the mentally ill population, police officers dealing with the homeless often have few options; not only is shelter space limited, but most shelters refuse to admit the large percentage of homeless who are also mentally ill or alcoholic.

Clearwater, Florida, a community of 100,000 residents that regularly draws another 20,000 tourists during the beach season, recently experienced an upsurge in problems related to street people—thefts, drugs, prostitution,

---

EXHIBIT 10-2 Reaching Out to the Mentally Ill in St. Petersburg, Florida

After mental health advocates began to complain that the police did not understand mental illness and the interventions they should take when encountering such individuals, the police chief instituted a mandatory eight-hour curriculum for all of the agency's 550 officers—the first such training curriculum in the United States. The heart of the course is a four-step approach called CIAF—*calming the subject, investigating* and *assessing* the situation, and *facilitating* a solution. The training, developed by mental health professionals, teaches officers how to look at behavior, intellectual state, attitude, verbal indicators, and environmental factors to optimize the outcome for both the officer and the individual. Instructors emphasize that officers must treat individuals who are mentally ill or unstable with respect, understanding, and compassion, but always have the situation under control. As one observer stated about the program, the police are in effect "untrained mental health counselors. They're problem solvers for people with nowhere else to turn." Officer feedback concerning the training has been positive, and success stories from using the training are beginning to mount, which underscores its effectiveness.

Source: Ronald J. Getz, "Reaching Out to the Mentally Ill," *Law and Order*, (May 1999):51.

and vandalism. Additionally, these people were sleeping on private property; defecating and urinating on public streets; and engaging in public drunkenness, graffiti, and littering.[23]

The police department, which entered into community policing in 1983 and takes nontraditional approaches to tough problems, decided to get into the housing business. First, the city opened a homeless shelter that included a police substation; virtually every area organization and agency working with the homeless has a presence at the shelter, dealing with everything from mental problems to substance abuse and job placement. Everyone living in the shelter is required to enroll in the Salvation Army Intervention Program, follow strict rules, attend Alcoholics Anonymous meetings regardless of whether they are addicted, participate in counseling, and abide by a curfew. The department used money seized from drug operations to purchase a single-family home, which it in turn leases to a social service agency; the home is used to provide transitional living units for people leaving the shelter, thus facilitating their return back into their own living quarters. Dedicated phone lines allow each homeless person to get calls from prospective employers and set up interviews.[24] The city has seen a turnaround with its homeless problems. Businesses that once fought the shelters are now allies, and investors are putting money into nearby properties for new construction and to rehabilitate existing buildings. For another example of the homelessness problem, see Exhibit 10-3.

Alcohol-Related Crimes

Many of the problems that are discussed in this chapter involve alcohol abuse. Given the extent of this problem, however, it will be treated separately (alcohol abuse was also discussed as being a crime accelerator in Chapter 2).

More than 7 percent of the population age 18 and older, nearly 13.8 million U.S. citizens, have problems with alcohol, including 8.1 million people who are

---

EXHIBIT 10-3   Homeless-Related Crimes in San Diego

California's Otay River Valley is a massive tract of undeveloped land covering 8,000 acres. It is bordered by the cities of San Diego, Chula Vista, and Imperial Beach. Businesses surrounding the river valley suffered from burglary, panhandling, theft, and vandalism. People often illegally dumped trash and debris in the valley. Transients, perhaps as many as 300, lived at campsites in the valley in bamboo, metal, plywood, and tarpaulin huts. Many of the transients booby-trapped their campsites to ward off intruders. A large number of them also suffered from infectious diseases, such as AIDS and sexual and skin diseases, and some were mentally ill. Police response was reactive until an increase in crime was noted; transients were becoming more aggressive, and two young boys were found murdered in the area. After political pressure began to mount to remove the transients, a three-phase effort was developed, including the enforcement of trespassing laws, the cleanup of the property, and the restoration of the land that would discourage illegal camping. In addition to the cities that were stakeholders, the state of California, San Diego County, the U.S. Fish

and Wildlife Service, and the Army Corps of Engineers joined in the massive project. A prosecutor was assigned as legal counsel as well. Police issued trespassing warnings to transients, provided them with information about area homeless shelters and other services, and photographed the transients in case it became necessary to arrest them. Police also made three sweeps through the area to ensure that all trespassers had been warned, making nearly 100 arrests in the process for outstanding warrants and other offenses. Approximately 200 volunteers collected refuse from the area, a private waste-hauling company removed 31 tons of trash (with the use of donated trash containers), and a private landfill company agreed to waive $1,500 in dumping fees. Burglaries and related crimes dropped 80 percent after the evictions and cleanups. Before the project, San Diego police were spending about 3,000 hours per year on valley-related crimes; since the project's completion, that number has dropped to between 500 and 800 hours.

Source: Sampson and Scott, *Tackling Crime and Other Public Safety Problems*, pp. 109–110.

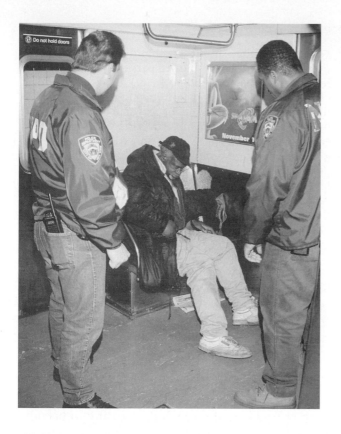

NYPD officers attend to a transient person found sleeping in the city's subway system. (*Courtesy* NYPD Photo Unit)

alcoholic; furthermore, alcohol contributes to 100,000 deaths annually.[25] The problem of alcohol in the United States is even more serious when viewed in terms of underage drinking, and where it leads; many youthful problem drinkers will eventually become adult alcoholics and commit crimes. Approximately 9.5 million drinkers are young, between the ages of 12 and 20; of this number, 4.4 million are binge drinkers, including 1.9 million heavy drinkers. Young people who begin drinking before age 15 are four times more likely to develop alcohol addiction than those who begin drinking at age 21. Alcohol is a factor in 35 percent of traffic fatalities involving persons ages 15 to 20.[26]

Portland, Oregon, police were recently compelled to focus on a specific type of beverage. Large (32- and 40-ounce) containers of fortified wine, each containing the alcohol equivalent of up to six drinks, contributed to problem street drinking in the Old Town/Chinatown district, causing many acts of fighting, disorderly conduct, harassment, littering, panhandling, and public urination and defecation. Four neighborhood convenience stores and four large chain stores—each selling from 60 to 100 cases of the wine per week—contributed to the area's problems by serving several hundred street drinkers. The police believed that restricting the drinkers' access to megasize beverages would reduce the problem.

Eventually, more than 100 retailers throughout the city volunteered to remove 16-ounce (or larger) beverages from their shelves. The impact in the neighborhood was huge: There was a 50 percent reduction in the number of detoxification holds and drinking-in-public incidents, and disorderly conduct incidents decreased 25 percent. Citizens reported that the neighborhood felt safer and looked better, and few people are now observed in the area with open containers.[27]

See Exhibit 10-4 for a discussion of alcohol problems in the Arctic.

EXHIBIT 10-4 Alcohol Problems in the Arctic

With the arrival of oil workers in the 1970s, alcohol consumption became a significant part of local culture in Barrow, Alaska. Two studies linked much of Barrow's premature deaths, violence, disease, and social disorder to alcohol abuse. Alaska state law provides for a local option on the sale of liquor, but mere prohibitions on alcohol sales had little impact on the problem. Data analysis revealed that in this small community of about 5,000 residents, there were 87 rapes by drunk men, 675 drunken assaults, 503 domestic disputes involving drunk spouses, 388 arrests for drunk driving, 229 arrests of drunk children, and 2,057 incidents in which people were taken into protective custody because of alcohol-induced incapacitation. Most problems were related to alcohol illegally imported and consumed by citizens who were binge drinkers. Police concluded that a total ban on alcohol was the only viable response. Such a ban was passed by city voters in October 1994.

Fetal alcohol exposure in pregnant women dropped from 45 percent to less than 10 percent, and alcohol-related calls for service to police declined by 81 percent. But the story does not end there on a happy note. The community then legalized alcohol in 1995, making the city "wet" again. The same alcohol-related problems recurred, at levels that were even higher than those preceding the ban. Furthermore, a proalcohol administration was elected into office, leading to a change in police administration as well. Police officers were ordered not to officially support the alcohol ban or release information about alcohol-related matters. Nonetheless, this problem-solving effort demonstrates a uniquely comprehensive and detailed analysis of the harm caused by alcohol, as well as an ambitious response strategy that might be unthinkable in many jurisdictions.

Source: Sampson and Scott, *Tackling Crime and Other Public Safety Problems*, pp. 53–55.

Domestic Violence

Domestic violence involves one person dominating and controlling another by force, threats, or physical violence. Traditionally, much of society and many police agencies turned their backs on the problem, refusing to become involved in "family quarrels." Accordingly, police rarely made arrests. Studies in the mid-1980s, however, found that arrests served as an independent deterrent to future violence, labeled the assailant's actions as criminal, and punished the attacker for his or her actions.[28] Communities with low unemployment rates were instructed to use a mandatory arrest policy; conversely, communities with high unemployment rates were urged to develop some alternative policies and not rely on arrest.[29] Today nearly all states have legislation mandating police officers to effect warrantless arrests where evidence of spousal assault is present. Unfortunately, however, domestic violence remains the most prevalent form of violence confronting our society today.

Domestic violence, like the other problems discussed in this chapter, must be viewed as a community-wide problem. Police can collect and analyze information about domestic violence and assist the community in becoming aware of its magnitude. Officers can also solicit community support in developing alternative strategies for combating it. Police must work closely with victims' advocates, social service agencies, and the judiciary (injunctive relief can be used to bar an abusive spouse from returning to the family residence). This is a quality-of-life issue, and—like problems such as drugs, gangs, or prostitution—if left unchecked it will fester and grow.

What can be done proactively about this problem? (See Exhibit 10-5 for one solution.) A growing number of promising COPPS practices have been identified. One Georgia police department, for example, trained county process servers to work with domestic violence survivors. Because many domestic violence incidents go unreported to the police, the person serving a restraining order is often the first authority to learn of a domestic violence situation. Officers can also encourage neighbors to anonymously report disturbances or signs of abuse. Religious organizations can be encouraged to reach

Recently the Largo, Florida, police department realized that its domestic violence (DV) efforts were of little avail; the community of 75,000 was receiving about 1,000 such calls per year, with only about 16 percent of them resulting in a prosecution. The department formed a partnership with a wide array of governmental agencies, private organizations, and citizen groups, with the goals of getting perpetrators into the justice or social services systems, providing survivor assistance, and finding ways to break the cycle and reduce the violence. Prosecution rates immediately increased to 85 percent. Following are other approaches used by the partnership.

- A DV Web site was established—the first of its kind in the United States.
- A mandatory arrest policy was initiated for DV perpetrators.

- A team of DV intervention specialists was established whose first priorities are the survivors and their families.
- A cellular phone program was begun to safeguard victims.
- A partnering among organizations from every spectrum of the community was begun to provide long-term solutions to reduce the number of incidents.

Although acknowledging the difficulty of obtaining measurable statistics on DV (long-term recidivism data are not yet available), the police department points to the permanent partnership it has formed with most of the stakeholders in DV issues.

Source: Adapted from Ronald J. Getz, "Largo Police Attack Domestic Violence," *Law and Order* (November 1998):44–45.

out to members who are victims. Substance abuse treatment can be arranged for abusers when alcohol and other drugs play a role in the violence.[30]

The Lapeer County, Michigan, sheriff's department reacted to a rise in domestic violence calls by using a unique approach. The department, in conjunction with a regional hospital, a citizens' group, and 17 other county agencies, formed a coalition that created a list of goals and objectives that serve as a foundation for reducing domestic violence in the county:

- Reduce to 10 percent or less the number of battered women and children turned away from emergency housing because of a lack of space.
- Reduce physical abuse directed at women by male partners to no more than 27 out of 1,000 couples.
- Ensure that a crisis intervention shelter and support resources are accessible to all regardless of ability to pay.
- Increase the number of physicians, nurses, social workers, teachers, and criminal justice professionals who receive training in identifying and referring victims.
- Establish a tracking mechanism to record the rate of assault injuries.[31]

The Regional Community Policing Institutes of the federal Office of Community Oriented Policing Services provide training in reducing domestic violence; training modules include facilitation skills, evidence gathering, safety planning, accessing and sharing information, and determination of the predominant aggressor.[32]

SCHOOL VIOLENCE

The recent increase in shootings on school campuses had all of America wondering what had happened to its children. In one six-year period, from July 1992 to June 1998, there were 225 school-associated violent deaths[33] (this figure excludes the April 1999 massacre of 13 people at Columbine High School in Littleton, Colorado). More recently, studies showed that there are

"What Has Happened to Our Children?"

about 128,000 victims of serious violent crimes at school; in fact, in 2000 there were 47 school-associated violent deaths in the United States.[34] At the present time, however, the prevalence of problem behavior at school seems to be declining, and students today tend to feel safer at school (although, as will be seen below, the problem of bullying is increasing and is one that is a serious concern).[35] Teachers are also victims of crime at school, but such crimes involve theft; teachers in urban schools are more likely to be victims of violent crimes.[36]

School safety does not involve any single method of control, such as metal detectors, surveillance systems, or swift punishment. Nor can we identify with certainty those students who will assault their teachers and peers. We do know, however, that school safety requires broad-based efforts, must involve students at an early age, and must be reinforced throughout their education.[37] Several strategies have been suggested for police and citizens to help prevent school violence:

- publicizing the philosophy that a gang presence will not be tolerated, and institutionalizing a code of conduct
- alerting students and parents about school rules and punishments for infractions
- creating alternative schools for those students who cannot function in a regular classroom

There is no single cause—or cure—for violence in the schools. (*Courtesy* Washoe County, Nevada, Sheriff's Office)

- training teachers, parents, and school staff to identify children who are most at risk for violent behavior
- developing community initiatives focused on breaking family cycles of violence, and providing programs on parenting, conflict resolution, anger management, and recovery from substance abuse
- establishing peer counseling in schools to give troubled youths the opportunity to talk to someone their own age
- teaching children that it is not "tattling" to go to a school teacher or staff member if they know someone who is discussing "killing"[38]

School Resource Officers (SROs) can also play an important role in a school's safety planning efforts. SROs can assess the schools' structure to determine where potential problems exist, help to address the social environment (by such means as setting high expectations for behavior, contributing to the development of codes of conduct, explaining what is illegal conduct, employing surveys to measure safety and security concerns of students and staff, and identifying bullies).[39]

The federal Office of Community Oriented Policing Services has a grant program designed to help police agencies hire new SROs and provides a maximum contribution up to $125,000 per officer position over a three-year period.[40]

A Related Problem: Bullying

While overall school violence has been declining, an old problem that seems to be widespread and perhaps the most underreported safety problem on school campuses is bullying. Bullying has two key components: repeated harmful acts, and an imbalance of power. It involves repeated physical, verbal, or psychological attacks or intimidation against a victim who is defenseless because of size or strength or is outnumbered. Between five and nine percent of students bully others with some regularity.[41]

To engage in problem solving with bullying, police should determine whether the school has a problem with it and how it is occurring; who offenders are, and how and where they are operating at the school; and who the victims are. Efforts should be made to increase student reporting of bullying; have trained supervisors monitor prone and less-supervised areas; consider staggering recess, lunch, and class-release time; and encourage administrators to provide teachers with classroom management training, where necessary.[42] Exhibit 10-6 discusses an excellent use of the S.A.R.A. problem-solving process for addressing the problem of bullying.

RENTAL PROPERTIES AND NEIGHBORHOOD DISORDER

Neighborhoods deteriorate one home at a time. This deterioration can have many root causes and be accelerated when drug houses, gangs, prostitutes, graffiti, abandoned houses and vehicles, and general neighborhood decay become commonplace. Public housing areas are particularly susceptible to such problems. The police must work in partnership with citizens, tailoring tactics to specific neighborhoods and assisting in their defense against crime and disorder.

A wide range of activities may be undertaken to attack neighborhood crime and deterioration. Herman Goldstein described some of the measures

EXHIBIT 10-6 S.A.R.A. Fights Bullying in Ohio

Unchecked disorderly behavior of students in South Euclid, Ohio, led the school resource officer (SRO) to review school data regarding referrals to the principal's office. The SRO found that the high school reported thousands of referrals per year for bullying and the junior high school had experienced a 30 percent increase in such referrals; police data revealed that juvenile complaints about disturbances, bullying, and assaults after school had increased 90 percent in the past 10 years. In the analysis phase, a survey, interviews, and focus groups (with students, teachers, and guidance counselors) conducted by academics from Kent State University's Justice Studies department provided much more information, and a geographic information system mapped hot spots in the schools. The main findings pointed to four areas of concern: the environmental design of school areas, teachers' knowledge and response to the problem, parents' attitudes and responses, and students' perceptions and behaviors.

Responses involved the SRO's working closely with other stakeholders to form a planning team, to develop a new school policy on bullying, and to open a new substation within the school next to a hot spot. Environmental changes included modifying the school bell times and increasing teacher supervision of hot spots; counselors conducted teacher training courses in bullying prevention; parent education including mailings and information about bullying and explanation of new school policy. Finally, student education focused on classroom discussions and assemblies conducted by the SRO.

The assessment found that bullying incidents dropped 60 percent in the hallways and 80 percent in the gym area. Surveys indicated positive attitudinal changes among students about bullying, and greater confidence that teachers would take action.

Source: Police Executive Research Forum, *Excellence in Problem-Oriented Policing: The 2001 Herman Goldstein Award Winners* (Washington, D.C.: Author, 2002), pp. 55–56.

---

that police may undertake when, for example, a public housing project is suffering from a rash of burglaries:

- Make efforts to apprehend those responsible for the burglaries.
- Counsel management regarding lighting, lock systems, landscaping that provides hiding places for burglars, fencing, appearance of buildings and grounds, and so forth.
- Refer uncorrected conditions that are in violation of the law to building inspectors, zoning authorities, or health authorities.
- Work with tenants, informing them of their rights vis-a-vis management, of various government services available to them, and of measures they can take to prevent crimes.
- Work with school authorities regarding any problem of truancy that may be related to burglaries, and with recreation and park authorities regarding any problem of idle youth.[43]

This list demonstrates what Goldstein observed: Once the police break out of the mold of looking only within the criminal justice system for solutions, "large vistas are opened to exploration" and the police can engage in a "far-reaching and imaginative search for alternative ways" to deal with recurring problems.[44] Exhibit 10-7 describes a problem of horrendous proportions in Santa Barbara, California, underscoring what can happen when landlords and management companies ignore their legal and moral responsibilities to their tenants.

As Goldstein mentioned, it is essential that property owners and landlords know their rights with respect to tenants. Because most drug activity occurs on rental property, prevention efforts must involve the property management community. Landlord-tenant training programs are being undertaken by a number of police departments to help owners and managers keep drugs and other criminal activities off their property.

EXHIBIT 10-7   Apartment Complex Crime in Santa Barbara, California

Police officers began looking into problems involving a local apartment complex, where tenants had complained about disturbances, an illegal auto repair shop, littering, and illegally built dwellings. The owner, who had 34 other properties in the city, resisted taking any corrective action and had never hired a property manager; as a result, nearly all of his properties were in disrepair and causing a tremendous drain on police resources. Health and safety codes were ignored, and apartments were overrun with cockroaches and rats. A number were also illegally subdivided, with up to 10 people living in a two-bedroom unit. Fire and building codes were also ignored, and there were excessive noise complaints and litter coming from the complexes. Children used abandoned vehicles in the parking lots as playgrounds. Officers found that 758 arrestees and 121 people with outstanding misdemeanor bench warrants listed the properties as their residences. Officers asked neighbors to keep logs of the problems at the properties for two months; officers also photographed the worst conditions and documented the rubble and running sewage. They suggested prosecuting the slumlord with an "unfair competition" charge, because his unlawful neglect of the properties gave him an unfair advantage over legitimately run properties. Officers enlisted the aid of a deputy from the district attorney's fraud unit and organized a task force that included representatives from several city and county prosecutor's, fire, and community development offices. Inspection teams took cameras and camcorders to the site, documenting 750 code violations. Media coverage focused community awareness on the site as well. With this evidence, a criminal court judge convicted the owner and ordered that, as a condition of his probation, he comply with all building codes and regulations; management by a management company was also ordered.

Source: Sampson and Scott, *Tackling Crime and Other Public Safety Problems*, pp. 14–18.

Such a situation occurred in 1989 in Portland, Oregon, when John Campbell, a resident of a quiet neighborhood, woke up one morning to find a crack house on his block. Campbell's frustration with the drug problem led him to investigate how landlords and neighbors could better detect and stem crime at rental properties. With the Portland police bureau's support—and after researching state and local laws and interviewing more than 40 people—Campbell developed an eight-hour training course for landlords and property managers. Since 1989 Campbell's crusade has resulted in more than 6,000 Portland-area landlords and property managers receiving this training. Furthermore, communities in other states have modified his approach to meet their particular needs.[45] Although such training programs vary, most include the following topics:

- an overview of what landlords and managers can do to keep neighborhoods healthy
- how to screen out dishonest applicants, while ensuring that honest applicants are encouraged to apply
- rental agreements and approaches that will strengthen the ability to evict tenants who are drug users or dealers
- warning signs of drug and other criminal activity, the drugs involved, and the behavior associated with using, growing, and dealing
- what to do if a clandestine drug lab is discovered
- the options and process of eviction
- how to work with the police
- rights and responsibilities under Section 8 (subsidized) housing[46]

For many poor urban families, public housing represents the only hope for housing of any kind. Disadvantaged by lack of education, skills, and health, the urban poor pass on public housing dependency from generation to generation. For young, single-parent families who cannot find decent, safe, and affordable temporary housing, severely distressed public housing becomes the permanent housing of last resort.

In most cases these young residents have the greatest need for affordable housing; they are also the most vulnerable, the most difficult to manage, and the most difficult for whom to provide security. Public housing residents ask that the police clear the hallways, stairways, lobbies, and streets of open-air drug sales. The police recognize that distressed housing can be difficult to patrol. Community policing offers the best hope for successful order maintenance in public housing. Sooner or later a housing authority police force will encounter problems. The conflict usually centers on crime problems, maintenance and repair issues, or such turf issues as who should enforce the "conduct" provisions of the lease.[47]

PROSTITUTION

Street prostitution constitutes an offense to the moral standards of the community. It creates a nuisance to passersby and nearby residents and merchants, and parking and traffic problems develop; the behavior may also foment other more serious crimes as well as the spread of sexually transmitted diseases, including AIDS. Street criminals such as prostitutes may also gather juveniles into their web.

Prostitutes often become brazen, know the law, and develop ways to avoid arrest and conviction. Therefore, police who undertake to address this problem need to perform a systematic inquiry into the extent and nature of the problem: How often are juveniles involved? How much crime (such as robberies of "johns") is related to prostitution? Is organized crime involved? Are prostitutes injuring others or being injured themselves? Answers to these and other related questions will help bring the problem into focus. Officers must also consider alternative strategies to thwarting problems. For example, New York City police officers enforced the mandatory seat belt law disproportionately against drivers in areas frequented by street prostitutes. Some jurisdictions now publish the names of johns in local newspapers and send letters to homes of registered owners of vehicles, warning the resident(s) that their vehicle was seen loitering in an area frequented by prostitutes.

At times the officers must also gather information from prostitutes themselves to bring a greater degree of order to the situation. The most severe problems associated with street prostitution can be reduced if prostitutes can be encouraged to bring juvenile prostitutes to police attention, expose those who rob their customers, and respect each other's turf.

Police problem-solving efforts for street prostitution must address both prostitutes' and clients' conduct, and include but are not limited to the following:

- enforcing laws prohibiting soliciting, patronizing, and loitering for the purposes of prostitution, while identifying and targeting the worst offenders
- establishing a highly visible police presence
- enhancing fines and penalties for prostitution-related offenses committed within specified high-activity zones
- banning prostitutes from geographic areas, and serving restraining orders and injunctions against the worst offenders

- imposing community service sentences in lieu of incarceration or fines (the former have been shown to be more effective)
- encouraging community members to publicly protest against prostitutes or clients (to intimidate prostitutes and their clients)
- educating and warning high-risk prostitute and client populations [certain groups are more vulnerable to becoming prostitutes (e.g., juvenile runaways) or being solicited (conventioneers, soldiers, and so on)] through billboards, lectures, signs, or media outlets
- suspending or revoking government aid to prostitutes (e.g., for housing, unemployment insurance, and/or disability)
- helping prostitutes to quit (e.g., by providing drug, mental health, housing, job, health care, and/or legal counseling and assistance)[48]

See Exhibit 10-8 for an example of how one community handled its prostitution situation.

OTHER SELECTED PROBLEMS

Next we look briefly at COPPS responses to three other kinds of public safety problems: cruising and street racing, false burglar alarms, and misuse and abuse of 911.

Cruising and Street Racing

Cruising may be loosely defined as repeatedly driving a motor vehicle in or near a congested area, within (and often during) a specified time period. What is meant by "repeatedly" and "specified time period" is determined by each municipality.

Cruising may seem on the surface to be a relatively harmless activity, and indeed people like to cruise for several reasons: socializing with friends,

---

EXHIBIT 10-8   Prostitution in Champaign, Illinois

Champaign, Illinois, had a chronic prostitution problem in its downtown area. Arrests provided only temporary relief, and the prostitutes were rarely convicted. Collateral crimes (theft, robbery, assaults, and "john rolling") caused a significant drain on police resources. Citizens complained that prostitutes used apartment building foyers, church parking lots, driveways, and private alleys to have sex. Ninety percent of the prostitutes were repeat offenders; 15 of them held the majority of all convictions. The city's antisolicitation ordinance, merely resulting in a fine, offered no long-term solution. Female officers dressed as prostitutes arrested johns for attempted patronizing, but the state attorney's office typically dismissed these cases because entrapment defenses were difficult to refute without evidence of the john's predisposition. The state legislature made a third prostitution conviction a felony, but often many years would pass before an offender would amass a criminal history that made her or him eligible for the enhanced felony sentencing. Finally, court-imposed travel restrictions were investigated. The police crime analysis unit found that 92 percent of 321 prostitution arrests over five years occurred in a 12-block downtown area. Armed with a pin map, police requested that the court impose travel restrictions on one chronic prostitute, thus keeping her away from the downtown area and potential customers. The judge agreed, and within two months Champaign courts imposed such restrictions on 13 chronic prostitutes, taking care of the recidivistic offenders; a state appeals court upheld the restrictions. The following year, the state legislature codified travel restrictions. Over the next year and a half, the city's street prostitution dropped by 90 percent. Limiting access to the area disrupted the market and separated prostitutes from their customers.

Source: Sampson and Scott, *Tackling Crime and Other Public Safety Problems,* pp. 14–18.

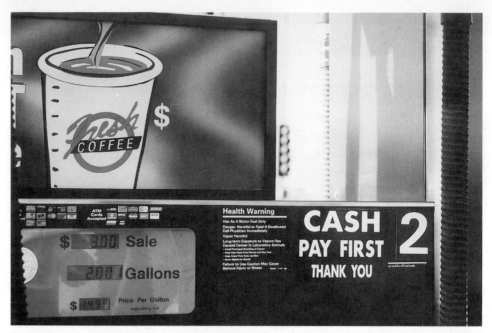

Gasoline station drive-offs (leaving without paying for gas) can account for a high number of calls for service. A prepay policy is one simple method for reducing this problem.

displaying driving ability, lack of other activities, and showing off cars.[49] But cruising has become intolerable in some communities, resulting in citizen harassment, vandalism, underage drinking, littering, urinating in public, trashing of parking lots, excessive noise, and general disorderly behavior. Police often have to devote large amounts of time to areas congested with cruisers and the attendant problems that arise.

Communities have responded with cruising ordinances, using citations and fines for cruising past a control or checkpoint more than a certain number of times during a specified time period. Some departments even enter license plate numbers into a computer, which alerts officers on seeing the same license plate a second or third time. Other communities have only aggravated the problem with their cruising ordinances, raising the ire of young and old alike who enjoy this activity. Therefore, some alternative measures have been used with greater success.

Arlington, Texas, rented a parking lot and posted a 10-mile-per-hour speed limit and two officers to patrol the area. Portland, Oregon, published a brochure on cruising and distributed it to cruisers in the affected areas. Topeka, Kansas, police located a "cruising zone" close enough to downtown to be acceptable to cruisers but not a nuisance to the community. Other communities have formed a Teen Court or some form of youth council to handle the violations that arise in the cruise area. See Exhibit 10-9 for another example of how a community dealt with the problem of cruising.

A companion traffic problem is *street racing*, which has existed for centuries (involving horses before automobiles) because of its thrills: the adrenaline rush, the ego boost, and the thrill of victory. However, given that this activity involves reckless driving, and the speed that today's vehicles are capable of reaching—and that even small autos can weigh 2,500 pounds—the risk

EXHIBIT 10-9   Cruising Trouble in Santa Ana, California

The street cruising problem in Santa Ana, California, became uncontrollable in the 1990s. On Sunday evenings 1,000 carloads of youths brought one six-block-long area in the community to a point of gridlock; this situation created a heightened sense of fear in the city because of associated criminal activity and rival gang violence (with 16 related homicides and more than 100 aggravated assaults in a two-and-a-half-year period). Traditional police responses failed and were expensive. Officers in the district formed a problem-solving team and developed a series of operation plans to address the issues. Police devised a traffic control scheme and used their legal authority to stop all traffic, identify drivers, and provide information on cruising violations. They entered driver and vehicle information in a computer database at the traffic control points and sent follow-up letters to registered vehicle owners to reinforce their warnings and to ensure that parents were informed of young drivers' activities. They also erected warning signs along the highways. On the first night of the operation, police stopped 70 percent of the cruising vehicles at checkpoints; during the next two nights, 83 percent were stopped. The number of returning cruisers diminished so much by the fourth night that the police suspended the checkpoints in favor of traffic stops. Cruising eventually ceased altogether. During the program, the police issued more than 2,000 personal warnings and sent more than 1,700 follow-up letters. The warning-and-education campaign turned out to be at least as effective as enforcement and was more efficient. Ninety percent of the cruisers warned on the first night did not return. There have been no cruising-related calls during the past two years, and crime associated with it has disappeared.

Source: Sampson and Scott, *Tackling Crime and Other Public Safety Problems,* pp. 14–18.

to drivers and spectators is exceptionally high. Unfortunately, some cities and states have not qualified street racing even as a misdemeanor; or, where there are laws against drag racing, racers can easily find an "amnesty jurisdiction" where such laws do not exist.[50]

Obviously, police everywhere support legislation that would tow vehicles involved in street racing and that allows the arrest of racers and spectators. Some cities have recently begun to view this matter very seriously. For example, in September 2002, the Los Angeles City Council urged Governor Gray Davis to approve legislation that would help the police department crack down on illegal street racing. It would take away racers' cars for 30 days (even on a first offense) and impose much more serious fines. The bill was signed into law by Governor Davis in September 2002.[51] In Wichita, Kansas, the police department recently contacted its Air Section to assist in street racing enforcement and used a digital camera to take aerial photographs; it also issued extra citations, engaged in surveillance, and collected reports about drag racing from businesses at common racing locations.[52] Finally, the San Diego police department used a "delayed response aimed at inducing ripples of paranoia within the city's illegal drag racing community."[53]

False Burglar Alarms

In the United States each year, police respond to about 38 million alarm activations. Most of the activations are burglar alarms, and about 98 percent of these alarms are false. As an example, Chicago police respond to more than 300,000 burglar alarms each year (98 percent of which are false), which translates to the equivalent use of 195 full-time police officers.[54]

The proliferation of electronic security systems for both commercial and residential use—estimates show between 18 and 21 million security alarm systems in the United States, with 1.5 million new systems added each year[55]—has brought with it a serious problem for police officers nationwide. False alarms, each of which requires about 20 minutes of police time, cost police departments about $1.5 billion each year.[56] Recent financial difficulties in some jurisdictions have forced police executives to reassess alarm responses, formerly provided free of charge.

Faced with budget cuts, an increasing number of police executives are charging business and residential owners for police responses to false alarms that are, in effect, wasted effort. A strategy of assessing fines for false alarms and the resulting termination of alarm use, now beginning to spread across the United States, obviously represents a major break with traditional police practices.

A problem-solving analysis for addressing burglar alarms would begin by asking the right questions:

- What percentage of the agency's alarm calls are false for business, residences, and government premises? What percentage are burglar alarms?
- What is the agency's true cost of responding to alarms?
- How many residential and commercial alarm systems are there in the juris-diction?
- At what rate do officers arrest burglars at alarm calls?
- Do some alarm companies have higher false alarm rates than others?[57]

Once the local problem is understood, responses may be implemented, such as the following:

- Require alarm companies to visually verify alarm legitimacy before calling the police.
- Charge a fee for service for all false holdup, burglary, and panic alarms.
- Establish an ordinance with escalating fines for false alarms.
- Publish alarm companies' false alarm rates on Web sites or elsewhere.[58]

Misuse and Abuse of 911

A police problem that is related to false alarms because of its misuse and abuse is 911 misuse and abuse, due to both unintentional and intentional calls. The United States 911 system handles 500,000 calls daily, or about 183 million an-nually, and unintentional, phantom wireless calls account for between 25 and 70 percent of all 911 calls in some U.S. communities. If a cell phone user inad-vertently presses the 9 or 1 key on a phone preprogrammed to dial 911, the phone automatically dials 911, even without the user having to press "send."[59]

Nonemergency 911 calls often constitute a large portion of all 911 calls as well; callers sometimes want to report an incident that was not an emergency or that does not require immediate police attention (e.g., the caller's car was broken into the previous night) as well as non-police-related matters, such as the time a football game begins, directions to a local event, the time of day, the day of garbage pickup, and so forth. People also call 911 to falsely claim an emergency or to deliberately hang up.[60] To problem solve 911 calls, the police must first analyze the problem by obtaining all available information about the incidents, offenders, location/times, and determining what percentage of 911 calls are wireless, misdials, hang-ups, nonemergencies, or pranks. Once the problem is analyzed, responses can be implemented, such as the following:

- requiring manufacturers to redesign wireless phones
- distributing phone button guards to reduce the accidental pressing of the 9 or 1 key
- prohibiting automatic 911 dialing

- funneling phantom wireless calls through an automated 911 answering system (during peak 911 calling periods, if no one is on the line the dispatcher can switch the call to a separate queue, and an automated attendant can ask the caller to press any number (or say yes) if an emergency exists; if the caller does not respond, the call is terminated)[61]

Exhibit 10-10 discusses how the San Diego police department addressed a 911 problem, and Exhibit 10-11 concludes the chapter with a discussion of how illegal dumping was halted in an Oklahoma county.

EXHIBIT 10-10   San Diego's Misuse and Abuse of 911

Officers in San Diego noticed that a high volume of 911 hang-ups were coming from pay phones in one block of the city's Southern Division. This area abuts Mexico and has the busiest border crossing in the world. Officers surveilled the 20 pay phones on the block—phones belonging to six different owners—and spoke with community members and taxi and bus drivers, and determined that diversionary calls (unlicensed taxi drivers were calling 911 to divert police away from their passenger pick-up points at the border, and drug dealers were also making such calls), prank calls (by late-night revelers returning to the U.S. from Mexico), and misdials (people returning to the U.S. from Mexico trying to call their families were dialing 911 instead of 011, the international access number) were the three main causes. The police alerted business owners to the severity of the problem, and that they were being diverted from crime-ridden areas to respond to false calls; the owners removed 10 of the phones and relocated others; officers also posted "no loitering" signs next to the phones. To address the misdialing problem, officers painted all the 9 keys red. As a result of these efforts, 911 calls dropped by 50 percent, and resulted in lower response times to other calls.

Source: Rana Sampson, *Misuse and Abuse of 911* (Washington, D.C.: U.S. Department of Justice, Office of Community Oriented Policing Services, September 2002), pp. 13–15.

EXHIBIT 10-11   Illegal Dumping in Oklahoma County

Sometimes the unincorporated portions of counties become an illegal dumping ground, spoiled by heaps of trash and even discarded appliances, tires, and household furniture. Such was the case recently in an area known as "No Man's Land" in Oklahoma County, which surrounds Oklahoma City. A new deputy sheriff position was assigned to attempt to quell the problem, by locating, investigating, and cleaning up illegal dumping sites.

First, the deputy received training in investigating and identifying the illegal dumping suspects, and worked with the district attorney's office to establish the evidentiary requirements for successful prosecution. Popular dumping sites were identified and undercover surveillance was initiated. The deputy soon identified one individual who was being paid by several tire dealers to dump their used tires illegally, often in a river. An undercover operation was launched to catch tire dealers who improperly disposed of their tires. In a month's time, hundreds of used tires were seized and felony charges were filed against five persons from four tire dealerships. The success of the program resulted in the creation of the Environmental Crimes Unit in the county sheriff's office.

Source: "Proactive Policing: Strategies That Work," *The Police Chief* (January 2003):20.

SUMMARY

This chapter has applied COPPS to the street, demonstrating how it works with specific crimes. The efficacy of COPPS in dealing with these problems was convincingly demonstrated. The police agencies described in this chapter and their peers across the United States are realizing many successes, breaking with tradition and attacking the contributing or underlying problems, while empowering neighborhoods to defend themselves against crime and deterioration.

NOTES

1. Zachary Tumin, "Managing Relations with the Community" (working paper 86–05–06, Program in Criminal Justice Policy and Management, John F. Kennedy School of Government, Harvard University, Cambridge, Massachusetts, November 1986), final page.

2. U.S. Department of Justice, Federal Bureau of Investigation, *Uniform Crime Reports: Crime in the United States—2001* (Washington, D.C.: Author, 2002), pp. 232–233.

3. Ellen Perlman, "The Meth Monster," *Governing* (January 2000):22.

4. Michael S. Scott, *Rave Parties* (Washington, D.C.: U.S. Department of Justice, Office of Community Oriented Policing Services, 2002), pp. 1–2, 13–14.

5. *http://www.portlandpolicebureau.com/news301/html* (Accessed May 27, 2003).

6. C. Ronald Huff, *Comparing the Criminal Behavior of Youth Gangs and At-Risk Youths* (Washington, D.C.: National Institute of Justice Research in Brief, 1998).

7. U.S. Department of Justice, National Criminal Justice Reference Service, "In the Spotlight: Gang Resources," *http://www.ncjrs.org/gangs/summary.html* (Accessed May 27, 2003).

8. S. Vantakesh, "The Financial Activity of a Modern American Street Gang." In *Looking at Crime from the Street Level: Plenary Papers of the 1999 Conference on Criminal Justice Research and Evaluation—Enhancing Policing and Practice through Research*, Volume 1 (Washington, D.C.: U.S. Department of Justice, Office of Justice Programs, National Institute of Justice, 1999).

9. Rana Sampson and Michael S. Scott, *Tackling Crime and Other Public Safety Problems: Case Studies in Problem Solving* (Washington, D.C.: U.S. Department of Justice, Office of Community Oriented Policing Services, 1999) p. 63.

10. Ibid., p. 64.

11. Ibid., p. 67.

12. Ibid., p. 68.

13. Ibid.

14. James Lasley, *"Designing Out" Gang Homicides and Street Assaults* (Washington, D.C.: U.S. Department of Justice, National Institute of Justice Research in Brief, November 1998), pp. 1–4.

15. Deborah Lamm Weisel, *Graffiti* (Washington, D.C.: U.S. Department of Justice, Office of Community Oriented Policing Services, 2002).

16. Ronald J. Getz, "Reaching Out to the Mentally Ill," *Law and Order* (May 1999):51.

17. Robert Rosenblatt, *Law Enforcement and the Mentally Ill* (Washington, D.C.: Regional Organized Crime Information Center, 2002).

18. Ibid.

19. *www.tri-statercpi.org* (Accessed May 27, 2003).

20. Donald G. Turnbaugh, "Curing Police Problems with the Mentally Ill," *The Police Chief* (February 1999):52.

21. David L. Carter and Allen D. Sapp, "Police Response to Street People: A Survey of Perspectives and Practices," *FBI Law Enforcement Bulletin* (March 1993):5–10.

22. Peter Finn, *Street People*. United States Department of Justice, National Institute of Justice, Crime File Study Guide (Washington, D.C.: USGPO, 1988), p. 1.

23. Ronald J. Getz, "A Positive Police Program for the Homeless," *Law and Order* (May 1999):93–96.

24. Ibid.

25. National Council on Alcohol and Drug Dependence, *Alcoholism and Alcohol-Related Problems: A Sobering Look* (Washington, D.C.: Author, 2000).

26. U.S. Department of Justice, Office of Juvenile Justice and Delinquency Prevention, OJJDP Fact Sheet, *Combating Underage Drinking* (Washington, D.C.: Author, February 1998), p. 1.

27. Sampson and Scott, *Tackling Crime and Other Public Safety Problems*, pp. 57–59.

28. Lawrence Sherman and Robert A. Berk, "The Specific Deterrent Effects of Arrest for Domestic Assault," *American Sociological Review* 49 (1984): 261–271.

29. Jacob R. Clark, "Where to Now on Domestic-Violence? Studies Offer Mixed Policy Guidance," *Law Enforcement News* (April 30, 1993):1.

30. "Taking a Problem-Solving Approach to Domestic Violence." In *Domestic Violence: 1995–1998 Edition* (Washington, D.C.: Community Policing Consortium, 1998), p. 4.

31. Ronald J. Kalanquin, "Coalition Works to Curb Rising Rate of Domestic Violence in Lapeer County." In ibid., p. 5.

32. *www.cops.usdoj.gov/* (Accessed May 27, 2003).

33. Gene Marlin and Barbara Vogt, "Violence in the Schools," *The Police Chief* (April 1999):169.

34. National Center for Education Statistics, "Indicators of School Crime and Safety, 2002,"

http://nces.ed.gov/pubs2003/schoolcrime (Accessed May 27, 2003).

35. Ibid.

36. Margaret Small and Kellie Dressler Tetrick, "School Violence: An Overview," *Journal of the Office of Juvenile Justice and Delinquency Prevention* 8(1) (June 2001):3–13.

37. Ira Pollack and Carlos Sundermann, "Creating Safe Schools: A Comprehensive Approach," *Journal of the Office of Juvenile Justice and Delinquency Prevention* 8(1) (June 2001): 13–20.

38. Marlin and Vogt, "Violence in the Schools," p. 169.

39. Center for the Prevention of School Violence, "School Resource Officers and Safe School Planning," *http://www.ncsu.edu/cpsv/srossp.htm* (Accessed May 27, 2003).

40. *www.cops.usdoj.gov* (Accessed May 27, 2003).

41. Rana Sampson, *Bullying in Schools* (Washington, D.C.: U.S. Department of Justice, Office of Community Oriented Policing Services, March 2002), pp. 1–2.

42. Ibid.

43. Herman Goldstein, *Problem-Oriented Policing* (New York: McGraw-Hill, 1990), pp. 44–45.

44. Ibid., p. 44. See also *Keeping Illegal Activity out of Rental Property: A Police Guide for Establishing Landlord Training Programs* (Washington, D.C.: U.S. Department of Justice, Bureau of Justice Assistance, March 2000).

45. Sampson and Scott, *Tackling Crime and Other Public Safety Problems*, pp. 13–14.

46. See, for example, Campbell Resources, Inc., *The Landlord Training Program: Keeping Illegal Activity out of Rental Property* (Portland, Ore.: Author, 1992), p. 2.

47. W. H. Matthews, *Policing Distressed Public Housing Developments: Community Policing Could Be the Answer* (Washington, D.C.: U.S. Department of Housing and Urban Development, Crime Prevention and Security Division, no date).

48. Michael S. Scott, *Street Prostitution* (Washington, D.C.: U.S. Department of Justice, Office of Community Oriented Policing Services, August 2001).

49. Boise Police Department Planning Unit, *Downtown "Cruising" in Major U.S. Cities and One City's Response to the Problem* (Boise, Id.: Author, 1990), pp. 1–2.

50. Portland, Oregon, Police Bureau Web page, *http://www.portlandpolicebureau.com/news302.html* (Accessed May 4, 2003).

51. Personal communication, Bill Murray, Los Angeles Community Policing, June 6, 2003, *http://www.lacp.org/Articles*.

52. *http://www.wichitagov.org* (Accessed May 27, 2003).

53. "SDPD's Drag-Net puts the brakes on street racers," *Law Enforcement News,* (November 15, 2002):5.

54. Rana Sampson, *False Burglar Alarms* (Washington, D.C.: U.S. Department of Justice, Office of Community Oriented Policing Services, August 2001), pp. 1–2.

55. Ibid., p. 2.

56. Ibid., p. 6.

57. Ibid., pp. 9–10.

58. Ibid., pp. 13–17.

59. Rana Sampson, *Misuse and Abuse of 911* (Washington, D.C.: U.S. Department of Justice, Office of Community Oriented Policing Services, September 2002), pp. 1–7.

60. Ibid.

61. Ibid., pp. 13–15.

INTRODUCTION

Some writers have manifested concerns with and criticisms of community oriented policing and problem solving (COPPS). This chapter examines these concerns—we have termed them the "devil's advocate" positions toward COPPS. Although several reservations were lodged against COPPS in the early stages of its development, they have probably been reduced or eliminated during the intervening years; however, we believe it is important for these concerns to be considered and addressed.

This chapter addresses nine concerns that have appeared in the literature. The concern is first described; then it is followed by a response, with some impressions of how COPPS, when implemented and practiced in a thoughtful and appropriate manner, addresses each stated concern.

—11—

THE "DEVIL'S ADVOCATE"

Addressing Concerns with COPPS

Pessimism, when you get used to it, is just as agreeable as optimism.
—ARNOLD BENNETT

THE ISSUES

Following are the nine general concerns and criticisms about COPPS:

1. Is there a true "community"?
2. Is this a proper role for police?
3. Does the concept violate the political neutrality of police?
4. Can COPPS work when it cannot cure the underlying societal problems of crime and disorder?
5. Does the concept require too much officer discretion?
6. Is this simply a faddish, costly gimmick?
7. Do officers possess the intellectual capacity and temperament to sustain the concept?
8. Can police departments change from within?
9. Will adequate evaluations be done of COPPS?

Some of these concerns overlap in varying degrees. Two more concerns are addressed at the chapter's end, including the recent phenomenon in policing termed "zero tolerance," and whether COPPS will continue to exist when federal funds are no longer available to assist in providing such initiatives.

Is There a True "Community"?

The community organizing role of the police in community policing tends to assume there is a viable "community" to organize. Some writers, however, question the ability of the police to create a feeling of community where none exists.[1] Legitimate concerns have also been lodged about the ability of COPPS to work in neighborhoods that are severely crimeridden and occupied with more reticent and fearful citizens. As stated by James Q. Wilson and John J. DiIulio,

> Much is made these days of "community oriented" policing. Both of us have written favorably about it and the problem solving, police–neighborhood collaboration that lies at its heart. But the success stories are always in communities in

Block parties help establish a "sense of community" by providing an opportunity for neighbors to get acquainted. (*Courtesy* Minneapolis, Minnesota, police department)

which the people are willing to step forward and the police are willing to meet them halfway. Where open-air drug markets operate every night, where Uzi-toting thugs shoot rivals and bystanders alike, it is a brave or foolhardy resident who will even testify against a criminal, much less lead an anticrime crusade.[2]

A related concern is that community organizing efforts may help organize only the middle class. Early COPPS experiments in Houston, Chicago, and Minneapolis found they were more successful among middle-income people, homeowners, and whites than among the poor, renters, and racial minorities.[3]

The question is whether the police will be able to organize communities that have disintegrated. Extremely poor neighborhoods may lack any organized community life, have an extremely transient population, and contain powerless people who do not have the ability to work with the police. As Samuel Walker put it, this may be "the *paradox* of community policing: The communities that need it most are least able to take advantage of it" (emphasis in original).[4] Another argument is that there are many groups in society who do not want a continued police presence.

Response

Neighborhoods do exist where there is very little sense of "community," particularly in highly transient areas or multicultural areas where language or police–community relations are problematic. In these areas, people may be extremely reluctant to step forward, to attend neighborhood meetings, or to assist the police in other ways to address problems. These people may also, for various reasons, hold their police in low regard.

Such situations will require that the police and other governmental agencies shoulder a much larger brunt of the responsibility for neighborhood problem solving. The police must hope that, over time, citizens assume some civic responsibility and engage in the "communitarianism" spirit, which was discussed in Chapter 3.

Furthermore, some cities—especially relatively young cities that have grown rapidly in recent years—may not have communities or neighborhoods in the traditional sense, or a long-term identification with the neighborhood or community institutions. It has been shown, however, in examples presented in earlier chapters, that COPPS can function in the most dismal of neighborhoods. Granted, these neighborhoods are a greater challenge than those with fewer "broken windows," but COPPS can function in any locale where citizens are tired of problems going unsolved. Programs such as Secret Witness and police storefronts can help reduce citizens' anxiety about working with the police to curb disorder.

Is the "community" a city, a block, a neighborhood? Can police and citizens share decision making and power in the community? What happens when community interest in solving problems fades?[5] These are questions that sociologists could debate indefinitely. This question/concern did not originate, however, with attempts to implement COPPS. A lack of a sense of community, anonymity, a mixture of lifestyles, and tensions have existed ever since people began living in groups. Still, despite strained relationships, people have always looked for order and to the police for solutions to their most troublesome problems.

Furthermore, as noted in Chapter 4, the community remains a largely untapped resource for identifying and reducing problems. Eliciting the help of the community should be a major objective in police efforts to identify and solve problems. Community surveys and other interactions by the police help to focus COPPS's efforts and empower communities to learn to police themselves.

Is This a Proper Role for the Police?

Another issue in the community policing debate involves the proper role of police: *Should* police officers function as community organizers, working on community problems that do not directly involve crime (such as garbage, graffiti, and abandoned vehicles)? Is this the proper function for a police officer? Some believe there are serious dangers in the community policing expansion of the police role, given our Anglo-American heritage of limits on police power. Some critics ask whether police officers should be going door to door, calling on law-abiding citizens who have not summoned the police. They worry that they will turn into political advocacy groups who will lobby for candidates or issues that the police support.[6]

There are also reservations about the potential for community policing to "weaken the rule of law" in the sense of equal protection and evenhanded enforcement, which "may lessen the protection afforded by law to unpopular persons."[7] The requirement that police become more decentralized is seen as a threat to the rule of law.

Another concern has been whether public safety will decline under community policing. Naysayers contend that the efficacy of using the public in the battle for crime control is untested. Of a related nature is the argument that the concept is "soft" on crime because of its very nature, because the police fear using any forceful action that would anger the community and jeopardize the gains from community policing. They ask, "Can the police put on a velvet glove and keep their iron hand in shape?"[8]

At the same time, there is concern with what is perceived as the "big brother" nature of community policing—the increased use of closed-circuit television, police coming into homes to make security inspections, and police asking about neighborhood problems. Skeptics also worry about the ease with which computer-stored information could be obtained.

Response

These concerns are, to a degree, a matter of policy choice for each community. A community may choose the COPPS model or subscribe to the traditional crime-fighting role of policing. COPPS advocates, however, believe that the police *should* take the initiative to identify emerging problems and offer solutions. They are in a unique position to collect and analyze data and quickly attempt to deal with problems rather than wait until problems become ominous in nature. The police should be more vocal in addressing problems and in presenting options to, and being advocates for, the community.

Also, as noted in Chapter 2, COPPS is simply a response to the major concerns and fears of Americans, most of whom do not fear being a victim of a major crime, but fear lesser crimes involving neighborhood disorder: drug violations, gang activities, noise, strangers, fighting, physical disorder (such as litter, graffiti, junk cars), and so forth. Here the police are analogous to the medical profession: Whereas physicians treat people who are in *physical* disorder, police have opportunities to assist people who are in *social* disorder, often in fear of the problems surrounding them. The police, like physicians, are in a unique position to intervene when peoples' lives are in disarray and to work with them to solve personal crises.

Some writers suggest that not all members of society want the same level of police service or visibility. This begs the questions: "But don't *all* citizens want neighborhood disorder eliminated? To have the freedom to leave their homes at night believing they are secure? To not have to douse the lights early to avoid becoming targets of area shootings? To be able to use the parks and streets instead of turning them over to gangs and drug dealers?" The answers to these questions override the concern by some that not all individuals want the same police service or visibility. COPPS offers the hope for a better quality of life.

In response to the concern or criticism that COPPS is "soft" on crime, *no one* recommends that crime be ignored under COPPS; the laws must still be enforced, and COPPS is not soft on crime. This concept is founded on prevention and control.

Another concern with COPPS follows the old expression, "Why aren't you chasing bank robbers instead of writing me a traffic ticket?" Critics claim that although community policing calls for foot patrols and neighborhood newsletters, there are international drug dealers and a globalization of crime and policing. They add that this concept "needs re-thinking when the broken windows in your neighborhood result from actions of drug lords in the Andes."[9]

To assume that neighborhood newsletters and foot patrols fail to deal with important issues, such as major crime, misses the point. Police do not exist in a vacuum; information is, and has always been, the lifeblood of policing, and it is critical to its success. Furthermore, the police belong in America's neighborhoods as much as they belong in the poppy fields of Turkey or on boats and planes watching our borders. Officers patrolling neighborhoods and business districts on foot are not on public relations excursions; they are seeking to maintain order and provide public safety. Indeed, these officers often glean important information that assists them in eradicating crimes and arresting criminals. The police cannot chase major drug lords and ignore neighborhoods any more than they can ignore drug lords and concentrate only on neighborhood order maintenance.

Finally, computerized data is the wave of the future; we bank, buy, research, and initiate personal relationships on the World Wide Web. Access, security, and privacy are major concerns, and police and other governmental agencies need to ensure that individual rights are not violated.

The police are definitely *not* apolitical. (*Courtesy* Washoe County, Nevada, Sheriff's Office)

Does the Concept Violate the Political Neutrality of Police?

Should the police be used to define and shape community norms? Should police officers be used as agents of informal social control? Some writers believe that this violates the political neutrality of the police and that it would be dangerous to give those with the power to enforce laws the additional authority to enforce norms.[10] Pessimists assert that "there is great potential for troublesome political entanglements, particularly when police are asked to take sides in battles between interest groups, neighbors, or racial bigots."[11] They also note that police traditionally arrested, constrained, warned, and deterred; now, however, under the COPPS philosophy, the police "advise, mediate, lecture, organize, participate, cooperate, communicate, reach out, solicit, and encourage."[12]

Other writers worry that some community policing programs will give influential citizens control over the police. They believe the objectives of improved community relations, creative problem solving, and crime prevention are the greatest threat to this neutrality. And, the argument goes, because the police must focus not only on the symptoms of crime but also on its root causes, the police have become politically involved in various agencies.[13] This concern includes the possibility that police will be led more and more to behave like politicians, developing powers of patronage and even advising how grant and local monies should be distributed.

Response

Regarding the concerns that COPPS will allow the police to become politically involved in various agencies and be led more and more to behave like politicians, this is precisely the kind of ingenuous and innovative work we would hope to see from our police officers.

Does society expect police to be apolitical? The police are not, nor have they ever been, politically neutral, at least in a partisan sense. Nor does society appear to want them to be neutral. They are decidedly *not* neutral when they form coalitions and work with prosecutors and political bodies (city councils, county commissions, state legislatures), or in lobbying efforts for new laws. They also lead drives for bond issues for more personnel and new stationhouses and represent neighborhoods in parking, traffic control, and other projects.

What we *do* ask of our police, however, is that they be equitable and fair to the public. It is also important that agencies proactively enact disciplinary policies that are based on standards of fairness, consistency, and equity so that the organization, the involved officer, and the public's interest are protected.

Can COPPS Work When It Cannot Cure the Underlying Societal Problems of Crime and Disorder?

Those who raise this issue obviously believe that because COPPS can neither eliminate crime nor attack its underlying causes (such as poverty, prejudice, broken homes, and peer influences), it is a doomed undertaking. Some even question whether, for this reason, the police are the proper agency to fulfill the goals of community policing. For them, the questions are whether the police should be working to solve *any* nonlegal problems (and should instead strictly be law enforcers) and whether social service functions should be removed from the police function.[14]

Response

This concern is particularly vexing. Is it implying that the United States should abandon its attempts to curb drug dealers and addicts, arrest serial murderers, or provide for the homeless because these groups represent social problems beyond control? The deep-seated problem with drugs may never be resolved, yet there are many neighborhoods in which the police and the community have worked together to rid the area of drug dealers and significantly improve living conditions.

No one has suggested that COPPS is a panacea to all our social ills. No modern police Moses is going to lead society to the Promised Land, nor can our police achieve world peace. COPPS does offer, though, our best hope for dealing efficiently and effectively with a variety of conditions that plague our neighborhoods and cause people to live in fear. Bright police leaders are willing to reengineer their agencies to provide better service and a more representative government. And young, educated, and energetic officers possess the skills to mobilize communities and coordinate the efforts of the police, other agencies, and the community in identifying and eradicating problems. Agencies across the nation are providing examples of their successes with COPPS.

As we noted in Chapter 4, it is important that the police pursue the resolution of major problems in the context of "small wins" rather than attempt to address problems on a massive scale. Some problems are too deeply ingrained, or too rooted in other complex social problems, to be eliminated. Some community problems must be broken down into smaller, more controllable problems.[15]

Does the Concept Require Too Much Officer Discretion?

Some police executives are concerned with the increased use of discretionary authority of patrol officers, and that greater intimacy with the public may threaten officer accountability (in other words, lead to graft).[16] Concern is also apparent that under community policing, officers may be encouraged to use any method at all to "handle" a neighborhood problem. Certain tactics could violate the rights of individual citizens (especially members of groups whom community residents do not like).[17]

Pessimists also emphasize that the police have traditionally not been in a policy-making position—a responsibility reserved for the legislatures and governing bodies. Thus, another worry is that community policing will "weaken" the rule of law. By expanding the use of discretion, community policing "can easily be read as bending the law so as not to offend. Local commanders may begin to think it is more important not to alienate loud voices than to protect quiet ones."[18]

Response

The police have always been in the field without being subject to direct supervision, while wielding tremendous authority and making difficult decisions that affect the lives of others. This is now assumed to be a necessary aspect of their job. No one expects the police to work without discretion and totally within the letter of the law—for example, to cite all traffic violators for driving a few miles per hour over the speed limit. As noted previously, we do require that they use discretion in a professional, fair, and equitable manner. We know that police have used informal means of problem solving for centuries.

Much of the reserve of knowledge possessed by the patrol officer has gone untapped. We hire the best persons we can for the job and then ask them, as Herman Goldstein put it, to behave like "automatons" when they arrive at work, following orders and regulations blindly and generally being treated like children.[19] Indeed, the many applications of the COPPS philosophy have shown that patrol officers can and do implement informal commonsense solutions to problems that work.

The job of the patrol officer has become much broader than it was in the past, and officers must use a greater range of discretion to deal with community problems and a wider range of community resources in responding to incidents. The time has come to release their creativity and allow their problem-solving skills to unfold.

Finally, in this era of increased use of citizen review boards, the specter of civil liability, and judicial review, police officers have become more accountable with their discretionary authority than ever before. The COPPS approach encourages and facilitates even greater accountability on the part of the police. Officers are forced to think through how they respond to problems and be prepared to justify their decisions to higher authorities within the department. This reduces the risk of arbitrariness and value judgments that may be illegal or improper.[20]

Is This Simply a Faddish, Costly Gimmick?

Some critics have wondered whether this concept is nothing more than "putting old wine in new bottles," arguing that it is a set of aspirations wrapped in a slogan, or a "trendy phrase spread thinly over customary reality."[21] In the same vein, some have described the community oriented approach as simply "fuzzy feel good politics" that has not been effectively implemented, with too much of it transpiring in "the boardroom and not on the boardwalk."[22] For others, community policing is akin to learning that the "emperor has no clothes."[23] And, for still others, it is merely "helping little old ladies across the street." In sum, for many persons COPPS is little more than a public relations gimmick.

Another concern is that community policing will squander community resources if police are spread too thinly, attempting to provide services for which other social agencies are statutorily responsible. To address this problem, several departments are increasingly using civilians as police assistants, performing a variety of jobs once performed by more costly, sworn personnel.

To disregard COPPS as a "trendy phrase spread thinly over customary reality"[24] is to ignore the efforts of numerous agencies that have successfully implemented COPPS and co-opted partnerships with the community to identify and resolve neighborhood problems. It also ignores the following facts: The federal government invested nearly $9 billion in community policing; scholarly publications abound on the subject, and college degrees are now being offered in the discipline; police academy and in-service curricula have changed significantly to include COPPS instruction; many agencies have changed their entire organization's strategic plans and methods of recruiting, hiring, and promoting to include the principles of COPPS; and, as detailed in Chapter 14, agencies worldwide have followed very similar paths to changing their strategies toward COPPS.

Also ignored is the degree to which the implementation of COPPS has transformed these agencies. In many cases it involved major internal changes, including the creation of new mission statements and department values, organizational restructuring, geographic reorganization, realignment of ranks, changes in promotional policies and operational policies, developing new recruiting practices, and providing new training programs. It also required the development of partnerships with the community, other government agencies, private business, and other police agencies. No past efforts at new programs in policing have had such significant impacts on agencies.

Concerning the costs associated with community policing, it is not the objective of COPPS to further obligate officers to issues that are better handled by other agencies. In fact, the opposite is true. The objective of COPPS is for officers to enlist the cooperation of agencies to handle the problems for which they are better equipped and more responsible. A problem oriented approach also provides officers with the tools to reduce both calls for service *and* crime—a further example of fiscal accountability and efficiency.

Some authors have maintained that care should be given in considering whether police personnel are "ready to fulfill the demands of such a role."[25] Community and problem-solving policing, it has been noted, requires line officers to

> alleviate specific problems, which they have helped to identify by orienting themselves to the needs of the community, with *creative* and *innovative solutions* in a fair, just, and legal manner. This requires certain skills, including problem conceptualization, synthesis and analysis of information, action plans, program evaluation, and communication of evaluation results and policy implications. . . . [S]uffice it to say that the sensitivity and demands of the role of community policing require an individual with a high degree of intelligence, open-mindedness, and nonprejudicial attitudes (emphasis in original).[26]

Many of the skills required of line officers do involve a certain degree of cognitive and logical ability. Police chief executives must endeavor to explore ways to tap the inventive nature of the rank-and-file.

Patrol officers have always possessed tremendous amounts of information concerning what is occurring in their communities—information about people (law-abiding and otherwise) and their streets and neighborhoods. According to Herman Goldstein, the street cop

> should have a detailed understanding of such varied problems as homicides involving teenage victims; drive-by shootings; and carjacking; and . . . at the micro

A police officer's job requires a high level of education and specialized technical training. (*Courtesy* NYPD Photo Unit)

level, a beat officer should have in depth knowledge about the corner drug house; the rowdy teenage gang that assembles at the convenience store each Friday night; and the panhandler who harasses passersby on a given street corner.[27]

To not attempt to utilize this resource to the fullest extent possible seems irrational.

We now have a better educated assemblage of police personnel than ever before. To intimate that police officers do not have the cognitive capacities to work within or carry the mandate of COPPS is nonsensical and insulting. The task of training officers on the problem-solving process (S.A.R.A.), and to facilitate neighborhood meetings and to mobilize community efforts is no more difficult than many of the other technical skills for which we hold police accountable. Chris Braiden, former superintendent of the Edmonton, Alberta, police department in Canada, complained that police live in cognitive prisons and are controlled by convention. He suggests that a "bureaucratic garage sale" is needed to correct this problem.[28]

For all of these reasons, to intimate that police are not educationally sophisticated enough to implement and evaluate this approach is groundless and unsupported.

Can Police Departments Change from Within?

Some authors have asserted that the current movement toward community policing attempts to change old policing philosophies, organizational designs, and management practices. This is a significant development, because it means that those agencies truly interested in adopting community policing must abandon longstanding traditional methods. It has been suggested that COPPS might eventually be seen as another "failed attempt at reform, much like team policing."[29] Problems are also anticipated with getting mid-level police managers to accept significant changes to the status quo. They maintain that if team policing was any indication, the answer will likely be less than favorable. Under this view, for community policing to work, there will have to be changes in organizational structure, management style, and personnel.

Skeptics worry that community policing makes supervision within police organizations ends- rather than means-based, that executives rate officers by their ability to achieve general objectives: management by objective, which now, in their view, permeates community policing. They believe that we will see "work schedules become more flexible, paperwork less detailed, dress more casual, contacts with citizens more offhand, supervision more collegial, and working behavior less rule-oriented."[30] According to this view, this "negotiated" policing may undermine professionalism, substituting responsiveness to community opinion with exogenous standards.

Response

We dealt with the subject of changing the culture of the police department in Chapter 7. There is a need, however, to respond here to the concern that old policing philosophies, organizational designs, and management practices may be too well entrenched to change.

COPPS requires a fundamental change in the way police view their mission. So long as the agency's traditionalists understand that the department is serious about community policing—and the message is constantly reinforced from the top—they can become an integral part of making the concept work.[31] As one writer observed, "Moving ahead doesn't mean forgetting where you've been. It means acknowledging that where you've been is not the only place you can go."[32]

Policing needs chief executives who are willing to do things that have not been done before, or, as another writer put it, "risk takers and boat rockers within a culture [policing] where daily exposure to life-or-death situations makes officers natural conservators of the status quo."[33] Departments must also find ways to free officers from the "tyranny of 911."

Changing an agency from the reactive, incident-driven mode to COPPS is a complex endeavor. As we noted in Chapter 6, four principal components of implementation profoundly affect the way agencies do business: leadership and administration (which includes roles of the chief executive, middle managers, and first-line supervisors), human resources (recruiting and training in particular, as well as the issue of labor relations), field operations (including decentralization and the roles of detectives and patrol personnel), and external relations (such as the community, local government agencies, service providers, business, and the media).

Will Adequate Evaluations Be Done of COPPS?

A caveat for many observers of community policing lies in the manner in which its work is to be evaluated. (Note that Chapter 12 deals entirely with the evaluation of COPPS strategies.) They note that if the police attempt to implement community policing while primarily using traditional "quantity-based evaluation criteria," the program will not be successful. Quality- and community-based criteria, they argue, including citizen attitudes and fear of crime issues (measured, at least in part, by community surveys), will need to become an integral part of how police effectiveness is measured.[34] Robert Friedmann added that perhaps

> the biggest drawback of the concept of community policing lies in impreciseness or overreach. It seems to include anything that has to do with the "community." What, after all, is community policing? Is it public policing? Is it a strategy? How does it blend with other strategies or other orientations? What is to be changed? Crime rates, fear of crime, attitudes of citizens toward police? Or cooperation with the police? What are acceptable levels of crime? And for what types of crime?

How, and by whom, are they defined? Who is to do what? Does the rookie or the experienced police officer do "community work"?[35]

Chris Offer also faulted the evaluations that have been done of community policing, saying there is no evidence that no other variables caused the change, that the change is long term, and that there even has been change.[36]

Response

For the first time in the history of modern policing, agencies are seriously considering the importance of qualitative assessments, and more evaluation is now being done than ever before—indeed, evaluation is highly encouraged. For example, the Department of Justice Office of Community Oriented Policing Services (COPS) requires that 10 percent of every problem-solving grant be devoted to project evaluation, and the National Institute of Justice has been given funds by the COPS office to conduct evaluations of problem-solving initiatives across the United States. Through this process a lot of information is being collected and much is being learned, both scientifically and anecdotally.

Some would go further and argue that data concerning crime statistics, clearance rates, and calls for service are unnecessary. The problem with traditional policing was that these "boilerplate" measurements were the *only* data gathered and were the sole basis for performance measurements. Research has shown that the majority of a police officer's activity (roughly 80 percent) involves nonpolicing activities. Therefore, it is important that systems are developed to shift evaluative efforts to better assess both the individual officer and agency. The police have already begun evaluating themselves differently.

As will be seen in Chapter 12, efforts are also being made to include COPPS efforts in evaluations of officers' performance. The S.A.R.A. process guides officers through problem solving and helps them to identify and evaluate the underlying conditions contributing to crime and disorder. With this information, officers are better prepared to consider their responses. In some cases, arrests may be required; however, in other matters, simply improving the environmental factors contributing to crime may be the best response. Officers also learn which agencies both inside and outside their own jurisdiction or government can assist them with a problem. Officers engaged in COPPS efforts learn how important other agencies and the community are in addressing crime and disorder.

Other Concerns: Zero Tolerance and Existing without Federal Funds

Following are discussions of two associated concerns that do not necessarily fit into the previous categories: zero tolerance, and whether COPPS can exist without the availability of federal funding to assist with such services.

Zero-Tolerance Movement

Recently, some agencies have adopted "zero tolerance"—the back-to-basics, hard-nosed, "get tough" approach to crime by the police. The best-known and most frequently cited example of this approach is the recent experience in the New York City police department (NYPD). The primary lesson from the NYPD's approach to disorder-type crimes in downtown Manhattan was that a sustained and aggressive crackdown on disorder and minor crime will result in tremendous crime decreases.37 According to the NYPD, significant improvements in crime control were realized as a result.

As Gary Cordner observed, however, this phenomenon "may pose the biggest threat of all to problem-oriented policing."[38] Cordner believes that

U.S. Department of Justice
Office of Community Oriented Policing Services

COPS 100,000 OFFICERS FUNDED

COPS office funding assisted many agencies in taking the first step toward implementing COPPS. The future success of those agencies will be determined by their ability to implement COPPS agencywide. (*Courtesy* U.S. Department of Justice)

zero tolerance represents a perversion of problem oriented policing, because it is usually employed without the benefit of careful problem identification or analysis, without any effort to identify underlying conditions and causes, and without careful consideration of possible alternatives. It returns policing to an overreliance on law enforcement.

Several points should be made about the NYPD's recent successes with the city's crime rate. First, several other initiatives were simultaneously undertaken by the department, including the CompStat meetings at which commanders were held more accountable for reviewing crime statistics in their precincts and making disorder-type crimes their priority, and the addition of more than 10,000 officers during the 1990s (some of whom were a result of amalgamations with other special police agencies, but many of whom were simply new personnel). Furthermore, it is possible that zero tolerance had an impact in New York City because prior enforcement levels were quite low.[39]

It is also notable that San Diego, California, experienced almost exactly the same crime decrease as New York City without adding substantially more officers. Indeed, whereas New York achieved 25 fewer reported Part I crimes for each additional officer hired, San Diego achieved 322 fewer Part I crimes reported per new officer—a return on its investment that was 13 times better than New York's. San Diego operates on a skeleton crew compared with New York, has about the same crime rate, and is one of the nation's primary devotees of COPPS. As Gary Cordner noted,

It is tempting to assert, therefore, that [problem oriented policing] is at least as successful as zero tolerance, and that it is much less costly. It would appear that problem-oriented policing requires fewer officers than traditional, enforcement-oriented policing. Fiscal conservatives should be flocking to it.[40]

Life Beyond the Office of Community Oriented Policing Services

Recent COPPS literature often presents questions and concerns about the fate of COPPS once federal funding expires for the Office of Community Oriented Policing Services. The question surfaces as to whether COPPS is sufficiently entrenched to sustain itself or, alternatively, whether the strategy will be cast aside. To borrow from Gregory Berg, many people are concerned that policing might revert to its old ways:

> We will muddle through, crisis to crisis, forever attempting to circle the wagons. We will lose our talented people to attrition or the dulling of their spirit. We will lose the faith and respect of those we are sworn to serve.[41]

It is probably true that COPPS initiatives in many jurisdictions will not realize the attention they received during the life of federal funding. In most cases, this is because those initiatives were never properly or earnestly implemented in the first place. Catchy COPPS acronyms may have been coined that were merely intended as window dressing. Indeed, some COPPS initiatives were probably undertaken in name only, involving the assignment of a few specialist officers or bicycle patrols with a misguided emphasis on community relations rather than collaborative problem-solving partnerships. Such "false advertising" and cosmetic changes will result only in short-lived successes. In addition, those agencies that attempted to implement COPPS with limited support of leadership and without substantive changes in the organization as noted in Chapter 6 will also find long-term success to be difficult.

If COPPS is to continue into the future, police executives must be determined to keep COPPS functional and must believe that COPPS works—with or without federal monies. Furthermore, they should take into consideration the capabilities and potential achievements of the problem-solving officers. As Aurora, Illinois, police commander Michael J. Nila stated, many officers have been "rescued" by COPPS:

> We now have police officers interacting with the citizens, and because they are able to do more long-term problem solving and see the results of their labors, the officers' job satisfaction is much higher than under traditional policing.[42]

SUMMARY

This chapter set out nine concerns with the COPPS concept and presented for each concern what we believe are countervailing responses. Even the most cautious scholars such as David Bayley, who wrote that community oriented policing was "more rhetoric than reality,"[43] have considerable optimism. Bayley wrote, "I do not believe that community policing should be abandoned. Its goals are worthwhile and its practice responsive to defects in current police performance."[44]

Some pessimism will always remain with the COPPS concept, as there was with the policing innovations of Robert Peel and August Vollmer. We believe, however, that this skepticism is healthy and establishes increased police effectiveness, accountability, and professionalism as policing enters a new era in problem solving and partnership with the community and other organizations.

NOTES

1. Samuel Walker, *The Police in America: An Introduction* (2nd ed.) (New York: McGraw-Hill, 1992), p. 189.

2. James Q. Wilson and John J. DiIulio, "Crackdown," *The New Republic* 201 (July 10, 1989):21–25.

3. See Wesley G. Skogan, *Disorder and Decline: Crime and the Spiral of Decay in American Neighborhoods* (New York: Free Press, 1990), p. 95.

4. Walker, *The Police in America*, p. 190.

5. Herman Goldstein, *Problem Oriented Policing* (New York: McGraw-Hill, 1990), p. 25.

6. David Bayley, "Community Policing: A Report from the Devil's Advocate." In *Community Policing: Rhetoric or Reality?*, Jack R. Greene and Stephen D. Mastrofski (eds.) (New York: Praeger, 1988), pp. 225–237.

7. Ibid., pp. 231–232.

8. Ibid., p. 228.

9. William F. McDonald, "Police and Community: In Search of a New Relationship," *The World and I* (March 1992):463.

10. Lisa M. Riechers and Roy R. Roberg, "Community Policing: A Critical Review of Underlying Assumptions," *Journal of Police Science and Administration* 17 (1990):109.

11. McDonald, "Police and Community," p. 457.

12. Bayley, "Community Policing," p. 231.

13. C. Short, "Community Policing—Beyond Slogans." In *The Future of Policing*, T. Bennet (ed.) (Cambridge, England: Institute of Criminology, 1983).

14. See ibid., p. 112.

15. Karl E. Weick, "Small Wins: Redefining the Scale of Social Problems," *American Psychologist* 39 (January 1984):40–49.

16. George L. Kelling, Robert Wasserman, and Hubert Williams, *Police Accountability and Community Policing* (Washington, D.C.: National Institute of Justice, 1988).

17. Bayley, "Community Policing," pp. 225–237.

18. Ibid., p. 232.

19. Goldstein, *Problem Oriented Policing*, p. 27.

20. Ibid., pp. 43, 47.

21. David Bayley, "Community Policing as Reform: A Cautionary Tale," in *Community Policing*, Greene and Mastrofski (eds.), pp. 47–67.

22. Jack Greene, quoted in "Community Policing Six Years Later: What Have We Learned?" *Law and Order* (May 1991):53.

23. Chris Offer, "C-OP Fads and Emperor without Clothes," *Law Enforcement News* (March 15, 1993):8.

24. Bayley, "Community Policing as Reform," pp. 225–226.

25. See Riechers and Roberg, "Community Policing," pp. 105–114.

26. Ibid., p. 111.

27. Herman Goldstein, "The New Policing: Confronting Complexity" (paper presented at the Conference on Community Policing, U.S. Department of Justice, National Institute of Justice, Washington, D.C., August 24, 1993).

28. Chris Braiden, "Community Policing: Nothing New under the Sun." In *Community Oriented Policing and Problem Solving* (Sacramento, Calif.: California Department of Justice, 1992), p. 21.

29. Roy R. Roberg and Jack Kuykendall, *Police and Society* (Belmont, Calif.: Wadsworth, 1993), p. 443.

30. Bayley, "Community Policing," p. 234.

31. Robert Trojanowicz and Bonnie Bucqueroux, "The Community Policing Challenge," *PTM* (November 1990):40–44, 51.

32. Jerald R. Vaughn, *Community-Oriented Policing: You Can Make It Happen* (Clearwater, Fla.: National Law Enforcement Leadership Institute, no date), p. 8.

33. Mike Tharp and Dorian Friedman, "New Cops on the Block," *U.S. News and World Report* (August 2, 1993):23.

34. See A. Lurigio and D. Rosenbaum, "Evaluation Research in Community Crime Prevention: A Critical Look at the Field." In *Community Crime Prevention*, D. Rosenbaum (ed.) (Beverly Hills, Calif.: Sage Publishers, 1986), pp. 19–44.

35. Robert R. Friedman, "Community Policing: Promises and Challenges," *Journal of Contemporary Justice* 6 (May 1990):84.

36. Chris Offer, "C-OP Fads," p. 8.

37. Gary Cordner, "Problem-Oriented Policing versus Zero Tolerance." In *Problem Oriented Policing: Crime-Specific Problems, Critical Issues, and Making POP Work*, Tara O'Connor and Anne C. Grant (eds.) (Washington, D.C.: Police Executive Research Forum, 1998), pp. 303–313.

38. Ibid., p. 304.

39. Ibid.

40. Ibid., p. 312.

41. Gregory R. Berg, "Promises versus Reality in Community Policing," *Law and Order* (September 1995):148.

42. Quoted in Keith W. Strandberg, "The State of Community Policing," *Law Enforcement Technology* (October 1997): 45.

43. Bayley, "Community Policing," p. 225.

44. Ibid., p. 236.

INTRODUCTION

A 75-year-old woman rose to her feet at a town meeting in a midwestern city to offer a suggestion on how an open-air drug market problem might be addressed. "You know," she said, "if you add one more street light per block, you might just get rid of these thugs selling drugs. They're like rats. They prefer the dark." The city manager's office and the police department designated the 16-block neighborhood as a test zone, used Community Development Block Grant money to purchase three new street lights per block for the high-crime area, and gathered data on reported crimes and drug trafficking. After three months (and still a year later), there were significant decreases in all monitored crimes for the area. The desired outcomes were achieved.[1]

This case study shows that the police, citizens, community leaders, and evaluators, working together—with community oriented policing and problem solving (COPPS) strategies—can create and evaluate change. With sound techniques and measurable results, communities can solve problems and demonstrate that the solutions employed were effective.

—12—

EVALUATING COPPS INITIATIVES

Not everything that counts can be counted; and not everything that can be counted counts.
—ALBERT EINSTEIN

This chapter begins by discussing the general rationale for evaluating COPPS generally. Next we examine the kinds of criteria to be used in evaluating COPPS, including several types of measures to be used. Then we review the role of evaluation in problem solving, including some of the questions that might be asked prior to commencing this task. Next is a review of criteria that might be employed for assessing the individual officer's problem-solving skills, and we include a rating scale. Following is the use of surveys—community, neighborhood, and individual patrol officers—to obtain input for evaluative purposes. We conclude the chapter with two case studies of COPPS evaluations (other examples of evaluative efforts are provided throughout the chapter as well).

This chapter provides only rudimentary coverage of response evaluation; this is a challenging undertaking, one that is best accomplished by people who are specially trained in this function and who understand evaluation research methodology. Those persons who are interested in engaging in further inquiry should read *Assessing Responses to Problems: An Introductory Guide for Police Problem-Solvers*, published by the federal Office of Community Oriented Policing Services; some of the information provided in this chapter draws from that booklet.

RATIONALE FOR EVALUATION

Rigorous evaluation is an essential component of the problem-solving process (S.A.R.A., discussed in Chapter 4). Ohio's Office of Criminal Justice Services even gives an annual award to the law enforcement agency in that state for the best "creation or adaptation of an evaluation tool for measuring the impact of community policing efforts in the community."[2] Program evaluation is used to inform decision makers, clarify options, reduce uncertainties, and provide feedback to decision makers and stakeholders about the program being evaluated. It is, therefore, decision oriented and focuses on what is intended and accomplished.[3]

Furthermore, evaluations provide knowledge; key decision makers in the jurisdiction need a gauge of the strategy's impact and cost effectiveness. Assessing progress will inform top management whether necessary changes in the culture and in support systems are indeed taking place. Until rigorous evaluations are completed, there will be no clear verdict on whether the COPPS approach makes a difference in controlling crime and disorder. An evaluation also helps ascertain whether a crime prevention initiative has achieved such goals as reducing crime and the fear of crime, raising the community's quality of life, and determining whether it is worthy of continued funding.[4]

It should be noted that few police agencies possess persons adequately trained and educated for conducting program evaluations. Therefore, it is normally best to go outside the agency to obtain the services of an evaluator—one who understands the complexity of the task, often someone with an academic orientation.[5] The police need good research. There is a demand for outcomes. It is no longer good enough for the police to say they made X number of arrests or wrote thousands of tickets. There are thus occasions when the police agency should acquire the services of one who is well grounded in research methodology.[6]

USING THE PROPER CRITERIA

The Old Versus the New

The evaluative criteria employed in the professional policing model, such as crime rates, clearance rates, and response times, have been problematic when applied to the professional model itself and are even less appropriate for the COPPS model. These measures do not gauge the effect of crime prevention efforts, and do not capture much of the work that police do or how they do it. A decrease in the reliance on these quantitative measures of police success is also important because communities differ in the services they desire, depending on the particular characteristics of individual communities.[7] Evaluating COPPS requires measurements that better reflect the objectives of this strategy.[8]

Some new indicators for success include identifying and solving local crime and disorder problems through a police–community consultation process; higher reporting rates for both traditional crime categories and for nontraditional crime and disorder problems; reducing the number of repeat calls for service from repeat addresses; improving the satisfaction with police services by public users of those services, particularly with victims of crime; increasing the job satisfaction of police officers; increasing the reporting of information of local crime and disorder problems by community residents and increasing the knowledge of the community and its problems by local beat officers; and decreasing the fear of personal victimization.[9]

Three General Criteria

According to the Community Policing Consortium, three major criteria can assist in evaluating a problem-solving effort: effectiveness, efficiency, and equity.

Effectiveness

An effective COPPS strategy has a positive impact on reducing neighborhood crime, allays citizen fear of crime, and enhances the quality of life in the community. It accomplishes this by combining the efforts and resources of the police, local government, and the community.[10] Assessing the effectiveness of problem-solving efforts includes determining whether problems have indeed been solved and how well the managers and patrol officers have used the community partnership and problem-solving components of COPPS.

Assessment should not only focus on whether the problem has been effectively eradicated or reduced but also on the manner in which this was

An officer's efforts to improve overall safety in a shopping mall may decrease crime and increase safety and profits for merchants. (*Courtesy* Community Policing Consortium)

accomplished. Solving problems does not always involve making arrests.[11] Improved quality of life is difficult to measure (and define), but it is an important goal of COPPS. Everyone desires a safe environment in which families can live and work. COPPS helps identify the fears, concerns, and needs at the neighborhood level. The factors that may determine "quality of life" may differ from neighborhood to neighborhood; removing signs of disorder—drunks, panhandlers, prostitutes, gang members—will enhance the quality of life. The absence of previous signs of neglect—abandoned vehicles, derelict buildings, garbage, and debris—offers a tangible indication that COPPS is working.[12]

Efficiency

Efficiency means getting the most impact from available resources. Evaluation measures determine whether available resources—including the police agency, local government and private agencies, citizen groups, and the business community—are being used to their fullest to solve any given problem.[13] If COPPS is to be successful, staunch partnerships and collaborative efforts must be established within the community.[14]

Employee job satisfaction also takes on a new significance in a COPPS organization. Patrol officers function more efficiently and effectively as catalysts and mobilizers of community support if they are highly motivated, given the necessary support, and appropriately rewarded for their efforts.[15] The need to survey the officers becomes evident in an organization where employee morale and satisfaction take on a greater level of meaning and importance.

Equity

Equity, the third major criterion for judging progress, has the most comprehensive impact on the success of COPPS. Equity is especially important because

The closure of a home can affect residents' feelings about safety and their overall quality of life.

officers work closely with the community and may be increasingly confronted with moral and ethical dilemmas.[16]

Equity has three separate dimensions in COPPS: (1) equal access to police service by all citizens; (2) equal treatment of all individuals according to the Constitution; "respect for dignity is incompatible with needless confrontation, excessive force, or discrimination;"[17] and (3) equal distribution of police services and resources among communities (it is critical that one community not be given preference over another).[18]

EVALUATION'S ROLE IN PROBLEM SOLVING

It is important to remember that evaluation and assessment are different. Evaluation is a scientific process for determining if a problem declined and if the solution caused the decline. Assessment occurs at the final stage of the S.A.R.A. problem-solving process. Evaluation begins at the moment the S.A.R.A. problem-solving process begins and continues through the completion of the effort.[19] Critical decisions about the evaluation are made throughout the process, as indicated in Figure 12-1. The left side of the figure shows the standard S.A.R.A. process and some of the most basic questions asked at each stage. It also draws attention to the fact that the assessment may produce information requiring the problem solver to go back to earlier stages to make modifications. The right side of Figure 12-1 lists critical questions to address to conduct an evaluation.

Asking the Right Questions

There are two types of evaluations, process and impact; both should be conducted, because they complement each other.

Types of Evaluations

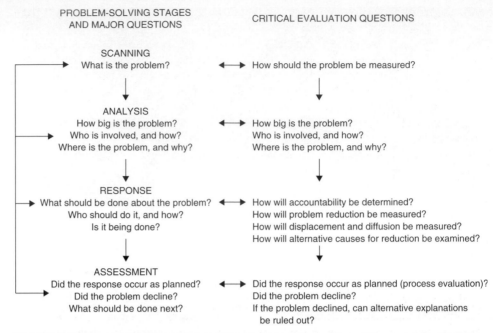

FIGURE 12-1. The Problem-Solving Process and Evaluation. (*Source:* John E. Eck, *Assessing Responses to Problems: An Introductory Guide for Police Problem-Solvers* [Washington, D.C.: U.S. Department of Justice, Office of Community Oriented Policing Services, 2002], p. 6.)

Process evaluations ask the following questions: Did the response occur as planned? Did all the response components work? A hypothetical example will assist in understanding process evaluations. A problem-solving team of officers, after a careful analysis, determines that in order to curb a street prostitution problem, after a crackdown in an area of town they will ask the city's traffic engineering department to make a major thoroughfare one-way, and create several dead-end streets to thwart cruising by "johns." Convicted prostitutes will be given probation under the condition that they do not enter the target area for a year. Finally, a nonprofit organization will help prostitutes who want to leave their line of work to gain the necessary skills for legitimate employment. The police, prosecutor, local judges, probation office, and traffic engineering departments all agree to this plan.

A process evaluation will determine whether the crackdown occurred and, if so, how many arrests police made; whether the traffic engineering department altered street patterns as planned; and how many prostitutes asked for job skills assistance and found legitimate employment. The process evaluation will also examine whether everything occurred in the planned sequence. Note that the process evaluation does *not* answer the question "What happened to the problem?"

To determine what did in fact happen to the problem, an *impact* evaluation is needed. An impact evaluation asks the following questions: Did the problem decline? If so, did the response cause the decline? Continuing with the prostitution example, assume that *during the analysis stage* vice detectives conduct a census of prostitutes operating in the target area. They also ask the traffic engineering department to install traffic counters on the major thoroughfare and critical side streets to measure traffic flow. This is done to determine how customers move through the area. The vice squad makes covert video recordings of the target area to document how prostitutes interact with potential customers. All of this is done before the problem-solving team selects a response, and the information gained helps the team to do so.

After the response is implemented, the team decides to repeat these measures to see if the problem has declined. They discover that instead of the 23 prostitutes counted in the first census, only 10 can be found. They also find that there has been a slight decline in traffic on the major thoroughfare on the weekends, but not at other times. However, there has been a substantial decline in side street traffic on Saturday nights. New covert video recordings show that prostitutes in the area have changed how they approach vehicles. In short, the team has evidence that the problem has declined after response implementation.[20] When conducting impact evaluations, it is important to remember that such efforts have two parts: measuring the problem, and systematically comparing changes in measures, using an evaluation design to provide the maximum evidence that the response was the primary cause of the change in the measure. It is best to decide during the scanning stage how to measure the problem. There are both quantitative and qualitative measures.

Quantitative measures involve numbers (e.g., the number of burglaries in an apartment complex during a period of time), and allow one to use math to estimate the response's impact (such as burglary rates drop 10 percent from before the response to after the response). Such measures can be counted before and after the response.

Qualitative measures allow comparisons, but do not involve any math. For example, suppose there is gang-related violence in a neighborhood. Analysis shows that much of the violence stems from escalating turf disputes, and that graffiti is a useful indicator of intergang tensions. The number of reported gunshots and injuries are counted the year before and the year after the response. These are quantitative measures. Photos are also taken monthly of gang graffiti hot spots both before and after the response. By comparing the photos, it is noted that before the response, graffiti was quite common; after the response, there is little graffiti. This qualitative information reinforces the quantitative information by indicating that the response may have reduced gang tension, or that gangs have declined.[21]

OFFICER PERFORMANCE EVALUATIONS

A major need of police agencies that have adopted COPPS is a performance evaluation system that is specifically intended for the street officer who is applying COPPS skills to crime and disorder issues. Exhibit 12-1 shows six steps for revising a police performance evaluation system.

Next we discuss 10 performance criteria for rating officers' skills and a rating scale that might be used to evaluate their efforts.

COPPS Skills, Knowledge, and Abilities

While not yet being done on a large scale (presently only about 14 percent of local police agencies, which employ about 35 percent of all officers, include problem-solving projects in the performance evaluation criteria for patrol officers),[22] supervisors should measure how well officers perform problem-solving functions during the course of their tour of duty. If officers are not familiar with the problem-solving process their performance will be deficient. Supervisors should work with officers to correct any deficiencies regarding the following performance criteria.

EXHIBIT 12-1 Steps for Revising Police Performance Evaluation Systems

Step 1: *Decide on the purpose(s) of the evaluation.* The purpose(s) to be served by an evaluation system will dictate both what and how officer behavior is measured.

Step 2: *Identify performance criteria.* Traditional measures of police performance do not capture the entirety of the community policing officer's role. New performance evaluations must reflect the work that the administration desires. A job analysis, identifying tasks typically performed by an employee (such as learning about beat problems and area residents, and developing means of problem solving), might be included. Related activities (such as conducting neighborhood meetings or analyzing crime data) might also be performed.

Step 3: *Define effective behavior.* Each police agency must define effectiveness individually as it relates to its own vision, mission, values, goals, and objectives. Input from officers, supervisors, and citizens may be required to determine what effective policing is, depending on realistic expectations of what they can accomplish.

Step 4: *Decide who should be evaluated.* Several officers and supervisors may be jointly responsible for a certain geographic area or beat, working as a team to solve problems therein. The extent to which officers are working in teams or groups must be considered for evaluation.

Step 5: *Decide who will participate in the evaluation process.* Many different constituencies may provide input to the evaluation of community policing officers, with supervisors being the primary source of evaluation. Other officers who in rank are equal to, above, or below the officer to be evaluated may also provide input. Citizen feedback should also be considered.

Step 6: *Develop or revise instrumentation and rating scales.* Remember that much of the community policing officer's work is of a qualitative nature and thus not easily reduced to numbers. As performance criteria change, and community policing "behaviors," such as communication and innovation, are modified, so should the performance evaluation instrument and the rating scales.

Source: Adapted from Meghan S. Chandek, "Meaningful and Effective Performance Evaluations in a Time of Community Policing," *The Journal of Community Policing* 2 (Spring 2000):7–24. This article includes examples of sample tasks and activities, definitions of effectiveness, quantifiable community policing activities, and an officer performance evaluation scale.

- *Time management:* using uncommitted time to scan neighborhoods and identify problems; balancing problem-solving efforts with other responsibilities
- *Awareness:* knowledge of problems in assigned areas, and taking steps to stay informed via citizen contact, familiarity with current events, reviewing departmental information, and sharing information with colleagues
- *Communication:* eliciting information from colleagues, supervisors, and citizens to facilitate problem solving; conveying information in a clear, concise manner
- *Analysis:* ability to relate symptoms to underlying circumstances; identifying factors that cause incidents to occur and knowing what questions to ask
- *Judgment:* identifying legitimate alternatives that can be used as responses in addressing problems; selecting the best alternative based on resource availability, ease of implementation, and perceived effectiveness of response
- *Goal setting:* distinguishing between short- and long-term goals of response; identifying goals that are measurable; relating the goal to the problem
- *Planning:* preparing a legitimate action plan to implement a response; identifying responsibilities of participants, appropriate procedures, and a timetable
- *Coordination:* demonstrating competency in organizing efforts of participants involved in implementing responses
- *Initiative:* self-motivation for engaging in the problem-solving process and identifying and addressing problems; helping others when appropriate
- *Assessment:* properly identifying variables to assess; knowing the types of information to collect to assess results; describing implications of results attained[23]

A guide for evaluating COPPS officers' performance was developed by the Community Policing Consortium in Washington, D.C. (*Courtesy* Police Executive Research Forum)

PERSONNEL PERFORMANCE EVALUATIONS IN THE COMMUNITY POLICING CONTEXT

TIM OETTMEIER
MARY ANN WYCOFF

The supervisor's rating of subordinates' COPPS efforts must be accurately reflected on a rating scale. Five value descriptions have been developed to help establish reliability in this regard, as follows.

The Rating Scale

SUPERIOR skill performance: The officer's skill performance is consistently excellent as to quality, accuracy, thoroughness, and technical excellence. The officer has a superior understanding of what skills to use to accomplish assigned responsibilities. Officer initiates and completes responsibilities without prompting from the supervisor, and there is no doubt as to officer's exercise of sound judgment. Supervisor and officer work in consultation with each other when appropriate.

STRONG skill performance: Performance exhibited is above average. Work performed and skills displayed regularly exceed basic requirements. Officer demonstrates an advanced ability to apply skills to various responsibilities and projects and makes conscientious effort to adhere to procedures and standards. Sound judgment is always exercised, and officer is always willing to perform the skills to do the work—without instructions or directions from supervisor.

EFFECTIVE skill performance: Performance in response to each skill is acceptable. Officer has demonstrated the ability to perform problem skills effectively and efficiently in a consistent manner. Officer applies knowledge and skills while using sound judgment and is usually desirous and willing to perform skills with minimum instructions and directions from the supervisor.

MARGINAL skill performance: Performance is barely satisfactory, and skill performance is marginal. There is limited ability to perform the skill in association with appropriate activities. Officer frequently disregards performing the skill

COLUMBIA POLICE DEPARTMENT
MONTHLY PERFORMANCE EVALUATION REPORT

Supervisor's Name: _____ Time/Date: _____

Officer's Name: _____ Assignment/Shift: _____

Use the following criteria to assess an officer's ability to perform problem solving skills to address crime and disorder within assigned neighborhoods.

A B I L I T Y

	Poor		Marginal		Effective		Strong		Superior	
Time Management	1	2	3	4	5	6	7	8	9	10
Awareness	1	2	3	4	5	6	7	8	9	10
Communication	1	2	3	4	5	6	7	8	9	10
Analysis	1	2	3	4	5	6	7	8	9	10
Judgment	1	2	3	4	5	6	7	8	9	10
Goal Seeking	1	2	3	4	5	6	7	8	9	10
Planning	1	2	3	4	5	6	7	8	9	10
Coordination	1	2	3	4	5	6	7	8	9	10
Initiative	1	2	3	4	5	6	7	8	9	10
Assessment	1	2	3	4	5	6	7	8	9	10

Grand Total: _____

Final Classification

Check:

_____ Category 1: Poor .... 10 - 19
_____ Category 2: Marginal .... 20 - 49
_____ Category 3: Effective .... 50 - 69
_____ Category 4: Strong .... 70 - 89
_____ Category 5: Superior .... 90 - 100

_____   _____   _____   _____
Supervisor's Signature   *Date*   *Officer Signature*   *Date*

FIGURE 12-2. Columbia Police Department Monthly Performance Evaluation Report. (*Source:* Columbia, South Carolina, police department.)

properly or does not adhere to standards governing the skill and only occasionally exercises sound judgment in skill performance. Supervisor is often required to observe the officer performing the skill; instructions are usually needed. Performance is sufficient, inconsistent, occasionally effective, but only to a minimally acceptable degree.

POOR skill performance: Officer's skill performance causes supervisor great concern about officer's capabilities. Demonstration of skill is weak, leading one to question officer's understanding of what is expected and his or her ability to perform with consistent competency. Officer demonstrates signs of "going through the motions" and tends to act quickly, without regard to effects or consequences of actions. Supervisor spends an inordinate amount of time correcting officer's actions or telling officer what must be done.[24]

Figure 12-2 shows the Columbia, South Carolina, police department's monthly performance evaluation report form based on the preceding criteria.

USE OF SURVEYS

Social scientists and political pollsters survey the public to learn about social relations and predict future events. Government agencies use surveys to learn how people will react to new policies. In criminal justice, researchers use surveys to get a better understanding of crime and the fear of crime.[25]

This section discusses three types of surveys that police managers find increasingly useful: surveys of the community, of the physical environment, and of the street officers who are engaged in the work of COPPS. We do not include an in-depth discussion of survey research methodology; instead, we provide citations of some helpful resources in the Notes section at the end of the chapter.

Polling the Community

Why the Effort?

The public's perception of crime in the community should be an important part of any measurement of community life and of police performance within in a given community.[26] And no other sector of government in our society has more frequent and direct contact with the public than the police. It has been noted that

> Whatever the citizen thinks of the police, they can hardly be ignored. Whereas other public bureaucrats are often lost from the public's view, locked in rooms

Many agencies use neighborhood meetings as a method to evaluate their performance and to identify residents' needs and priorities. (*Courtesy* Arlington County, Virginia, police department)

filled with typewriters and anonymity, police officers are out in the world—on the sidewalks and in the streets and shopping malls, cruising, strolling, watching, as both state protectors and state repressors.[27]

Surveys are a vital part of a COPPS strategy. About one-fourth of local police departments, employing 50 percent of all officers, survey citizens in their jurisdiction.[28] Furthermore, as shown in Figure 12-3, citizen survey information is used for a variety of purposes—primarily to provide information to patrol officers, evaluate program effectiveness, and to prioritize crime-disorder problems. Given their position, role, and function in the community, it is all the more important that police agencies attempt to "feel the pulse" of their communities. The importance of surveying community needs cannot be overstated. Public opinion surveys provide vital information and feedback in the matter of the public's perception of officer performance and can assess the effectiveness of police department communication with the public. The mood of the public should be a vital consideration when police make public policy decisions.[29]

Police agencies have long used citizen surveys to measure performance and assess the quality of their work. Surveys have been used to evaluate random patrolling, rapid response to calls for service, patrol deployment schemes, and community policing strategies. Thus, although direct police use of surveys is relatively new, the application of survey research to management and policy questions is quite extensive.[30] In recent years, carefully developed surveys have been used to great advantage for measuring citizen attitudes toward police and citizen satisfaction with police services.

Methods and Issues

Those persons who are about to conduct community surveys will find a very valuable resource in a joint publication by the federal Bureau of Justice Statistics and the Office of Community Oriented Policing Services' *Conducting Community Surveys: A Practical Guide for Law Enforcement Agencies.*[31] This is a very good primer on the use of surveys by police agencies, discussing survey development and administration and ways to analyze and interpret survey results. Many other books have been written that are devoted exclusively to the subject of evaluation.[32] Individuals who are contemplating COPPS evaluations can review these texts to determine the best method to use given the nature of their operation. Following are several key issues to resolve before developing a questionnaire.

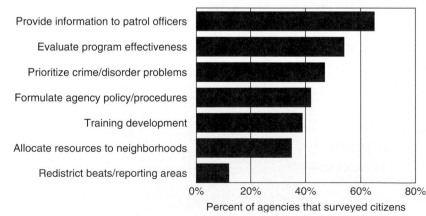

FIGURE 12-3. Uses of citizen survey information by local police departments, 2000. (*Source:* U.S. Department of Justice, Bureau of Justice Statistics, *Local Police Departments 2000* [Washington, D.C.: Author, January 2003], p. 17.)

- *What are the specific purposes of the survey and what kinds of questions are most likely to yield responses that are consistent with those purposes?* It is important to clarify the goals of the survey project to minimize the number of questions asked. Without clear goals the number of questions tends to mushroom. This increases the amount of time required to administer each survey, which is a burden on both interviewer and interviewee. In short, fight the temptation to include everyone's "pet" question.
- *How will the survey be administered—by mail, telephone, or in person?* There are three basic types of strategies: A questionnaire can be mailed to everyone in the sample to complete and return; the sampled respondents can be interviewed by telephone; or they can be interviewed in person (at home, in the office, on the bus, or wherever they are). Mail surveys are an inexpensive method of obtaining large sample sizes.[33] There are advantages and disadvantages to each type of survey that should be explored prior to determining which type is to be used.
- *How much time will it take to complete the survey, and is this a reasonable amount of time to impose on respondents?* Remember that completion of a survey is an intrusion on the time of others. Most people will allow such intrusion if the cause is worthwhile and the time burden is not too onerous. About 10 to 15 minutes to complete a questionnaire is reasonable; but if examining, say, problems involving drugs and violence, 30 to 40 minutes might be reasonable. The key is to be considerate about demands on others.[34]

Neighborhood Surveys

Neighborhood surveys are often employed by police officers in problem solving; usually such surveys are informal, but they can provide large amounts of information that is not available in crime statistics. Some evidence even suggests that door-to-door surveys by officers are enough to reduce crime and fear and enhance citizen attitudes toward police, independent of any information they gain or what police do with it. Surveys can also help measure the characteristics of neighborhood residents, the background of crime victims, or the background of offenders. Surveys also seek information on the "mental state" of the community, and they frequently address such issues as

- attitudes toward police performance
- fear of crime
- future plans and intentions
- concerns about specific problems
- suggestions for police actions

Surveys are also useful for gathering data on individuals' behaviors and experiences. Common topics addressed in surveys of this type include

- crime prevention actions taken
- experiences as victims of crime
- experiences with the police
- experiences with problems[35]

Surveys are useful in revealing characteristics of groups of people, such as

- the characteristics of people living in a neighborhood
- the background of victims of crimes
- the personal history of offenders[36]

In short, surveys can be used to achieve four goals:

- to gather information on the public's attitudes toward police and neighborhood priorities
- to detect and analyze problems in neighborhoods or among special population groups
- to evaluate problem-solving efforts and other programs
- to control crime and reduce fear of crime[37]

There are many alternative sources of information as well. For example, census data provide a great deal of information about neighborhoods. Characteristics of victims can be obtained from offense reports. Offender background information can be obtained from arrest reports.

Surveying Officers

Under COPPS, patrol officers become key decision makers and catalysts. And, as we commented earlier, employee morale and job satisfaction take on a new significance in a COPPS organization. Patrol officers function more efficiently and effectively as catalysts and mobilizers of community support if they are highly motivated, given the necessary support, and appropriately rewarded for their efforts. Job satisfaction will both affect and result from the success of the COPPS philosophy. As Montgomery County, Maryland (and former Portland, Oregon), police chief Charles A. Moose and his coauthors noted,

> With added responsibilities for police officers, job satisfaction becomes critical. If they are satisfied, they perform better and are able to support their agency's mission. Employee job satisfaction is not simply an indicator of success in community policing—it is a goal of community policing.[38]

Therefore, intraagency surveys can be invaluable for providing a look at the big picture of a COPPS initiative: the attitudes, opinions, and impressions of officers toward their jobs, the department, and the COPPS philosophy.

Officers can be asked a wide variety of questions concerning their knowledge and application of community oriented and problem-solving policing. Following is a sample of the subjects and questions that might be posed to officers.[39] Note that these items are only a sample of general and topical questions that might be considered. Actual questions should be carefully written for use in a survey and for the particular venue, and some sort of Likert Scale is needed to assess the direction and strength of feeling for each question.

The Role of the Police

- What is the role of the police in a community?
- Do you believe the increase in administrative responsibilities and paperwork has stripped you of your ability to expand COPPS initiatives? If yes, how?

Proactive Action

- In what ways does your department emphasize proactive action, reactive action, or a blend of the two?

Public Expectations

- In what manner does your community want its police force, first and foremost, to focus on reactive tasks? To respond rapidly to all calls for service? To reduce the fear of crime? Does the public want to be educated on crime prevention? To work with the police to solve problems of crime and disorder? (Note: This subject area has any number of possible items that could be included.)

- How much of your duty time is spent conducting administrative or paperwork functions? Responding to calls for service? Explaining crime-prevention techniques to citizens? Working with citizens to solve underlying causes of crime? Coordinating with other governmental agencies to improve police service or solve problems? (This subject area also has a wide range of possible questions.)

Perceptions of COPPS

- What have you been told about the purpose of COPPS (or, how valuable was the academy training in this regard)?
- What have you been told concerning the implementation of COPPS?
- How would you rate the quality of your department's in-service training concerning COPPS?
- Does COPPS increase, decrease, or have no impact on the risk of corrupt behavior by police?
- Will COPPS increase, decrease, or have no effect on the amount or seriousness of excessive force incidents?[40]

Co-Workers' Attitudes

- How do your co-workers feel about COPPS? About working with citizens to solve crimes? Crime prevention? Reducing the fear of crime? Sharing information with the community regarding police activities? The proactive style of policing?

Other Selected Issues

- To what extent do your citizens understand the problems of police?
- Describe the kinds of discretion you are given to carry out COPPS initiatives.
- Explain why you believe the investigative division or other specialized units are or are not more "elite" than the patrol division.
- Are COPPS activities and conventional policing activities given equal weight?
- How have the performance appraisal and promotional processes of your department been appropriate for a COPPS philosophy?

Analyzing the Data

To handle large sets of survey data (many questions answered by many respondents) a computer will probably be needed. Today computers are inexpensive, and user-friendly software programs are available for analyses. Also, police agencies can partner with local colleges and universities for assistance with data analysis. Someone will have to read each questionnaire, note how each question was answered, determine the code for each answer, and enter the codes into a data file. This must be done with care to minimize data entry errors.[41] Once the data have been entered, there are four types of analyses to be performed.

1. *The characteristics of the sample must be determined.* During this most basic stage of data analysis, the frequency, central tendency (the average, or typical responses to a question; includes the mean, median, and mode), and dispersion of responses (i.e., standard deviation or variance) to each question is calculated.
2. *A determination is needed of how representative the sample really is of the population being studied.* The principal method for checking representativeness is by comparing answers to a few of the questions with information known about the population. If there are no substantial differences, the sample is likely representative of the entire population under study. It may not always be possible to make such a comparison, however.

3. *An investigator may want to make inferences from the sample to the population it represents.* There are two types of inferences that can be made about the population based on sample data. First, characteristics of the population can be determined from what is learned from the sample. Second, one can determine whether there are relationships among the characteristics of members of the population (for example, whether the age and sex of a person have an influence on fear of crime).

4. *The investigator may want to determine whether there are relationships between or among the attitudes, behaviors, and characteristics identified in the sample population.* When analyzing relationships, social scientists usually talk about variables. Two variables can be causally or noncausally related. A noncausal relationship means that neither variable causes the other; they merely happen to be associated, perhaps because a third variable is causing both of them. In a causal relationship, one variable is causing the other. In statistical analysis, the causes are called *independent* variables, and the effects are the *dependent* variables.[42]

CASE STUDIES

The following two case studies provide views of COPPS evaluations for Chicago, Illinois, and Lawrence, Massachusetts.

Chicago, Illinois

The Chicago Alternative Policing Strategy (CAPS) initiative was field tested in 1993 in five selected districts (and later implemented on a citywide basis) to cultivate problem solving and to reorganize policing around the city's 279 police beats. In 1995 researchers found that perceived crime problems had decreased significantly in all five districts; furthermore, physical decay had declined in three districts, and citizen assessments of police had improved significantly.[43]

A more recent evaluation of CAPS was conducted in 1999 with funding by the U.S. Department of Justice and the Illinois Criminal Justice Information Authority. Some of the findings were as follows.

- Since 1996 recognition of CAPS had grown from 53 percent to 79 percent; awareness of the strategy had increased the most among young adults. The greatest source of information was television, with nearly 40 percent of Chicagoans recalling hearing about CAPS via that media outlet.

- Involvement continued to be strong among some of the city's poorest and most crime-ridden communities. Attendance at beat meetings was highest in predominately African American areas. Overall, 14 percent of Chicagoans said they had attended a beat meeting in the past year. The meetings, however, were weak at finding solutions to problems. Most actions were proposed by the police rather than residents, and residents were particularly ineffective at reporting back to the group about their recent problem-solving efforts.

- Police officers who attended beat community meetings reported satisfaction with the effectiveness of the meetings. More than three-quarters were happy with levels of attendance.

- Community policing had become a routine aspect of the city's life. Within the police department, the strategy was no longer described as "just smoke and mirrors."[44]

Lawrence, Massachusetts

Lawrence, Massachusetts, is a dense, urban center of 70,000 people, 28 miles north of Boston, whose residents live in an area of only seven miles. In the

1980s the Massachusetts Criminal Justice Training Council submitted a critical report concerning the operations of the Lawrence police department. A wide gap existed between the police and the public. The department's budget was cut as well. The department began to explore new philosophies for delivering police service and to generally reform its operations.

The police chief and a nine-member management team began rethinking their basic strategies. First, the police chief adopted total quality management (TQM, discussed in Chapter 3). Then a bilingual community questionnaire was designed to identify crime and disorder issues important to citizens. Next, a citizen advisory committee was established to get more direct input about the needs of the customers.[45] The management team then began to develop a "vision" for the department; from this process, new mission and values statements were written.

The department began to explore how to strategically address problems. The team chose the Arlington neighborhood, a 45-square-block area consisting mostly of multiple-family residential units, with relatively little single-family housing. A team of six community police officers (CPOs) was assigned to Arlington to seek citizen input, analyze problems, and develop intervention strategies. Questionnaires were again used to identify problems and concerns in the area. Returns of these questionnaires produced a lot of valuable information on drug dealers' operations and also raised the fear levels of dealers. A public education campaign was launched in the area, and police activity was enhanced.

The department believed it was important to develop an objective means of evaluating whether the strategy was worth the effort. A pre–post citizen survey approach was adopted with a random sample of households, using a 60-item questionnaire distributed to 3,676 households (with a 30.3 percent response rate). Responses to each question were given a numerical weight, and an average score was computed. The following formula was developed and helped obtain a fear index for the neighborhood:[46]

$$\frac{(\text{\# increased} \times 5) + (\text{\# same} \times 3) + (\text{\# decreased} \times 0)}{\text{Total responses}}$$

A disorder index was developed from the survey, based on the following formula:

$$\frac{(\text{\# big problem} \times 5) + (\text{\# problem} \times 3) + (\text{\# no problem} \times 0)}{\text{Total responses}}$$

Using this procedure, a summary measure of disorder for each neighborhood was obtained.

The findings indicated that Arlington residents experienced substantial reductions in their fear and perceptions of crime and disorder. The close attention to involvement of both staff and managers in the organizational change process and the carefully planned community intervention strategy make Lawrence an important case study in the systematic implementation of COPPS in a medium-sized city.[47]

SUMMARY

This chapter emphasized the fact that the evaluation of the impact of COPPS is critical; without such scrutiny this initiative may be jeopardized in the long term.

Although there is no one evaluation process that will work for all communities, this chapter offered some reasons, methods, and criteria for evaluating such a social intervention. The chapter also provided several examples of successful evaluations.

The philosophy and methods under COPPS are quite different from those of traditional policing and obviously require different measurements of performance.

NOTES

1. Adapted from the National Crime Prevention Council, *How Are We Doing? A Guide to Local Program Evaluation* (Washington, D.C.: Author, 1998), p. 5. This is a valuable resource for COPPS evaluations, including many examples of forms that may be used in the evaluation process (see, for example, Chapter II, "A Toolkit for Evaluation Design") and other types of information not commonly found in evaluation textbooks (such as communicating findings and results for maximum results).

2. *http://www.communitypolicing.org/publications/art bytop/w5/w5lee.htm* (Accessed May 27, 2003).

3. Ibid., p. 3.

4. U.S. Department of Justice, Bureau of Justice Assistance, The Community Policing Consortium, *Understanding Community Policing: A Framework for Action* (Washington, D.C.: Author, 1993), p. 82.

5. Gloria Laycock, "Becoming More Assertive about Good Research," *Subject to Debate* (Police Executive Research Forum newsletter) 14 (July 2000):1.

6. Ibid., p. 3.

7. Community Policing Advisory Committee, *Community Policing Advisory Committee Report* (Victoria, British Columbia, Canada: Author, March 1993), p. 61.

8. Barry Leighton, "Visions of Community Policing: Rhetoric and Reality in Canada," *Canadian Journal of Criminology* (July/October 1991):75–87.

9. Ibid.

10. U.S. Department of Justice, *Understanding Community Policing*, p. 86.

11. Ibid., pp. 87–89.

12. Ibid., p. 90.

13. Ibid., p. 91.

14. Ibid., pp. 92–93.

15. Ibid., p. 93.

16. Ibid., p. 97.

17. Edwin Delattre and Cornelius Behan, quoted in ibid., p. 99.

18. Ibid., pp. 101–102.

19. John E. Eck, *Assessing Responses to Problems: An Introductory Guide for Police Problem-Solvers* (Washington, D.C.: U.S. Department of Justice, Office of Community Oriented Policing Services, 2002), p. 5.

20. Ibid., pp. 7–9.

21. Ibid., pp. 13–14.

22. U.S. Department of Justice, Bureau of Justice Statistics, *Law Enforcement Management and Administrative Statistics: Local Police Departments 2000* (Washington, D.C.: Author, January 2003), p. 17.

23. Adapted from Columbia, South Carolina, Police Department, *Columbia Patrol Officer Performance Evaluation Workbook* (Columbia, S.C.: Author, March 1997), pp. 6–7; also see Timothy N. Oettmeier and Mary Ann Wycoff, *Personnel Performance Evaluations in the Community Policing Context* (Washington, D.C.: Community Policing Consortium, 1997).

24. Ibid., pp. 8–9.

25. Police Executive Research Forum, *A Police Practitioner's Guide to Surveying Citizens and Their Environment: Monograph* (Washington, D.C.: U.S. Department of Justice, Bureau of Justice Assistance, 1993), p. 1.

26. Richard D. Morrison, "What Effect Is Community Policing Having on Crime Statistics," *Law Enforcement Technology* (October 1998):26.

27. N. D. Walker and R. J. Richardson, *Public Attitudes toward the Police* (Chapel Hill, N.C.: Institute for Research in Social Science, 1974), p. 1.

28. U.S. Department of Justice, *Law Enforcement Management and Administrative Statistics*, p. 17.

29. Mervin F. White and Ben A. Menke, "A Critical Analysis on Public Opinions toward Police Agencies," *Journal of Police Science and Administration* 6 (1978):204–218.

30. Ibid., p. 1.

31. Deborah Weisel, *Conducting Community Surveys: A Practical Guide for Law Enforcement Agencies* (Washington, D.C.: U.S. Department of Justice, Bureau of Justice Statistics and the Office of Community Oriented Policing Services, 1999).

32. See, for example, Carl A. Bennett and Arthur A. Lumsdaine, *Evaluation and Experiment* (New York: Academic Press, 1975); Ronald Roesch and Raymond R. Corrado (eds.) *Evaluation and Criminal Justice Policy* (Beverly Hills, Calif.: Sage, 1981); Malcolm W. Klein and Katherine Teilmann Van Dusen, *Handbook of Criminal Justice Evaluation* (Beverly Hills, Calif.: Sage, 1980); and Richard H.

Price and Peter E. Politser, *Evaluation and Action in the Social Science Environment* (New York: Academic Press, 1980).

33. See, for example, Ken Peak, "On Successful Criminal Justice Survey Research: A 'Personal Touch' Model for Enhancing Rates of Return," *Criminal Justice Policy Review* 4(3) (Spring 1992):268–277; Don A. Dillman, *Mail and Telephone Surveys: The Total Design Method* (New York: Wiley, 1978); Arlene Fink and Jacqueline Kosecoff, *How to Conduct Surveys: A Step-by-Step Guide* (Beverly Hills, Calif.: Sage, 1985); Floyd J. Fowler, *Survey Research Methods* (Newbury Park, Calif.: Sage, 1988); Abraham Nastali Oppenheim, *Questionnaire Design, Interviewing, and Attitude Measurement* (New York: St. Martin's Press, 1992); Charles H. Backstrom and Gerald Hursh-Cesar, *Survey Research* (2nd ed.) (New York: Macmillan, 1981).

34. Police Executive Research Forum, *A Police Practitioner's Guide*, p. 22.

35. Ibid., p. 8.

36. Ibid., pp. 8–9.

37. Ibid.

38. Charles A. Moose, Wendy Lin-Kelly, Steve Beedle, and Brian Stipak, "Evaluating Community Policing with Employee Surveys," *The Police Chief* (March 2000):44.

39. Adapted from the Royal Canadian Mounted Police, Community Policing Branch, *R.C.M.P. Community Policing: Blending Tradition with Innovation* (Ottawa, Ontario, Canada: Author, 1992).

40. "Abuse of Police Authority in the Age of Community Policing: What Police Say" (Washington, D.C.: Police Foundation, *http://www.policefoundation.org/docs/recentresearch.html* (Accessed May 27, 2003).

41. For a more detailed introduction to analyzing data in policing, see John Eck, *Using Research: A Primer for Law Enforcement* (Washington, D.C.: Police Executive Research Forum, 1984).

42. Adapted from Police Executive Research Forum, *A Police Practitioner's Guide*, pp. 31–34.

43. U.S. Department of Justice, National Institute of Justice Research Preview, "Community Policing in Chicago: Year Two" (October 1995):1–2.

44. Institute for Policy Research, *Northwestern Study Shows Great Strides in Community Policing Program* (Evanston, Ill.: IPR News, May 1999), pp. 1–2. A 120-page report on Years Five–Six of CAPS is available at: *http://www.new.edu/IPR/news/CAPS99 release.html*.

45. Allen W. Cole and Gordon Bazemore, "Police and the 'Laboratory' of the Neighborhood: Evaluating Problem-Oriented Strategies in a Medium Sized City," *American Journal of Police*, forthcoming.

46. Ibid., p. 24.

47. Ibid., p. 31.

INTRODUCTION

Henry Miller is correct: Example is an efficacious means by which to disseminate information and move the world. This chapter provides case studies of community oriented policing and problem solving (COPPS) initiatives. Featured are case studies of COPPS activities in 21 jurisdictions: seven "large" (more than 250,000 population), nine "medium-sized" (between 50,000 and 250,000 population), and five "small" (less than 50,000 population). Also discussed in lesser detail are COPPS initiatives in federal and state agencies.

–13–
SELECTED AMERICAN APPROACHES

Example moves the world more than doctrine.
—HENRY MILLER

LARGE COMMUNITIES

Austin, Texas

Austin, located in central Texas, has about 465,000 residents; the city's police department (APD) consists of approximately 1,360 sworn officers. In the early 1990s, the APD began reviewing the COPPS philosophy and designed a strategy to incorporate the concept throughout the entire organization. A five-year transition was developed and submitted to the city council, and implementation was soon under way. Today, several ancillary programs have been implemented, including a leadership academy for citizens, a landlord training program, a citizen patrol program, and problem-solving projects for cadets at the academy and after graduation. For policing purposes, the city is separated into seven geographical area commands, each of which is subdivided into 10 to 12 districts staffed by seven shifts of officers.

Strong emphasis is placed on the use of technology. In the mid-1990s a Geographic Information System (GIS) was first employed to see where vehicles were being stolen and recovered. Success in this venture led the APD to incorporate GIS into the crime analysis unit, which soon noticed a pattern of burglaries of churches and residences that were occurring overnight and midweek. A victim told police there was a group of homeless persons who were committing burglaries, and officers went to an area where such persons clustered. Upon arriving, they noticed two transients who were examining some goods; questioning by officers revealed that they had just stolen the articles from a vehicle. The officers learned where they normally fenced their goods: from a woman operating a nearby taco cart. The men agreed to be confidential informants in lieu of arrest, setting into motion a six-week investigation that busted up the largest fencing operation in the history of Austin. In fact, an undercover operation with officers posing as shoplifters determined that three taco carts operated by the woman and three accomplices were receiving stolen property. The four were arrested for engaging in organized crime, three homes were raided, and 395 items were seized along with $62,000 in cash; residential burglaries in the downtown area were reduced by 60 percent.[1]

See Exhibit 13-1 for a discussion of another Texas approach, in San Antonio.

EXHIBIT 13-1 COPPS in San Antonio, Texas

The San Antonio, Texas, police department has embraced COPPS for many decades through its Community Services, School Services, and Crime Prevention programs; storefronts; decentralized patrol substations; and downtown foot and bicycle patrol units. In 1995 the department went a step further, creating a special community policing unit called San Antonio Fear Free Environment (SAFFE), which is linked closely with community involvement programs. First established in 1995 with 60 officers and enlarged to 100 officers in 1996, the SAFFE unit focuses on identifying, evaluating, and resolving community crime problems with the cooperation and participation of community residents. Beginning in 2000 an additional 10 officers are being added to the unit each year for five years. SAFFE officers are not tied to radio calls but instead are able to establish and maintain day-to-day interaction with residents and businesses within their assigned beats to prevent crimes before they occur. SAFFE officers also act as liaisons with other city agencies, work closely with schools and youth programs, coordinate graffiti-removal activities, and serve as resources to residents.

Source: San Antonio police department Web page: *http://www.ci.sat.tx.us/sapd/COPPS.asp* (Accessed January 21, 2004).

Charlotte-Mecklenburg, North Carolina

The Charlotte-Mecklenburg police department (CMPD), with 2,000 staff members in a community of 650,000, is the largest local police agency between Washington, D.C., and Atlanta, Georgia. Its mission: "To build problem-solving partnerships with our citizens to prevent the next crime."

Technology is an important crime reduction tool, and CMPD takes pride in taking the use of technology to a new level; each officer is assigned a laptop computer in the police cruiser, and each can utilize the GIS, both of which allow officers quick and easy access to information for problem solving and to analyze events that have taken place. Their Web site is also a valuable tool.

The CMPD has undertaken major reorganization and redistricting. Reorganizing involved placing all patrol districts under the responsibility of just one deputy chief to allow for more consistent supervision countywide. Redrawing the 12 police district boundaries was a painstaking process that included a thorough review of calls for service data, manpower allocations, and extensive discussions with citizens and businesses—all of which were critical to reducing crime and enhancing the quality of life.

Recently CMPD was confronted with a serious problem that demonstrated the value of its use of and reliance on technology: the thefts of home appliances. Between the time when a certificate of occupancy (CO) was issued for a new home and when the new owners moved in, burglars were stealing a large number of home appliances that were already installed. Using geographic mapping and the Statistical Package for the Social Sciences (SPSS), CMPD was able to show contractors that a positive correlation existed between issuance of the CO and the thefts. Police advised builders to lock appliances in rented metal storage lockers and to wait until the day before closing the home purchase before installing the appliance. This approach quelled the problem.

CMPD also conducts annual citizen satisfaction surveys; recently the survey indicated that 82.6 percent of residents were satisfied or very satisfied with how the police served their neighborhoods.[2]

The CMPD's award-winning project involving domestic violence intervention is discussed in Appendix A.

Chicago, Illinois

Although we briefly discussed the Chicago police department's (CPD) mapping system in Chapter 4, its crime-prevention strategies in Chapter 5, and its COPPS evaluation in Chapter 12, here we discuss the evolution of its highly successful COPPS efforts.

St. Petersburg, Florida, neighborhood police officers attempt to get to know residents and youths on their beat. (*Courtesy* St. Petersburg, Florida, police department)

Because of soaring crime rates in the early 1990s, the city wanted a "smarter" approach to policing, one that mobilized residents, police officers, and other city workers around a problem-solving approach. Initiated at the highest levels, the Chicago Alternative Policing Strategy (CAPS) was instituted in April 1993 in 5 of the city's 25 police districts. Patrol officers were permanently assigned to fixed beats and trained in problem-solving strategies. Neighborhood meetings between officers and area residents were held, and citizen committees were formed to advise district commanders. In the fall of 1994 elements of CAPS began to be introduced in Chicago's other districts; citywide involvement in the strategy began in the spring of 1995. Now, a decade later, a long-term evaluation has found evidence of CAPS-related success with physical decay problems in three of the five initial experimental districts, as well as a decline in gang and drug problems in two districts and a decline in major crimes in two districts.

The police department promotes citizen participation through an aggressive advertising campaign that publicizes CAPS and encourages people to participate in beat meetings and activities. A recent survey found that nearly 80 percent of Chicagoans knew of CAPS, more than 60 percent knew of beat meetings in their neighborhood, and, of the latter group, 31 percent had attended at least one meeting.

Thousands of officers are assigned to teams dedicated to working in small beats. The department's dispatch policy was revised to enable officers to remain on their assigned beats for most of their duty shift. All of the city's sworn officers and their supervisors have been trained in problem solving.

Surveys have found that officers are generally optimistic about the impact of CAPS on their work and on the community, about their own ability to engage in problem solving, and about the viability of community policing and problem solving.

CAPS has been recognized as one of the most ambitious COPPS initiatives in the United States; it has been cited as a model by numerous police experts and the federal government.[3] In February 2003, Mayor Richard M. Daley stated: "I believe that CAPS is a great program. CAPS is no longer a pilot program." The CPD superintendent, Terry Hillard, added, "It is the foundation of everything we do to create safer neighborhoods. Community policing in Chicago is here to stay because it delivers results."[4]

Fort Lauderdale, Florida

In June 1995 this south Florida city's police department set out to develop a COPPS initiative that would be used to guide the future of the entire agency in terms of how it provided police services. The COPPS initiative aimed to marshal community and governmental resources.

There have been several major accomplishments since the inception of COPPS, involving reclaiming neighborhoods and parks, and initiating nuisance abatement proceedings against problem properties.

In 2000, the FLPD officially changed the title of its Community Policing Initiative to the Community Support Division (CSD). This division, initially begun with 10 employees and now with 59, has become the centerpiece of COPPS efforts in FLPD. The components of CSD are: Crime Analysis Unit, Crime Prevention Unit, Narcotics Detection Dogs, Youth Services, Motor Unit, Administration, Code Enforcement, Alarm Reduction, and the Demonstration Center (the latter serving as a training center and meeting facility for both police and nonpolice). Through CSD, the FLPD emphasizes community-building strategies; threatened neighborhoods implement problem-solving plans to reduce crime and raise the quality of life. Calls for service decrease in CSD-targeted areas. Indeed, every resource that is available is used to address every negative element that contributes to neighborhood instability.[5]

St. Louis, Missouri

Since initiating a pilot COPPS project in a single neighborhood in the early 1990s,[6] a notable undertaking has been the department's efforts with COPPS "on the beat"—efforts in specialized functions. Following is a brief description of how COPPS has been mainstreamed into various aspects of police work.

Narcotics section: All narcotics detectives have been assigned to specific neighborhoods and are responsible for coordinating all POP responses to narcotics problems with patrol officers. Narcotics detectives focus their work on community hot spots. An innovative computerized tracking system for citizen-generated calls to a hotline was recently developed.

Auto theft unit: The auto theft unit works with COPPS officers to target certain neighborhoods for theft prevention. The expertise of the auto theft detectives and the community contacts of the patrol officers is combined to enhance police response to the problem.

Juvenile division: The juvenile division helps coordinate the department's School Assistance Grant, placing 14 uniformed patrol officers in selected high schools and middle schools and their neighborhoods; the department participates in the Substance Abuse Prevention Partnership. A COPPS response to family violence has also been developed.

Gang unit: After conducting a thorough study of gang activity in St. Louis, this unit developed educational materials for parents and school officials and conducted gang awareness training for patrol officers.

Mobile reserve unit: The mobile reserve unit identifies persistent problems of crime and disorder throughout the city, ranging from narcotics sales to graffiti to fights and disturbances. It also provides patrol support while officers are attending COPPS training.

Legal division: In-house counsel assists officers with their COPPS efforts, hearings to enforce building code violations, and condemnation proceedings on problem property.

In addition, a CAD flagging system notifies officers of safety alerts, ongoing COPPS projects, and hot spots. A computerized problem-solving database, revised policy on awards and recognition, and monthly COPPS newsletter are in place, and an Information Division was created that includes the library, the TV Section (which produces videotapes of crime problems, for training), Computer Center, and Planning and Development. A Performance Appraisal Review Committee of eight officers and supervisors prepares recommendations to the chief that are consistent with COPPS.

A recent addition has been the Neighborhood Stabilization Team (NST) concept. The NST serves as a catalyst for bringing together autonomous city departments, the police, and citizens to solve neighborhood problems. There are 27 NST officers, who serve in all 79 city neighborhoods; this function has a $1.9 million budget. The department also provides problem-solving training in conjunction with NST to teach police and nonpolice how to analyze, interpret, and act on neighborhood-level crime data.[7]

St. Petersburg, Florida

The Community Policing Division was formed following a November 1990 reorganization of the department.[8] Today COPPS in this agency of 539 sworn officers involves a department-wide philosophy with citywide deployment. Community policing areas (CPAs) cover every neighborhood, and a community police officer (CPO) is assigned to each CPA. CPOs are responsible for their area 24 hours per day, 7 days per week, and foster a partnership with the community; they identify hot spots and implement strategies to resolve them. CPOs work flexible schedules to meet the needs of the community; they might be in uniform and driving a marked police cruiser, or patrolling on a police mountain bike, or working in plainclothes.

Currently there are 41 CPOs assigned throughout St. Petersburg; in addition, 11 officers are assigned to the downtown area, two work at a large shopping mall, and two are posted at the city's public housing complexes, for a total of 56 CPOs. There are also zone officers assigned throughout the city, whose primary duty is to respond to calls for service. Zone officers are encouraged to partner with the CPO in their assigned area, forming a "team" for each of the shifts. Furthermore, most of the detectives are given geographical responsibilities, thus allowing them to become part of the "team" to address emerging crime problems.[9]

Like many other incident-driven police agencies, San Diego treated symptoms while the underlying problems continued to grow. Communication between the top and the bottom of the organization was not occurring in an effective and timely manner. The decision was made that officers could more effectively deal with underlying problems.

Since the early 1970s community policing has been San Diego's guiding philosophy.[10] The San Diego police department (SDPD) entered neighborhood policing in a major way by forming STOP (Selected Tactics of Policing). Ten patrol officers formed a team to combine traditional policing with COPPS to target crime. Neighborhoods on two beats in midcity were selected as target locations. SDPD also became involved in a Neighborhood Policing Restructuring Project to strengthen and expand neighborhood policing throughout the department by developing a plan to convert the police "beat" system from a census tract basis to a community-based format, and by incorporating problem solving into all department levels and functions.

To professionalize problem solving as an accepted policing strategy, the SDPD and the Police Executive Research Forum founded the annual National Problem Oriented Policing Conference. As many as 1,500 participants from around the world attend this conference, which has a rich blend of hands-on advice combined with the most recent research in the field.[11]

Recent examples of neighborhood policing in San Diego include

- A revitalized Neighborhood Watch program, consisting of community coordinators, watch coordinators, and block captains all working toward a common goal
- Citizens' Patrol groups throughout the city, acting as eyes and ears to observe suspicious activities and report problems
- Safe Streets Now!, working to get rid of nuisance properties through civil remedies
- the Drug Abatement Response Team, involving the city attorney, housing inspectors, and police in identifying properties that have a long history of ongoing narcotics activities (in a recent six-month period, more than 70 drug houses were targeted for abatement action)

Also, in February 1997 the SDPD adopted a strategic planning process as a means to improve organizational management. The process was opened to community members, other city employees, and police employees. In the first phase of developing a three- to five-year strategic plan, nearly 215 people had a voice in the goals and objectives the SDPD would pursue. In the second phase, begun in November 1997, plans were developed to put the overall strategies into action.[12]

Appendix A contains a description of a recent successful problem-solving endeavor in San Diego concerning a school truancy problem.

MEDIUM-SIZED COUNTIES AND CITIES

Arlington County, Virginia, is an urban community of approximately 26 square miles, located across the Potomac River from Washington, D.C. Being both a residential community and an employment center, its population swells from about 187,000 residents to about 265,000 each workday with the influx of commuters.

Using federal and state community policing grants, five community-based teams were deployed to diverse communities throughout the county.

Teams consisting of up to 24 officers and 3 supervisors establish a cooperative relationship with the community and identify broad-based strategies to address crime problems. Additionally, Community Resource Officers in each of the county's schools act as a part of the faculty, serving as instructors (teaching antidrug and antigang classes), enhancing the schools' security efforts, and coordinating Neighborhood Watch programs.

Geographic accountability is a management and motivational tool to facilitate agencywide implementation of COPPS. Officers are responsible and accountable for specific "turf" rather than a particular shift. Four districts were created, and the department's 10 police beats follow the natural boundaries of its civic organizations. This design enhances department-wide communications and encourages neighborhood focus. Officers are assigned to fixed areas for extended periods of time and are responsible for their specific areas 24 hours per day, seven days per week. In addition to responding to both emergency and nonemergency calls for service, they are responsible for preliminary criminal investigations, special event planning, and school liaisoning. The middle managers within the department have been identified as the key players in making COPPS work.

The department's COPPS efforts have resulted in a significant reduction in crime and calls for service. The department is also working aggressively to develop a technology strategy that will support its new geographic policing strategy. Through another recently funded grant, the department hopes to develop a technology infrastructure to support the requirements of beat officers engaged in problem solving.[13]

Concord, California

In the fall of 1992, the Concord police department (CPD) assembled a group of employees into a task force to develop the framework for a unique version of community policing; over the next decade, the CPD refined COPPS so that it reflected the needs of the community and was a "way of being" in public safety service. Thus, COPPS is an evolutionary process that seeks to join the police and community in reducing crime and enhancing the quality of life.

Officers, first-line supervisors, and middle managers are all held accountable for solving problems and are evaluated in annual performance evaluations; their pay is directly tied to their effectiveness. Part of this evaluation concerns the amount of time spent in problem-solving efforts. Of paramount importance are the *results* obtained by the officers in these endeavors. However, the fact that a problem was not eradicated is not viewed as being ineffective, per se; rather, it is the analysis of *why* the problem was not solved that offers more satisfying long-term solutions. Automated crime statistics are made available to the public around the clock, and officers go into the community to serve as mentors and trainers concerning COPPS.

The CPD has learned, and counsels others, that it takes time for institutional transformation to occur; the mindset of employees must change and accept COPPS as a "way of being" in order to accomplish the agency's mission.[14]

Hayward, California

Hayward has a population of about 120,000 and 160 sworn police officers. The 1990s were marked by increases in crime, drug trafficking, gangs, and traffic problems. Like other communities, Hayward's growing social ills contributed to the evolution of an incident-driven policing system in which "random patrol produces random results" and rapid response was a key priority. Realizing that the authority of the Hayward police department (HPD) was centralized

Hayward, California, police work closely with other city agencies to resolve neighborhood problems. (*Courtesy* Hayward, California, police department)

and stifled the creativity of employees, the department began developing a new approach to policing, believing it was time for law enforcement to change.

The Hayward Plan—officially known as Community Oriented Policing and Problem Solving (COPPS)—was activated and incorporated into all routine police functions (HPD's methods for changing its culture and mission statement are described in Chapter 6). New means of responding to calls for service were developed to free up officer time for problem solving. Officers are "managers" of their beats, encouraged to engage in responsible, creative ways to bring about problem resolution. They meet and talk with residents to build and nurture partnership and commitment as well as to explore viable solutions and seek out available resources.

The Hayward model is intended to be flexible, effective, and responsive to the needs of that community, stressing the importance of partnerships, problem solving, and visionary leadership. The process, the department acknowledges, requires considerable time, planning, and cooperation by everyone concerned. Such a comprehensive change in philosophy dictates a new policing style and "ushers in an exciting era."[15]

Lansing, Michigan

Lansing's police department (LPD) began its COPPS efforts in 1990. The city is divided into 18 geographic team areas with assigned officers, investigators, and command staff. As the philosophy evolved, the LPD recognized a critical need to better communicate crime and health as well as basic social service needs to the community. Accordingly, a seamless network was created between the police problem-solving teams, various service providers, and community members. A digital link provides all Lansing and Tri-County residents access to information related to crime problems, health care, and basic needs such as housing, food, and clothing. A citywide Internet-accessible e-mail system made it searchable by the community, police, and government Web sites. An information referral database was also created, allowing anyone with Internet access the ability to connect to nearly all services. Users can search over 600 agencies that provide basic services.

In order to enhance the users' ability to identify neighborhood problems, a GIS was implemented. This system was given reported crime locations, parks locations, parcel mapping for identification of registered properties, and county health data. Citizens can also contact their police team to provide information that may lead to the solving of a crime in their neighborhood. The effectiveness of all these efforts is evaluated by measurable questions, analysis measures, and specific evaluator resources to determine whether or not the goals of LPD were met in a timely and satisfactory manner.[16]

Lincoln, Nebraska

The city of Lincoln has formed a Problem Resolution Team (PRT) composed of a group of representatives from key public agencies and neighborhood associations, including the city police department, victim and witness unit, attorney's office, building and safety department, housing authority, and urban development office, as well as the county health and social services departments. The team has several functions:

- Gathering information relevant to cases—the team assembles relevant documents that pertain to a complaint or problem, such as reports, correspondence, or other records.
- Sharing information among public agencies—at regular meetings cases are shared among the team.
- Developing action plans or strategies—team members discuss possible strategies for resolving problems, finalizing action plans, and making specific assignments by consensus. Each team member coordinates the activities of his or her own agency that are necessary to fulfill its portion of the action plan.
- Keeping citizens informed about the status of cases and outcomes of city actions.
- Making recommendations to city officials to improve city practices or policies.

The PRT is currently developing a computer program that will match the police computer-aided dispatching and other agency responses at specific locations to those that are flagged as public housing properties. Another program is being developed that will alert area police captains about excessive calls-for-service locations in order to identify problems before they become entrenched.

Perhaps the jewel in the crown of Lincoln's community policing efforts is the Quality Service Audit—a partnership between the Lincoln police department and the Gallup organization. This audit is an ongoing, systematic survey of citizen perceptions regarding the quality of the city's police services; it seeks to provide officers with feedback about their contacts with citizens and to provide strategic information to police managers.[17]

Each year, student interns from the University of Nebraska and other area colleges, working at the police department, complete more than 6,000 telephone surveys with Lincoln residents who have recently received police services. Crime victims, drivers in traffic accidents, and even persons who have been arrested or ticketed by the police are surveyed using 10 questions developed by Gallup. The department requires all new officers to receive audit feedback as a condition of their employment; officers with more than three years of service are allowed to participate voluntarily. Only aggregate data are provided to managers, and narrative comments are provided to the officers on a monthly basis.[18]

Although surveying citizens is not a new approach under COPPS, this concept is given exceptional importance and sophistication in Lincoln. As the mayor and police chief state,

The tendency to overvalue workload data and underutilize measures of quality service may result in an organizational milieu that rewards a sort of fast driving, rapid response policing which retards efforts to improve relationships with the public, build citizen trust, and implement or encourage a community based style of policing. Overemphasis on statistics can be detrimental if an agency does not make a concerted effort to also utilize data about the quality of services provided.[19]

The city received a $50,000 federal grant from the National Institute of Justice to study how its audit system affects officers' behavior.

Reno, Nevada

Reno is located on the northeastern slopes of the Sierra Nevada mountain range. It is a 24-hour gaming community, consisting of 80 square miles and about 190,000 population (swelling to more than 250,000 persons with the influx of tourists for gaming and during special events).

In April 1987, the Reno police department (RPD) reorganized its entire agency toward implementing a new community policing strategy. The city was divided into three geographic areas, and officers and supervisors were assigned to teams in neighborhoods. Every employee (sworn and non-sworn) attended a 40-hour course in community policing.

A vision statement, "Your Police—Our Community" was adopted to stress the importance of collaborative problem solving. New mission and values statements were also developed by a committee of employees. Hiring, promotional systems, selection for special assignments, personnel evaluation systems, and individual awards and decorations reflected officers' knowledge of COPPS and related performance.

COPPS training was included in the recruit academy and infused into a new national field training model, called the "Reno Model Police Training Officer Program." Annual in-service training courses were designed to improve officers' COPPS skills, and all officers were certified in crime analysis and crime

In the Kids Korner program in Reno, Nevada, beat officers and medical personnel visit low-income rental motels to identify children who are truant and in need of medical and social services. (*Courtesy* Reno, Nevada, police department)

prevention through environmental design (CPTED). An advanced COPPS mentoring course was designed to create a cadre of "super" trainers. During this 40-hour course, patrol officers are sent into the field with a trainer and are taught higher problem-solving skills. A computer program was developed to track COPPS projects in neighborhoods.

A new city manager adopted a community-oriented government approach to services. Monthly neighborhood advisory board meetings included representatives of various city agencies and the police department working with residents to resolve problems. Problem solving and CPTED training has been extended to other city agencies that work closely with officers in neighborhoods.

The department supplements its service to neighborhoods with more than 60 senior volunteers who are trained to perform crime analysis functions for field officers, monitor school crossings, and distribute crime prevention materials, among other tasks.

An annual community survey provides vital information by measuring residents' perceptions of police performance, personal safety, and other concerns. The results are presented to the entire department in briefings, and responses to community concerns are developed.

Most recently, the RPD has incorporated COPPS into its training for homeland defense. The RPD feels it is important that officers understand that their knowledge of a beat, its residents, and its problems is at the heart of good policing and is the best weapon against the threat of domestic terrorism.

Savannah, Georgia

In 1991 Savannah's police department began a plan of COPPS implementation that necessitated the hiring of 34 new officers and a reorganization from a centralized command to a system of precincts housed in four different locations. Several programs were then initiated under the COPPS umbrella.

1. *Showcase Neighborhood Program:* The city improved livability in depressed neighborhoods by becoming partners with area residents. Police worked with citizens to identify problems and establish priorities for eliminating them. For this effort, the city won an award from the U.S. Conference of Mayors.

2. *Horse and bicycle patrols:* Public interest led to the development of horse patrols in 1987 in the downtown area (later they were used in targeted problem neighborhoods). Bicycle patrols, also begun downtown, were eventually used successfully in a number of COPPS initiatives. The emphasis of the bicycle patrol is now on problem solving.

3. *Police ministations:* One officer was assigned to each of four public housing areas that experienced high crime rates. Each ministation sponsors a Boy Scout troop and makes constant checks on shut-ins and the elderly.

Since the initiation of COPPS, other new programs have evolved. The Volunteer Program uses 20 actively participating volunteers, and a Citizens Police Academy consists of a 10-week, one-day-per-week course on the operation of the Savannah police department. The department considers COPPS a continually evolving process of changing the way it does business, forcing officers to open their minds to new ideas and change attitudes concerning the delivery of services—all of which, it is hoped, will result in long-term benefits for the police and citizens alike.[20]

Spokane, Washington

Spokane is unique because of its geographic location and regional orientation. Although the current city population is about 185,000, the city is the urban center of the Spokane–Coeur d'Alene area, which has a combined population of more than 450,000. Many demands for city services are generated daily from a nonresident population base, which includes out-of-state workers, surrounding county residents, and Canadian visitors.

Like most police agencies dealing with increasing violent crimes, more drug-related offenses, and limited staff and resources, the Spokane police department (SPD) had fallen into the reactive, incident-driven, call-to-call policing model. Officers became seriously stressed, with as many as 40 officers at one time off work because of fatigue-related illnesses.

In late 1991 the department created a strategic planning team to mold its future and identify and remedy obstacles to change. Members met regularly to tackle separate issues; a monthly department newsletter was created as well. The department then teamed with the Washington State Institute for Community Oriented Policing (WSICOP) to focus on the COPPS philosophy, develop community partnerships, strengthen informal social control, expand police and community empowerment, and increase social and cultural awareness. Written surveys were distributed to police employees and 1,200 citizens.[21]

Also in late 1991, spurred by the tragic abduction of two local girls, citizens were sparked by their grief to form a task force to address neighborhood problems. They approached the city council and proposed to open a neighborhood police substation, staffed by community volunteers, as a central distribution point for information on crime and disorder as well as problem solving. The city council and police chief supported the idea, and on May 1, 1992, the facility opened; four years later, there were nine "COPS Shops" in the city, with four more in planning stages. The volunteers take police reports, deal with nuisances, disseminate resource information, register bicycles, aid victims, and sponsor guest speakers and "get together" nights. Since the original COPS facilities opened, crime rates have declined significantly.[22]

Tempe, Arizona

Tempe is a growing suburb of Phoenix and the most densely populated city in the state, with about 156,000 residents in a 40-square-mile area. City departments have a reputation for interdepartmental cooperation and problem solving, and citizen surveys have repeatedly indicated the city has an excellent quality of life.

The Tempe police department (TPD) employs 256 sworn officers. In response to the changing public safety needs of the city, the TPD initially introduced COPPS on one beat to demonstrate how COPPS strategies could be used to reduce drug demand and overall crime and disorder. This Innovative Neighborhood Oriented Policing (INOP) project was eventually used as a model for citywide implementation of COPPS strategies.[23]

TPD first ensured that officers had the flexibility to solve problems (using the S.A.R.A. model). Patrol officers worked as a self-directed team, sharing information, problem solving, and scheduling with a COPPS philosophy. Officers were in the beat area for extended time periods.

TPD's first task was to perform a comprehensive and detailed profile of the target area using community and business surveys measuring demographic characteristics, fear of crime, perception of quality of life, and so on. Next, the department involved business owners, residents, neighborhood organizations, other city departments, and social service agencies in project coordination. The team of beat officers then used a variety of intelligence and information sources to support drug enforcement and demand reduction efforts. Newsletters, meetings, and a citizen hotline were used to disseminate information.

An evaluation component was developed by an independent consulting agency to assess INOP's implementation, process, and impact. Although the impact on the community has yet to be determined, the project's impact on the department has been significant. The agency believes that once it made the commitment to INOP, there was no turning back. Changes in organizational structure, management and supervisory roles, policies, goals, recruitment practices, evaluation and award systems, and the COPPS information system are permanent.

A feature of COPPS in Tempe is the department's elaborate system for geographic deployment of patrol officers, allowing officers within a geographic area to have varying schedules. Such deployment provides officers with better information about their beats, increases officer job satisfaction as they take ownership of areas and solve problems, holds officers accountable for their geographic areas, and allows the community to become more involved in solving problems in their neighborhoods.[24] Tempe officers are scheduled individually, rather than by squads, to facilitate greater coverage during peak times. This system has been quantitatively shown to yield higher correlations between calls for service and available staffing.

SMALL COMMUNITIES

Arroyo Grande, California

With a complement of 29 staff members, the Arroyo Grande police department advertises the fact that should citizens visit their newly expanded police facility, they will not find COPPS written as a specific program, or a COPPS officer or unit; rather, their COPPS philosophy is based on a "Value Based Policing" philosophy that involves every member of the organization.

The agency has developed an organizational culture that seeks to form true partnerships with the community's various stakeholders in order to provide a better quality of life for all residents. The department's operations attempt to anticipate and solve problems before they erupt into major issues. Some examples of COPPS initiatives include

- Employee Participation Program
- Community Advisory Council
- Adopt-a-School Program
- Juvenile Diversion Program
- Bicycle Patrol Program
- Citizen Academy
- Crime Prevention/Neighborhood Watch
- Citizens Assisting Police (CAP) Volunteer Program
- Parent Project (for parents of high-risk children)
- Crime Prevention through Environmental Design (CPTED)
- DARE and Drug Free Zone
- Neighborhood Officer Program
- Community Services Program
- Foot Patrol Program
- Teen Citizen Academy

Several police agencies have visited or contacted the department concerning its COPPS initiative and these programs, and the California Peace Officer Standards and Training (POST) has used the department's programs as a resource for developing its training.

The Neighborhood Officer Program in Arroyo Grande is a major aspect of COPPS. This program is unique in that instead of assigning a few officers to cover districts or beats across the city as their primary assignment, each patrol officer is responsible for a particular neighborhood as an ancillary duty, thereby involving the entire uniformed division in the program. Patrol officers, while on duty, respond to calls for service but also pay attention to ongoing problems in their assigned neighborhoods. The officers act as liaisons between citizens and the department and coordinate problem-solving projects in their areas. The neighborhood officer also meets with individuals and organizations regarding disturbances, juvenile problems, and a variety of civil problems, and attempts to solve these problems with creativity or appropriate enforcement methods.[25]

Elmhurst, Illinois

Elmhurst is a city of 43,000 in the southern portion of Illinois, where the police attempt to provide citizens with "one-stop shopping" convenience. The police department has a cadre of officers who can handle the full range of citizens' needs, including noise complaints, broken street lamps, fallen trees, and other problems. When possible, officers handle problems themselves, or, if need be, the problem is communicated to an appropriate city agency. Steps have been taken to ensure that officers have a stake in the policing process. Each officer has policy- and procedure-making power. They even test and select department equipment and uniforms, and they have developed a new design for police vehicles.

Perhaps a unique aspect of Elmhurst's COPPS strategy lies in its approach to officer evaluation. Instead of relying on traditional quantitative criteria, such as number of arrests, the department uses what it calls "community sensing mechanisms." The chief actively seeks feedback from elected government officials and residents. Random callbacks are conducted to gauge citizen satisfaction with officers and calls for service. In addition to letters to the chief, other sources of input that are given weight include newspaper articles, editorials, and comments from the local chamber of commerce.[26]

Gresham, Oregon

Gresham has seen dramatic growth, burgeoning housing and commercial development, and increasing demands for governmental services. With 72,000 residents, Gresham is the fourth-largest city in Oregon. Issues such as drug abuse, gang activity, theft, and violent crime forced a transition from the traditional policing model.[27]

The department became Oregon's first COPPS agency in 1992 as part of the department's five-year strategic plan.[28] A new mission was developed, along with the following activities: forming partnerships with many segments of the community; solving problems through a comprehensive process involving a chief's forum, zone advisory groups, and a neighborhood association; empowering citizens; and responding to underlying problems and conditions that cause crime. To design a foundation that would reflect the agency's values, the department conducted a public opinion survey; reconfigured its six patrol districts into three service delivery zones; assigned a lieutenant and team officers to each zone to further develop partnerships with neighborhood associations, schools, and businesses; and received donated office space, furnishings, and materials for zone offices. These efforts led to overall decentralization, greater initiative and empowerment among all levels of staff and officers, and heightened awareness

Huntington Beach, California, police found bicycle patrol to be an efficient and effective method of delivering services to beach recreation areas. (*Courtesy* Huntington Beach, California, police department)

of community concerns and priorities. Several "success stories" have resulted from Gresham's COPPS strategy:

- establishment of a community services center
- placement of a School Resource officer, a DARE officer, and a Gang Enforcement officer at each of the two Gresham-area school districts
- implementation of the Desk Officer Program to reduce response time to lower-priority calls and enable more face-to-face contact between officers and citizens
- eviction of drug dealers and overall cleanup of apartment complexes
- voter approval of a three-year, $2 million levy that will, in part, allow for the hiring of nine new officers, three Community Resource Specialists, and one Community Policing Analyst[29]

Orange County, Florida

Tourists are an often-forgotten population in our communities. Orlando, Florida, is the number one tourist destination in the world, with a 78-square-mile tourist corridor. There is also a plethora of criminals seeking to take advantage of unsuspecting victims, many of whom experience armed robbery and theft when items are stolen from their automobiles and hotel rooms. The items most frequently stolen are expensive video cameras, foreign passports, and money.

The Orange County Sheriff's office developed a Tourist Oriented Police Service (TOPS) program that offers tourists the same services that are available to locals as well as tourist-oriented services: crisis intervention, assistance with crimes compensation, interaction with foreign consulates, language translation services, and accompaniment throughout the criminal justice system. A tourist advocate is assigned to the patrol unit, and deputies assigned to TOPS make themselves accessible to tourists by leaving their cars, horses, and motorcycles so that they can walk their beats and interact with visitors. The sheriff's office has also developed a training video to teach hotel and business employees how to prevent crimes against tourists.[30]

Pittsburg, Kansas

Pittsburg is located in the southeast corner of the state and is a university town of about 20,000. The region is known as the "Little Balkans" because it was populated in the late 19th century by immigrants from European Balkan countries who came to work in the coal mines and smelters. In the latter part of the 20th century, Pittsburg experienced another wave of immigrants, this one mostly made up of Hispanics who also sought the American Dream in the heartland, in local factories and businesses. But the community was not mentally or structurally prepared for this influx and its subsequent demands on local resources. The police began hearing cries to "get those Mexicans out of Pittsburg"—even by people whose own grandparents or great-grandparents had lived in the community for 50 years without ever learning to speak English.

Sensing the growing tension, the police realized they could either do nothing and face serious problems of crime and disorder, as several other midwestern communities had, or proactively assist the assimilation of the new residents into the community. The police chief opted for the latter option, and with a local female activist (who is bilingual) formed the organization PACO, Pittsburg Area Community Outreach. This body evolved into a 29-person board of directors representing a cross-section of the community who donated their time and professional resources to projects that promoted integration of, and interaction with, the immigrants. The city mayor, an attorney, provided free legal advice to the immigrants, while other board members and citizens focused on helping them to understand the community. On five occasions, PACO invited an immigration expert from out of state to assist them with their immigration questions and needs at no cost, and the Mexican consulate from Kansas City was invited to provide Mexican passports and identification cards to them; meeting facilities in a municipal auditorium were provided by the city. The county health department sent nurses to the meetings to screen the immigrants for high blood pressure, HIV, and other health problems, as well as to dispense free flu shots. The public schools, library, adult education center, and other social services agencies provided assistance as well. The bilingual woman who cofounded PACO became very involved with translating marriage and birth certificates for the immigrants, which the police chief notarized as necessary.

To date, more than 250 immigrants have benefited from these services, and PACO has sponsored or supported more than 50 community projects. As a result of these efforts, the police chief was recognized by the U.S. Department of Justice and the U.S. attorney general for the department's commitment to community outreach and police–community relations.[31]

FEDERAL AND STATE AGENCIES

A Federal Approach

Several federal agencies are also engaged in COPPS. One example is the U.S. Customs Service's Strategic Problem Solving (SPS) initiative, which is composed of the following six elements.

1. Identify problem.
2. Determine objective/expectation (involves determining and stating the goals, objectives, or expectations in measurable terms).
3. Develop alternative solutions to problems through brainstorming.
4. Analyze and select alternatives.
5. Implement the alternatives.
6. Monitor outcomes.

Since the Customs Service began using SPS in 1996, more than 350 projects have been initiated across the United States. The Office of Strategic Problem

In many jurisdictions, partnerships and training between local and federal law enforcement agencies and private business have proved instrumental in combating crime. (*Courtesy* Community Policing Consortium)

Solving rewards team members for their successes in dealing with a wide range of problems, such as

- officer safety at land ports of entry
- stolen vehicle exportations at major seaports
- internal smuggling conspiracies involving airlines, railroads, and shipping company employees
- drug smuggling across land and via air travel

SPS has proven to be an effective tool because it brings together interdisciplinary teams of subject matter experts who are encouraged to be creative in developing solutions to problems.[32]

State Police and Universities

The Delaware State Police Rural Community Policing Unit has been in existence since mid-1994. Rural community policing is not common among state police agencies. The demographics of Delaware, however, make this an ideal venue for this concept. Sussex County, the most rural county in Delaware, has communities with high crime rates and few resources to assist the residents of these communities. The purpose and goal of the state police Rural Community Policing Unit is to reduce crime and provide resources to eight targeted communities in Sussex County. The unit is composed of four full-time troopers. The unit engages in activities such as conflict resolution, peer leadership, drug awareness, and Neighborhood Watch.

Calls for service in the targeted communities declined about 10 percent after the first year of the COPPS initiative, and other notable accomplishments include working with outside agencies to improve homes, streets, and water systems; obtaining a computerized information system from the state department of health to locate available health resources and job information; giving bicycle helmets and infant or child car seats to parents; and joining with local physicians to provide free physicals for youths attending camps.[33]

State colleges and universities across the nation are also involved with COPPS, including Harvard University (see Exhibit 13-2). Many college and university police departments, such as those at Harvard, Northwestern University,[34] University of North Dakota,[35] and Eastern Connecticut State University[36] have their own Web pages for describing their COPPS approach to the public; such Web sites also discuss such matters as the agency's history, philosophy, purpose, goals and objectives, and COPPS initiatives.

Some COPPS initiatives are instituted statewide. For example, Maryland needed a comprehensive statewide approach to pool resources and form partnerships among state and local governments along with business and community leaders. This approach considers a geographic focus on crime. Hot spots exist in urban, suburban, and rural parts of Maryland. To increase the

---

EXHIBIT 13-2   A New Policing Model for Harvard University

Harvard University's decision to restructure resulted in a significant transformation of the Harvard University police department (HUPD). Begun in 1997, the HUPD revised its management structure to reflect the needs of the COPPS approach, emphasizing

- familiarity with the community through a "neighborhood beat cop" system that builds on frequent, positive interactions with students, faculty, staff, and visitors

- a concentration on crime prevention
- a team approach to problem solving
- increased training at all levels of the agency
- a unified management philosophy governing decision making at all levels of the department

Source: Harvard University Web page: *http://www.news.harvard.edu/specials/policing/policing.html* (Accessed October 20, 2000), p. 4.

EXHIBIT 13-3   California Highway Patrol's Corridor Safety Program

The California Highway Patrol's (CHP) Corridor Safety Program has been credited with saving hundreds of lives on many dangerous rural roadways. The corridor under consideration involved California state routes 41 and 46, which are rural east-west highways connecting California's Central Valley to the central coast region. Scanning revealed this corridor had been the locale of 976 collisions—including 48 fatalities—during a four-year period. The CHP formed a task force to complete a thorough analysis of this problem; this analysis revealed that the main causal factor was unsafe turning movement, which included drifting out-of-lane, overconnecting off the road, and crossing over the center line into oncoming traffic. Also identified were inadequate shoulders and improper signage. A large Spanish-speaking farm worker population also raised questions of motorists' knowledge of traffic signs and laws as well as laws concerning drinking and driving.

Responses involved the task force's development of a detailed action plan, which had four facets: enforcement, emergency services, engineering, and public education. Patrol was enhanced along the corridor, and a CHP helicopter was permanently assigned to the area. Emergency roadside call boxes were installed, and emergency service providers found ways to deliver services more quickly. Several engineering projects were implemented along the corridor, including the widening of medians, treating outside shoulders with rumble strips, improving overall signage and striping, and adding daytime headlight sections. The CHP mounted an extensive public education campaign, which included the dissemination of two million color flyers about safe driving habits, safe-driving posters being placed in restaurants and recreational areas, and kick-off news conferences conducted to remind motorists to drive safely.

These efforts were quite successful. Injury accidents were reduced by nearly one-third, and over a five-year period it is estimated that the program has saved 21 lives and prevented 55 injuries.

Source: Police Executive Research Forum, *Excellence in Problem-Oriented Policing: The 2001 Herman Goldstein Award Winners* (Washington, D.C.: Author, 2002), pp. 5–14.

quality of life for citizens, several interrelated statewide initiatives were developed, which included assistance from the state Multi-Agency Response Teams, HotSpot Communities and its component initiative Operation Spotlight, and statewide HotSpot Computer Mapping.[37]

Exhibit 13-3 discusses the work of a well-known state law enforcement agency: the California Highway Patrol's (CHP) Corridor Safety Program, which won a Herman Goldstein Award in 2001 for excellence in community policing (the CHP also won this award in 2002; that effort is described in Appendix A).

SUMMARY

A common thread running through most if not all of the COPPS approaches in this chapter is the realization by the police that new strategies were necessary for addressing crime and neighborhood disorder. The cities and counties discussed in this chapter have demonstrated that the path to attaining a full-fledged COPPS initiative involves a complete transformation in ideology and more than mere rhetoric or putting officers on footbeats or on bicycles. This path may not be an easy one, but it has been shown that the rewards can be substantial.

NOTES

1. Kathleen Woodby and Tess Sherman, "Austin, Texas, Police Department Takes a Bite Out of Burglary with GIS," *http://www.esri.com/news/arcnews/spring03articles/austin-texas-police.html* (Accessed May 28, 2003).

2. Charlotte-Mecklenburg police department Web site, *http://www.charmeck.org/Departments/Police/About+Us/Home.htm* (Accessed May 28, 2003).

3. Chicago, Illinois, police department Web page: *http://www.ci.chi.il.us/CommunityPolicing.htm*, October 20, 2000.

4. City of Chicago, Office of the Mayor, Press Release, February 15, 2003, *http://w6.ci.chi.il.us/mayor/2003Press/newspress0215capsrallyaustin.html* (Accessed May 28, 2003).

5. Ft. Lauderdale police department, "Community Support Division," *http://ci.ftlaud.fl.us/police/cpipaul.html* (Accessed May 28, 2003).

6. Michael S. Scott, personal communication, December 23, 1993.

7. St. Louis, Missouri, police department, *http://stlouis.missouri.org/5yearstrategy/app_c(crime).html* (Accessed May 28, 2003).

8. Information provided by Donald S. Quire, St. Petersburg, Florida, police department, January 31, 1994.

9. St. Petersburg, Florida, police department Web site, *http://www.stpete.org/police/commpol.htm* (Accessed May 28, 2003).

10. Bob Burgreen and Nancy McPherson, "Implementing POP: The San Diego Experience," *The Police Chief* (October 1990):50–56.

11. Ibid., p. 17.

12. San Diego police department Web page: *http://www.sannet.gov/police/sdpd* (Accessed November 26, 1997).

13. Arlington County, Virginia, Web page: *http://www.co.arlington.va.us/pol/comm/htm* (Accessed October 20, 2000).

14. Laura M. Hoffmeister, "Best Practices of Community Policing: The Concord Experience." In *Best Practices of Community Policing in Collaborative Problem Solving* (Washington, D.C.: The United States Conference of Mayors, June 2001), pp. 32–36.

15. California Department of Justice, Attorney General's Office, Crime Prevention Center, *COPPS: Community Oriented Policing and Problem Solving* (Sacramento, Calif.: Author, November 1992), pp. 43–46.

16. David C. Hollister, "'In Touch': Neighborhood Stabilizing Data Improving Low Income Citizens Quality of Life." In *Best Practices of Community Policing in Collaborative Problem Solving* (Washington, D.C.: The United States Conference of Mayors, June 2001), pp. 95–99.

17. Mike Johanns and Tom Casady, "Quality Service Audit Improves Community-Based Policing," *U.S. Mayor* (April 7, 1997):3.

18. Community Policing Journal (Fall 1996):14.

19. Johanns and Casady, "Quality Service Audit Improves Community-Based Policing," p. 3.

20. Information provided by Dan Reynolds, Savannah, Georgia, police department, December 9, 1993.

21. Information provided by Robert C. Van Leuven, Spokane, Washington, police department, December 14, 1993.

22. Ellen Painter, "Tragedy Sparks Community Policing in Spokane, Washington," *Community Policing Exchange* (May/June 1995):5.

23. Tempe, Arizona, Police Department, "Overview": *http://www.tempe.gov*, November 26, 1997.

24. Tempe, Arizona, Police Department, *Geographic Deployment of Patrol* (Tempe, Ariz.: Author, 1993).

25. "Community oriented policing in Arroyo Grande": *http://www.thegrid.net/agpd/community.html*, November 26, 1997.

26. Steve Anzaldi, "Adapting to Needs: Community Policing around the State," *The Compiler* (Chicago: Illinois Criminal Justice Information Authority, Fall 1993), p. 8.

27. Gresham, Oregon, Police Department, "A Call for Challenge: Community-Based Policing" (Gresham, Ore.: Author, no date), p. 1.

28. Gresham, Oregon, Police Department, "Community Policing: Vision, Mission, Values" (Gresham, Ore.: Author, no date), p. 2.

29. Information provided by Gerald Johnson, Acting chief of police, Gresham, Oregon, police department, October 27, 1993.

30. Greta Snitkin, "Tourist Victim Advocacy: Servicing Your Extended Community," *Sheriff Times* (Spring 1997):1, 8.

31. Mike Hall, chief of police, Pittsburg, Kansas. Personal communication, March 12, 2003.

32. *http://www.customs.treas.gov/enforcem/sps.htm*.

33. *http://www.state.de.us./dsp/rural/htm*.

34. *http://www.new.edu/up/community.html*.

35. *http://www.operations.und.nodak.edu/Op/police/CoP.htm*.

36. *http://www.ecsu.ctstateu.edu/depts/police/cops/html*.

37. Danny Shell, Maryland State Police, "The 8th Annual International Problem Oriented Policing Conference: Problem Oriented Policing 1997," November 16, 1997, San Diego, California.

INTRODUCTION

The world has become a global village. Through technology, rapid intercontinental travel, and high-technology communications systems, we are virtual neighbors around the planet. Even very disparate countries can learn from, and have shared much with, one another.

It has been said that the comparative approach provides the opportunity to "search for order."[1] This chapter does so by comparing the work of community oriented policing and problem solving (COPPS) in foreign venues with that in the United States. It will be seen that COPPS has indeed gone international and is now the operational strategy of many police agencies around the globe.

First we "travel" to Canada, looking at the country generally, then viewing COPPS in Burnaby and with the Royal Canadian Mounted Police (problem-solving efforts in Ontario are also discussed in Exhibit 14-1). Next we look at some of the earliest community policing efforts in Japan, then move on to Australia, where COPPS is having a major effect across that country. Great Britain is our next stop. The chapter concludes with a brief look at COPPS in some other venues, including Scotland, the Isle of Man, Israel, Hong Kong, New Zealand, and the Netherlands. Other venues are discussed in five more exhibits spread throughout the chapter.

Much can be learned from examining the activities and approaches undertaken in each venue. The reader is encouraged to determine whether there are common elements of COPPS in these countries, and to compare each with the American strategy as it is described in earlier chapters. We discuss in the chapter summary whether common denominators exist and the presence of an international understanding and application of the concepts around the world.

—14—

IN FOREIGN VENUES

COPPS Abroad

The world is but a school of inquiry.
—MICHEL DE MONTAIGNE

CANADA

Canada stretches nearly 5,000 miles from east to west, touches both the Atlantic and Pacific Oceans, embraces four million square miles, covers six time zones, and has 10 provinces. More than 30 million people reside in Canada, 90 percent of whom are within 100 miles of the southern border, near the United States. They speak more than 60 languages and are members of 70 ethnocultural groups.[2]

More than 56,000 sworn officers work in about 400 independent police services in Canada, translating to about one officer for every 520 Canadians. Of the total number of officers, about one-quarter are members of the Royal Canadian Mounted Police (RCMP, discussed later), and 16 percent work for the three independent provincial police forces—the Ontario Provincial Police (see Exhibit 14-1), the Surete du Quebec, and the Royal Newfoundland Constabulary. More than half (56 percent) of Canada's police officers work in 361 independent municipal police services. The average size of a Canadian police service is 141 sworn personnel.[3]

Community policing is now the official approach to policing across Canada, at all levels of government. The most widely recognized "police service of

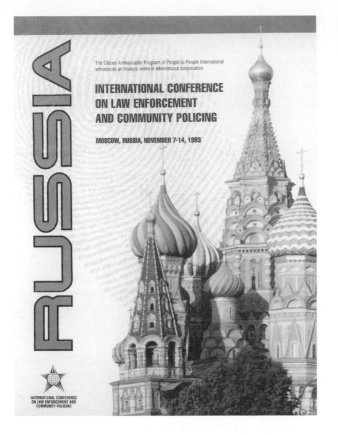

The fall of communism led Russia and other countries to explore more democratic forms of policing, as illustrated by this International Conference on Community Policing brochure.

excellence" in Canada is the City of Edmonton Police Service, which pioneered a demonstration project on neighborhood foot patrol in 1993. Edmonton is considered by many to be the "Mayo Clinic of policing" and is perhaps the model of a very modern police service.[4]

But the question of whether community policing has succeeded in Canada is yet to be answered. Despite its widespread adoption, there has been little in the way of comprehensive, rigorous evaluations of community policing in Canada, which lacks a police research arm that would be equivalent to the U.S. Police Executive Research Forum, Police Foundation, or National Institute of Justice.[5] It is believed, however, that four challenges still confront community policing in Canada.

EXHIBIT 14-1   Community Policing in Ontario

The Ontario Provincial Police (OPP) have created an impressive Web site that describes in detail (in both English and French) its Community Policing Development Centre. The site describes its community policing strategy, including the differences between COPPS and traditional policing, and an explanation of what is termed "P.A.R.E.": problem identification, analysis, response, and evaluation. It also provides the agency's mission (including the use of police–community "prevention partnerships" and teams), objectives, and strategic implementation plan; provides a news bulletin; and provides an extensive guide to problem solving with an online "How Do We Do It" manual. COPPS service delivery is customized for each neighborhood, which guarantees that police services will best meet community needs. A "Just for Kids" page is available, as well as an "Honour Roll" of citizens and police, a slate of current programs, OPP recruitment information, wanted/missing persons information, and links to other governmental agencies.

Source: OPP Web site: *http://www.gov.on.ca/opp/english* (Accessed May 29, 2003).

EXHIBIT 14-2   "Showdown at the Playground" in Vancouver

A 2001 recipient of the Herman Goldstein Award for Excellence in Problem-Oriented Policing was a problem-solving project in Vancouver, British Columbia, Grandview-Woodland Community Policing Centre. Grandview Park, a one-square-block area of Grandview-Woodland, is adjacent to a large community center that houses an elementary high school, a day care center, and various community services. The neighborhood is also next to Downtown East-side (DTES), an area plagued by drug use and drug dealing. DTES, which is comprised of about 20 square blocks, is one of Canada's poorest areas and also has one of the highest needle-based drug-user populations and HIV drug infection rates in North America. Analysis of the problem was accomplished from several perspectives, including the social dynamics of the problem population, the park structure and its effect on criminal behavior, past police responses, and community meetings and surveys.

Responses included the use of plainclothes operations to identify the drug dealers, area citizens willingly opening their homes to officers as observation points, and a volunteer foot patrol that provided information about drug dealing. The Park Board was asked to help to control graffiti and litter, and youths were hired for these efforts as well as to paint murals. Suggestions from Simon Fraser University criminology students helped horticulturists understand CPTED and how the park should be changed; they eliminated obstructed sightlines, severely pruned covered areas, and replaced low bushes where drug dealers hid drugs. Furthermore, the local animal control center stepped up its enforcement of unleashed dogs used by drug dealers to intimidate residents.

An assessment revealed that these efforts generally resulted in decreases in 911 calls and other calls for service to the area, as well as increases in numbers of arrests for trafficking and in drugs seized. Significantly, people began bringing their children to the playground once again.

1. The police have yet to overcome the unrealistic expectations and demands placed on them by the public that they provide rapid emergency response while providing order maintenance services—what one author described as demanding both a "Green Beret" and a "Peace Corps" role of the police.[6]
2. Community policing in Canada carries a bias toward dealing with local problems at a time when drug smuggling, money laundering, and other crimes demand national and international focus.
3. The police are still challenged to move beyond the traditional criteria for police success: arrests, clearance rates, and response times.
4. Police need to take advantage of a brief window of opportunity to implement and prove the effectiveness of COPPS before a fiscal crisis of government drives policing back to the reactive, incident-driven, traditional form of policing.[7]

Project Metrotown in Burnaby

Burnaby comprises an area of about 38 square miles on the southwest coast of Canada, and has approximately 194,000 residents. The Royal Canadian Mounted Police (RCMP)—Burnaby Detachment received a 2002 Herman Goldstein Award for its work in decreasing crime in three apartment buildings and the surrounding area.

The problem began in 1998 when rampant drug dealing became common around the Metrotown SkyTrain station. Honduran nationals were coming to Canada, claiming refugee status; a large number began occupying the three apartment buildings in Burnaby. The problem soon became complex, involving a marked increase in calls for service as well as an organized crime problem. After working through the S.A.R.A. problem-solving process, charging 30 persons with trafficking, and reducing calls for service at the apartments and the surrounding area by 40 percent, the RCMP had successfully addressed the problem—or so they thought. By mid-1999 the problem had returned, with a resurgence of calls for service to the area. Again, town meetings were held and solutions were sought. Many problem-solving activities were undertaken, including court orders barring certain persons from the premises.

This time the police got the community more involved and opened a community police office in the area, used volunteer bike patrols and a citizens' watch, redesigned the train station to make it less attractive to loiterers, and employed a joint task force of police departments whose officers patrolled the train station area. Following this renewed effort, the problem-solving approach was a success, resulting in more than 200 drug trafficking charges in the area and deportations of many traffickers.

This venue's situation and its eventual success shows the need to revisit a problem with a problem analysis.[8]

The Royal
Canadian
Mounted Police

Community policing efforts of the Royal Canadian Mounted Police have been making significant strides in its smaller detachments, where COPPS has been operational for a long time. In September 1993 the RCMP resolved to pilot a detachment-wide COPPS initiative in one of its largest areas—Burnaby, British Columbia—with a population of about 150,000 and approximately 150 officers.[9]

The RCMP mission statement is shown in Box 14-1. The official view is that the adoption of community policing allows the RCMP to become more responsive to the needs of the communities it serves.

The RCMP also believes that "the open management style under this philosophy allows all officers to make appropriate informed decisions and take action, giving the RCMP [the] flexibility needed to provide completely responsive, integrated, and relevant police service."[10] The primary elements of the strategy include the following (note that there is a strong problem oriented policing flavor):

- *Direct service delivery*—working with the community to identify its problems; resolving the identified problems; empowering officers to make decisions and take action; and making patrol, enforcement, and investigative work effective and directed.
- *Changing the administrative organization*—decentralizing, using modern management concepts (such as problem solving, innovative resource deployment,

BOX 14-1

Mission Statement of the Royal Canadian Mounted Police

RCMP community policing is . . .

a partnership between the police and the community, sharing in the delivery of police services.

With this valuable community cooperation, the RCMP pledges to . . .

- Uphold the principles of the Canadian Charter of Rights and Freedoms.
- Provide a professional standard of service.
- Ensure all policing services are provided courteously and impartially.
- Work with the community and other agencies to prevent or resolve problems that affect the community's safety and quality of life.
- Act with the Canadian justice system to address community problems.
- Promote a creative and responsible environment to allow all RCMP members to deliver community services.

Source: Vancouver, B.C., Royal Canadian Mounted Police, *RCMP Community Policing: Strategic Action Plan Update, 1992–1995* (June 1993), p. 9.

risk management, flattening organizational hierarchy, and participatory management); creating an enhanced generalist career path; reducing the paper burden; and utilizing citizen satisfaction surveys.[11]

COMMUNITY POLICING IN JAPAN

The Earliest Community-Based Approach

Japan—with its Showa Constitution containing many articles that are similar to those found in the Fourth, Fifth, Sixth, and Eighth Amendments to the U.S. Constitution[12]—can lay claim to possessing the oldest and best-established community policing system in the world. Japan initiated its system immediately after World War II out of a combination of traditional culture and American democratic ideals. According to Jerome Skolnick and David Bayley, four elements seem to be at the core of this philosophy: (1) community-based crime prevention, (2) reorientation of patrol activities to emphasize non-emergency servicing, (3) increased accountability to the public, and (4) decentralization of command.[13] Next we briefly discuss these four elements.

Each of Japan's 47 prefectures has its own autonomous police force, and together they employ about 220,000 officers—on densely populated islands totaling about 144,000 square miles and 127 million people.[14] If community policing began with *community-based crime prevention*, the Japanese experience offers several valuable insights. One of the basic reasons Japanese policing works as well as it does is that the officers daily deal face-to-face with citizens and, therefore, have become a part of the community, rather than being separated from the people in a vehicle. Also, Japanese neighborhood crime-prevention associations (the Japanese tradition of the *gonin-gumi*, a group of five people in a neighborhood) have generally given Japanese culture a much closer relationship between people and their neighbors.

With regard to Japanese police *patrol activities*, people in Japan seem not to have the same "we versus they" perceptions about the police as Americans have.[15] Thus, the Japanese appear to be far more willing than Americans to accept police presence. As a result, Japanese police place heavy emphasis on order maintenance and crime prevention, aiding the community to resolve problems that could lead to disorder.[16] A major part of this effort includes the counseling services that are part of every Japanese police station. All police stations assign an experienced older officer, usually a sergeant, to provide a wide range of general counseling, ranging from family disputes to questions about contracts and indebtedness. Trained in dispute resolution, the police are able to provide a helpful, informal conciliation.[17]

If the police and the community are to become coproducers of an orderly society, police must have *closer accountability to the public* and begin to share power with the community they serve, beginning with closer relations with community groups, clubs, churches, and civic organizations to help obtain information, define priorities, and aid in planning effective strategies.[18]

If all of this is to be accomplished, however, the fourth major element in COPPS must be developed: *decentralization of command*. Providing neighborhood police centers and beat offices as well as giving officers greater discretion to develop responses to community problems form the nucleus of this strategy. This has been one of the strengths of the Japanese system.[19] Patrol officers in Japan are under even closer supervision than are rank-and-file officers in the United States. Yet the *kobun-oyabun* (a kind of student–mentor relationship) between the Japanese patrol officers and their superiors allows the officers a great deal of input into decisions about local problems.

Japanese officers perform their duties in a neighborhood koban. (*Courtesy* Office of International Criminal Justice)

The Koban

Like the *chusai-san* (a rural police officer, who is required to visit each household twice per year and works with citizens to solve area problems), the urban police officer in Japan visits neighborhood households and does police business in the koban. These police boxes are the foundation of the sense of security of the people, and they function as the bases of police functions closest to the citizens. Officers prepare and disseminate crime bulletins and provide citizens with tips concerning crime prevention, stories of good deeds by children, and opinions of residents.[20] Exhibit 14-3 provides a case study of the work of koban police.

A koban may be found every few blocks; there are about 15,000 kobans across the country, 6,000 of which are residential in nature. There are also *mobile police-boxes* or wagons that assist the koban as needed, and temporary kobans are established at times as well.[21] The Japanese police try to keep the

---

EXHIBIT 14-3   Work of the Japanese Koban

A police officer of the police box of the Sendai Higashi police station, Miyagi Prefecture, visited once a week and took care of a 75-year-old woman who had no relatives in the neighborhood, suffered from diabetes, and had problems with her legs. One day the officer called on the woman and got no answer. Knowing that this was unusual and because of her physical state, the officer entered the home to check on her welfare. He found the woman lying unconscious and assisted in hospitalizing her. Then the officer tried to find the woman's relatives and determined that she had a niece living in Sendai. As a result, the aged woman was able to obtain better care with the help of her niece.

---

number of people for which a koban is responsible to less than 12,000, and the area less than four-tenths of a square mile. No koban may be less than six-tenths of a mile from another one. They are often put in areas with more than 320 criminal cases per year, more than 45 traffic accidents, and a high volume of pedestrian traffic.[22]

Kobans are usually storefront offices or tiny buildings resembling sentry stations. They consist of a reception room with a low counter or desk, telephone, radio, and wall maps; a resting room for personnel, often with a television set; a small kitchen or at least a hotplate and refrigerator; an interview room; a storeroom; and a toilet.[23] The officers' work shifts are long; they spend 24 hours at the koban every three days. From a tour of duty in a koban, officers move on to detective work, traffic patrol, riot police, and other specialized assignments.[24] The koban officer also

> has a wealth of . . . data on the jurisdiction . . . such as lists of people working late at night who might be of help as witnesses to crime, of people who are normally cooperative with the police, of people who own guns or swords, of all rented homes and apartments that might serve as hideouts for fugitives of people with criminal records, and of people with mental illness; organizational charts of gangs in the police station jurisdiction (sometimes with photographs of all the gangsters); lists of old people in the area living alone who should be visited periodically . . . and of all bars, restaurants, and amusement facilities in the jurisdiction; a short history of the koban; and a compilation of the total population, area, and number of households in the jurisdiction.[25]

Herein lies a fundamental difference between the Japanese and American police: Whereas American police come to the home only when called by citizens, their Japanese counterparts are constantly watchful of, informed about, and involved with the people in their neighborhoods.

AUSTRALIA'S POLICING STRATEGY

This section describes COPPS efforts in four Australian jurisdictions—Queensland, South Australia, Toowoomba, and Tasmania—while Exhibit 14-4 discusses a day in the life of an Australian officer in the bush.

"Stopbreak" in Queensland

Data analysis by Queensland, Australia, police in 1996 revealed that residential burglaries had increased 176 percent during the past 20 years, and 66 percent during one five-year period. Burglaries represented one in five of all criminal offenses. Analysis revealed two contributing factors to the burglary problem: a lack of proper security measures and the ease with which stolen goods could be "fenced" for profit. It was no wonder that many of the 3.4 million citizens of Queensland, Australia's second largest state, no longer felt safe in their homes.

Furthermore, there were disturbingly high rates of repeat victimization and low rates of offender apprehension. The police also concluded that "even if the number of police patrols were doubled, the typical dwelling or business would still only be under surveillance for an average of 60 seconds per day."[26]

A response—termed *Stopbreak*—was developed to address the primary contributing factors. A proactive COPPS philosophy was adopted on several levels. The police were trained in proper security audit techniques, and "hot spots" were examined to reduce repeat victimization and home burglaries in general. Citizens were advised concerning crime prevention and proper security

EXHIBIT 14-4   A Day in the Life of an Australian Bush Officer

Policing Australia's remote Aboriginal communities requires diplomacy and an ability to work in some of the most physically challenging regions in the world. Australia is using more and more women for these tasks in the bush. As a case in point, Sgt. Tanya Woodcock is responsible for maintaining harmony among the 2,500 traditional indigenous people on the two islands of Bathurst and Melville. She acts as a mediator in tribal and family disputes, and is also adept at sidestepping crocodiles. Following is an account of Woodcock's typical day. At 8:00 A.M., she checks the computer system at the police station, located near her home on Melville Island, to see if anything has happened overnight; she devotes about two hours to this task. At 10:00 A.M., she is in her four-wheel-drive vehicle, heading to the various communities. By noon she is in Milikapiti community, which has an Aboriginal

community police officer. By 3:00 P.M. Woodcock is headed back to the police station. Although armed, officers do not carry their firearms into these traditional communities, because it alarms their sense of stability. The biggest problem for the police is violent crimes against the person, usually fueled by alcohol or drug abuse. Another problem to this tropical paradise comes from Mother Nature: the weather. Ferocious cyclones do occur, and during such times it is Woodcock's responsibility to warn the remote communities' 2,500 residents. Toward this end, she has developed, and plays on local television stations, a videotape that warns residents of impending cyclones and what to do if the area is hit.

Source: http://www.bbc.co.uk.crime/fighters/dayinthelife/bushofficer .shtml (Accessed May 29, 2003).

An Australian police officer takes a crime report at a neighborhood station.

measures they could take in their homes. Victims were referred to victim support organizations, and homes and businesses that had been targets of repeat burglaries had temporary, portable silent burglary alarms installed. These alarms were linked to police headquarters.

An assessment found that officers and victims alike indicated that the strategies were substantially positive in nature, and a majority of victims implemented at least one of the security measures recommended by the police.[27]

Operation Mantle in South Australia

In the late 1990s the South Australia Police (SAPOL) employed a problem-solving approach across metropolitan Adelaide. Prior to Operation Mantle, law enforcement strategies lacked integrated approaches for dealing with high-level and low-level drug trafficking; furthermore, drug supply reduction measures predominantly aimed at the high level were unsuccessful in reducing the supply of illicit drugs. This operation employed three strategies: use of intelligence-driven problem-solving policing methods that take account of harm minimization in an effort to reduce mid- and low-level drug trafficking; fostering and maintaining alliances with government agencies and the community to enhance the integrated approach; and ensuring good communication and intelligence flow within and between tactical units and SAPOL. The operation's integrated approach to drug enforcement included the establishment of regional tactical investigation teams that targeted low-level and mid-level traffickers and that also sought closer collaboration with a range of agencies to improve harm minimization and treatment options.

The operation appears to have had an impact on drug-related crime. The impact was not spectacular, nor was it expected to be. Operation Mantle stabilized the trafficking rates, a significant achievement in light of the previously projected increases in such crimes. These results are felt to echo Herman Goldstein's contention that the best that should be expected is a minimization of the problem, a reduction of the adverse effects, and a lessening of consequent suffering.[28]

A Pilot Project in Toowoomba

In the mid-1990s the Criminal Justice Commission and the Queensland Police Service established a two-year beat policing pilot project in the city of Toowoomba in southeastern Queensland. The impetus for the project was a governmental report that recommended the adoption of COPPS.

This project was designed to promote a community-based policing style, characterized by localized, problem oriented service delivery. The key features of the project were to be the following:

- assignment of officers to two defined beat areas on a long-term basis; the officers were to reside in these beat areas as well
- provision of most policing services by the locally based officers
- use of foot patrols by the beat area officers
- inclusion of proactive policing activities as part of the normal duties of the officers
- introduction of a negotiated response strategy[29]

The pilot project was based on COPPS initiatives in the United States and Canada and was designed to incorporate a problem-solving orientation into the normal duties of the police officers, so they could focus on the underlying conditions generating calls for service (CFS) and develop strategies to address those conditions. Management and beat officers provided strong support for the problem oriented approach.

After the two-year period ended, the Criminal Justice Commission in Brisbane determined that the number of CFS generated by the top 10 addresses in the bcat areas decreased over the first 12 months of the project, that the problems handled by the beat officers ranged from prowlers and alcohol-related incidents to disputes between neighbors, and that the two most common strategies employed by the beat officers to resolve problems were "removing the problem" and preventive activities such as fixing street lighting.

TASMANIA

Tasmania is located off of the southeastern portion of Australia and is an island state of that country. It is composed of 26,383 square miles and about 360,000 people. The Tasmanian police vision is "To be widely recognized as a premier policing service." Toward that end, the police conduct a number of community-based activities, including Crime Stoppers, Bush Watch, Neighbourhood Watch, Business Watch, Safety House, Officer Next Door Program, Police in Schools, and Adopt-a-Cop. These programs are supported by officers from the state office in the island capital of Hobart. This state office is assisted by various geographic district Community Policing sections around the state. Community policing officers are involved in attending the schools, regattas, agricultural shows, and various expositions around the state. Community policing officers also provide crime prevention advice, recruitment information, drug education, security audits, and historical displays.[30]

COPPS IN GREAT BRITAIN

There are 41 police forces in England and Wales. There are 27 county police forces, 8 combined police areas (where 2 or 3 counties have been united for policing purposes), and 6 metropolitan forces.[31] Almost all police forces in this region are introducing or are actively considering the introduction of COPPS in some form.[32]

Indeed, COPPS has progressed to such a level in Great Britain that the Home Office in London has published dozens of monographs on the subject, including two that are highly significant in the field: the Police Research Group's *Problem-Oriented Policing: Brit POP*, 1996, which described the early stages of a development project implementing problem oriented policing in one division in Leicestershire, and *Brit POP II: Problem-Oriented Policing in Practice*, published in 1998, which highlighted "the lessons learned over the past two to three years for introducing and maximizing the benefits from POP."[33]

A Guiding Philosophy

The philosophy of community oriented policing in Britain, as well as several important aspects of its practice (such as neighborhood-based patrols) can be traced to the formation of professional policing in the nineteenth century and the ways in which the police mandate was established and legitimated.[34]

Early architects of British policing established the idea that effective policing can be achieved only with the consent of the community.[35] From the 1970s onward, arguments in favor of greater use of foot patrol have assumed an increasingly important place in public debate about policing in Britain. Community surveys have found that more foot patrol is clearly what most people want. So there has been a return to the bobby on the beat—a virtually unanimously accepted goal of public policy.[36] Foot patrol remains a key feature of community oriented policing in Britain.

Exhibit 14-5 discusses one community's program.

Early Initiatives

Sir Kenneth Newman, who served as commissioner of Scotland Yard from 1982 to 1987, brought to the job a new intellectual dimension and a willingness to challenge existing police practices. He launched many planning initiatives, including authorizing his staff in 1983 "to evaluate the feasibility of adopting the 'Problem Oriented Approach' in the Metropolitan Police."[37]

Four problems were selected for study: Asian gangs, shopping victims (on a specific street), prostitutes (in a specified area), and motor vehicle crime. An evaluation of the studies found that COPPS had the potential to improve police performance.[38] The studies demonstrated that the potential for the implementation of COPPS was severely limited unless greater flexibility was introduced into the organization. The Metropolitan Police organization is centralized in its policy making, and management communications are designed by "line" or territory, not by problem. Newman stated in a letter to the force in 1984 that "the structure of our hierarchy [was] hindering more than helping the good work done on the ground." He concluded that "too much energy and effort are wasted in keeping the organization going instead of serving the mainline job of policing" and that "there is a tendency for our organization to try to cope with problems through superficial changes in the bureaucratic system, rather than looking for real solutions."[39] Thus, Newman sought to reduce the rigidity of the organization. In 1985 he wrote that

> The aim of the Metropolitan Police will . . . be to work with other agencies to develop . . . a "problem solving" approach to crime prevention, where, rather than merely dealing with individual acts of law-breaking, careful analysis is made of the total circumstances surrounding the commission of types of crime, taking account of wide-ranging social and environmental factors, in order better to understand—and counter—the causes of those acts.[40]

Today, undoubtedly the key issue concerning COPPS in Britain is accountability. Public opinion is especially intense in London, where no local control over the police exists and there are about 30,000 sworn officers. Critics are calling for greater role definition for community constables and a greater permeation of

---

EXHIBIT 14-5 West Mercia Constabulary's Four Tracks of Policing

West Mercia Constabulary serves 1.1 million people in Herfordshire, Worcestershire, and Shropshire counties in England, which spread out over 2,868 miles. The constabulary has developed a policing model known as the "four tracks of policing," which sets out a strategic approach to implementing COPPS. The first track, local policing, stresses the constabulary's commitment to local policing and local partnerships to achieve effective solutions to local problems. The second track, responsive policing, focuses on the constabulary's duty to respond appropriately to requests for assistance and to provide adequate resources for emergency situations. The third track, targeted policing, concentrates on using intelligence-based policing operations to solve specific problems. Finally, the fourth track, policing partnerships, recognizes that no matter how effective the constabulary may be with the other three tracks, it is vitally important to work with communities to develop shared solutions.

Source: Workshop presentation, Constable David C. Blakely, The 8th Annual International Problem Oriented Policing Conference: Problem Oriented Policing 1997, November 15, 1997, San Diego, California.

A British constable provides a tourist with directions at Parliament Square in London.

the community philosophy throughout the police organization and in its operations. They also argue that if concrete progress is to be made, the mechanics of community policing need to be made visible and the principles they embody openly and skeptically debated. In short, for many to this point the community approach to policing in Britain has been more rhetoric than reality.

The Role of Constables

Britain's constables have a mandate to control crime. They are to "penetrate the community in a multitude of ways in order to influence its behavior for illegality and toward legality."[41] The officer's primary role is defined as being concerned with crime and criminals, and his or her effectiveness is to be judged by the amount of information passed on to colleagues. The emphasis is largely on crime fighting and law enforcement, and contact with the public is to be fostered mainly in terms of its contribution toward meeting these ends.[42]

Public input is growing concerning the police task, however. Almost all of the 41 police authorities in England and Wales now have established formal police–community consultative committees. Some of the issues addressed by the committees are maintaining mutual trust between the police and the public; maintaining community peacefulness and improving quality of life; promoting greater public understanding of policing issues, such as causes of crime and police procedures and policies; examining patterns of complaints against officers; fostering links with local beat officers; and developing victim support services.[43]

For Britain's police, Neighborhood Watch forms the most common and popular form of community-based crime prevention. Neighborhood Watch programs have grown immensely in Britain. At the instigation of the Home Office, roughly 300 crime prevention advisory panels were established within Britain's 41 police force jurisdictions from 1985 to 1988. And, in terms of patrol deployment, referred to as "general duties," foot beats returned in large measure after being virtually eliminated in favor of motorized units in the early 1970s. By the late 1980s the London Metropolitan Police had assigned 5 percent of its officers to "home beats" as "community constables." These constables were charged with developing an intimate knowledge of their beats, encouraging crime prevention, patrolling on foot, and building closer rapport with the community.[44]

See Exhibit 14-6 for another example.

Contemporary Approaches

A number of recent attempts in Great Britain have introduced problem-solving strategies in England and Wales. Following is an overview of past implementations of COPPS in five police forces. The lessons learned from these five locations were used to implement COPPS in Leicestershire.[45]

In London, the *Metropolitan Police* experiment involved the formation of a project team to define and diagnose specific problems, such as prostitution and motor vehicle crime, in four pilot sites. The problems were then addressed by dedicated teams that developed responses. Following riots in an area in *Northumbria* known for high crime and poor police–community relations, police established a dedicated COPPS unit to develop tactics; beat officers were given greater discretion and were encouraged to manage their time and think proactively to get to the root causes of the local problems. In *Thames Valley*, police graded call responses in order to "buy time" for COPPS, so that dedicated beat officers could identify problems. In *West Yorkshire*, COPPS was introduced in Killingbeck, Leeds, with the formation of two cohesive groups of beat officers who shared information and brainstormed local problems. The *Surrey Constabulary* has a long history of interest in COPPS.

Implementation of COPPS in *Leicestershire* and other subsequent venues was made difficult by the variations in the forms of COPPS adopted in the previously mentioned locations. Administrators had to decide between a wide or narrow geographical spread, a short- or long-term lifespan of the initiative, problem identification from the top down or bottom up, the introduction of problem-solving teams or the adoption of COPPS by all officers, and the identification of

---

EXHIBIT 14-6   Problem Solving in Merseyside

The impetus to pursue a problem-solving policing style in Merseyside, England, was stimulated by an operation to combat its increasing number of shootings. A project team was established in mid-1997 to consider how the problem-solving approach could be adopted across the entire force. The team produced a clearly defined philosophy of problem-solving policing; systems and structures that would support the adoption of problem-solving policing; a clear definition of the skills needed to deliver this policing style, with subsequent training needs; and a plan (and its costs) for implementation of the approach. The first task was to visit police agencies that had publicly professed to be using problem-solving policing to some degree. Next, a comprehensive internal consultation program was conducted to establish the current extent of problem-solving activity within the force, introduce the concept of problem solving, identify potential issues that would need consideration in order to adopt effective problem solving, and identify peoples' views on possible solutions to these issues. One-to-one interviews were conducted with all officers and heads of other operational and support departments. A series of focus group meetings was held with a cross-section of front-line staff from each police district, as well as with other citizens and agency heads—a very lengthy process. There was widespread support for adopting a problem-solving approach. Two areas appeared to be fundamental to the process: the identification of problems (including the provision of up-to-date information) and the need for training. Eventually the team produced recommendations in five broad areas: structure and organization of the force, systems and processes, information technology, human resources, and marketing. The adoption of COPPS as an "umbrella" philosophy in Merseyside represented a fundamental shift in policing.

Source: Adapted from Brian Gresty and Geoff Berry, "Problem-Solving Policing: The Merseyside Philosophy." In *Focus on Police Research and Development* (London: Home Office Police Research Group, 1998), pp. 12–13.

---

problems by the police or by the community and external agencies. In relation to these questions and concerns, the following premises of successful COPPS implementation have become accepted in Great Britain.

- COPPS can create more time for officers, because the source of problems is dealt with and CFS reduced.
- Deliberately and systematically introduced, COPPS can build on existing partnership work and yield increased benefits from it.
- Humane and efficient responses to individual incidents can occur alongside COPPS.
- Regardless of COPPS, the police still have to provide a wide-ranging service to the public, for which they will have to maintain their response to non-crime-related incidents.
- Police officers will find COPPS rewarding, and gradually the police culture will accept the centrality of COPPS.[46]

Cleveland Police and Problem Youth

Cleveland Police is the smallest force in the United Kingdom, covering an area of about 24,000 acres in northeast England. The Cleveland force employs 1,500 officers. Hartlepool is the most northerly city in the force area, located on the northeast coast, with a population of 90,000. Cleveland, and Hartlepool in particular, is at the top of almost every poverty index in the country. Most of the problems, furthermore, are centered on the Raby Gardens Housing Estates.[47]

In the late 1990s the police began looking at school truancy rates in Hartlepool: Fifty percent of the youths were offenders (the highest in the United Kingdom). One-half of the youths involved in crime were regularly absent from schools, and 58 percent of the youths had behavioral problems. Specifically, the youths of the Raby Estates area had low self-esteem; there was also a huge schism between the younger and older residents of the area and a lack of parental interest and control. These problems had existed for a number of years, and the police had, by their own admission, been merely "papering over the cracks" where these problems were concerned. The formation of a community policing team was the first movement toward forging a partnership with the community.

First, officers interviewed citizens who had contacted the police concerning problems with youths of the area; it was emphasized that they needed to identify who the youth were and what they were doing. The police promised extra policing and to try to ascertain whether something could be done for the youths. Interviews with the youths determined that they were bored and disillusioned with life. The police approached several public and private agencies to obtain funding to change things. Second, police identified the potential ringleaders and troublemakers and invited them and their friends from the Estates to a series of meetings. Eventually, the "Raby Rebels" was formed; it was composed of and run, policed, and organized by the young people. The Rebels formulated a set of rules that included behavioral boundaries. Meanwhile, legal proceedings were commenced against families who would not take control of their youths.

The most significant breakthrough for the police came when, at one of the Raby Rebels' meetings, the main complainants arrived. The complainants spoke to the group, explaining their side of the matter in a calm, positive way. They offered their support for the youths in the form of fundraising so the group could continue. This signaled the beginning of a new community spirit. After the meetings there were fewer calls per week pertaining to the youths.

COPPS IN OTHER VENUES

Scotland

Although overall crime had been decreasing in the Strathclyde region of Scotland, many of its 2.25 million citizens perceived that crime rates were increasing dramatically. Violent crimes, however, were increasing; and it became part of the culture of the west of Scotland to carry knives. The Strathclyde police—an amalgamation of six police forces in west central Scotland and the largest in the country—decided that it had to find a solution to the fear and violent crime problems.[48]

The Spotlight Initiative, the first program of its kind in the United Kingdom, was implemented with a "listening tour," as police sought to learn which types of crimes were of major concern to the public. The police learned that minor crimes—litter, graffiti, and disorderly gangs shouting obscenities, smashing bottles, and carrying weapons—worried them the most. From this, four fundamental principles of the initiative developed: It must address public concerns, fully exploit corporate partnerships, address serious crimes through concentration on minor crimes, and feature maximum presence of officers on the beat. Eleven major crimes were spotlighted as well.

Division commanders were immediately instructed to seek improved environmental clean-up resources to rid their areas of litter and graffiti. A media coverage campaign was launched to boost the public's and police officers' confidence. To attack minor crimes, the department made greater use of intelligence and crime management systems, employed new technology (such as satellite tracking systems, telephone bugs, and high-definition night-time cameras), and worked with every group with a legitimate interest in reducing crime.

On the day the program was operationalized, officers arrested almost 400 men and women in a series of dawn raids, targeting people who had "forgotten" to appear in court or for whom bench warrants had been issued. Police searched 43,000 people for weapons in the first three months (with the number of people carrying weapons declining about 50 percent). Truancy rates at local schools declined dramatically. The department installed a series of closed-circuit cameras in high-crime areas. Crime declined as well, and more drugs were recovered than ever before. The department was quite pleased with its results.[49]

Isle of Man

Even very small countries have COPPS. One such example is the Isle of Man—part of the British Isles and situated midway between England, Scotland, Ireland, and Wales—which has a land mass of only 227 square miles, measures 33 miles by 13 miles, and is occupied by only 73,000 people.

The Isle of Man Constabulary has large aims, however. Its 2000/2001 Policing Plan reveals its vision:

> We will provide a world-class, community-based policing service to the whole of the Island's community. Cooperation, consultation, and a partnership approach will drive all that we do, helping to make the Island an even safer place in which to live. Our aim: to be a world-class police service. What we will offer: community-based policing excellence.

The constabulary's values statement is also brief but powerful:

> Ours is an organization that is open, honest, and caring. The organization itself, and those who work for it, view integrity as being vital to our success.

A constable from the Isle of Man converses with a citizen while walking a footbeat in a city's business district. (*Courtesy* Isle of Man police department)

And its policing style and philosophy are as follows:

> We aim to provide excellence in all that we do. Our policing style will be friendly, approachable, and neighborly, offering the best possible service to the whole of the Island's community. The main driver will be a problem solving approach, both internally and externally.[50]

These may seem to be ambitious statements, but when one views these words in conjunction with the total package of materials that the constabulary has developed and disseminated to its populace—as well as its *Strategic Plan, 2000–2003*—as part of an "extensive program of modernization underpinned by the philosophy of continuous improvement," there can be little doubt as to the sincerity of the organization's resolve.

Israel

In the mid-1990s the police in Israel, providing services to about 5.5 million people, decided to change from a basically reactive form of policing to COPPS, knowing it would not be easy. The national police force had been, for the previous 20 years, engulfed in security duties by virtue of terrorist and other emergency matters. Because of a shifting of police resources to antiterrorist and bomb-disposal units, efforts to reduce crime at the local station level had not been successful, and domestic violence and family abuse had become particularly problematic.[51]

A strategic plan was developed to implement COPPS. A new headquarters unit was established to implement the planned change, beginning with a "bottom-up" approach that would start with the station level and officers in the field, because they best knew the communities' problems. In phase one, the local police and mayors of many communities were approached and asked if they were willing to undertake the change to COPPS. Their enthusiasm was usually high. Then the officers and selected community leaders were trained in the working principles of COPPS. Such training included explanations of the need for the police and the public to collaborate, and the problem-solving approach to analyzing and addressing problems.

A three-day planning workshop was then held with the police and with community and local organizations and associations. Each police station's mission statement was developed, and local problems and needs were scanned, prioritized, and analyzed. The strategic plan was then developed, including timetables, responsible persons, and needed resources. Each police station was to work on 10 objectives during a six-month period.[52]

By the second year of its implementation across Israel, more than 50 communities had undergone the shift to COPPS. Cities were "rewarded" by being allowed to send one person abroad to study COPPS in other countries. Furthermore, the shift to COPPS had advanced to such an extent that the decision was made to effect the shift at the senior management (police headquarters) level. The atmosphere there, however, was not so enthusiastic, being more of a "business as usual" attitude, while the local police stations went about their "quiet revolution." Planning workshops were provided and headquarters' objectives were developed, leading to greater acceptance of the new philosophy. Community Policing Centers were set up in neighborhoods to decentralize services, and a major organizational change occurred, resulting in a greater flattening of the force, to empower local levels and to provide more efficient and effective police services.[53]

Hong Kong

Hong Kong's population is about 6.4 million, making it one of the most densely populated places in the world—up to 25,000 people per square mile in the urban areas.[54]

Hong Kong began practicing some forms of COPPS in the 1960s, with its early policing style being typical of British colonial policing. The result was a series of police–community relations initiatives that were launched in the late 1960s, with a view to improving police–public relations, developing popular trust, and cultivating public support for crime control. During 40 years of evolution of community policing, the Hong Kong police force has undergone six stages, involving five major community policing schemes with different focuses:

1. the Police Community Relations Officer (PCRO), a community relations program, focusing on the promotion of police–public relations
2. the Neighbourhoods Police Unit (NPU), a crime control device with the objective of providing convenient locations for the public to report criminal activities to the police and offer support for combating crime
3. the Junior Police Call (JPC), centering on the control of juvenile delinquency and including a range of activities and programs for youth
4. the Police School Liaison (PSL), dealing with juvenile crimes in school by working with students, authorities, and teachers
5. the Neighbourhood Watch (NW), which organized local residents' efforts to control and prevent burglaries and sexual offenses[55]

The first stage of community policing for Hong Kong occurred from 1968 to 1973. With the relaxation of police–public tension as the theme, the police established the Police Public Information Bureau. The second stage was the adoption of a community orientation in crime control that signaled Hong

Kong's entering the era of community policing. The focus was on two-way communication, and the PCRO marked the first major attempt by the police to reach community members and involve them in crime fighting.

The third stage was the rapid growth of community policing across Hong Kong. The PCRO was quickly expanded to cover every police district, and the JPC, the PSL, and the NPU concepts were launched. The fourth stage was the retrenchment of the police–community relations effort briefly from 1983 to 1985. The focus was on the reorganization of tight police resources for effective crime control. NPUs were replaced by a small scale of Neighborhood Police Coordinators (NPCs)—viewed widely as a step backward from the force's previous police strategy.

The fifth stage involved reassessment, during which community policing was under a severe test in a tight resource situation. There was a lack of consensus among police administration concerning the proper role of community relations activities within the broader context of crime control. The introduction of NW and the restoration of PSL indicated, however, that community policing had remained a preferred strategy for policing the society. The sixth stage was reorientation, with community relations affirmed as the key aspect of the policing strategy. The focus of this stage has been the improvement of the police's public image and collaborative police–public working relationships for crime control.

Today, the PCROs have taken an active role in liaisoning with community leaders, and the NPC police have attempted to work with community members. The JPC officers have devoted their full attention to approaching young people, and the PSLs have engaged most of their time in keeping close contact with schools and schoolchildren. The NW is probably the weakest among all of these programs in terms of communication with the community. Police officers seem more approachable through the NPU and NPC concepts, and the PCRO remains the backbone of the police dedication to COPPS.

Despite these favorable reports, however, there are problems. Although the force recognizes the need for harmony with the public, the organizational commitment to COPPS still appears to be limited because of the lack of a long-term vision for the strategy. There is a strong temporary outlook for the NPU, the PSL, and the NW concepts, and a shortage of well-thought-out action for the PSL and NW schemes. There has not been any rigorous evaluation of the effectiveness of any of these approaches. Furthermore, because of a lack of incentive measures to motivate police officers for COPPS work, they evidence a lack of knowledge and commitment.

Several lessons can be learned from this case study. Hong Kong entered into community policing nearly four decades ago for the primary purpose of obtaining public support for ordering the society. Five major policy schemes have evolved to translate this strategy into action, but they have met with limited success. This lack of progress in the force's COPPS strategy and the limited performance of its policy initiatives are mainly due to the force's pragmatic approach of using COPPS initiatives for the sole purpose of crime control and prevention. Without proper public support, consultation, and participation, COPPS will fall short in attempting to provide a mechanism for addressing crime and disorder.

New Zealand

COPPS has been designated as the principal operational strategy for the delivery of police services by the New Zealand police, as set forth in the organization's Corporate Plan of 1994–1995. The police mission statement is "To serve the community by reducing the incidence and effects of crime, detecting and apprehending offenders, maintaining law and order and enhancing public safety."[56] Its values statement is to "Maintain the highest level of integrity and professionalism; respect individual rights and freedoms; consult with, and be responsive to, the needs of the community; uphold the rule of law; and be culturally sensitive."[57] Furthermore, its strategic goals for 1993 to 1998 included the implementation of community oriented policing and states that COPPS "will remain the primary policing strategy for service delivery . . . aimed at reversing the upward crime trends of the last three decades."[58]

The New Zealand Police COPPS strategy includes the following.

- *Change style of policing:* Police as individuals and groups work to form a partnership with the community, identify issues and problems, innovate solutions, and share perspectives with the community.
- *Localize resources:* Establish smaller police stations in major areas and community policing centers in communities.
- *Enhance patrol and investigation strategies:* Determine and implement patrol objectives and strategies, adopt appropriate patrol assignments according to time of day and so on, and establish community-based investigators (who will focus on communities rather than type of crime).
- *Engage in problem solving:* Apply the S.A.R.A. model.
- *Adopt a new management style:* Managers are to have a commitment to COPPS, encourage bottom-up innovation, and attend COPPS training and education.[59]

THE NETHERLANDS

Significant changes in Dutch society have ushered in a period of considerable experiment and innovation. The Netherlands is a small country (its population is 16 million), with virtually open borders, a multicultural population, and a high standard of living. Its police are regionalized in 25 forces, with one national service for certain national tasks. Amsterdam, with 5,600 officers, is the largest regional force. The policing style is generally laid back, fairly tolerant, nonviolent, and negotiation plays a vital role. Dutch officers are normally well trained and speak several languages.

The most recent step in the development of COPPS in the Netherlands has been the introduction of the community beat officer. In the new philosophy, the proximity to the public, citizen involvement in dealing with crime problems, and police working with local public and private agencies are given great importance. New is the extensive cooperation with external partners and strong involvement of citizens in determining what issues should be addressed. But perhaps most important is the shift in responsibility. Whereas the former beat constable was "just an ordinary cop," the community officer is held responsible for "organizing security" in his or her area. If he or she needs assistance from colleagues in specialized departments, those specialists are obliged to help. Responsibility is thus pushed down to a lower level in the organization.

Recently, Amsterdam—the capital city of the Netherlands with a population of 800,000—experienced growing problems. Amsterdam is a major tourist center, with many headquarters of companies and businesses, a diverse population, a large number of retail stores, a renowned red light district, and "coffee shops" where soft drugs can be purchased. Street crimes began increasing on busy streets and in public transport and nightspot areas.

It was decided to establish one police district for the entire inner city area, with six neighborhood teams consisting of 700 officers. As part of this new inner city district, a special support team of 75 officers was tasked with the responsibility of maintaining public order in the entire district. Officers in this team could be sent into places where temporary disruptions of public order were anticipated. This team was to regain authority and bring back a sense of norms, with a low tolerance for small breaches of law (such as is espoused in James Q. Wilson and George Kelling's "broken windows" theory, discussed in Chapter 5). For instance, urinating in public became public enemy number one after such behavior was held even to be undermining the foundations of the historic sixteenth century buildings in the downtown area (today, portable urinals are placed at such "hot spots"). This zero-tolerance approach to infractions contradicted a long tradition of leniency towards deviance of the social order.

A fundamental question is whether this new policy is compatible with COPPS. It is argued that the "community" agrees that the police should take strong action against those who do not comply with community norms and laws. Conversely, some residents believe that the city has given the area away to the tourist industry and the "night-time economy," and that newcomers are complainers who want to take away the fun of the area.

Given the large number of noisy drunken youths, motorists massively ignoring traffic regulations, numerous pickpockets targeting tourists, local drug addicts who shoot up and deal in drugs in the area, homeless and mentally ill individuals who become aggressive on the streets, the police had to do something. Still, the police try to put on a "personal face" and get involved in community meetings and cooperate with other agencies and the local government in dealing with these social problems that have become more complex than just crime.[60]

SUMMARY

This chapter discussed COPPS as it has developed internationally. Several common themes or practices are identifiable: the taking of police from their "mechanized fortresses" and putting them into closer contact with the public (together engaging in the use of problem-solving methods), decentralizing the organization to areas and neighborhoods, developing a sense of "community," and sharing decision making (empowerment) with the public. We also saw that some venues initiated a pilot project before implementing the concept department-wide; another common denominator seemed to be the need for sound evaluations of community and problem oriented policing to determine what works.

Finally, this chapter has shown that the community and problem-solving approach is not that different in foreign venues from what it is in the United States. Perhaps most important, this chapter demonstrated that we are indeed learning from, and sharing with, one another. We are a "global village"; we hope this spirit of scholarly interaction will continue. We should also be mindful, however, that the foreign experience is not necessarily a recipe for Americans to replicate; rather, it can serve as a point of departure in considering what is feasible.[61] These venues offer an opportunity for us to examine issues that might arise as COPPS continues to spread across the United States.

NOTES

1. Mark Kesselman, "Order or Movement? The Literature of Political Development as Ideology," *World Politics* 26 (1973):139–154.
2. Barry Leighton, "Community Policing: The Canadian Experience" (paper presented at the Third Research and Development Conference, Toronto, Canada, etc. April 10, 1996).
3. Ibid.
4. Ibid.
5. Ibid.

6. Ibid.

7. Ibid.

8. *http://burnabynow.com/102202/news/102202nn16 .html* (Accessed May 29, 2003).

9. Vancouver police department, application for the Herman Goldstein Award for Excellence in Problem-Oriented Policing, April 1999.

10. Greg Saville, personal communication, October 11, 1993.

11. Vancouver, B.C., Royal Canadian Mounted Police, *RCMP Community Policing: Strategic Action Plan Update, 1992–1995* (June 1993), pp. 3–5.

12. Richard J. Terrill, *World Criminal Justice Systems: A Survey* (5th ed.) (Cincinnati: Anderson, 2003), p. 373.

13. Jerome H. Skolnick and David H. Bayley, *Community Policing: Issues and Practices around the World* (Washington, D.C.: National Institute of Justice, 1988).

14. Terrill, *World Criminal Justice Systems*, pp. 378–380.

15. Ted D. Westermann and James W. Burfeind, *Crime and Justice in Two Societies: Japan and the United States* (Pacific Grove, Calif.: Brooks/Cole, 1991), p. 157.

16. Ibid.

17. David H. Bayley, *Forces of Order: Police Behavior in Japan and the United States* (Berkeley, Calif.: University of California Press, 1991), p. 87.

18. Westermann and Burfeind, *Crime and Justice in Two Societies*, p. 159.

19. George L. Kelling, Robert Wasserman, and Hubert Williams, "Police Accountability and Community Policing," *Perspectives on Policing*, No. 7 (November). U.S. Department of Justice. (Washington, D.C.: U.S. Government Printing Office, 1988).

20. "Community Police Activities of Japan" (Tokyo: National Police Agency of Japan, 1992), pp. 2, 9.

21. Ibid., p. 5

22. David H. Bayley, *A Model of Community Policing: The Singapore Story* (Washington, D.C.: U.S. Department of Justice, National Institute of Justice, 1989), p. 8.

23. Skolnick and Bayley, *Community Policing*, p. 9.

24. Bayley, *Forces of Order*, Ch. 2.

25. W. Ames, *Police and the Community in Japan* (Berkeley, Calif.: University of California Press, 1981), p. 39.

26. New South Wales Bureau of Criminal Statistics, 1996.

27. *Stopbreak*. Queensland Police Service, North Coast Region, application for the Herman Goldstein Award for Excellence in Problem-Oriented Policing, 1999.

28. Paul Williams, Paul White, Michael Treece, and Robert Kitto, "Problem-Oriented Policing: Operation Mantle—A Case Study, " *Australian Institute of Criminology: Trend and Issues in Crime and Criminal Justice*, No. 190 (February 2001):1–6.

29. Criminal Justice Commission, *Toowoomba Beat Policing Pilot Project: Main Evaluation Report* (Brisbane, Australia: Author, 1995), p. ix.

30. *http://www.police.tas.gov.au/police/police2001.nsf.W .Resources* (Accessed May 29, 2003).

31. Her Majesty's Stationery Office, "Police Reform: A Police Service for the Twenty-First Century" (June 1993):41.

32. Adrian Leigh, Tim Read, and Nick Tilley, *Brit POP II: Problem-Oriented Policing in Practice* (London: Home Office Police Research Group, 1998), p. 1.

33. Ibid., p. iii.

34. Mollie Weatheritt, "Community Policing: Rhetoric or Reality?" In *Community Policing: Rhetoric or Reality?* Jack R. Greene and Stephen D. Mastrofski (eds.) (New York: Praeger, 1988), pp. 153–174.

35. Ibid., pp. 155–156.

36. Ibid., p. 161.

37. Quoted in Herman Goldstein, *Problem Oriented Policing* (New York: McGraw-Hill, 1990), p. 54.

38. M. A. Hoare, G. Stewart, and C. M. Purcell, *The Problem Oriented Approach: Four Pilot Studies* (London: Metropolitan Police, Management Services Department, 1984), Summary.

39. Ibid., p. 55.

40. Kenneth Newman, *The Principles of Policing and Guidance for Professional Behavior* (London: The Metropolitan Police, 1985), p. 12.

41. Quoted in ibid., p. 165.

42. Ibid., pp. 153–174.

43. Ibid.

44. Skolnick and Bayley, *Community Policing*, p. 30.

45. Adrian Leigh, Tim Read, and Nick Tilley, *Problem-Oriented Policing: Brit POP* (London: Home Office Police Research Group, 1996), pp. 4–5.

46. Ibid., pp. 39–40.

47. Cleveland Police, Throston Community Policing Team, *Raby Rebels Youth Project*, application for the Herman Goldstein Award for Excellence in Problem-Oriented Policing, 1998.

48. Arthur G. Sharp, "Putting a Shine on 'Spotlight,'" *Law and Order* (November 1999):75.

49. Ibid.

50. Isle of Man Police Constabulary, *Strategic Plan 2000–2003* (Isle of Man:Author, 2000), pp. 2–3.

51. Ruth Geva, "Community Policing in Israel," *The Police Chief* (December 1998):77.

52. Ibid.

53. Ibid., p. 80. Also, for an excellent discussion of community policing in Israel, which explains the difficulties in encountering resistance of traditional military-style organizational culture as well as a lack of organizational commitment to community policing, see David Weisburd, Orit Shalev, and Menachem Amir, "Community Policing in Israel: Resistance and Change," *Policing: An International Journal of Police Strategies and Management* 15(1) (2002):80–109.

54. *http://hongkongnet/Directory/Facts/Population/population.html* (September 17, 2000).

55. Hong Kong Police, *Community Policing in Hong Kong: An Institutional Analysis* (Hong Kong: Author, no date).

56. New Zealand Police, *Corporate Plan, 1994–1995* (no date, author, or location given), p. 7.

57. Ibid., p. 10.

58. New Zealand Police, *Strategic Plan, 1993–1998, Reference Version* (no date, author, or location), p. 2.

59. Ibid., pp. 16–17.

60. Maurice Punch, Kees van der Vijver, and Olga Zoomer, "Dutch 'COP': Developing Community Policing in the Netherlands," *Policing: An International Journal of Police Strategies and Management* 25(1):(2002)60–79.

61. Bayley, *A Model of Community Policing,* p. 29.

INTRODUCTION

It has been said that the only thing that is permanent is change. Perhaps more than anything else, this book has demonstrated that axiom. Even the historically tradition-bound domain of policing has been shown to be dynamic, as is the general American society in which it exists.

But much work remains to be done. The question that should be at the forefront of our minds, and that of the police, is: "What will the future bring?" This question becomes even more poignant and ominous when we consider the world's present state of affairs.

Our choice is either to ignore the future until it is upon us, or to try to anticipate what the future might bring and gear our resources to cope with it. Predicting the future is not easy, however. Many variables, such as war, terrorism, high technology, and economic upheaval, can greatly affect even the most sound predictions and established trends. What we hope to do in this chapter, therefore, is to try to explain why a future orientation is important for community oriented policing and problem solving (COPPS), and discuss some areas in which the police must be foresighted. Indeed, this chapter poses more questions than it answers.

Thus we begin by considering why it is important to study the future in policing, and then look at several forecasts and questions for policing in this era of COPPS. Several fundamental aspects of COPPS are considered, with a number of issues posed in the areas of personnel, technology, and organizational structure. The chapter concludes with a case study.

—15—

LOOKING FORWARD WHILE LOOKING BACK

The Future

At every crossing on the road, each progressive spirit is opposed by a thousand appointed to guard the gates of the past.
—MAURICE MAETERLINCK

WHY CONSIDER THE FUTURE?

We all think about the future as a normal part of everyday living. We attend classes to better our future life, schedule meetings and appointments, consider our retirement programs, prepare notes for classes and speeches, and even pay our bills as a hedge against problems on the morrow. The trouble is that when the future finally arrives, we often find that it has had a way of being far different from our expectations; we simply did not plan effectively.

The future is therefore a dynamic and amorphous concept, making us unsure of what lies ahead. To use the driving experience as an analogy, we must constantly look at and be aware of several aspects of the road ahead—our speed and that of other drivers, traffic signals and signs, weather and road conditions—in order to reach our destination. And we certainly cannot afford to plummet into the next century with our eyes firmly fixed on the rearview mirror!

And so it is with police administration generally, as well as with COPPS. Historically, the primary role of many administrators in the public sector has seemingly been to maintain the status quo. But on close inspection we realize that reliance on the status quo will not prepare us for the future. Previous chapters of this book, dealing with all kinds of issues, have made clear the need for having strategies for future problems. We have learned from changing demographics and crime, terrorist attacks, riots, financial cutbacks, natural and manmade disasters, strikes, and other exigencies that we must anticipate the future, plan for the unknown, and expect the unforeseen. Furthermore, factors such as locale, political environment, and economics will determine how an agency and its employees will view and react to the future.

For 45,000 years humankind huddled in the darkness of caves, afraid to take that first step into the light of day. Police leadership must now be out in front, pointing the way for others to follow, not waiting for someone else to set the pace.[1] These administrators also shoulder the responsibility for seeing that the best and brightest individuals are recruited, trained, and become the best they possibly can be in their performance. And they must have a vision for how those individuals—and the ever-evolving high technology that they will be using—may be directed in the most efficient, just manner.

Defining solutions to the problems facing future police service is difficult at best. This challenge is made even more difficult because of the fact that, for some police leaders, the future is the next fiscal year, while for others it is a three- to five-year span of time toward which they have set into motion a strategic planning process; but for others, the future is next Friday and means surviving without a crisis until their next day off. Any discussion of the future must include the short term as well as the long term and give attention to operational issues, administrative issues, the community, and the basic philosophy of policing.

FORECASTS AND QUESTIONS FOR THE COPPS ERA

Several Fundamental Issues

The first priority for the police who adopted COPPS was to realize that the conventional style of reactive, incident-driven policing employed during the professional era had several drawbacks. That former type of police department was hierarchical, impersonal, and rule-based, and most important policy decisions were made at the top; line officers made few decisions on their own. Some departments may continue to struggle with the decision to initiate, and the challenges of implementing, COPPS; this approach may be passed off as a fad, or implemented as a series of temporary programs, simply to take advantage of the available federal funding and create a positive image.

Although this book has looked at COPPS from many different perspectives, many fundamental questions remain. For example, will more police agencies make a commitment to implement this strategy? Some authors point to what they believe are several unfavorable social forces that militate against the future of COPPS: local governments being pushed toward a more legalistic, crime-control model of policing; a public that is less willing to pay more taxes to address fundamental social problems; and a public policy that does not allow the police to focus on the root causes of crimes, but rather on their symptom—criminal conduct—through aggressive strategies rather than through COPPS.[2] How many agencies have demonstrated the link between community policing and the quality of the communities they serve? How many have embraced community policing to gain a share of available federal dollars? Will community policing endure without federal funding? How many agencies will consider the importance of COPPS in a new world that carries the constant threat of domestic terrorism (discussed below)?

Similarly, this book has also mentioned in several chapters the federal office of Community Oriented Policing Services (COPS), created by the Violent Crime Control and Law Enforcement Act of 1994, which has helped many agencies to

A bumper sticker funded by the federal office of Community Oriented Policing Services shows the relationship between COPPS and homeland defense.

implement COPPS, added tens of thousands of officers to the beat, and provided them with technical assistance, technology, equipment, and training. As with any federally funded program, however, the duration of this office's survival remains in question, and any police agency whose COPPS efforts hinge on or revolve around federal funds may find itself in desperate straits in the future.

Another central issue with respect to COPPS concerns community partnerships. Much of society, including the police, has come to realize that the police cannot function independently to address crime and disorder. The challenge to leaders, now and in the future, is to develop meaningful and lasting partnerships rather than the superficial relationships that exist in many communities. For many police officers, the concept of partnership means simply attending occasional neighborhood association meetings or occasionally visiting neighborhood leaders who live on their beat. Partnerships for the sake of partnership do not endure; they will only work when the mutual benefits to the parties involved are well defined, well understood, and attainable. Furthermore, it must be remembered that partnerships must include other city and county departments, businesses, and social service agencies; these entities are vital if COPPS is to survive and thrive. Other important issues include whether police chief executives will change the culture of their agencies, decentralize their department (pushing decision making downward), invest in the necessary technology for locating "hot spots," and develop the necessary mechanisms to support COPPS.

Other challenges involve police personnel policy, including recruitment, selection, training, performance appraisals, and reward and promotional systems. It is also necessary that police unions work with administrators to effect the kinds of changes that are needed for COPPS. In addition to these personnel challenges, other related and traditional personnel problems are not likely to go away either. Such matters as the need for more women and minorities in police service, unionization and job actions, civilianization, accreditation, and higher education will not be resolved in the near future. A related need and challenge involves bringing more people of different ethnicities into policing, including Russians, South Africans, Baltic nationalities, and Asians. Some metropolitan areas, such as Los Angeles, are composed of people of more than 100 cultures. Furthermore, changing societal values, court decisions concerning the rights of employees, and the Peace Officers' Bill of Rights will make leadership increasingly challenging. How these issues are addressed could be critical, not only to the future of COPPS but also to policing in general.

COPPS and Homeland Defense

Regarding terrorism and policing after September 11, 2001, it is important to note the principle of policing that must NOT change in the future: recruiting candidates who are or show very strong promise of becoming intellectually and morally qualified to bear the public trust, thorough and unhurried training, and effective supervision. History has shown that departure from these practices damages police agencies; September 11 did not change the need for any of this.[3] And while traumatic events like the September 11 attacks can cause police organizations to fall back on more traditional methods of doing business, and even abandon COPPS altogether for seemingly more immediate security concerns, COPPS should play a central role in the defense of our homeland. Because COPPS helps to build trust between police and their communities, deals more effectively with community concerns, and helps the police to develop knowledge of community activity, the problem-solving model is well suited to the prevention of terrorism. Departments can use a wide variety of data sources to proactively develop detailed risk management and crisis response plans.[4]

Homeland Security Advisory System
http://www.homelandsecurity.org/

Red: **Severe**	✓ **Complete recommended actions at lower levels** ✓ Listen to radio/TV for current information/instructions ✓ Be alert to suspicious activity and report it to proper authorities immediately ✓ Contact business/school to determine status of work/school day ✓ Adhere to any travel restrictions announced by local governmental authorities ✓ Be prepared to shelter in place or evacuate if instructed to do so by local governmental authorities ✓ Discuss children's fears concerning possible/actual terrorist attacks
Orange: **High**	✓ **Complete recommended actions at lower levels** ✓ Be alert to suspicious activity and report it to proper authorities ✓ Review disaster plan with all family members ✓ Ensure communication plan is understood/practiced by all family members ✓ Exercise caution when traveling ✓ Have shelter in place, materials on hand, and review procedure in **Terrorism: Preparing for the Unexpected** brochure ✓ Discuss children's fears concerning possible terrorist attacks ✓ If a need is announced, donate blood at designated blood collection center
Yellow: **Elevated**	✓ **Complete recommended actions at lower levels** ✓ Be alert to suspicious activity and report it to proper authorities ✓ Ensure disaster supplies kit is stocked and ready ✓ Check telephone numbers and e-mail addresses in your family emergency communication plan ✓ If not known to you, contact school to determine their emergency notification and evacuation plans for children ✓ Develop alternate routes to/from school/work and practice them
Blue: **Guarded**	✓ **Complete recommended actions at lower levels** ✓ Be alert to suspicious activity and report it to proper authorities ✓ Review stored disaster supplies and replace items that are outdated ✓ Develop an emergency communication plan that all family members understand ✓ Establish an alternative meeting place away from home with family/friends
Green: **Low**	✓ Obtain copy of **Terrorism: Preparing for the Unexpected** brochure from your local Red Cross chapter ✓ Develop a personal disaster plan and disaster supplies kit using Red Cross brochures Your Family Disaster Plan and Your Family Disaster Supplies Kit

The federal office of Community Oriented Policing Services assists police with understanding the Homeland Security Advisory System color codes.

A Metamorphosis?

Some futurists see COPPS addressing several of these issues in the future, with policing undergoing a metamorphosis in the following ways.

- Ethics and ethical leadership will be woven into everything the police do: the hiring process, field training officer programs, decision-making processes. There will be increased emphasis on accountability and integrity within police agencies as policing is elevated to a higher standing, reaching more toward being a true profession and, concomitantly, the majority of officers being required to possess a college degree.

- Formal awards ceremonies will concentrate as much (or more) on improving citizens' quality of life as on felony arrests or other high-risk activities.

- Communications will be greatly improved through internal "intranets," containing local and agency operational data, phone books, maps, calendars, calls for service, crime data sheets, speeches, newsletters, news releases, and so forth.

- Major cities will no longer require policing experience of the chief police executive (being recruited from private industry). The head of the future police agency will essentially be recognized as a CEO with good business sense as a trend toward privatization of certain services becomes more prevalent. Knowledge will continue to increase at lightning speed, forcing the CEO to be involved in trend analysis and forecasting in order to keep ahead of the curve.

- The rigid paramilitary style currently effective will become obsolete, replaced by work teams consisting of line officers, community members, and business and corporate representatives.

- The current squad structure will give way to more productive, creative teams of officers who, having been empowered with more autonomy, will become efficient problem solvers, thus strengthening ties between the police and the citizenry.

- Neighborhoods will more actively participate in the identification, location, and capture of criminals.[5]

Role of the Rank-and-File

It would be a tremendous oversight to fail to mention the role of rank-and-file officers among the changes to be witnessed in future police service. For many reasons—including the fact that future generations will have been raised to be at ease and fluent with information technologies, as well as their entering a police service that is much more involved with collective bargaining—future generations of police officers will be vastly different from those of the past.

In the past—particularly under the professional model of policing—while undergoing the academy phase of their training, recruits adopted a new identity and a system of discipline in which they learned to take orders and not to question authority. Indeed, much of the emphasis was on submission to authority. Recruits learned that loyalty to fellow officers, a professional demeanor and bearing, and respect for authority were, and still are, highly valued qualities. That theme—and the police executive's set of expectations for recruits—must change, however. In the future, officers will be hired only if they can think critically, plan, and evaluate. At the same time, chiefs, sheriffs, commanders, and even sergeants will wield less coercive power and control and filter less information; instead, they will be encouraged to ask questions and engage in lifelong learning, and move into enhanced roles as coaches, supporters, and resource developers.[6]

People entering police service in the future will not usually possess military experience with its inherent obedience to authority, but they will have higher levels of education and will tend to be more independent and less responsive to traditional authoritarian leadership styles. These recruits will have been exposed to more participative, supportive, and humanistic approaches; they will want more opportunities to provide input into their work and to address the challenges posed by problem solving. The autocratic leadership style of the past professional era of policing will not work today or in the future. The watchwords of the new leadership paradigm are coaching, inspiring, gaining commitment, empowering, affirming, being flexible, bearing responsibility, self-managing, power sharing, and being autonomous and entrepreneurial. Therefore, a major need for police leadership will be the surrendering of power to lower-ranking employees in a flattened organizational hierarchy (discussed below).

Police officers of the future will also function in very different ways and on very different terms than officers of the past. Given existing technologies and what they bode for the future, every officer will function with few time and space constraints, because all officers will be equipped with a pager, cellular phone, personal data assistant, and laptop computer with software that includes encryption programs, sophisticated databases, and search engines. These officers will be able to have "real-time" chats with officers from other agencies or in other states or even countries. Every rookie, before going on the streets, will be thoroughly computer literate and able to use crime analysis software.[7]

With such tools, it is easy to envision an officer's home, car, or convenience store becoming his or her workplace. Identification of suspects in the field will take a quantum leap with electronic telecommunication of fingerprints, scanning of retinal patterns, and facial ratio and heat patterns that say positively, "This is the bad guy." Officers will also access maps and data; be able to bring up any call, crime type, or problem by geographic area; and sort this information and compare similar incidents. They will be able to touch their computer keys and ask for the top 10 crimes in their beat area, while receiving instant crime analysis for use in deployment and other operational decisions. All civilians will likewise be trained in computer use.[8]

Exhibit 15-1 provides an example of what one community has done to formally plan for the future.

EXHIBIT 15-1   Twenty-First Century Police Department: Naperville, Illinois

Over the past decade, companies in the manufacturing, entertainment, and defense industries have used a tool called "process mapping" to help them describe, analyze, and, ultimately, improve how their organizations operate. Recently, members of the city of Naperville, Illinois, police department and 23 other police agencies were invited to attend training in process mapping, which involves the development of three different flowcharts that visually depict the series of activities involved in carrying out one of the organization's major functions.

- The as-is map describes the organization as it currently exists. This map is based on interviews and observations of people and is used to diagnose waste, duplication of effort, coordination of problems, or breakdowns in the flow of information.
- The should-be map makes short-term changes to reduce waste, remove duplication, and improve coordination and flow of information. This map is based on management analysis of the as-is map

and suggestions gathered from field personnel during interviews.
- The could-be map describes the ideal process for the future. This map is based on the organization's vision and highlights the long-term changes that are needed to get there.

As an example, Naperville is focusing on "crime solving" as the major function to be mapped and is focusing on one crime type: burglary. Process mapping allows the agency to increase the clearance rate for crimes by identifying areas where new work methods or organizational changes might improve police ability to investigate crimes and arrest offenders. It also makes more widespread and effective use of automation and technology by identifying areas where work processes can be improved, such as automated case reporting.

Source: City of Naperville, Illinois, Web page, "Twenty-First Century Police Department," 1997, pp. 1–2. *http://www.naperville.il.us* (Accessed April 29, 2003).

High Technology

In previous chapters we mentioned technology as it relates to crime analyses and determining hot spots. But other challenges come with technology as well. Certainly the advent of computer crime has changed with the world of policing, posing new and extraordinary challenges. The current high-tech revolution in our homes and offices has not only enhanced our lives but also opened a whole new world for the criminal element. Pornographers and pedophiles are now on the Web, as well as people who trade stolen credit card numbers, rig auctions, create viruses, and devise baby adoption scams, among many other crimes. Computer crimes will increase dramatically, including such crimes as cyber-terrorism, identity theft, credit card fraud, consumer fraud, stock market–related fraud, and industrial espionage; these crimes may well become the next national crime-fighting obsessions.

Many police organizations lack the in-house computer expertise to install or run software and equipment. Many agency executives feel that they only hire people to be police officers, not to be computer programmers or database experts. But as the nature of crime changes, people with such skills are not only desirable but are also a *necessity* as a problem-solving aid.

Exhibit 15-2 shows what might very well be a wave of the future: "online communities" for improving COPPS.

Flattening the Organization

An area of debate among futurists concerns organizational structure. Increasing numbers of executives—particularly in the very paramilitary, hierarchical police organizations—are beginning to question whether or not the traditional "pyramid" shaped bureaucracy will be effective in the future. Others believe that flattening the organizational structure is ill-advised, and the focus should instead be on accountability at all levels. Nonetheless, communication within the pyramid structure is often confronted with many barriers and frustrated by the levels of bureaucracy; perhaps the organizational structure, the argument

Laptop computers and video cameras are advanced technologies that are being installed in patrol vehicles by many agencies. (*Courtesy* Kris Solow, City of Charlotte, North Carolina)

EXHIBIT 15-2 On-line Communities Improve COPPS

When a neighbor recently posted a shaky though unmistakable photograph of a burglar skulking from a house on the Web site of a neighborhood in southeast Washington, D.C., community policing forever changed there. The photo helped police arrest a suspect, and it established on-line neighborhood communities as a way for citizens and beat officers to interact. "Parking your patrol car on the block and walking up and down, knocking on doors, that's just so Flintstones," said Lt. Keith Roch. "It makes no sense to do that when you can talk to 2,000 people on-line at once." The District recently obtained a $283,000 federal grant to create a network of interactive Web sites for each of the city's areas, which will also provide on-line access to records and statistics for each neighborhood and block. The police are mindful, however, that face-to-face contact can never be replaced, and that on-line connections between police and residents also can raise sticky issues. For example, such high-tech communication might leave less-connected residents in the dark; also, officers assigned to "patrol" their beats electronically may walk their beats less often. Furthermore, on-line forums can become conduits for libelous neighborhood gossip. Nonetheless, the District and other communities are moving ahead with plans to expand their on-line connections with the people they protect, and believe that the benefits far outweigh potential detriment.

Source: Adapted from Petula Dvorak, "Online Communities Improve Neighborhood Policing," *http://washingtonpost.com/ac2/wp-dvn?pagename=article&node=&contentld-A336* (Accessed April 28, 2003).

goes, could be changed to a more horizontal design to facilitate the flow of information and ideas. Indeed, the spread of COPPS has allowed many police executives to flatten their organizations.

Advancements in hand-held computer devices will greatly enhance supervisors' management and communications capabilities. (*Courtesy* Reno, Nevada, police department)

It may be fairly said that several questions for the future remain concerning COPPS:

- Will those police organizations that have not as yet done so come to believe that they alone cannot control crime and truly enlist the aid of the community in this endeavor?

- Will police chief executives that have not as yet done so acquire the innovative drive necessary to change the culture of their departments, implement COPPS, flatten the organizational structure of their department, and see that officers' work is properly evaluated?

- Will police organizations become learning organizations (discussed in Chapter 8) that can adapt to change and evolve with the times?

- Will police executives have the necessary job security to accommodate COPPS? Should at-will employment of chiefs place COPPS at risk?

- Will those departments that are not as yet doing so work with their communities, other city agencies, businesses, elected officials, and the media to sustain COPPS?

- Will police unions work with administrators to effect the changes needed for COPPS?

- Will police employees, sworn and civilian, who have not yet done so realize that the traditional "sacred cow" reactive mode of policing has obviously not been successful and cannot work in the future?

- Can those police organizations, from top to bottom, become more customer- and value-oriented?

- Will police executives and supervisors that have not as yet done so come to develop the necessary policies and support mechanisms to support COPPS, including recruitment, selection, training, performance appraisals, and reward and promotional systems?

- Will those police executives and supervisors agencies that have not as yet done so begin viewing the patrol officer as a problem-solving specialist, and give street officers enough free time and latitude to engage in proactive policing?

- Will those agencies that have not as yet done so come to view COPPS as a department- and citywide strategy? Will they invest in technology to support problem oriented policing?

- Will those agencies attempt to bring diversity into their ranks, reflecting the changing demographics and cultural customs of our society?[9]

Only time, and the proper effort, will determine the answers to these questions.

CASE STUDY

To tie it all together, the following case study—which can be viewed as including many perspectives examined in this book's preceding chapters—will assist the reader in conceptualizing some of the primary elements of COPPS, both contemporary and future, and to consider some of the major challenges one faces when looking at COPPS for today and the future.

A neighboring community, Gotham City, has a number of new department heads, with varying levels of experience. Recent crime, budget, and other crises, including the relatively new emphasis on homeland defense, have underscored the need for that city to address these problems by the most effective and efficient means. Because you are your police agency's most knowledgeable employee about COPPS, your chief of police has assigned you to go to Gotham City and conduct a comprehensive workshop there concerning this concept, taking as much time is required. Your presentation must include information concerning how this strategy should be viewed philosophically, planned and implemented, and evaluated; how both police and non-police personnel, both inside and outside the organization, will be trained in the concept and the problem-solving process; what cultural changes, both internal and external to the police organization, will be necessary, and how it will have a customer orientation; and, given that all of this foundation has been properly laid, how COPPS and the agency should be functioning in five to ten years.

SUMMARY

The cup is half full/the cup is half empty. Should we be optimistic or pessimistic about the nation's future? One thing that is for certain is that our society is changing. This chapter has examined the future, including the need for police generally to plan for it as well as some prognostications for the COPPS strategy. As noted above, peering into the future raises as many questions as it provides answers. This is obviously a very exciting and challenging time to be serving in the policing service.

The years ahead are not likely to be tranquil, either inside or outside the halls of the police agency. Many dangers and issues now exist that increasingly compel us to "read the tea leaves" with greater trepidation.

Today's police leaders must not wait for someone else to set the pace. Bold leadership is essential today to prepare for the future of police reform. More than ever before, police leaders must shoulder the responsibility for seeing that the best and brightest individuals are recruited, trained, and then become the best they possibly can be. Police administrators can benefit greatly by anticipating what the future holds so that appropriate re sources and methods may be brought to bear on the problems ahead; what is certain is that they can no longer be resistant to change or unmindful of the future.

But challenges have always been present for the men and women of our society who have chosen to wear the badge.

NOTES

1. William L. Tafoya, "The Changing Nature of the Police: Approaching the 21st Century," *Vital Speeches of the Day* 56 (February 1990):244–246.

2. Roy Roberg, John Crank, and Jack Kuykendall, *Police and Society* (2nd ed.) (Los Angeles: Roxbury, 2000), pp. 521–522.

3. Edwin J. Delattre, "Principles of Policing After September 11," *Subject to Debate* 16 (9) (Washington, D.C.: Police Executive Research Forum (September 2002), p.1.

4. Rob Chapman and Matthew C. Scheider, "Community Policing: Now More Than Ever," *http://www.cops.usdoj.gov/default.asp?Item=716* (Accessed April 29, 2003).

5. Kenneth J. Peak, *Policing America: Methods, Issues, and Challenges* (4th ed.)(Upper Saddle River, N.J.: Prentice Hall, 2003), pp. 414–415.

6. Dave Pettinari, "Are We There Yet? The Future of Policing/Sheriffing in Pueblo—Or in Anywhere, America," *http://www.policefuturists.org/files/het.html* (Accessed February 13, 2001).

7. Ibid.

8. Ibid.

9. Peak, *Policing America*, pp. 415–416.

APPENDICES

Although many examples of COPPS initiatives are dispersed throughout the text, here we briefly provide three case studies that specifically concern police application of problem-solving techniques. Readers wishing to learn more about these and other problem-solving efforts are encouraged to see *Excellence in Problem Oriented Policing,* published by the Police Executive Research Forum, Washington, D.C. in November 2002. It presents the winners of the prestigious Police Executive Research Forum's 2002 Herman Goldstein Award for Excellence in Problem-Oriented Policing.

The first case study, involving a problem-solving initiative by the California Highway Patrol, won the Herman Goldstein Award for 2002; the other two were finalists. All of the venues discussed followed the S.A.R.A. process of problem solving, as discussed in Chapter 4 and other chapters.

SAFETY AND FARM LABOR VEHICLE EDUCATION (SAFE) PROGRAM: CALIFORNIA HIGHWAY PATROL

——————A——
AWARD WINNING PROBLEM-SOLVING CASE STUDIES

SCANNING: On the early morning of August 9, 1999—the peak of harvest season in California's Central Valley—15 farm workers climbed into a 1983 van to go to work; soon thereafter the van slammed into a commercial vehicle making a U-turn on the road, killing 13 of the van's passengers. The van's driver, who had a lengthy record of driving violations, was arrested for operating the vehicle while under the influence.

Unfortunately, collisions of farm labor vehicles were not uncommon in this area during the peak season (May through September), when about 300,000 farm labor jobs are available; with this influx comes increased traffic congestion, road infractions, and operating of unsafe vehicles.

ANALYSIS: Analyzing farm labor vehicle collisions proved challenging for the California Highway Patrol (CHP) due to discrepancies in how data were recorded. At a minimum, however, thorough data analysis showed an estimated 187 farm labor collisions, with 20 fatalities and 121 injuries, from 1997 through 1999. On average, traffic fatalities were 42 percent higher in the area during the peak harvest months. An examination of the relevant statutes and regulatory laws showed room for improvement: For example, farm labor vehicles were exempt from the state's mandatory seatbelt law. Furthermore, language barriers and the farm-working culture affected outreach efforts and hindered efforts to improve farm worker safety.

RESPONSE: With the support of the California Highway Patrol, the California State Legislature passed two bills to enhance the safety of farm workers and their vehicles. These laws made provisions for:

- the mandatory use of seatbelts for farm works in farm labor vehicles
- strengthening the safety and nonpunitive inspection and certification requirements for these vehicles
- increasing CHP's personnel strength to work specifically with farm labor vehicles
- a coordinated public education campaign, using town meetings and print and electronic media to announce inspection dates and places, and to inform the farming community about licensing and safety requirements

ASSESSMENT: In 2002, for the first time in a decade, there were *no* farm worker fatalities resulting from farm labor collisions; in addition, collisions involving these vehicles decreased 73 percent. These positive results have continued as of July 2003.

MIAMI, FLORIDA, ATTACKS A MAJOR PRODUCE MARKET PROBLEM

SCANNING: Miami, Florida's, Allapattah Produce Market is the center for the commercial shipping of fresh produce for the southeastern United States. Local supermarkets, cruise ships, and "mom and pop" stores rely on the market for their daily produce as well. Over several years the quality of life declined and crime (burglaries, robberies, drugs, vandalism, and so on) rose to previously unseen levels in this 3-by-5-block area. A large homeless population was thriving and contributing to the crime, disorder, and fear of the area, and business operators had allowed their facilities to deteriorate. Garbage-strewn parking lots, vacant lots, improper disposal of rotted produce, and overflowing garbage bins led to pollution, sanitation, and health hazards. Traffic problems also abounded.

ANALYSIS: Officers analyzed calls for service and crime statistics for the market and surrounding neighborhoods, noting an average of 23 business burglaries a month in the market; they also interviewed patrol officers and code enforcement personnel. They found that the location and layout of the market contributed to the traffic congestion and noise problems. The fundamental problem at the market was that businesses had been allowed to operate with very little oversight by organizations charged with regulating health, sanitation, and pollution problems. The vendors' illegal disposal of unusable produce attracted homeless persons and drug dealers to the area. Nearby residents suffered from criminal victimizations, traffic congestion, and decreasing property values.

RESPONSE: A response plan was designed to mitigate the problems, causes, and underlying conditions. The following goals were established for the response plan.

1. Significantly reduce the pollution and improve sanitation and health standards.
2. Reduce traffic congestion and enhance the market's transportation infrastructure.
3. Reduce criminal activity in the area and fear of crime in the surrounding residential neighborhoods.
4. Reduce the home population in the area.
5. Promote a partnership between the commercial entities and Miami officials.

A key component of the plan was an increased presence of police and code enforcement personnel, particularly to explain the response plan to business owners and vendors—who were urged to comply with code requirements by constructing locked, fenced enclosures around their individual trash bins.

A business owners association was formed, and, to alleviate the traffic problems, officers worked with the commercial truck operators to develop improved parking, unloading, and turnaround facilities. A complete road redesign project was initiated for the market area.

As the project moved forward, homeless persons moved out of the area and officers and business owners spearheaded a series of area beautification projects (with the assistance of a $600,000 state grant), including improvements in landscaping, lighting, and signage. Officers and business association owners also produced a video for vendors that explained proper disposal of garbage.

ASSESSMENT: The overall reported crime rate and calls for service in and around the target area declined, with reported business burglaries decreasing from an average of 23 per month to fewer than 5 per month. The transient population disappeared almost entirely, and traffic congestion was significantly reduced. Health and sanitation hazards were also reduced or eliminated; nearly all businesses were brought into compliance with codes and regulations. New businesses were attracted to the area, and annual sales of all businesses in the market increased.

DOMESTIC VIOLENCE INTERVENTION PROJECT CHARLOTTE-MECKLENBURG, NORTH CAROLINA

SCANNING: For several years the Charlotte-Mecklenburg, North Carolina, police department had made domestic assaults a priority and worked to analyze those cases, intervene, and reduce its occurrence in the community. In October 2000, however, an officer working a particularly serious domestic assault case became concerned about the overall number of domestic assaults in his patrol district for that year: 305 domestic assaults, or 30 percent of the total assaults for that year. He began looking for previous reports involving the victim and suspect in this specific case, and found a number of reports for such other "indicator" offenses as vandalism and communicating threats; trouble followed this couple around the county. This examination of the case reports indicated that, rather than a repeat call location being the "hot spot" for crime, he surmised that tracking the *participants* might be a better indicator of future violence.

ANALYSIS: A much more thorough analysis of domestic assault reports showed that the average victim had filed nine previous police reports, most involving the same suspect but sometimes crossing police district boundaries. Many of the prior reports were for other indicator crimes, such as trespassing, threatening, and stalking. Most repeat call locations were domestic situations. It became clear that it was best to regard the victim and suspect as hot spots instead of the traditional fixed geographic location.

RESPONSE: Officers developed a tailored response plan for each repeat offense case, including zero tolerance of criminal behavior by the suspect and the use of other criminal justice and social service agencies. A Police Watch program was implemented, in which systematic zone checks of both the victim's residence and workplace were made when appropriate. A Domestic Violence Hotline voice mail system for victims was also initiated, which victims could use to report miscellaneous incidents involving a suspect. Officers developed detailed case files and created a separate database with victim/offender background data. The database tracks victims and offenders as hot spots moving from one address to another and across patrol district boundaries.

ASSESSMENT: Repeat calls for service were reduced by 98.9 percent at seven target locations. Domestic assaults decreased 7 percent in this targeted patrol district, while increasing 29 percent in the rest of the city. Only 14.8 percent of domestic violence victims in the project reported repeat victimization, as opposed to a benchmark figure of 35 percent. No complaints against officers were generated by officer contacts with officers.

The following pages show the Community Service Survey formerly used by the Fort Collins, Colorado, police department (FCPD) and adopted by many other police agencies. Respondents may complete the survey via the Internet, clicking on their responses.

For items 3 and 4, which ask how safe the city and the respondent's neighborhood are, possible responses are "no response," "very safe," "above average safety," "average safety," "below average safety," and "very unsafe."

For item 5, which asks how often certain activities or crimes occur in the respondent's neighborhood, possible responses are "no response," "never," "rarely," "sometimes," "often," and "constantly."

For items 6, 7, and 8, dealing with rate of satisfaction with the FCPD in different types of contact, possible responses are "no response," "very satisfied," "somewhat satisfied," "satisfied," "somewhat unsatisfied," and "very unsatisfied."

For item 9, asking whether respondents would support different types of police responses to nonemergency type calls, possible responses are "no response," "yes, this is acceptable," and "no, this is not accceptable."

Item 10 asks respondents to indicate whether they agree or disagree with several statements concerning police activities and programs; possible responses are "no response," "strongly agree," "somewhat agree," "agree," "somewhat disagree," and "strongly disagree."

For item 11, regarding the importance to the community of various police department programs, possible responses are "no response," "very important," "important," "somewhat important," "not very important," and "unimportant."

B

A COMMUNITY SURVEY IN FORT COLLINS, COLORADO

Fort Collins **POLICE**

Community Service Survey

Dear Members of the Fort Collins Community:

We at Fort Collins Police Services are interested in your thoughts and ideas! We know our citizens are concerned about crime and safety in their neighborhoods. We also know that the citizens of this community have some excellent ideas about how to deal with these important issues. We are asking for your assistance in identifying problems to which you believe we should be responding differently. In addition, we are interested in your opinion of our current performance. Please assist us by completing the following survey. It should only take about 20 minutes to complete. Thank you for your help!

Sincerely,

Dennis Harrison, Chief of Police

A printed version of this survey is also available if you would prefer. If you'd like us to mail one to you, or if you would like to speak to someone about the survey you may call Officer Bud Bredehoft at (970) 221-6830, or send him e-mail at lbredehoft@ci.fort-collins.co.us.

Your Neighborhood

Please complete this survey based upon where you live in the City of Fort Collins. You may answer all of the questions, or as many as you'd like.

1. Where do you live in Fort Collins?
Use the map and select the area number which includes the area in which you live: (The areas extend beyond the map along the streets indicated by the thick black area boundary lines)
`No Response ▼`

1a. I do not live in Fort Collins, but I work or attend school in area:
`No Response ▼`

2. What is your age group?
`No Response ▼`

3. How safe of a place to live is Fort Collins?
`No Response ▼`

4. How safe of a place to live is your neighborhood?

No Response ▼

5. Let us know how often the following activities or crimes occur in your neighborhood:

Abandoned/Junk Cars: No Response ▼

Graffiti: No Response ▼

Loud Parties or Noise: No Response ▼

Speeding Cars: No Response ▼

Unsupervised Juveniles/Youth: No Response ▼

Littering: No Response ▼

Vandalism: No Response ▼

Aggressive Panhandling/Begging: No Response ▼

Public Intoxication: No Response ▼

Vagrancy/Loitering: No Response ▼

Fighting: No Response ▼

Unlawful Discharge of a Weapon: No Response ▼

Thefts From Autos: No Response ▼

Other Thefts: No Response ▼

Burglary: No Response ▼

Auto Theft: No Response ▼

Personal Assaults: No Response ▼

Illegal Drug Activity: No Response ▼

Domestic Violence: No Response ▼

Sexual Assault & Rape: No Response ▼

Criminal Gang Activity: No Response ▼

Hate Crimes: No Response ▼

Additional comments: [text box]

Contact with the Police

6. Rate your level of satisfaction with the Fort Collins Police in the following areas:

How often an officer patrols your neighborhood: [No Response ▼]

General police service in your neighborhood: [No Response ▼]

7. If you personally had contact with Fort Collins Police Services within the past 12 months, rate the level of service you received based upon the following type(s) of contact you had:

Called 911 for emergency assistance: [No Response ▼]

Called for a non-emergency reason: [No Response ▼]

Dealt with a police officer in person: [No Response ▼]

Spoke on the phone with an officer: [No Response ▼]

Received a traffic citation: [No Response ▼]

Was stopped by the police but not cited: [No Response ▼]

Contacted a Police Services employee who was not a police officer: [No Response ▼]

Other personal contacts not listed above: [text box]

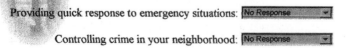

What could we have done to improve your contact(s) with Police Services? [text box]

Service Expectations

8. Rate your level of satisfaction with the Fort Collins Police in the following areas:

Providing quick response to emergency situations: [No Response ▼]

Controlling crime in your neighborhood: [No Response ▼]

Source: Reproduced by permission of the Fort Collins, Colorado, police department.

As part of the review and updating process of its community policing strategic plan, the Portland police bureau solicits citizen input concerning how goals are to be achieved. Citizens may complete the survey via the Internet or using conventional means.

Following is the bureau's two-page "Community Policing Strategic Plan Suggestions" survey instrument on the Internet.

COMMUNITY POLICING STRATEGIC PLAN SUGGESTIONS

A STRATEGIC PLAN SURVEY IN PORTLAND, OREGON

The Portland Police Bureau is asking for your ideas in order to create a working draft of the 1998–2000 Strategic Plan. You do not need to be an expert on past strategic plans to provide valuable information; a good idea of what public safety efforts are working and what still needs attention is all that is needed. Thank you for your assistance on this project.

First Name

Last Name

Organization

Address

City

State

Zip

Phone

E-mail [   ]

These comments (check one):

☐ are my personal opinion

☐ reflect the views of my organization or unit

1. In the last two years, what activities or programs have substantially contributed to reducing crime and the fear of crime in Portland? Give examples of ones that stand out.

[   ]

2. What activities or strategies are particularly important to work on in the next two years? These can be existing efforts that should continue, new ones that should be implemented or existing efforts that need more attention.

[   ]

Use the "Submit" button to send us your comments.

(Submit)

If you wish to respond in greater detail by mail, please attach this page as a cover sheet.

Return replies to:

Strategic Plan
Portland Police Bureau
1111 S.W. 2nd Ave., Room 1552
Portland, OR 97204

Fax: 823-0289

Interoffice: B119/R1552

INDEX

approaches, 124–25
  Baltimore, Maryland, case study, 134
  chief executives, 125–26
  first-line supervisors, 126
  middle managers, 126
  participatory management, 141
Managers, of offenders, 74
Marriage, societal stability and, 32
MDMA (ecstasy), 200–201
Media, involvement with COPPS
  programs, 175
Mentally ill, 204–05
Merseyside, Great Britain, 286
Methamphetamine labs, 198
Metropolitan Police Act (1829), 1, 2
Mexicans, 193. See also Chicanos; Hispanics
Michigan City, Indiana, (Internet
  education program), 187
Middle class, community organization
  and, 223
Middle managers
  accountability for problem solving, 260
  COPPS curriculum for, 171
  role in changing agency culture, 146–47
  role in COPPS implementation, 126
Midtown Community Court (New York),
  57–58
Military model
  COPPS curriculum and, 171
  criticized as basis for policing, 139
  obsolescence of, 300
Military, role in protection against
  terrorism, 24
Minorities. See social diversity
Mission statements
  COPPS implementation, 123
  Montgomery County, Maryland, 132
  Royal Canadian Mounted Police, 277
Modeling
  as basis for change, 139
  change, 141
  human resource management, 127
Montgomery County, Maryland (COPPS
  implementation), 131–33
Mount Pleasant, South Carolina, (COPPS
  implementation), 122

Naperville, Illinois, 301
Narcotics. See drugs
National Commission on Law Observance
  and Enforcement, 9
National Conference of Christians and
  Jews (NCCJ), 11
National Institute on Police and
  Community Relations (NIPCR),
  11–12
National Police Chiefs Union, 7
National Prison Association, 10
Native Americans
  cultural diversity, 191
  terminology for, 193
NCCJ (National Conference of Christians
  and Jews), 11
NDS (Neighborhood Defender Service),
  57
Needs assessment, 121–22, 166
Neighborhood Assistance Office, 131
Neighborhood Defender Service
  (NDS), 57

Neighborhood surveys, COPPS evaluation, 247–48
Neighborhood Watch programs, 95, 111,
  259, 285–86
Neighborhoods
  Arroyo Grande, California case study,
    267
  communitarianism and, 45
  destabilizing, 32
  deterioration of, 211–12
  lacking sense of community in, 223
  participation in police work, 300
  police integration with in late
    nineteenth century, 6
  safety of, 40–41
  San Diego case study, 259
  Savannah, Georgia, case study, 264
  as unit of analysis, 17
Netherlands, COPPS initiatives, 292–93
New York City, zero-tolerance movement
  and, 232–33
New York model for policing, 3–5
  civil disorders of 1840s–1870s and, 5
  Peel's Principles as basis of, 3
  political ties of police, 4
New Zealand, COPPS initiatives, 291–92
Newman, Oscar, 95–96
Newman, Sir Kenneth, 284
NIPCR (National Institute on Police and
  Community Relations), 11–12

Objectives, COPPS implementation, 123
Obstacles, COPPS implementation,
  134–36, 172–73
Offenders
  "rule setting" and, 106
  deflecting, 106
  monitoring repeat, 111
  problem analysis triangle, 73
Oliver, Willard, 21
Olson, Robert K., 189–90
On-line communities, 303
Ontario, Canada, (COPPS initiatives), 275
Operation Mantle in South Australia, 282
Orange County, Florida, (COPPS case
  study), 268
Organizational skills, officer evaluation, 242
Organizations
  COPPS implementation and, 135
  flattening hierarchical structure,
    302–03
  formula for change, 139–41
  learning organizations, 158
  values of, 143
Osborne, David, 54–55

Participatory management, 141
Partnerships. See collaboration
Patrol cars, 9
Patrol personnel. See street officers
Patrols, Japanese emphasis on, 278. See
  also foot patrols
PBL (problem-based learning), 158–59,
  169–70
Peel, Sir Robert, 2
  effectiveness of policies, 93, 98
  movement to professionalize police in
    England, 1

principles, 2–3
Peel's Principles, 2–3
PERF (Police Executive Research Forum),
  13, 164
Personnel management, 154–55
PIO (public information officer), 175
Pittsburg, Kansas, (COPPS case study),
  268–69
Place, problem analysis triangle, 73
Planning. See strategic planning, COPPS
Planning skills, officer evaluation, 242
Planning team, 120
Police Executive Research Forum (PERF),
  13, 164
Police Foundation, 13
Police officers
  evaluating, 241–45
  surveys, 248–50
  training, 158–59
Police reports, 86–87
Police Training Officer (PTO) program,
  160–61
"The Policeman as a Social Worker"
  (Vollmer), 8
Policewomen, 10. See also women
Policing
  agency culture. see agency culture
  alternatives to (1960s), 14
  changes required by COPPS approach,
    230–31
  collaboration with communities,
    47–48, 59–60
  community justice system and, 55–59
  community role of, 224–25, 248
  COPPS. see community oriented policing
    and problem solving (COPPS)
  COPPS approach compared with
    traditional, 64–66, 79
  crime rate as measure of effectiveness,
    11
  discretion of police and, 227–28
  history of, in COPPS curriculum, 168
  Internet resources for, 164
  minorities and, 179–81, 185–86
  new realism in contemporary studies, 14
  New York model. see New York model
    for policing
  patrols, 111
  political neutrality of, 226–27
  POP. see problem oriented policing (POP)
  professional model. see professional
    model of policing
  temperament and intellectual
    capacities and, 229–30
  terrorism and, 23–24
Policing a Free Society (Goldstein), 67
Policing, evolution of, 1–28
  British contributions, 1–3
  call for new approach, 17
  community policing via Internet, 24–25
  community problem solving model,
    18–23
  crime commissions and early studies,
    9–10
  efficiency and control emphasized,
    10–11
  homeland security, 23–24
  limitations of professional model
    (1960s), 12–17